THE RISE OF AI AGENTS

THE RISE OF AI AGENTS

INTEGRATING AI, BLOCKCHAIN TECHNOLOGIES,

AND QUANTUM COMPUTING

Petar Radanliev

✦ Addison-Wesley

Boston • Columbus • New York • San Francisco • Amsterdam • Cape Town
Dubai • London • Madrid • Milan • Munich • Paris • Montreal • Toronto • Delhi • Mexico City
São Paulo • Sydney • Hong Kong • Seoul • Singapore • Taipei • Tokyo

ISBN-13: 978-0-13-535294-6
ISBN-10: 0-13-535294-0

3 2025

Front Cover Credit - CoreDESIGN/Shutterstock

Director, ITP Product Management
Brett Bartow

Executive Editor
James Manly

Managing Editor
Sandra Schroeder

Development Editor
Christopher A. Cleveland

Senior Project Editor
Mandie Frank

Copy Editor
Chuck Hutchinson

Technical Editor
Omar Santos

Editorial Assistant
Cindy Teeters

Designer
Chuti Prasertsith

Composition
codeMantra

Indexer
Timothy Wright

Proofreader
Jennifer Hinchliffe

The integration of AI agents based on the Q-learning type of reinforcement learning, with quantum computing represents a potential leap toward artificial general intelligence (AGI) and the technological singularity, a point where AI surpasses human intelligence, fundamentally transforming society and becomes the highest form of intelligence on the planet. Quantum algorithms, such as Grover's and Shor's, will exponentially enhance AI's capacity for optimization and cryptographic analysis, accelerating AGI's evolution. This immense new power won't be easy to control, and that raises significant security concerns, particularly in cryptographic resilience. The fastest solution lies in post-quantum cryptography, like lattice-based and hash-based cryptography, which ensures that even quantum-powered AI cannot compromise data integrity. But that is not sufficient, and we can expect breaches. We need to be able to audit cyber attacks. Blockchain technology, through its decentralized and immutable ledger, offers a transparent, immutable ledger for recording transactions and AI decisions, providing accountability and safeguarding against the misuse of AGI. By addressing these challenges, we can harness the benefits of AGI while mitigating the risks associated with the singularity.

—Dr Petar Radanliev, University of Oxford, August 2024

Contents

Preface

The combination of artificial intelligence (AI), quantum computing, and blockchain technologies brings us ever closer to the development of artificial general intelligence (AGI) and the potential advent of a technological singularity. This book is the culmination of extensive research conducted across these domains, shaped by my experiences at leading institutions such as MIT, Imperial College London, and most recently, the University of Oxford. Throughout my academic and professional journey, I have been deeply engaged in addressing the critical security, plus ethical and practical challenges that accompany these rapidly advancing technologies.

At the University of Oxford, my research has been particularly focused on examining the vulnerabilities inherent in AI systems as they progress toward AGI. I lead projects that develop AI-driven cybersecurity models designed to detect and mitigate advanced threats, including those posed by quantum computing. These models are essential for advancing the security of AI deployments, ensuring that as AI systems increase in capability, they do so within frameworks robust enough to withstand the new risks introduced by quantum technology.

Moreover, my work at Oxford has centered on the integration of blockchain technology with AI systems to create transparent and accountable decision-making processes. One significant project involved the development of a blockchain-based system that records AI decisions made through reinforcement learning algorithms, such as Q-learning, ensuring that these decisions are secure and verifiable. This integration is needed for maintaining trust in AI systems, particularly as they begin to operate autonomously in critical sectors such as finance, healthcare, and national security.

The emergence of quantum computing has introduced profound challenges, particularly the potential to break traditional cryptographic systems, thereby compromising the security of AI models. My research has been dedicated to developing NIST-compliant post-quantum cryptographic frameworks that are designed to protect AI systems against the unprecedented computational power of quantum algorithms. These frameworks are indispensable for preserving the integrity of AI-driven processes in a post-quantum world, ensuring that AI systems remain secure as they advance toward AGI.

To address these concerns, in this book, I have worked on forecasting how, despite the emergence of AGI, humanity can integrate blockchain and quantum technology with AI agents to prevent the risk of a technological singularity event. Blockchain, known for its role in cryptocurrencies, offers a way to record every decision an AI system makes in a secure, tamper-proof ledger. This means that as AI becomes more capable of making decisions on its own, whether in finance, healthcare, or even national security, we can ensure that these decisions are transparent and accountable.

This book is my attempt to make these complex but crucial topics accessible to a wider audience. I believe it is important for everyone, not just specialists, to understand the potential of, and the risks associated with, the technologies that are rapidly shaping our future. Whether you're a technologist, a policymaker, or simply someone interested in the future, I hope this book provides you with valuable insights into the challenges and opportunities that lie ahead.

I wish to extend my deepest gratitude to the Fulbright Commission, whose fellowship has played a crucial role in advancing my research and provided invaluable opportunities for collaboration with leading experts in the field. Their support has been instrumental in the development of the ideas and frameworks presented in this book.

I am also profoundly grateful to my colleagues at the University of Oxford, whose insights and collaboration have greatly enhanced the depth and scope of this work. Their contributions have been vital in ensuring that this book reflects the latest advancements in AI, blockchain, and quantum computing and also anticipates and addresses the critical challenges that lie ahead.

Goals/Objectives/Approach of the Book

The primary aim of this book is to provide a thorough and accessible exploration of the development and implications of AI agents, particularly in relation to their integration with quantum computing and blockchain technologies. The focus is on how AI agents, enhanced by advanced reinforcement learning techniques and secured through post-quantum cryptographic methods, can be responsibly developed and deployed in a world approaching artificial general intelligence (AGI) and the potential onset of a technological singularity. This book adopts an interdisciplinary approach, drawing together insights from AI research, cryptography, cybersecurity, and blockchain technology to create a cohesive narrative. It leverages the latest research in AI agent development, NIST-approved post-quantum cryptographic standards, and the role of blockchain in ensuring transparency and accountability in autonomous systems. Through this approach, the book seeks to provide readers with a detailed understanding of the technical and ethical challenges involved in creating and managing AI agents that are both powerful and secure.

Targeted Reading Audience

This book is crafted to cater to a diverse audience, primarily targeting academic researchers in the fields of artificial intelligence, quantum computing, and blockchain technologies. It is also designed to be accessible to policymakers, legal practitioners, and professionals in cybersecurity and AI who seek to understand the technical intricacies and broader implications of AI agents as they integrate with emerging technologies. The detailed analysis and real-world examples provided will be particularly valuable to graduate students in computer science, cybersecurity, and related disciplines. Furthermore, this book will serve as an insightful resource for anyone interested in exploring the future of AI agents, especially in the context of advancing toward artificial general intelligence and the associated challenges of security, ethics, and transparency.

Book Organization

Chapter 1: Introduction to AI Agents, Blockchain, and Quantum Computing

This opening chapter lays the groundwork for the book by introducing the fundamental concepts of AI agents, blockchain, and quantum computing. It provides a comprehensive overview of these transformative technologies, elucidating their individual significance and the potential impact of their convergence. The chapter is crafted to be accessible to a broad readership, ensuring that readers acquire a solid understanding of these technologies before engaging with more complex discussions. The narrative also introduces Jovan, a fictional character whose experiences with these technologies serve to illustrate their real-world applications and implications throughout the book. The chapter begins by exploring the evolution of AI from basic rule-based systems to sophisticated AI agents capable of autonomous decision-making, facilitated by advancements in neural networks and reinforcement learning. It then expands into blockchain technology, emphasizing its role in securing and verifying the vast data processed by AI agents through decentralized, immutable ledgers. The discussion extends to quantum computing, highlighting its potential to exponentially enhance the computational power available to AI agents, enabling them to tackle previously unsolvable problems. This chapter sets the stage for the rest of the book.

Chapter 2: The Advance of Artificial Intelligence into AI Agents

Chapter 2 provides a detailed exploration of the evolution of artificial intelligence into AI agents, focusing on key methodologies such as reinforcement learning, Q-learning, and neural Turing machines (NTMs). The chapter traces AI's progression from early machine learning, highlighting the shift from symbolic AI to data-driven approaches that enabled the development of autonomous decision-making agents. Reinforcement learning, with a focus on Q-learning, is examined for its role in teaching AI systems to optimize decisions through interaction with their environment. The chapter also introduces NTMs, which combine neural networks with memory capabilities, significantly enhancing the ability of AI agents to handle complex, sequential tasks. This chapter sets the foundation for understanding how these advancements have paved the way for the development of more sophisticated AI systems, capable of complex problem-solving and closer to achieving artificial general intelligence.

Chapter 3: Digital Trust in AI Agents and Blockchain Technologies

Chapter 3 provides a detailed examination of how blockchain technology underpins digital trust for AI agents in decentralized environments. It begins by analyzing blockchain's role in creating immutable and tamper-proof records, which are crucial for ensuring the integrity and transparency of AI agent operations. The chapter focuses on Ethereum and Hyperledger, exploring how these platforms enable the automation of AI functions through smart contracts and permissioned networks. It specifically addresses the integration of AI with blockchain via smart oracles, which allow AI agents to access real-time external data, and automated contracts, which enable the autonomous execution of agreements based on this data. The chapter also delves into the technical challenges of integrating AI and blockchain, particularly in maintaining data privacy, managing scalability, and ensuring robust security. By linking these technologies to practical applications in finance, supply chain management, and healthcare, the chapter offers a precise analysis of the mechanisms that build and sustain digital trust in AI-driven systems.

Chapter 4: Quantum Computing and AI Agents

Chapter 4 provides a precise analysis of the impact quantum computing will have on the capabilities of AI agents. It begins with a detailed examination of quantum principles such as superposition, which allows qubits to represent multiple states simultaneously, and entanglement, which enables instant state correlation between qubits, vastly increasing computational power. The chapter specifically addresses the role of qubits in achieving quantum supremacy, where quantum systems surpass classical computers in tasks like factoring large integers using Shor's algorithm, which threatens current RSA encryption, and speeding up unstructured database searches with

Grover's algorithm, reducing search complexity. The discussion also covers the technical challenges, such as qubit decoherence, which leads to loss of quantum information, and the ongoing development of quantum error correction techniques essential for stable quantum computations. The chapter concludes by projecting how these quantum advancements will enhance AI agents, particularly in breaking traditional encryption methods, optimizing large-scale computations, and handling massive datasets with unprecedented efficiency.

Chapter 5: Decentralised AI Agents

Chapter 5 provides a focused analysis of how AI enhances blockchain technology to create more secure and efficient systems. The chapter begins by examining the specific mechanisms through which blockchain's decentralized ledger and immutable records reinforce the integrity of AI agents in distributed networks. It details how AI algorithms optimize blockchain operations, particularly through neural chain technologies that improve transaction processing speed, enhance scalability, and refine consensus mechanisms. The chapter offers concrete examples, such as AI-driven fraud detection in financial transactions and automated data verification in healthcare records, showcasing the practical applications of AI-blockchain integration. Additionally, it addresses the technical challenges, including the computational overhead of AI models on blockchain networks and the complexities of ensuring data privacy in a decentralized environment. The chapter concludes by outlining future advancements, such as the development of more efficient consensus algorithms and the potential for AI-driven smart contracts to autonomously manage complex, multi-party transactions.

Chapter 6: Quantum AI Agents

Chapter 6 provides an in-depth analysis of the integration of quantum computing with AI, focusing on the specific advancements this convergence enables in AI agents. The chapter begins by detailing how quantum phenomena, such as superposition and entanglement, are utilized to exponentially increase computational efficiency in AI tasks that involve large-scale data processing. It thoroughly examines quantum machine learning (QML) techniques, especially quantum neural networks (QNNs), which allow AI agents to perform complex pattern recognition and optimization tasks far more efficiently than classical neural networks. The chapter also explores the direct impact of quantum algorithms like quantum support vector machines and quantum principal component analysis on enhancing the performance of AI models. It addresses technical challenges such as qubit decoherence, quantum noise, and the need for robust quantum error correction methods, all critical to the practical implementation of quantum AI. The chapter concludes by projecting how emerging developments in quantum hardware, such as the improvement of qubit fidelity and the creation of scalable quantum processors, will further revolutionize AI agents, particularly in applications like cryptography, financial modeling, and precision medicine.

Chapter 7: Blockchain, Quantum Computing, and AI Agents

Chapter 7 provides a precise examination of the integration of AI agents with blockchain and quantum computing to establish quantum-resilient security systems. It begins by detailing how AI agents implement lattice-based cryptographic schemes, such as NTRUEncrypt and FrodoKEM, to secure blockchain networks against quantum attacks. The chapter then explores the use of AI in optimizing quantum key distribution (QKD) protocols, particularly BB84 and E91, for secure communication. Specific focus is given to how AI agents manage the distribution and authentication of quantum keys within blockchain frameworks, ensuring resistance to quantum-based threats. The chapter also investigates the practical challenges of incorporating quantum-resistant algorithms, like CRYSTALS-Kyber and SPHINCS+, into blockchain ledgers, and the role of AI in automating these processes. It concludes by addressing the complexities involved in scaling quantum-resistant solutions, particularly the computational overhead and integration difficulties within existing blockchain infrastructures.

Chapter 8: Ethics of AI Agents

Chapter 8 offers a focused analysis of the ethical challenges in deploying AI agents and quantum technologies, specifically addressing how to mitigate algorithmic bias and protect privacy in quantum computing environments. It begins by identifying precise sources of bias in AI models, such as underrepresented minority groups in training datasets and the design of decision thresholds that disadvantage specific demographics. The chapter then details concrete methods to counteract these biases, including dataset rebalancing techniques, adversarial training to minimize discrimination during model development, and applying fairness constraints like demographic parity in post-processing. It also examines the privacy threats posed by quantum computing, particularly its capacity to break RSA and ECC encryption, and explores the use of specific lattice-based cryptographic algorithms, such as Kyber and Dilithium, alongside quantum key distribution (QKD) protocols like BB84, to secure sensitive data. The chapter further discusses how these technologies must be implemented within stringent ethical frameworks to prevent deepening existing inequalities or infringing on personal privacy. The chapter concludes by addressing the necessity for rigorous governance, focusing on the development of international standards and policies to manage the ethical implications of these advanced technologies effectively.

Chapter 9: Legal Frameworks and Global Standards Shaping the Future Development of AI Agents

Chapter 9 provides a detailed examination of the legal and regulatory frameworks governing AI agents, blockchain, and quantum computing, with a focus on specific regulations and standards. It begins by analyzing the European Union's Artificial Intelligence Act, which classifies AI systems into four risk categories—unacceptable, high, limited, and minimal—and mandates compliance requirements for high-risk AI, including transparency and accountability measures. The chapter contrasts this with the United States' sector-specific regulatory approach, such as the FDA's guidance on AI in medical devices and the FTC's focus on AI in consumer protection. It also explores China's AI regulations, including the New Generation Artificial Intelligence Development Plan, which aligns AI policy with national strategic goals. The chapter further examines international standards from ISO and IEEE, detailing specific standards like ISO/IEC 23894 for AI governance and IEEE 7010 for AI transparency. It discusses the challenges of regulating quantum computing, particularly in managing its dual-use capabilities for both civilian and military applications, and the critical need for post-quantum cryptographic standards like NIST's selected algorithms (e.g., Kyber, Dilithium) to protect data from quantum threats. The chapter concludes by emphasizing the importance of dynamic, adaptive regulatory frameworks that can keep pace with technological advancements while balancing innovation with ethical and security imperatives.

Chapter 10: Societal Impact and the Rise of Autonomous AI Systems

As the final chapter, Chapter 10 offers a comprehensive analysis of the long-term societal impacts of AI agents and quantum computing, with a focus on future predictions. The chapter begins by examining the transformative role of AI in industries such as transportation, where advancements in autonomous vehicles, including real-time decision-making algorithms and sensor technologies, are poised to revolutionize safety and efficiency. In healthcare, AI's contribution to improving diagnostic accuracy through advanced deep learning models and its potential in personalized medicine are critically assessed. The chapter also explores the disruptive potential of quantum computing in finance, particularly in complex financial modeling and data optimization, and its implications for cybersecurity as quantum algorithms threaten to break current encryption standards. Ethical and regulatory challenges are thoroughly addressed, emphasizing the need for robust frameworks to manage AI accountability in critical applications and the urgent development of post-quantum cryptography to protect sensitive data. The chapter concludes with future predictions, discussing the potential economic ramifications of AI-driven automation on job markets, the risk of widening social inequalities, and the importance of adaptive policy measures and international collaboration to ensure these technologies benefit society as a whole while mitigating associated risks.

Register your copy of *The Rise of AI Agents* on the InformIT site for convenient access to updates and/ or corrections as they become available. To start the registration process, go to informit.com/register and log in or create an account. Enter the product ISBN (9780135352946) and click Submit. If you would like to be notified of exclusive offers on new editions and updates, please check the box to receive email from us.

Acknowledgments

The completion of this book would not have been possible without the support, encouragement, and contributions of many individuals and institutions. First and foremost, I would like to express my deepest gratitude to the University of Oxford, where the research and writing of this book took place. The intellectual environment and the collaborative spirit at Oxford have been instrumental in shaping the ideas presented in these pages. I am especially thankful to Professor David De Roure, whose mentorship and insightful guidance have been invaluable in refining my research focus and broadening my understanding of the complex intersections between artificial intelligence, quantum computing, and blockchain technologies.

I am particularly grateful to my students at the Department of Computer Science, whose curiosity, enthusiasm, and thoughtful questions have greatly enriched this work. Their perspectives and engagement have pushed me to refine and clarify my arguments, and I deeply appreciate their contributions throughout this journey.

I would like to extend my sincere thanks to the Fulbright Commission for awarding me a fellowship, which provided me with the invaluable opportunity to collaborate with leading experts and broaden my research horizon. I am especially grateful to the US Embassy in Skopje, whose support was crucial in facilitating my Fulbright experience. The fellowship experience was essential in the development of the multidisciplinary approach that underpins this book.

Special thanks are due to my family and friends, whose patience and understanding have been unwavering throughout this journey. I am particularly grateful to my nieces, Charlotte and Rachel, and my nephew, Robert, whose love and encouragement have been a constant source of strength during the long hours of research and writing. Their presence has been a joyful reminder of the importance of balance and the support that family provides in the pursuit of academic and professional goals.

Lastly, I would like to thank the technical editor for the time and technical expertise, and the Pearson team, especially James Manly, Christopher Cleveland, and Mandie Frank for their patience, guidance, and support. This book is the result of collective effort, and I am truly grateful to everyone who has contributed to its creation. Any errors or omissions remain entirely my own.

About the Author

Dr Petar Radanliev is a Professional Masters Programme Project Supervisor in AI and cybersecurity at the University of Oxford's Department of Computer Science. Previously, he was a research associate in AI and cybersecurity at the University of Oxford's Department of Engineering Science. He earned his PhD in 2013 and conducted post-doctoral research at Imperial College London, the University of Cambridge, and the Massachusetts Institute of Technology. His primary research areas encompass artificial intelligence, cybersecurity, post-quantum security, and blockchain security. Before his academic career, Petar spent ten years as a cybersecurity manager for RBS—the largest bank in the world at the time, and five years as a lead penetration tester for the Ministry for Defence.

PART I

FOUNDATIONS OF ADVANCED TECHNOLOGIES

Part I introduces the intersection of artificial intelligence, blockchain, and quantum computing. This part of the book provides a detailed examination of the initial integration of these advanced technologies, expanding into individual intricacies and the synergies between them. The AI section extends through the evolution of AI, covering the transition from machine learning to deep learning and highlighting the pivotal roles of neural networks and neural Turing machines. The blockchain section presents insights into distributed ledger technologies such as Ethereum and Hyperledger and the incorporation of AI in blockchain systems. The final chapter of this part engages in cutting-edge advancements in quantum computing, exploring complex concepts such as quantum mechanics, qubits, quantum supremacy, and quantum algorithms. Part I lays the groundwork for understanding the interconnected nature of these technologies, thereby shaping the future of technological progress.

Introduction to AI Agents, Blockchain, and Quantum Computing

Chapter Objectives

The first chapter focuses on an educational aspect of artificial intelligence (AI), blockchain, and quantum computing. The aim is to provide a foundational understanding for grasping this technological trio's subtleties. By the end of this chapter, you will be able to

- **Understand the Fundamental Concepts**: Gain a basic comprehension of AI, blockchain, and quantum computing, appreciating their individual characteristics and overarching principles.

- **Appreciate the Importance of Integration**: Recognize the significance and potential of integrating AI, blockchain, and quantum computing and how their synergy could lead to groundbreaking advancements.

- **Decipher Complex Technologies**: Understand the particulars of these technologies, obtaining clarity on how they operate both independently and in conjunction.

- **Understand the Key Areas of Focus**: Understand critical aspects such as neural networks in AI, smart contracts in blockchain, and quantum entanglement in quantum computing, understanding their roles and impacts within their respective domains.

- **Set the Background for the Following Chapters**: Establish the groundwork for deeper exploration in subsequent chapters, preparing for an all-inclusive understanding of how these technologies interact and the possibilities they unlock.

- **Identify Key Innovations and Trends**: Recognize the latest advancements and emerging trends in AI, blockchain, and quantum computing, appreciating their current and future potential.

- **Recognize the Challenges and Opportunities**: Identify the challenges these technologies pose when integrated and their opportunities for various sectors, including cybersecurity, finance, and healthcare.

- **Forecast the Future Landscape**: Acquire insights into how the convergence of AI, blockchain, and quantum computing is shaping the future of technology, preparing for the advanced concepts discussed in the following chapters.

In this chapter, you will gain a far-reaching understanding of the core principles of AI, blockchain, and quantum computing and begin to comprehend the profound impact that their integration can have on various industries and aspects of our lives.

Fictional Story (Part 1): The Story of Jovan

In the Year 2024:

In the vibrant metropolis of Neo-Eden, young Jovan thrived in a world filled with boundless curiosity for the marvels of the universe. His parents, pioneers in tech development, fostered his fascination with tales of AI neural networks that could mirror human emotions, quantum computers unraveling complex cosmic enigmas in mere minutes, and blockchain systems that formed the bedrock of global digital identity.

Jovan's school was a utopia of cutting-edge technology. AI avatars brought historical events to life with breathtaking realism within its virtual realm. One moment, he could engage in a debate with a virtual iteration of Winston Churchill; the next, he would find himself strolling across a digitally re-created terrain of Mars.

In the Year 2034:

At 20, Jovan attended a university where the buildings were aware, powered by advanced AI that optimized energy use and environmental settings. His interest in AI had deepened, particularly in the field of emotional intelligence networks (EINs)—AI systems that understand and respond to human emotions with empathy.

Jovan worked on a project developing quantum holography, enabling people to send lifelike 3D images of themselves across the globe, revolutionizing communication. He also dabbled in blockchain-based voting systems, ensuring secure and transparent democratic processes.

In the Year 2044:

Now a pioneer in quantum blockchain systems, Jovan, at 30, had developed an unbreakable security protocol even by quantum computing standards. This technology underpinned the Mars Colonization Project, ensuring secure communication and transactions between Earth and Mars.

Jovan's personal life was also touched by technology. He and his partner, whom he met through a sophisticated AI match-making system that analyzed deep personality traits and preferences, raised their child in a smart home where IoT devices seamlessly integrated to create a living environment that adapted to their moods and needs.

In the Year 2064:

At 50, Jovan's dream project came to life. The neural quantum interface (NQI)—a device enabling direct brain interaction with quantum computers—had become a reality. It allowed humans to extend their consciousness into space, experiencing distant worlds through quantum simulations. This technology had profound implications for space exploration, education, and entertainment.

AI and quantum computing have also revolutionized medicine. Nanobots, controlled through advanced AI systems, can now perform intricate surgeries, and quantum genetic mapping offers personalized medical treatments at a genetic level.

In the Year 2084:

Jovan saw the world as a symphony of humanity and technology as an elder. Cities were living eco-systems powered by quantum fusion reactors and administered by AI governments that ensured efficiency and fairness. Interstellar travel was now a reality, with quantum teleportation gates allowing travel to distant galaxies.

His final contribution was an AI system integrated with quantum consciousness, designed to preserve Earth's knowledge and guide humanity toward sustainable and ethical use of technology.

The Foundations of AI Agents

In this opening chapter, we begin an engaging tour into the world of artificial intelligence (AI) agents, which are set to become key players in the digital society. This book uses a novelistic approach to guide you through complex concepts, making them accessible even to those without a technical background. The story-driven narrative allows us to explore the emergence of AI agents—sophisticated systems capable of autonomous decision-making—by examining the technologies that enable their existence.

The chapter sets the stage by introducing three key technologies: artificial intelligence, blockchain, and quantum computing. Each of these fields has evolved separately, contributing unique strengths that, when combined, lead to the creation of AI agents with capabilities far beyond what was previously imaginable.

We begin by examining artificial intelligence, the core of these agents, which has changed from basic rule-based systems into advanced neural networks capable of learning, adapting, and perform-ing tasks with human-like intelligence. This section explains how AI's ability to process and analyze vast amounts of data underpins the development of AI agents, enabling them to operate in real-time environments, make informed decisions, and learn from experience.

Next, we turn to blockchain technology, which is crucial for ensuring the security and transparency of data managed by AI agents. Blockchain's decentralized nature provides a secure framework for recording and verifying the vast amounts of data that AI agents process. This section highlights how the immutability of blockchain records allows AI agents to operate in environments where trust and security are paramount, such as in financial transactions and supply chain management.

Following this, the chapter explores quantum computing, a technology that significantly enhances the computational power available to AI agents. Quantum computing's ability to process complex algorithms at unprecedented speeds allows AI agents to tackle problems that were previously unsolvable, such as predicting financial markets with greater accuracy or simulating molecular interactions for drug discovery. This section will clarify how the integration of quantum computing not only accelerates AI's processing abilities but also introduces new levels of security through quantum-resistant encryption methods.

As the chapter progresses, it becomes clear that these technologies do not just coexist—they converge to create AI agents that are more powerful, secure, and capable of addressing complex challenges across various industries. The discussion on the convergence of AI, blockchain, and quantum computing illustrates how these agents are poised to revolutionize sectors like healthcare, finance, and cybersecurity by offering solutions that are more efficient, transparent, and resilient than ever before.

Throughout the chapter, fictional narratives are interwoven to bring these concepts to life. These stories provide concrete examples of how AI agents might function with emerging technologies in real-world scenarios, making the material more relatable and helping you to see the practical implications of the technologies discussed. For instance, you will encounter scenarios where AI agents manage secure voting systems, enhance personalized medicine, and even contribute to large-scale climate modeling, all thanks to the foundational technologies explored in this chapter.

By the end of this chapter, you will have a solid understanding of the fundamental technologies that give rise to AI agents and how these agents can potentially transform various aspects of our lives. This foundational knowledge is crucial as the book progresses, leading deeper into each technology and exploring their ethical implications, real-world applications, and the future challenges they present. The rest of the chapter prepares you for a wide-ranging exploration of how these agents are being developed, what makes them unique, and how they will shape the future of technology and society.

Technological Innovations That Shape the Development of AI Agents: AI/ML, Blockchain, and Quantum Computing

In relation to how AI agents are developing, three technological innovations stand prominently at the forefront: AI, blockchain, and quantum computing. These technologies represent a significant leap in our ability to process information, secure data, and solve complex problems. However, the convergence of these fields is the place where their true transformative potential lies, promising a synergy poised to redefine our technological capabilities and applications in unprecedented ways.

The Emergence of Artificial Intelligence

From its origins in the mid-20th century to its current status as a keystone of modern technological innovation, artificial intelligence has journeyed from theoretical science to ubiquitous aspects of daily life. At its essence, AI involves the creation of machines capable of performing tasks that typically require human intelligence. This intelligence includes learning, reasoning, problem-solving, perception, and understanding language.

Early AI and the Advent of Neural Networks

AI began with simple algorithms designed to mimic basic human problem-solving and decision-making processes. These early AI systems were primarily rule-based, programmed to respond to specific inputs with predetermined responses. However, the advent of neural networks marked a significant paradigm shift. Neural networks, inspired by the structure and function of the human brain, allow AI systems to learn from vast amounts of data. They can make decisions and predictions based on patterns and experiences rather than just preprogrammed rules.

Applications and Impact

This evolution from rigid algorithms to adaptive learning models has dramatically expanded AI's capabilities and applications. Today, AI systems range from virtual assistants like Siri and Alexa, which have become integral to millions' daily routines, to more sophisticated applications in predictive analytics in finance, personalized medicine, and autonomous vehicles.

AI's impact is seen in various sectors. In healthcare, AI algorithms analyze medical records and imaging data to assist in diagnoses and treatment plans. In finance, AI is used for fraud detection, risk assessment, and algorithmic trading. Moreover, in autonomous vehicles, AI's advanced decision-making algorithms are crucial in navigating complex traffic environments.

Blockchain: Decentralized Trust

Blockchain technology has gained recognition for its significant role in developing and overseeing cryptocurrencies like Bitcoin (Nakamoto 2008). However, its impact extends beyond financial applications. This innovative technology signifies a fundamental shift in storing, organizing, and conducting digital data transactions.

Beyond Cryptocurrencies

Blockchain's initial association with Bitcoin has often overshadowed its broader applications. Beyond its role in cryptocurrencies, blockchain offers a decentralized and secure ledger system. This distributed database maintains a continuously growing list of records, known as blocks, linked and secured using cryptography.

Each block within a blockchain contains a cryptographic hash of the previous block, a timestamp, and transaction data, making the data within each block resistant to unauthorized modification. This feature has profound implications for applications requiring transparent and trustworthy record-keeping.

Expansion into Various Sectors

Blockchain technology has extended its influence beyond financial transactions to change various sectors. It plays a crucial role in supply chain management by ensuring the authenticity and traceability of products. Blockchain secures the electoral process against fraud in voting systems, making democracy more transparent and accountable.

One of the most innovative aspects of blockchain is the development of smart contracts. These are self-executing contracts, with the terms of the agreement between buyer and seller being directly written into lines of code. Smart contracts automate and enforce contractual agreements with a level of efficiency and security previously unattainable, extending blockchain's utility to virtually any scenario that requires contractual agreements, from real estate transactions to legal processes.

Quantum Computing: A Leap into the Future

Quantum computing is a new approach to processing information that harnesses the principles of quantum mechanics. It represents a paradigm shift from classical computing and has the potential to tackle some of the most intricate problems that are currently beyond the capabilities of traditional computers. These problems could include simulations of complex molecules for drug discovery, optimization of large-scale systems, and cryptography resistant to quantum attacks. Quantum computing's ability to process vast amounts of data simultaneously through quantum bits (qubits) opens up new frontiers in computation and problem-solving.

The Advent of Quantum Computing

The concept of quantum computing dates back to the 1980s, but significant progress was made in the 21st century. While it is still in the early stages of development compared to AI and blockchain, quantum computing has demonstrated immense potential in various fields.

The critical distinction between quantum and classical computing lies in their approach to processing information. Classical computers utilize bits (0s and 1s) for processing, whereas quantum computers utilize quantum bits, or qubits. Qubits possess the unique ability to exist simultaneously in multiple states due to superposition and entanglement, enabling quantum computers to process many possibilities simultaneously.

Transforming Industries

The potential of quantum computing to change our understanding in many fields, such as cryptography, material science, and pharmaceuticals, is immense. Quantum computing can factor large numbers exponentially faster than classical computers, which could render current encryption methods obsolete while paving the way for new, highly secure cryptographic techniques. In material science, quantum computing facilitates the simulation of molecular structures at an unprecedented level, offering opportunities to discover new materials with customized properties.

In the pharmaceutical industry, quantum computing accelerates drug discovery and personalized medicine by enabling the modeling and analysis of complex biological processes, leading to more effective treatments tailored to individuals.

The Convergence

The simultaneous development and integration of artificial intelligence, blockchain technology, and quantum computing unlocks unprecedented potential for innovation and transformation across industries. This convergence (see Figure 1-1) is not just a hypothetical concept; it is actively reshaping various fields and pushing the boundaries of what we once thought possible.

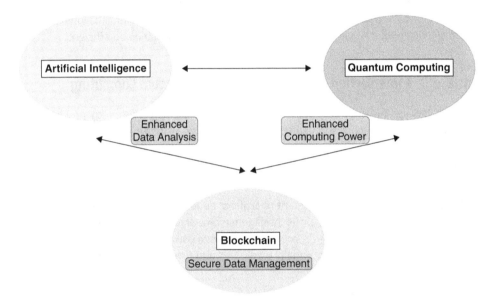

Figure 1-1
Convergence of AI, Blockchain, and Quantum Computing

AI and Blockchain Synergy

The integration of AI with blockchain technology is a significant step forward. AI's ability to process and analyze vast datasets can enhance the efficiency of blockchain networks. Moreover, AI can learn from the data secured on blockchains, enabling more intelligent decision-making. Blockchain, in turn, provides a secure and transparent framework for managing the complex data and decision-making processes involved in AI systems. This ensures trust and accountability in AI-driven systems.

This integration is particularly impactful in sectors such as finance and healthcare. In finance, AI-driven predictive analytics, combined with blockchain's tamper-proof record-keeping, transforms transactions and trades. In healthcare, AI's ability to analyze patient data for personalized treatment is bolstered by blockchain's capacity to manage patient records, ensuring privacy and data integrity securely.

Quantum Computing Boosting AI and Blockchain Capabilities

Quantum computing's integration with AI and blockchain further amplifies these technologies' capabilities. Quantum computing's ability to process massive datasets can dramatically accelerate AI's learning and problem-solving capabilities. This makes AI systems more efficient and effective, particularly in areas like machine learning, where large datasets are crucial for training algorithms.

Quantum computing offers new forms of security and efficiency for blockchain. The development of quantum-resistant algorithms ensures the protection of blockchain networks against potential quantum attacks. Additionally, quantum computing's speed and processing power can significantly enhance the performance of blockchain networks, making them more scalable and efficient.

Future Potential of the Intersection of AI, Blockchain, and Quantum Computing

As AI advances in understanding and interpreting complex data, blockchain technology provides a secure and transparent way to record and verify transactions. At the same time, quantum computing has the potential to solve complex problems at an unprecedented speed. Together, these technologies promise to create a future where technology is a powerful tool and a transformative force that shapes the world in ways we have yet to imagine.

The future of AI is moving toward the development of artificial general intelligence, or AGI (Goertzel 2007), AI that can understand, learn, and apply its intelligence broadly and flexibly, and perform any intellectual task that a human can do. AGI would be capable of complex decision-making and problem-solving in unfamiliar situations, potentially leading to significant advancements in various fields.

As the development of AGI nears reality, the conversation naturally extends to what may lie beyond this milestone. AGI represents a significant leap forward, enabling machines to perform a wide array of intellectual tasks on par with human capabilities. However, the next stage in this evolution is artificial superintelligence (ASI) (Bostrom 2014), which would not only replicate but exceed human intelligence across all domains. ASI is anticipated to possess unparalleled abilities in scientific creativity, problem-solving, and social interaction, potentially unlocking new frontiers in knowledge and innovation that are currently beyond human reach.

The integration of ASI with emerging technologies like blockchain and quantum computing could further amplify its transformative potential. Quantum computing's extraordinary processing power could accelerate ASI's capacity to solve the most intricate problems, while blockchain could provide the necessary frameworks to ensure secure, transparent, and ethical deployment of such advanced intelligence. As we explore the future potential of AI, blockchain, and quantum computing, it is crucial to consider how these technologies might converge to create systems of intelligence that not only surpass human abilities but also require careful consideration of their ethical implications and the governance structures necessary to harness their power responsibly. This convergence could redefine our technological landscape, pushing the boundaries of what is possible and compelling us to rethink the very nature of intelligence, security, and human-machine interaction in the future.

Blockchain's future is envisaged to extend its reach far beyond current applications. Its integration with other emerging technologies, such as AI and the Internet of Things (IoT), will lead to more secure, efficient, and intelligent systems. These integrated systems can autonomously execute transactions and contracts, manage complex supply chains, and even govern intricate data networks such as those needed for smart cities. Future blockchain technology could provide open source and decentralized identity verification, making it more secure and user-friendly, potentially eliminating identity theft and fraud. It may also underpin voting systems globally, ensuring the integrity and transparency of electoral processes.

In quantum computing, the future promises to address some of the world's most intricate and pressing problems. Quantum computing could enable the creation of new materials with tailored properties, the development of highly effective drugs by accurately simulating molecular structures, and the resolution of complex optimization problems in logistics and manufacturing. Furthermore, quantum computing may benefit fields like climate modeling, allowing us to predict and mitigate the effects of climate change more effectively. It also holds the potential to accelerate the development of fusion energy, offering a clean and virtually limitless energy source.

Integration Case Studies and Theoretical Models

In healthcare, IBM's Watson (D. F.-I. J. of R. and Development and 2012, n.d.; … and 2010 2010; Beltzung 2013; Resonance and 2014, n.d.; Chandrasekar 2014; Zadrozny et al. 2015; Baker 2011; B. L.-I. J. of R. and Development and 2012, n.d.; Yang, Chesbrough, and Hurmelinna-Laukkanen 2020; Gliozzo et al. 2017), an AI system, is used to analyze patient data and provide personalized treatment options. As explored by companies like Google and IBM, quantum computing further enhances this by simulating molecular interactions at an unprecedented scale, leading to faster and more efficient drug development. This synergy paves the way for treatments tailored to individual genetic profiles, potentially transforming healthcare delivery.

In the financial sector, AI algorithms are integrated with blockchain to enhance fraud detection and risk management. Mastercard, for example, uses AI to analyze transaction data on its blockchain network for anomalies that suggest fraudulent activities. This integration allows for real-time, secure, and efficient transaction processing, significantly reducing the incidence of fraud.

Companies like IBM and Maersk use blockchain and AI to improve supply chain transparency and efficiency. Their solutions track the movement of goods globally, using AI to predict and manage logistics issues and blockchain to provide an immutable record of transactions and product journeys. This integration has significantly improved supply chain resilience, reduced costs, and enhanced consumer trust.

Quantum computing introduces the possibility of unbreakable encryption, addressing one of the significant challenges in cybersecurity. Companies like ID Quantique are already exploring quantum key distribution (QKD), which uses quantum mechanics principles to secure communication channels. Combined with AI-driven threat detection systems, this represents a significant advancement in securing digital communication against cyber threats.

The integration of these technologies is aiding in the fight against climate change. Quantum computing's advanced computational capabilities, combined with AI's pattern recognition skills, are being used to create more accurate climate models. These models help scientists and policymakers better understand and predict climate change, leading to more effective environmental policies and strategies.

In the automotive industry, companies like Tesla and Waymo are integrating AI with advanced computing techniques to develop autonomous vehicles. Quantum computing's potential to process complex algorithms rapidly can enhance the decision-making capabilities of AI in these vehicles, improving safety and efficiency.

These case studies and theoretical models demonstrate the individual strengths of AI, blockchain, and quantum computing and highlight their profound impacts on integration. The synergy of these technologies is transforming existing industries and paving the way for new technological paradigms and solutions to some of the world's most challenging problems.

In healthcare, AI can analyze vast amounts of patient data for personalized treatment, secured on a blockchain for privacy and integrity. Quantum computing could further enhance this by allowing the simulation and analysis of complex biological processes, leading to drug discovery and disease treatment breakthroughs. This integration could see AI predicting health issues before they manifest, blockchain securely managing patient data across global systems, and quantum computing enabling the discovery of cures for previously incurable diseases.

In the financial sector, AI's predictive analytics and blockchain's security could transform transactions and trading. Quantum computing could be utilized to solve complex financial models, optimize portfolios, and enhance risk management, potentially revolutionizing the entire industry. This use would allow for more secure and efficient transactions, reduce fraud, and provide transparency previously unseen in the financial world.

The field of cybersecurity could benefit significantly from the integration of these technologies. AI's ability to detect and respond to threats, combined with blockchain's secure record-keeping and quantum computing's potential to create unbreakable encryptions, could lead to the development of nearly impenetrable cybersecurity systems. These systems could result in a digital world where data breaches are a thing of the past and privacy is upheld at the highest standard.

The Ethical and Societal Implications

The integration of these technologies raises questions about privacy, security, and the ethical use of AI. We need to ensure that these technologies are used for the betterment of society. This includes developing frameworks and guidelines to manage AI decision-making processes, ensuring transparency in blockchain applications, and setting standards for quantum computing use to prevent misuse.

Society must prepare for the changes these technologies will bring. This effort includes upskilling the workforce to meet the new demands of a technology-driven world and ensuring equitable access to these technologies. It also involves creating awareness about the potential and limitations of AI, blockchain, and quantum computing, fostering an informed public discourse about their use and impact.

These technologies can solve some of humanity's most complex problems, create new industries, and transform existing ones. However, governance and policy will be crucial in guiding the development and application of these technologies. The promise of a future shaped by the integration of these technologies is one of a more connected, efficient, and intelligent world. It is a future where technology enhances human capabilities, addresses pressing global challenges, and opens up new possibilities.

Summary

This chapter provided a broad overview of AI, blockchain, and quantum computing, exploring their evolutions, current applications, and future potential. We examined the convergence of these technologies and the vast opportunities this integration presents across various sectors. We also explored the ethical and societal implications, highlighting the need for responsible development and application. As we stand at the brink of this new technological era, the combined power of AI, blockchain, and quantum computing is poised to lead us into a future that extends beyond our current imagination. The following chapters will explore each technology in more detail, further unpacking the intricacies and possibilities of this exciting technological convergence.

References

C Thompson - Times Magazine (June 2011). http://www. nytimes, and undefined 2010. 2010. "What Is IBM's Watson." *Whsfilmfestival.Com*. http://www.whsfilmfestival.com/Walpole_High_School_Film_Festival/Grammar_Articles_files/Smarter%20Than%20You%20Think%20-%20I.B.M.'s%20Supercomputer%20to%20Challenge%20'Jeopardy!'%20Champions%20-%20NYTimes.com.pdf.

Baker, S. 2011. *Final Jeopardy: The Story of Watson, the Computer That Will Transform Our World*. https://books.google.com/books?hl=en&lr=&id=CwLSrDUoVB0C&oi=fnd&pg=PP1&dq=Watson+and+Jeopardy!+by+IBM+(2011)&ots=TPZ0AN5zB2&sig=7nl37ZkwaS_vV6HohOQqSucZ5wM.

Beltzung, Louise. 2013. "Watson Jeopardy! A Thinking Machine." https://citeseerx.ist.psu.edu/document?repid=rep1&type=pdf&doi=e123d71b927bddd5fd5873023804f06894b2831f.

Bostrom, Nick. 2014. *Superintelligence: Paths, Dangers, Strategies*. 9780198739838th ed. Vol. 0198739834. Oxford: Oxford University Press.

Chandrasekar, Raman. 2014. "Elementary? Question Answering, IBM's Watson, and the Jeopardy! Challenge." *Resonance* 19 (3): 222–41. https://doi.org/10.1007/S12045-014-0029-7.

Development, BL Lewis - IBM Journal of Research and, and undefined 2012. n.d. "In the Game: The Interface between Watson and Jeopardy!" *Ieeexplore.Ieee.Org*. Accessed October 20, 2023. https://ieeexplore.ieee.org/abstract/document/6177728/.

Development, DA Ferrucci - IBM Journal of Research and, and undefined 2012. n.d. "Introduction to 'This Is Watson.'" *Ieeexplore.Ieee.Org*. Accessed October 20, 2023. https://ieeexplore.ieee.org/abstract/document/6177724/.

Gliozzo, A, C Ackerson, R Bhattacharya, and A Goering. 2017. *Building Cognitive Applications with IBM Watson Services: Volume 1 Getting Started*. https://books.google.com/books?hl=en&lr=&id=7W0pDwAAQBAJ&oi=fnd&pg=PR5&dq=Watson+and+Jeopardy!+by+IBM+(2011)&ots=_BcdP51oRk&sig=KlFnqRXFU2w0ShhHUnJiUhF-JeM.

Goertzel, Ben. 2007. "Human-Level Artificial General Intelligence and the Possibility of a Technological Singularity. A Reaction to Ray Kurzweil's The Singularity Is Near, and McDermott's Critique of Kurzweil." *Artificial Intelligence* 171 (18): 1161–73. https://doi.org/10.1016/j.artint.2007.10.011.

Nakamoto, Satoshi. 2008. "Bitcoin: A Peer-to-Peer Electronic Cash System." *Decentralized Business Review*, 21260.

Resonance, R Chandrasekar -, and undefined 2014. n.d. "Elementary? Question Answering, IBM's Watson, and the Jeopardy! Challenge." *Springer*. Accessed October 20, 2023. https://idp.springer.com/authorize/casa?redirect_uri=https://link.springer.com/article/10.1007/s12045-014-0029-7&casa_token=YvPwOZBqloAAAAAA:NJQM01wcZCpFDAZk3yaBn15X3BPFgx_H5QrbDdfJOSnI1z5PirgFsS6GcpDocyyeFKwBqTTNmNEsQJPB.

Yang, J, H Chesbrough, and P Hurmelinna-Laukkanen. 2020. "The Rise, Fall, and Resurrection of IBM Watson Health." https://oulurepo.oulu.fi/bitstream/handle/10024/27921/nbnfi-fe2020050424858.pdf?sequence=1.

Zadrozny, WW, S Gallagher, … W Shalaby - Proceedings of the 46th, and undefined 2015. "Simulating IBM Watson in the Classroom." *Dl.Acm.Org*, February, 72–77. https://doi.org/10.1145/2676723.2677287.

Test Your Skills

Multiple-Choice Questions

These questions are designed to test understanding of the key concepts, focusing on the societal impacts, challenges, and future implications of AI in autonomous systems.

1. Which of the following technologies plays a key role in ensuring the security and transparency of transactions in a decentralized system?

   A. Artificial intelligence

   B. Quantum computing

   C. Blockchain

   D. Internet of Things (IoT)

2. Which technology is creating machines capable of tasks requiring human intelligence?

   A. Quantum computing

   B. Blockchain

   C. Artificial intelligence

   D. Digital encryption

3. What distinctive feature is associated with blockchain technology?

   A. High-speed data processing

   B. Immersive virtual reality creation

   C. Secure and transparent record-keeping

   D. Advanced biological simulations

4. What differentiates quantum computing from classical computing?

   A. The use of binary bits (0s and 1s)

   B. The employment of quantum bits (or qubits)

   C. The implementation of cryptographic hashes

   D. The reliance on deep learning algorithms

5. Neural networks serve which of the following functions in artificial intelligence?

   A. Securing data transactions

   B. Facilitating machine learning from data

   C. Developing decentralized databases

   D. Conducting quantum simulations

6. Which of the following sectors is significantly impacted by AI's predictive analytics?

    A. Logistics

    B. Finance and healthcare

    C. Automotive manufacturing

    D. Agricultural production

7. Which technology has evolved from rule-based systems to adaptive learning models?

    A. Blockchain

    B. Quantum computing

    C. Artificial intelligence

    D. Cybersecurity

8. The combination of AI and blockchain technology is particularly influential in which areas?

    A. Tourism and entertainment

    B. Education and training

    C. Finance and healthcare

    D. Art and design

9. What societal challenge is highlighted about advanced technological integration?

    A. Increased urbanization

    B. Enhanced entertainment experiences

    C. Job displacement risks

    D. Changes in culinary trends

10. Blockchain technology is primarily characterized by its ability to

    A. Speed up Internet connectivity.

    B. Enhance virtual reality experiences.

    C. Provide secure, transparent record-keeping.

    D. Increase the processing power of computers.

11. What role do neural networks play in the field of AI?

    A. Data encryption and security

    B. Enhancing graphical user interfaces

    C. Facilitating machine learning from vast data

    D. Conducting automated system diagnostics

12. What is the role of governance and policy in developing these technologies?

    A. Secondary to market forces

    B. Essential for guiding responsible development

    C. Irrelevant in the face of rapid innovation

    D. Focused solely on economic benefits

2

The Advance of Artificial Intelligence into AI Agents

Chapter Objectives

This chapter looks at the evolutionary journey of artificial intelligence (AI) and machine learning (ML) into AI agents, charting its progress from the early days to the advanced stages of deep learning. This exploration includes a detailed study of significant methodologies such as reinforcement learning, Q-learning, and the innovative concept of neural Turing machines (NTMs). Through this chapter, you will achieve the following objectives

- **Trace AI's Historical Progression**: Understand the evolution of artificial intelligence, beginning with its early concepts and leading up to the sophisticated algorithms that define the field today.

- **Comprehend the Transition from Machine Learning to Deep Learning**: Gain insights into how AI progressed from basic machine learning techniques to the more complex structures of deep learning, identifying key milestones and breakthroughs in this transition.

- **Explore Reinforcement Learning and Q-Learning**: Delve into the specifics of reinforcement learning and Q-learning, understanding their fundamental principles, applications, and impact on AI.

- **Understand Neural Turing Machines**: Acquire a comprehensive understanding of them, appreciating their significance in bridging the gap between traditional Turing machines and modern neural networks.

- **Analyze the Evolutionary Impact on Current AI Applications**: Examine how these advancements have shaped current AI applications, particularly in fields requiring complex decision-making and problem-solving.

- **Recognize the Challenges and Breakthroughs**: Identify the challenges encountered in AI's evolution and the groundbreaking solutions that have propelled the field forward.

- **Evaluate the Future Potential of AI Evolution**: Assess future developments in AI, considering the current trajectory and emerging trends in machine learning and neural networks.

- **Reflect on the Broader Implications of AI's Evolution**: Consider the broader implications of these advancements in AI on society, technology, and industry, preparing for the exploration of more complex applications and ethical considerations in later chapters.

By the end of this chapter, you will have a thorough understanding of AI's historical and technical progression, equipping you with the knowledge to understand its current state and potential future developments. This chapter investigates the profound developments in AI, tracing its inception and focusing on the transition from machine learning to deep learning. Additionally, it explores the advancements in reinforcement learning, Q-learning, and neural Turing machines, each representing a significant leap in our quest to create machines capable of learning, reasoning, and decision-making. These advancements have paved the way for a deeper understanding of cognitive processes and the potential for creating more advanced and autonomous systems.

In the early days, machine learning, a subset of AI, emerged from the desire to shift from explicit programming of computers to a paradigm where machines could learn from data. The founding work in the 1950s and '60s, including Frank Rosenblatt's Perceptron (Rosenblatt 1958; Minsky and Papert 2017; Bourlard and Kamp 1988), laid the foundation for what would evolve into modern ML. This marked the beginning of algorithms that could make predictions or decisions based on data input.

Before ML took center stage, AI development was dominated by symbolic AI, which focused on encoding intelligence through logic and rules. These systems excelled in environments with clear, well-defined rules but needed help with the complexity and ambiguity of real-world data. The limitations of symbolic AI, such as its inability to learn from data, eventually led to the pursuit of more adaptable, data-driven approaches.

This chapter is designed to understand how the foundational advancements in AI have directly influenced the development of AI agents—autonomous systems capable of complex tasks that once required human intelligence.

The section opens with a look at the historical milestones in AI, starting from simple machine learning models to more advanced deep learning techniques. This progression isn't just a series of technical achievements; it's a journey that has enabled the creation of AI agents capable of processing large volumes of data, identifying patterns, and making decisions. These abilities are foundational for AI agents as they navigate real-world environments and interact with humans in increasingly sophisticated ways.

Next, the chapter delves into specific AI methodologies like reinforcement learning (Lapan 2018) and Q-learning (Watkins and Dayan 1992). These approaches are vital for teaching AI systems how to make decisions and improve over time through trial and error. For AI agents, this means the ability to adapt to new situations and refine their actions based on feedback, which is crucial for tasks such as autonomous driving, robotics, and financial modeling. Understanding these learning processes is key to grasping how AI agents evolve and become more effective in their roles.

The chapter also covers neural Turing machines, a significant advancement that combines neural networks with memory capabilities. This development is particularly relevant for AI agents that need to remember and use past information to make better decisions in complex and changing environments. NTMs are paving the way for AI agents that can perform tasks requiring cognitive flexibility and long-term information retention, such as planning and problem-solving.

The ability to train more complex models has been critical in enhancing the capabilities of AI agents, allowing them to handle more sophisticated tasks and improve their decision-making processes. This section highlights how these technological advancements support the infrastructure necessary for AI agents to operate effectively.

As AI agents become more prevalent, issues such as transparency in decision-making and the ethical implications of their actions come to the forefront. This discussion is essential for anyone involved in the development or deployment of AI agents, as it provides a framework for thinking about the broader impact of these technologies on society.

The Rise of Neural Networks and Deep Learning

The concept of neural networks, a cornerstone in AI, dates back to the 1940s, with early models like the McCulloch-Pitts neuron. However, the pivotal development came with the Perceptron in 1958, demonstrating the potential of machines to learn from data. Despite facing challenges and periods of slowed progress, neural networks have become a fundamental element in AI. In Figure 2-1, we can see the timeline of AI development from 1940 until the present.

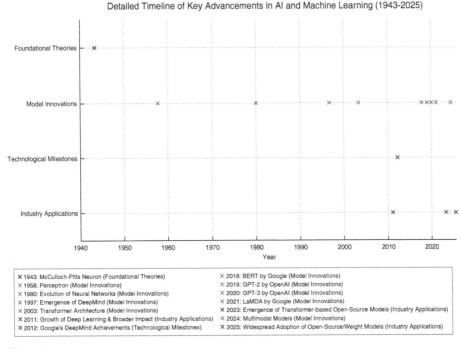

Figure 2-1
Timeline of Neural Networks and Deep Learning Development

Neural networks possess the remarkable ability to learn and recognize complex patterns. Their layered structure enables them to process input data and identify intricate patterns and correlations, proving invaluable in applications such as recognizing speech patterns, interpreting visual data, and understanding natural language. The breakthrough in neural networks arrived with the development of deep neural networks (DNNs), which comprise multiple layers of neurons and allow the network to model complex, high-level abstractions. This has paved the way for significant advancements, such as Google's DeepMind (Chang et al. 2016), which developed a deep neural network that accurately identifies objects in images and enhances user experience in applications like Google Photos.

Deep learning is a specific approach within machine learning based on artificial neural networks and represents a revolutionary leap in AI. It transcends the limitations of traditional machine learning algorithms by employing networks with many layers, enabling the system to learn from vast amounts of data. The rise of deep learning has been facilitated by the exponential increase in computational power and the availability of large datasets, making it possible to train deep neural networks effectively. This has profoundly impacted various fields, including natural language processing, autonomous systems, and healthcare, where deep learning has transformed diagnostics and treatment, showcasing its potential to augment human expertise.

In Figure 2-2, the timeline diagram visually represents the concepts and historical development discussed in the text, focusing on the evolution of neural networks and deep learning from the 1940s to the present. The timeline includes critical elements such as early models, the development of layered structures, breakthroughs with deep neural networks, and the impact on various fields. This visual representation shows the growth and significance of neural networks and profound learning in AI.

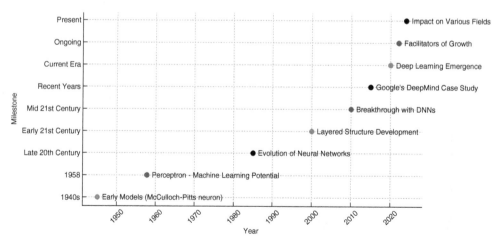

Figure 2-2

Timeline of Neural Networks and Deep Learning Evolution

The timeline diagram in Figure 2-2 illustrates the evolution of neural networks and deep learning. It starts in the 1940s, highlighting the introduction of early models like the McCulloch-Pitts neuron. In 1958, the development of the Perceptron was demonstrated, validating the potential of machines to learn from data. Moving toward the late 20th century, we observe the evolution of neural networks, a period marked by challenges and gradual progress. In the early 21st century, the diagram indicates the development of layered structures, crucial for pattern recognition and data processing. Advancing to the mid-21st century, we see the breakthrough with deep neural networks, introducing multiple layers of neurons. The recent years focus on case studies, such as Google's DeepMind, showcasing practical applications. The current era is defined by the emergence of deep learning, surpassing traditional machine learning. Ongoing developments emphasize the facilitators of growth, such as computational power and large datasets. Finally, the present day reflects the impact on various fields, including healthcare, autonomous systems, and natural language processing. This diagram offers a clear, chronological perspective of how neural networks and deep learning have evolved and influenced the field of AI.

Computational Power and Big Data

The rise of deep learning has been facilitated by two critical factors: the exponential increase in computational power and the availability of large datasets. The advent of graphics processing units (GPUs) and tensor processing units (TPUs) has provided the necessary computational resources to train deep neural networks effectively. Simultaneously, the digital age has seen an explosion of data, providing the extensive datasets required for training these networks.

Following the significant advancements brought about by GPUs and TPUs, a new area of research and development gaining considerable attention is the use of application-specific integrated circuits (ASICs) for AI workloads. Unlike GPUs and TPUs, which are designed to handle a wide range of tasks, ASICs are custom-built hardware designed to perform specific tasks with high efficiency. Recent studies and industry trends suggest that ASICs could potentially outperform traditional GPUs in specific AI applications, especially in areas where power, efficiency, and speed are paramount.

ASICs offer several advantages, such as reduced power consumption and increased processing speed for specific tasks, making them particularly appealing for large-scale AI models and data centers where energy efficiency is critical. This has sparked discussions on whether the future of AI hardware may shift away from the dominance of general-purpose processors like GPUs to more specialized, task-specific solutions like ASICs. The ongoing research into ASICs is exploring how these chips can be optimized for different AI workloads, potentially leading to significant computational power and efficiency breakthroughs, further accelerating the pace of AI innovation.

A notable example of deep learning's impact is in natural language processing (NLP). OpenAI's GPT (Generative Pre-trained Transformer) models have demonstrated remarkable capabilities in generating human-like text, translating languages, and composing poetry and prose. These models, trained on diverse Internet text, have pushed the boundaries of what AI can achieve in understanding and generating human language.

Deep learning has significantly impacted the development of autonomous systems, particularly in the automotive industry. Tesla, for instance, employs deep learning algorithms in its Autopilot feature, enabling vehicles to navigate complex driving scenarios with increasing autonomy. These systems rely on deep neural networks to process and interpret vast amounts of sensory data, making split-second decisions that mimic human driving instincts.

In healthcare, deep learning is transforming diagnostics and treatment. Google Health's deep learning model can detect breast cancer in mammography screenings more accurately than human radiologists. This breakthrough illustrates deep learning's potential to augment human expertise, leading to earlier and more accurate diagnoses.

The rise of neural networks and deep learning marks a monumental stride in AI's journey. From early models mimicking essential brain functions to advanced systems capable of complex tasks, this evolution signifies a fundamental shift in how we approach problem-solving and decision-making in machines. As deep learning continues to evolve, it promises to unlock further capabilities in AI, driving innovation across various domains, from healthcare to autonomous vehicles and beyond.

While deep learning offers immense benefits, it poses challenges and ethical considerations. These models' "black box" nature, where the decision-making process is not always transparent or interpretable, raises concerns in critical applications like healthcare and criminal justice. Furthermore, the requirement for large datasets poses privacy concerns, while the computational demands raise environmental issues.

Reinforcement Learning: Learning Through Interaction

Reinforcement learning (RL) is a unique branch of machine learning that focuses on learning through interaction with the environment. Unlike traditional supervised and unsupervised learning, RL relies on trial and error to learn. At the core of RL is the concept of an "agent" who knows how to make decisions by taking actions within an environment to achieve a specific goal. The agent's learning process is guided by a system of rewards and penalties, similar to a feedback loop, which helps determine the best actions or "policy" needed to accomplish its objective. This process mirrors how humans and animals learn from their experiences, making it suitable for problems involving sequential decision-making and strategic planning.

Figure 2-3 illustrates RL and its wide-ranging applications. RL's heart lies in the interaction between the agent and the environment. The agent engages in actions within the environment and receives feedback through state and reward. The learning process is exemplified through trial and error, focusing on sequential decision-making and strategic planning.

The diagram in Figure 2-3 enumerates various applications of RL, encompassing game playing (e.g., AlphaGo), robotics (e.g., Boston Dynamics robots), autonomous vehicles (e.g., Tesla), healthcare (e.g., treatment optimization), finance (e.g., algorithmic trading), and energy management (e.g., smart grids). This illustrative diagram serves to simplify the concept of RL and its diverse applications, thereby enhancing the comprehension of the fundamental principles and real-world impacts of reinforcement learning.

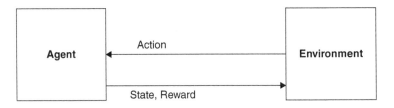

Learning through Trial and Error
- Sequential decision-making
- Strategic planning

Applications:
- Game playing (e.g., AlphaGo)
- Robotics (e.g., Boston Dynamics)
- Autonomous vehicles (e.g., Tesla)
- Healthcare (e.g., treatment optimization)
- Finance (e.g., algorithmic trading)
- Energy (e.g., smart grids)

Figure 2-3
Reinforcement Learning (RL) and Its Applications

The practical applications of RL are extensive, spanning multiple industries and disciplines. One of the most celebrated achievements in RL is Google DeepMind's AlphaGo. This AI program gained global recognition when it defeated Lee Sedol, a world-champion Go player, in a five-game match. The complexity of Go, with its vast number of possible positions, made it an ideal problem for RL. AlphaGo's victory showcased the ability of RL algorithms to tackle complex, strategic issues that require a deep understanding of long-term consequences and planning.

In robotics, RL has been crucial in developing systems capable of autonomous decision-making and complex task execution. For example, Boston Dynamics has developed robotic systems that can navigate complex terrains and perform intricate tasks, learning to adapt to changing environments through RL. These robots learn to optimize their actions for functions ranging from warehouse management to search and rescue operations through continuous interaction with their environment.

The automotive industry has leveraged RL in the development of autonomous vehicles. Companies like Tesla and Waymo use RL algorithms to teach cars how to navigate roads, respond to dynamic traffic conditions, and make split-second decisions. RL enables these vehicles to learn from vast amounts of driving data, honing their ability to make safe and efficient driving choices in real-world conditions.

RL algorithms are being explored in healthcare for personalized treatment plans and drug discovery. RL models can analyze patient data and clinical responses to develop tailored treatment strategies. For instance, RL optimizes chemotherapy regimens, balancing treatment efficacy with minimizing adverse effects. RL finds applications in algorithmic trading and risk management in the financial sector. Financial institutions use RL to develop trading algorithms that adapt to market changes and identify profitable trading opportunities. For example, hedge funds employ RL models to predict stock market trends and execute trades that maximize returns while managing risk. The energy sector utilizes RL to optimize consumption and distribution. RL algorithms help manage and balance energy supply and demand, leading to more efficient and sustainable energy systems. For instance, RL is used to optimize the operation of smart grids, ensuring the efficient distribution of renewable energy sources.

RL consists of two primary components: the agent and the environment. Figure 2-4 illustrates the concept, emphasizing its nature of learning through interaction. The diagram features the agent and the environment as primary components. Two prominent arrows represent the interaction between the agent and the environment. The arrow from the agent to the environment signifies the action taken by the agent. Conversely, the arrow from the environment to the agent depicts the reward/penalty that the agent receives as a consequence of its action.

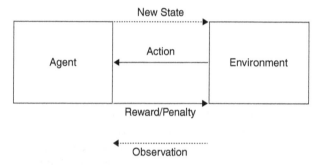

Figure 2-4
Reinforcement Learning: Learning Through Interaction—Agent Interacts with Environment Using Actions and Receives Rewards/Penalties

The diagram in Figure 2-4 captures the essence of RL's cyclical process of action, observation, and feedback, a fundamental aspect of learning through interaction in various domains such as strategic games, autonomous driving, and robotics.

Recent advancements in reinforcement learning have heralded the advent of innovative methodologies that integrate human and AI-generated feedback to optimize the learning process and enhance model alignment. A noteworthy example is reinforcement learning from human feedback (RLHF), wherein human evaluators are systematically embedded within the training pipeline. This approach allows the agent to iteratively refine its policy based on human judgment, which guides the learning process by assigning rewards or penalties that mirror human preferences. RLHF has demonstrated particular efficacy in domains requiring alignment with complex human values, such as the training of language models where ethical considerations and nuanced decision-making are crucial.

Extending the principles of RLHF, reinforcement learning with AI feedback (RLAIF) utilizes AI-generated feedback as a scalable alternative or complement to human input. RLAIF employs pretrained AI models to evaluate the agent's actions and provide feedback that simulates, or even augments, human evaluation. This approach not only reduces dependency on human involvement but also enhances the efficiency of the training process by enabling continuous, high-frequency feedback. RLAIF has shown significant promise in areas such as natural language processing and autonomous systems, contributing to real-time model refinement and improved policy generalization.

The implementation of these advanced techniques is exemplified by tools such as CriticGPT, which employs AI-driven feedback mechanisms to furnish a consistent and scalable framework for reinforcement learning. CriticGPT, for instance, dynamically assesses the agent's decisions and adjusts its feedback in a manner that aligns the model's behavior with the desired outcomes, thus proving itself as a potent instrument for the fine-tuning of complex models (see Figure 2-5).

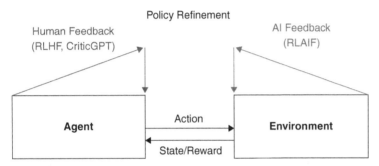

Figure 2-5
Advanced Reinforcement Learning System Integrating Human and AI Feedback for Policy Refinement

These advancements in reinforcement learning, through the integration of human and AI feedback mechanisms, are critical for the development of highly reliable and ethically aligned AI systems. By incorporating such methodologies, reinforcement learning can achieve greater robustness in policy learning, particularly in scenarios demanding a balance between efficiency, safety, and ethical considerations. This progress is pivotal in pushing the boundaries of AI applications across various high-stakes domains, including autonomous driving, healthcare, and strategic gameplay, where the implications of decision-making are profound.

With its unique approach to learning through interaction, RL has opened new frontiers in AI. From mastering strategic games to driving autonomous vehicles, RL continues to push the boundaries of what machines can learn and achieve. As we move forward, integrating RL with other AI techniques and continuously improving its algorithms promise even more incredible advancements, making RL a cornerstone in the ongoing evolution of intelligent systems.

Despite its wide-ranging applications, RL faces challenges, particularly regarding data efficiency and transfer learning. RL models often require significant data to learn effectively, and transferring learned policies to new but related tasks remains a complex issue. Addressing these challenges is crucial for RL's continued growth and application in real-world scenarios.

Q-Learning: An Off-Policy RL Algorithm

In artificial intelligence, Q-learning represents a fundamental shift in machine learning, enhancing the ability of AI systems to learn optimal policies through temporal difference learning.

The theoretical foundation of Q-learning is based on the Markov decision process (MDP), a framework for modeling decision making in situations where outcomes are partly random and partly under the control of a decision maker. In Q-learning, the algorithm aims to learn a policy that maximizes the cumulative reward by iteratively updating its Q-values. The Q-value represents the expected utility of taking a particular action in a given state, allowing the agent to make decisions optimizing long-term rewards. This approach enables the agent to learn the best course of action through trial and error, ultimately leading to more effective decision-making in complex environments.

Central to Q-learning is its update rule, formulated as:

$$Q(s,a) \leftarrow Q(s,a) + \alpha[r + \gamma \max a' Q(s',a') - Q(s,a)]$$

Here, α signifies the learning rate, γ the discount factor, s the current state, a' the current action, r the immediate reward, and s' the subsequent state. This rule allows the Q-values to converge toward the optimal policy iteratively.

It might be easier to understand this process in a diagram. Hence, Figure 2-6 provides a comprehensive diagram illustrating the concepts and applications of Q-learning. The diagram is structured to provide an overview of Q-learning as an off-policy reinforcement learning algorithm, highlighting the core concept of temporal difference learning and its connection to Markov decision processes. Additionally, the diagram expands into the theoretical foundation of Q-learning in MDPs, emphasizing the decision-making process in uncertain environments.

The diagram in Figure 2-6 includes detailed Q-learning algorithm components, including a flowchart or formula display showing the Q-learning update rule with explanations of each parameter (α, γ, Q-values, states, actions, and rewards). It also represents the iterative process of updating Q-values toward the optimal policy. The diagram covers various applications of Q-learning. These applications include automated trading, how Q-learning processes historical market data for trading decisions, and robotics, showcasing Q-learning's role in autonomous navigation and path optimization. The diagram depicts the integration of deep neural networks and Q-learning in advanced gaming scenarios.

In addition, the diagram in Figure 2-6 addresses the challenges and solutions associated with Q-learning. It illustrates significant challenges, such as the "curse of dimensionality" and the "exploration-exploitation dilemma." It depicts solutions, such as function approximation in Deep Q Networks (DQNs), ε-greedy strategy, and the Upper Confidence Bound (UCB).

The diagram in Figure 2-6 looks at the prospects and potential integration of Q-learning with emerging technologies, such as neuromorphic computing and federated learning. Finally, the diagram illustrates Q-learning's role and evolution in AI and machine learning, including its conjunction with deep learning. It provides a comprehensive view of Q-learning in the AI landscape.

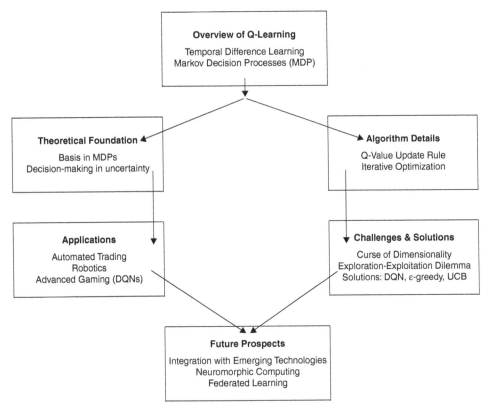

Figure 2-6
Q-Learning: An Off-Policy Reinforcement Learning Algorithm

Q-learning has been instrumental in automated trading, developing algorithms that execute trades based on predictive analytics. For example, in algorithmic trading platforms, Q-learning algorithms process historical market data to identify profitable trading opportunities, adapting to market volatility and anomalies. This has proven a valuable tool in the financial markets, enabling automated trading systems to make informed decisions based on historical patterns and market conditions.

Q-learning has also been successfully applied in robotics and exceptionally autonomous robotic navigation. It enables robots to find the best paths in dynamic environments, such as warehouse robots utilizing Q-learning to optimize route planning amidst changing obstacles, thus enhancing operational efficiency. This application of Q-learning showcases its adaptability and effectiveness in solving complex navigational challenges in real-world scenarios.

Another area where Q-learning has demonstrated remarkable capabilities is in advanced gaming through deep q networks. DQNs, agents integrate Q-learning with deep neural networks and have been utilized in playing complex games such as Atari 2600 games. The algorithm learns to play games at a superhuman level by processing raw pixel inputs and selecting appropriate actions, showcasing the potential for Q-learning to excel in highly dynamic and complex environments.

Despite its strengths, Q-learning confronts challenges, primarily when dealing with environments exhibiting high-dimensional state spaces, leading to the "curse of dimensionality." Addressing this challenge necessitates advanced function approximation techniques, where deep learning integrates with Q-learning, as seen in DQNs. Another challenge is the exploration-exploitation dilemma, which is critical in environments where sampling diverse experiences is computationally expensive or impractical. Techniques such as the ε-greedy strategy and Upper Confidence Bound have balanced exploration and exploitation. These challenges highlight the need for continued research and innovation to improve further the applicability and effectiveness of Q-learning in various domains.

Integration with Emerging Technologies

The combination of Q-learning with emerging technologies is an exciting frontier. For example, integrating Q-learning with neuromorphic computing can advance energy-efficient AI systems. Furthermore, incorporating Q-learning into federated learning paradigms could lead to decentralized, privacy-preserving AI applications.

As an off-policy RL algorithm, Q-learning is a cornerstone in the evolving landscape of AI and machine learning. Its adaptability to diverse environments and ability to learn optimal policies independently of the agent's actions underscore its importance. As AI advances, Q-learning, especially in conjunction with deep learning, will undoubtedly continue to play a crucial role in the quest to create more intelligent and autonomous systems. Exploring Q-learning's potential in new domains, and its integration with cutting-edge technologies, offers promising opportunities for future research, with the potential for significant breakthroughs in AI.

Neural Turing Machines: Bridging AI and Memory

Neural Turing machines (NTMs) are a groundbreaking fusion of neural networks and traditional Turing machines' external memory capabilities. This amalgamation empowers NTMs to process data and store and retrieve information, enabling them to tackle intricate tasks that necessitate memory. By mimicking a Turing machine's sequential access to memory, NTMs could revolutionize the field of artificial intelligence.

Despite their immense potential, NTMs encounter challenges due to their complexity and substantial computational demands. Integrating memory into neural networks demands sophisticated algorithms and significant processing power. Yet, their unique ability to learn sequential tasks and effectively utilize stored information positions NTMs as a critical advancement in AI, particularly in domains that mandate complex reasoning and long-term planning.

NTMs offer a promising avenue for addressing real-world problems that require memory-augmented neural networks. Their capacity to learn from sequential data and utilize stored information presents an exciting opportunity for developing intelligent systems capable of handling complex tasks more efficiently and accurately. Furthermore, the fusion of neural networks with memory capabilities opens the door to various applications, ranging from natural language processing to robotics.

Future Directions

We are witnessing exciting progress in the AI field. This growth includes more complex designs for neural networks, improved learning methods, and a closer integration of humans and machines. The future of neural networks may draw inspiration from the human brain, potentially utilizing *spiking neural networks* that mimic our brain's functionality. Additionally, we may see the emergence of "quantum neural networks" that can rapidly process information on a large scale.

Advancements in AI learning methods are anticipated, particularly in reinforcement learning and deep learning areas. These improvements aim to make AI more efficient and effective, addressing current challenges such as learning from limited data and applying learned knowledge to new but similar tasks.

A key focus for future AI is ensuring that AI systems make decisions transparently and ethically, especially in critical areas such as healthcare, finance, and autonomous vehicles. AI is also expected to work more effectively alongside humans, enhancing creative work and daily activities by understanding and predicting human needs.

One of the primary goals of AI is to develop systems that excel in various tasks, not just one specific function. This type of AI, known as artificial general intelligence (AGI) (Goertzel 2007), would significantly advance, offering capabilities similar to human thinking.

AI is expected to be increasingly used to combine different fields of study, leading to discoveries. For example, integrating AI with biology could result in new approaches to treating illnesses, while combining AI with materials science could lead to developing new materials and energy solutions. AI is also expected to focus more on assisting people.

Summary

This chapter reviewed AI's evolution, from its roots in machine learning to the cutting-edge realms of deep understanding, reinforcement learning, Q-learning, and neural Turing machines. These developments illustrate the rapid progress in AI and hint at the transformative potential AI holds for the future—a future where AI could redefine our understanding of intelligence and capability. Subsequent chapters will examine these areas more deeply, offering a more granular view of their mechanisms, challenges, and societal impacts.

References

Bourlard, H., and Y. Kamp. 1988. "Auto-Association by Multilayer Perceptrons and Singular Value Decomposition." *Biological Cybernetics* 59 (4): 291–94.

Chang, H. S., M. C. Fu, J. Hu, and S. I. Marcus. 2016. "Google DeepMind's AlphaGo: Operations Research's Unheralded Role in the Path-Breaking Achievement." *OR/MS Today* 43 (5). Accessed October 20, 2023. https://go.gale.com/ps/i.do?id=GALE%7CA471000820&sid=googleScholar&v=2.1&it=r&linkaccess=abs&issn=10851038&p=AONE&sw=w.

Goertzel, B. 2007. "Human-Level Artificial General Intelligence and the Possibility of a Technological Singularity. A Reaction to Ray Kurzweil's The Singularity Is Near, and McDermott's Critique of Kurzweil." *Artificial Intelligence* 171 (18): 1161–73. https://doi.org/10.1016/j.artint.2007.10.011.

Lapan, Maxim. *Deep Reinforcement Learning Hands-On: Apply modern RL methods, with deep Q-networks, value iteration, policy gradients, TRPO, AlphaGo Zero and more.* Packt Publishing Ltd, 2018.

Minsky, M., and S. A. Papert. 2017. "Perceptrons: An Introduction to Computational Geometry." *Perceptrons*, January. https://doi.org/10.7551/MITPRESS/11301.001.0001.

Rosenblatt, F. 1958. "The Perceptron: A Probabilistic Model for Information Storage and Organization in the Brain." *Psychological Review* 65 (6): 386–408. https://doi.org/10.1037/h0042519.

Watkins, C. J. C. H., and P. Dayan. 1992. "Q-Learning." *Machine Learning* 8 (3–4): 279–92. https://doi.org/10.1007/BF00992698.

Test Your Skills

Multiple-Choice Questions

These questions are designed to test understanding of the key concepts, focusing on the societal impacts, challenges, and future implications of AI in autonomous systems.

1. What was a critical factor in transitioning from symbolic AI to machine learning in the early days of AI's evolution?

    A. The development of quantum computing

    B. The inception of neural Turing machines

    C. The introduction of Frank Rosenblatt's Perceptron

    D. The emergence of deep learning algorithms

2. What marks the significant development in neural networks leading to modern AI?

    A. The creation of the McCulloch-Pitts neuron in the 1940s

    B. The development of the Perceptron in 1958

    C. The advent of quantum neural networks

    D. The introduction of spiking neural networks

3. Which of the following best describes the impact of deep learning in AI?

    A. It enabled AI to surpass the limitations of traditional machine learning algorithms.

    B. It reduced the need for large datasets in training models.

    C. It simplified the computational requirements for training neural networks.

    D. It focused on rule-based algorithms rather than data-driven approaches.

4. Reinforcement learning (RL) is distinct from other machine learning approaches because it does which of the following?

    A. Relies on labeled data for training

    B. Focuses on learning through interaction and trial and error

    C. Uses predefined rules for decision-making

    D. Prioritizes unsupervised learning techniques

5. What is a primary challenge faced by reinforcement learning models?

    A. Limited ability to process visual data

    B. Difficulty in transfer learning and data efficiency

    C. Lack of applications in real-world scenarios

    D. Inability to work with sequential decision-making

6. Q-learning, a fundamental shift in machine learning, primarily addresses which of the following?

   A. The limitations of supervised learning algorithms

   B. The integration of memory in neural networks

   C. Learning optimal policies through temporal difference learning

   D. The challenge of processing sensory data in autonomous systems

7. Neural Turing machines (NTMs) represent a significant advancement in AI because they do which of the following?

   A. Eliminate the need for large datasets in model training

   B. Combine neural networks with the memory capabilities of traditional Turing machines

   C. Focus solely on rule-based decision-making

   D. Are primarily used in the development of quantum computing

8. What future direction is anticipated for AI based on this chapter?

   A. Phasing out deep learning in favor of symbolic AI

   B. Drawing inspiration from human brain functionality, possibly through spiking neural networks

   C. Limiting AI applications to noncritical areas

   D. Focusing only on reinforcement learning methods

9. The main challenge associated with the "black box" nature of deep learning models is

   A. The inability to process large datasets.

   B. The difficulty in interpreting the decision-making process.

   C. The limitation of applying these models to real-world scenarios.

   D. The reliance on supervised learning methods.

10. What distinguishes Q-learning from other machine-learning techniques?

   A. It uses labeled data for decision-making.

   B. It relies on a trial-and-error approach to learn optimal policies.

   C. It focuses on sequential decision-making processes.

   D. It emphasizes temporal difference learning.

11. How has deep learning impacted the healthcare sector, as mentioned in the chapter?

    A. By simplifying administrative tasks

    B. By enhancing drug discovery processes

    C. By improving diagnostic accuracy, such as in breast cancer detection

    D. By replacing human decision-making in treatment plans

12. The "curse of dimensionality" is a challenge primarily associated with which of the following?

    A. Symbolic AI

    B. Neural Turing machines

    C. Q-learning

    D. Reinforcement learning

13. The concept of neural Turing machines (NTMs) is revolutionary because it does which of the following?

    A. Eliminates the need for reinforcement learning

    B. Combines external memory capabilities with neural networks

    C. Focuses exclusively on supervised learning methods

    D. Reduces the computational demands of AI models

14. What primary goal is identified in the chapter regarding AI's future potential?

    A. To focus solely on the development of autonomous vehicles

    B. To develop artificial general intelligence (AGI) with capabilities similar to human thinking

    C. To restrict AI applications to noncritical areas of technology

    D. To revert to the basics of machine learning

3

Digital Trust in AI Agents and Blockchain Technologies

Chapter Objectives

This chapter is an in-depth survey of digital trust and blockchain technologies. It provides a detailed analysis of distributed ledger technologies, offering a comprehensive examination of Ethereum and Hyperledger. Furthermore, the chapter expands into the integration of AI agents in blockchain, explicitly focusing on smart oracles and automated contracts. By the end of this chapter, you will have gained a thorough understanding of the technical workings, potential applications, and implications of these cutting-edge technologies, and you will be able to

- **Understand the Foundations of Blockchain Technology**: This chapter will help you gain a solid understanding of blockchain and how it establishes digital trust, laying the groundwork for exploring its various applications.

- **Explore Ethereum and Hyperledger**: Engage with the specifics of Ethereum and Hyperledger, two leading platforms in the blockchain domain, understanding their unique features, functionalities, and contributions to distributed ledger technology.

- **Comprehend the Integration of AI and Blockchain**: Learn about the innovative integration of AI with blockchain technology, mainly focusing on how AI can enhance blockchain functionality through smart oracles and automated contracts.

- **Analyze Smart Oracles**: Understand the concept of smart oracles, exploring how they operate and their role in bridging external data with blockchain networks.

- **Investigate Automated Contracts**: Examine the development and application of automated contracts, evaluating how they leverage AI to automate and enhance the efficiency and reliability of blockchain transactions.

- **Recognize the Challenges and Solutions in Blockchain Integration**: Identify the challenges faced in integrating AI with blockchain technology and the solutions developed to address these issues.

- **Evaluate the Implications of AI-Enhanced Blockchain**: Assess the broader implications of AI-enhanced blockchain technologies in various sectors, including finance, supply chain, and healthcare, considering both the opportunities and potential risks.

- **Predict Future Trends in Blockchain and AI Integration**: Anticipate future developments and trends in integrating AI and blockchain, considering how this synergy could evolve and shape future technological environments.

This chapter examines how blockchain technologies are related to establishing and maintaining trust, which is essential for AI agents to function effectively and securely in a decentralized digital environment. It discusses how blockchain serves as the backbone of trust for AI agents, ensuring that their operations are transparent, reliable, and resistant to tampering.

The chapter begins by introducing blockchain as a distributed ledger. For AI agents, this technology is crucial because it provides a secure and immutable record of transactions and interactions, making it possible for these agents to operate in environments where trust is not governed by a central authority but is instead distributed across a network. This distributed nature of trust is particularly important for AI agents that need to operate autonomously and make decisions based on data from multiple sources.

Next, we advance into specific blockchain platforms, such as Ethereum and Hyperledger, and their roles in supporting AI agents. Ethereum's smart contracts, for instance, allow AI agents to execute agreements automatically when certain conditions are met, without the need for human intervention. Hyperledger, with its permissioned networks, offers a secure and scalable solution for enterprise applications, where AI agents can interact within a controlled environment, ensuring that sensitive information is protected.

The integration of AI with blockchain is explored further through concepts like smart oracles and automated contracts. Smart oracles are critical for AI agents because they enable these systems to access and utilize real-world data in real time. By bridging the gap between on-chain and off-chain data, smart oracles enhance the decision-making capabilities of AI agents, allowing them to act on accurate and timely information. This capability is particularly relevant in scenarios like financial markets or supply chains, where AI agents must respond swiftly to external changes.

Automated contracts, powered by machine learning (ML) algorithms, represent another significant advancement. These contracts allow AI agents to automatically enforce agreements based on data-driven insights, making processes more efficient and reducing the potential for human error. This section highlights how the combination of AI and blockchain not only automates transactions but also ensures that they are carried out with a high degree of trust and security.

Throughout the chapter, the emphasis is placed on the challenges and opportunities that arise from integrating AI with blockchain. Issues such as data privacy, scalability, and the need for standardized protocols are discussed, providing a realistic view of the current state of the technology. These challenges are particularly relevant for the development of AI agents because they must navigate complex digital ecosystems while maintaining trustworthiness and efficiency.

The Essence of Blockchain as a Distributed Ledger

Traditionally, trust was based in big institutions like banks, legal systems, and governments. However, with blockchain technology, trust has moved to a system that is not controlled by one central authority. Blockchain, as a type of technology, challenges old ideas of trust by recording and synchronizing transactions across a network of different parts.

At its core, a blockchain is a type of technology where data is organized into blocks, each containing a unique code, a timestamp, and transaction data. This structure makes it hard to change data. Since each block is linked to the one before, changing one record would mean changing all the blocks after it, which is too hard to do on a well-distributed network. This unchangeable nature is one of the main things that makes people trust a blockchain.

Trust in blockchain depends on its rules, which ensure that all parts of the network agree on the system's state. Bitcoin, the first extensive use of blockchain, used the proof of work (PoW) system, where people solve challenging puzzles to ensure transactions are OK and to create new blocks. But PoW uses a lot of energy. Ethereum at first used PoW, but moving to Ethereum 2.0 means it's using proof of stake (PoS). In PoS, people who check things are chosen to make new blocks based on the number of coins they have and are willing to "stake" as a promise. This change deals with energy worries and opens new ways to make finance more efficient and bigger.

Ethereum is unique because it supports intelligent contracts, such as self-running contracts with terms written into code. Smart contracts do things independently, meaning we don't need intermediaries. Ethereum's primary computer language, Solidity, is the usual way to write smart contracts. Solidity makes it easier to create complicated apps for different industries, including finance and healthcare, and to make and move things, showing that Ethereum is valuable for more than just money.

However, Ethereum needs help, especially with its capabilities. The old Ethereum system could only process about 15 transactions in a second, less than other payment methods. Ethereum 2.0, with its change to PoS and creation of shard chains, wants to process a lot more transactions, maybe thousands in a second.

Another worry is Ethereum's move from PoW to PoS. This change is good for energy but brings new concerns about safety and security.

Ethereum does many things, but Hyperledger does things in a way that's more for big companies. Hyperledger is part of the Linux Foundation and has many ways to make blockchains that fit in with big businesses' needs. Unlike Ethereum, Hyperledger works with private blockchains and needs permission, which fits with what companies need to keep things private and follow the rules.

Hyperledger Fabric, part of Hyperledger, is unique because it can be changed to suit companies' needs. It has ways to keep things private and different ways for people to agree, run code, and manage who's who, making it suitable for many industries.

The big difference between Ethereum and Hyperledger Fabric is what they're used for and how they're made. Ethereum is known for being used for different things and working with smart contracts, whereas Hyperledger Fabric is set up for big companies and works with private blockchains that can be changed to suit companies' needs.

Ethereum and the Evolution of Blockchain Ecosystems

In the modern digital environment, Ethereum is more than just a cryptocurrency (Wood 2017). Created by Vitalik Buterin, this platform goes beyond currency and serves as a stronghold for intelligent contracts and decentralized applications (dApps). Unlike Bitcoin, which mainly functions as a digital currency, Ethereum introduces Solidity, a Turing-complete programming language (Buterin 2014). This allows developers to directly encode complex contractual terms into lines of code, marking a significant advancement over previous digital currency platforms.

Ethereum's architecture revolves around the Ethereum Virtual Machine (EVM), a global computer (Altarawneh et al. 2020). In this network, each node replicates transaction execution to maintain a consistent and synchronized ledger state. Ether, Ethereum's native token, fuels these transactions. The concept of "gas" in Ethereum measures computational efforts, ensuring efficient transaction processing and protecting against network abuse. Through its developmental phases—Frontier, Homestead, Metropolis, and Serenity—Ethereum demonstrates its commitment to scalability, security, and sustainability. The transition to Ethereum 2.0, moving from PoW to PoS, represents a significant step forward, particularly in addressing the energy-intensive nature of operations and improving transaction throughput.

However, Ethereum's journey in the blockchain space is complemented by the emergence of other blockchains, each carving out unique niches. Cardano, for instance, strides forward with a research-driven approach. Orchestrated by Charles Hoskinson, one of Ethereum's cofounders, Cardano aims to tackle the scalability, interoperability, and sustainability challenges inherent in earlier blockchain iterations. Ouroboros's PoS consensus algorithm presents a more energy-efficient and secure framework. Cardano also emphasizes the formal verification of smart contracts, ensuring higher security and reliability.

In another innovative twist, Solana makes its mark with high throughput and low transaction costs. It introduces the proof of history (PoH) mechanism, creating a historical record that timestamps events, thus facilitating greater scalability and efficiency. Solana has an impressive capability of handling thousands of transactions per second, significantly outperforming Ethereum's current capacity.

Cosmos (ATOM), known as the Internet of blockchains, envisions an interconnected blockchain ecosystem. It employs independent yet interoperable blockchains to solve scalability and interoperability issues. Cosmos utilizes the Tendermint consensus model, which decouples the application layer from the consensus and networking layers. This architecture offers a more adaptable and scalable solution, catering to various blockchain applications.

Several Layer 2 protocols have surfaced to address Ethereum's scalability issues. They operate atop the Ethereum blockchain to enhance transaction speed and cost-effectiveness. Arbitrum and Optimism employ Optimistic Rollups, assuming transactions are valid by default and running computations only in case of a challenge. This approach significantly increases throughput while leveraging Ethereum's security model.

zkSync utilizes zero-knowledge rollups (zk-Rollups), bundling transactions into a single process through zero-knowledge proofs. This approach dramatically reduces data per transaction, lowering fees and hastening processing times while maintaining robust security. Other solutions like Loopring use zk-Rollups for efficient trading and payments, and Plasma creates subsidiary blockchains linked to the main Ethereum chain, thereby alleviating the main chain's transaction load.

The integration of these technologies demonstrates a concerted effort to address the blockchain trilemma of scalability, security, and decentralization. While Ethereum remains a trailblazer in smart contract and dApp development, alternative blockchains like Cardano, Solana, and Cosmos bring diversity and innovation. These platforms, each with unique characteristics, contribute significantly to the evolving narrative of blockchain technology.

The emerging alternative blockchains and the development of Layer 2 solutions signify a maturing ecosystem. It is an ecosystem characterized by diverse, complementary technologies, each contributing to blockchain applications' robustness and multifaceted nature. In particular, Ethereum's Layer 2 scaling solutions represent a vital development in maintaining the platform's relevance and efficacy in the face of rapidly evolving blockchain technologies.

As the blockchain environment evolves, the interaction between Ethereum, its contemporaries, and Layer 2 solutions will undeniably shape the future of decentralized applications and smart contracts. This ecosystem's dynamic and innovative nature ensures that it remains at the forefront of digital transaction technology, constantly pushing the boundaries of what is possible in decentralized trust and digital contracts.

The blockchain ecosystem, led by Ethereum but enriched by various other technologies and platforms, is a testament to the innovative spirit of digital transaction technology. As we move forward, this ecosystem will continue to evolve, adapting to new challenges and opportunities and paving the way for a future where decentralized trust and digital contracts play a vital role in the digital economy.

Hyperledger: A Consortium for Enterprise Blockchain Solutions

Hyperledger stands out as a leading provider of enterprise blockchain solutions. Hosted by the Linux Foundation, Hyperledger differs from platforms like Ethereum, which target a wider audience. It is not a standalone blockchain but an umbrella project that includes a range of modular frameworks, each designed to meet specific business requirements. Notably, Hyperledger Fabric, Sawtooth, and Besu are well regarded for their unique capabilities and ability to adapt to various industrial applications.

Hyperledger Fabric is at the forefront of this suite and is renowned for creating permissioned networks. Participant identities are known in these networks, making it an ideal choice for scenarios where privacy and compliance are paramount. Fabric's architecture, built on pluggable consensus mechanisms, provides a flexible and scalable foundation, accommodating a diverse range of industrial applications. Its smart contracts, called chain code, offer a robust framework for automating and enforcing complex business agreements.

Complementing Fabric in Hyperledger's array is Sawtooth, which distinguishes itself with a focus on energy efficiency. Sawtooth employs the proof of elapsed time (PoET) consensus mechanism, a less energy-intensive alternative to traditional PoW systems. Its design supports permissioned and permissionless network configurations, demonstrating a versatility that caters to various enterprise needs. Sawtooth's approach to scalability and energy efficiency presents an attractive proposition for businesses mindful of their environmental impact and operational costs.

In contrast, Hyperledger Besu targets Ethereum-based applications, offering compatibility with public and private networks. This characteristic positions Besu uniquely, facilitating interoperability with Ethereum's public network while retaining the privacy and control of a permissioned system. It indicates the growing demand for flexible blockchain solutions that improve public transparency and private confidentiality.

The diagram in Figure 3-1 illustrates the essence of blockchain as a distributed ledger. It is divided into several sections to convey crucial points effectively. The top section represents the general structure of blockchain technology, highlighting how data is organized into blocks containing unique codes, timestamps, and transaction data. The middle section is divided into two parts, focusing on Ethereum and Hyperledger. It emphasizes their distinct features, changes in consensus mechanisms (such as the transition from PoW to PoS in Ethereum), and their suitability for different applications. The bottom section addresses additional concerns and features related to blockchain technology, including trust, scalability, environmental impacts, and security implications. This visual representation aims to provide a broad understanding of the intricate concepts associated with blockchain technology.

A new perspective emerges when evaluating these offerings against other enterprise blockchain solutions, such as R3's Corda and the Enterprise Ethereum Alliance (EEA). Corda, primarily serving the financial sector, excels in transactional privacy, a critical requirement in finance. However, its focus is narrower than Hyperledger's, which offers a wide range of industrial applications. On the other hand, the EEA leverages Ethereum's technology for business use. While it benefits from Ethereum's established technology and vast developer community, adapting a public blockchain for enterprise use can present challenges in customizability and privacy control, where Hyperledger's purpose-built enterprise solutions tend to have an edge.

Integrating AI into blockchain technology adds complexity and potential to these platforms. Smart oracles and automated contracts are two significant areas where AI reshapes blockchain functionality (Kumar, Nikhil, and Singh 2020). Traditional oracles, which act as intermediaries between blockchains and external data sources, are evolving into smart oracles with the integration of AI. This advancement allows for sophisticated data analysis, enhancing the accuracy and reliability of the information fed into blockchain networks. These capabilities are crucial in applications such as market predictions or automated compliance checks, where nuanced data interpretation is essential.

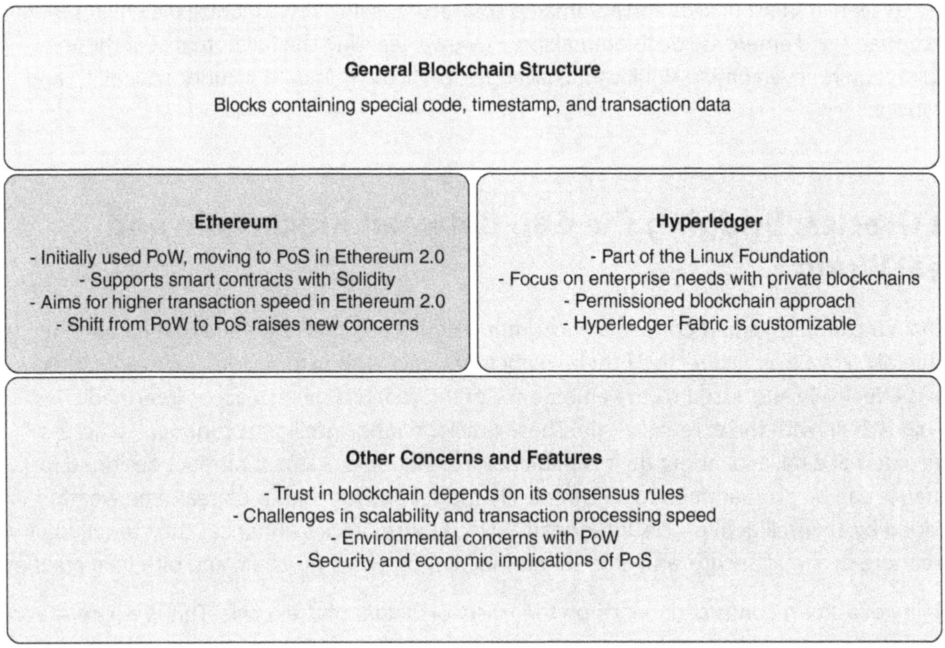

General Blockchain Structure

Blocks containing special code, timestamp, and transaction data

Ethereum

- Initially used PoW, moving to PoS in Ethereum 2.0
- Supports smart contracts with Solidity
- Aims for higher transaction speed in Ethereum 2.0
- Shift from PoW to PoS raises new concerns

Hyperledger

- Part of the Linux Foundation
- Focus on enterprise needs with private blockchains
- Permissioned blockchain approach
- Hyperledger Fabric is customizable

Other Concerns and Features

- Trust in blockchain depends on its consensus rules
- Challenges in scalability and transaction processing speed
- Environmental concerns with PoW
- Security and economic implications of PoS

Figure 3-1

The Essence of Blockchain as a Distributed Ledger

Another exciting development is AI-enhanced automated contracts. These contracts leverage machine learning algorithms to adapt and respond to changing conditions, enabling a more dynamic and responsive contractual framework. Such flexibility is particularly advantageous in sectors like logistics and finance, where contract terms often hinge on fluctuating external factors, such as market prices or inventory levels.

Integrating AI into blockchain has its challenges. Ensuring data privacy and security within this amalgamation is a complex task, given the immutable nature of blockchain records and the dynamic data requirements of AI algorithms. The computational intensity of AI presents scalability challenges for blockchain networks, necessitating ongoing research and development efforts to optimize their integration.

As these technologies evolve, there is a growing focus on interoperability between different blockchain platforms, as exemplified by Hyperledger Besu's compatibility with Ethereum. Such interoperability is crucial for fostering a collaborative and efficient blockchain ecosystem. The future trajectory of enterprise blockchain solutions seems geared toward platforms that can provide tailored solutions to specific industry problems and seamlessly interact with other blockchain systems and technologies.

Hyperledger's suite of blockchain solutions represents a far-reaching approach to addressing the diverse needs of enterprises. Compared with platforms like R3's Corda and the EEA, Hyperledger's breadth of industrial applicability and flexibility stands out. Additionally, the integration of AI into blockchain, as seen in smart oracles and automated contracts, is set to revolutionize the environment of digital contracts and enterprise decision-making. However, realizing the full potential of these technologies requires overcoming significant challenges, particularly in data security, scalability, and interoperability.

Smart Oracles: Bridging the Gap Between Blockchain and the Real World

In blockchain technology, smart contracts encounter a significant challenge due to their confinement within blockchain, which restricts their ability to interact with external data or events. This limitation is effectively addressed by the emergence of *smart oracles*, which act as intermediaries bridging blockchain with the external world. These oracles enable intelligent contracts to access and utilize external data, expanding their capabilities. For example, a smart contract designed for crop insurance can be programmed to automatically trigger payouts based on real-time weather data provided by an intelligent oracle. Integrating AI into these oracles enhances their functionality, ensuring a more dynamic, secure, and efficient connection between on-chain and off-chain realities.

The reliability of a smart contract depends on the trustworthiness of the oracle. This is where AI can be utilized. By integrating AI algorithms, smart oracles can analyze data from various sources, reducing the risks of inaccuracies and manipulation. Smart oracles represent a significant advancement from traditional oracles. These advanced entities use AI algorithms to gather, validate, and analyze data from various external sources. This enhanced capability is transformative, especially in automating data-driven processes that require interaction with the real world. For instance, consider a smart contract that oversees crop insurance. A smart oracle could automatically make payouts by analyzing weather data, turning what was once a manual, error-prone process into a streamlined, automated operation.

On the other hand, the reliability and integrity of smart oracles is crucial, as the authenticity of the data they provide is fundamental to the validity of the entire innovative contract process. The integration of AI is instrumental here, using sophisticated data analytics, machine learning, and possibly natural language processing to identify and validate relevant information. This technological advancement significantly reduces the likelihood of inaccuracies or manipulations, which have been persistent concerns with conventional oracles.

Oracles are essential for bringing real-world data into blockchain networks, thereby enabling smart contracts to function autonomously and accurately in response to external conditions.

Human oracles represent one of the most traditional forms of data verification within blockchain ecosystems. These individuals, often experts in specific fields, provide trusted data inputs for smart contracts. By leveraging their specialized knowledge, human oracles can verify, validate, and provide the necessary data for blockchain-based agreements. This approach is particularly useful in scenarios where subjective judgment or expertise is required, such as legal contracts or complex financial agreements. However, the reliance on human input can introduce a level of subjectivity and potential bias, which contrasts with the decentralized and automated nature of blockchain technology.

Software oracles, on the other hand, automate the process of data acquisition, making them one of the most commonly used types of oracles in blockchain applications. These oracles interface with various online sources, such as web APIs, to retrieve real-time data like market prices, flight statuses, and weather updates. The integration of software oracles into blockchain systems allows for the automation of processes that rely on external data, significantly enhancing the efficiency and scalability of smart contracts. This approach aligns well with the chapter's emphasis on the importance of automation and the reduction of manual intervention in blockchain transactions.

Hardware oracles extend the functionality of blockchain networks by interfacing with physical systems and technologies. These oracles capture real-world data through devices such as RFID sensors, IoT devices, and other physical monitoring systems. For example, in supply chain management, hardware oracles can track the movement of goods and ensure that smart contracts are executed based on the actual physical state of the items involved. This integration of physical data into blockchain networks underscores the chapter's discussion on the expanding role of blockchain in industries that rely heavily on real-world interactions and data.

Outbound oracles perform the critical function of transmitting data from blockchain networks to external systems. This allows smart contracts to interact with nonblockchain sources, thereby expanding the utility of blockchain beyond its native environment. For instance, a smart contract might trigger a payment in a traditional banking system or send a notification to a logistics provider. This highlights the importance of such interoperability in creating seamless, integrated systems that combine the strengths of blockchain with those of traditional technologies.

Inbound oracles, conversely, focus on feeding external data into blockchain networks. These oracles enable smart contracts to respond to specific external conditions, such as executing a buy order if an asset reaches a certain price. Inbound oracles are particularly valuable in financial applications where timely and accurate data is crucial for decision-making. The chapter's exploration of the integration of blockchain with external data sources is well exemplified by the role of inbound oracles, which ensure that blockchain systems remain responsive and relevant to real-world events.

Finally, *consensus* oracles offer a decentralized approach to data verification by aggregating information from multiple sources and using consensus algorithms to determine the most accurate and reliable data. This method reduces the risk of manipulation or error by relying on a collective agreement rather than a single source. Consensus oracles are particularly suited to applications where trust and accuracy are paramount, such as in decentralized finance (DeFi) and other blockchain applications requiring high security and integrity levels. The chapter's focus on the importance of decentralization in maintaining the integrity of blockchain networks is directly supported by the use of consensus oracles, which embody the principles of trustlessness and distributed verification.

Each type of oracle discussed contributes to the broader goal of integrating blockchain with real-world data, thereby enhancing the functionality and applicability of blockchain technologies across various industries.

The comparison of smart oracles with their predecessors and similar innovations such as Chainlink, Band Protocol, and API3 reveals the evolution and diversification of Oracle technology. Chainlink has emerged as a leading solution in this field, establishing itself as a decentralized oracle network that provides secure, tamper-proof data for intelligent contracts across different blockchains. It accomplishes this by gathering data from multiple independent sources, ensuring data integrity, and reducing risks associated with single points of failure.

Similarly, Band Protocol offers a decentralized Oracle system that focuses on scalability and facilitates cross-chain data sharing. It aims to deliver data to smart contracts quickly and efficiently, utilizing a simplified consensus mechanism.

API3 introduces the concept of decentralized APIs (dAPIs), aiming to provide high-quality, real-time data directly from sources to smart contracts, eliminating the need for intermediary oracles. This direct linkage approach seeks to enhance data security and transmission efficiency.

Integrating AI within smart oracles and developing oracle networks like Chainlink, Band Protocol, and API3 address the demand for more sophisticated, reliable, and versatile smart contract facilitators. While AI-augmented smart oracles excel in data accuracy and anti-manipulation, decentralized Oracle networks emphasize the importance of data integrity through a distributed approach. API3's direct connection model presents a streamlined, efficient solution for data transfer. However, the combination of AI and blockchain oracles faces challenges such as ensuring data security and privacy, maintaining scalability, and upholding the decentralized nature of blockchain. The computational demands of AI algorithms require careful integration to preserve efficiency and cost-effectiveness in Oracle operations.

Figure 3-2 shows a diagram illustrating the concept of smart oracles. The diagram is organized into distinct sections. First, it emphasizes the role of smart oracles as intermediaries, connecting blockchain technology with external data sources such as real-time weather data for crop insurance. Second, it highlights the enhancement of smart oracles through the integration of AI, improving their data analysis capabilities and reducing risks of inaccuracies and manipulation. Additionally, the diagram compares smart oracles with other advancements like Chainlink, Band Protocol, and API3, showcasing the evolution of Oracle technology.

Figure 3-2 discusses future developments in the field, focusing on data security, scalability, advanced machine learning models, quantum computing, and natural language processing. The diagram explains the transformation of AI-enhanced smart oracles into agents capable of sophisticated analysis, prediction, and autonomous decision-making. This diagram provides an all-inclusive overview of smart oracles and their significance in the blockchain ecosystem.

Looking to the future, as seen in Figure 3-2, the development of AI blockchain oracles is likely to be heavily influenced by advancements in AI and machine learning. Future AI oracles are expected to demonstrate enhanced predictive capabilities, utilizing advanced machine learning models to provide predictive analytics and decision-making support rather than just relaying information. For example, an AI oracle in a supply chain context might forecast potential disruptions based on real-time global events, enabling proactive logistics and inventory management adjustments.

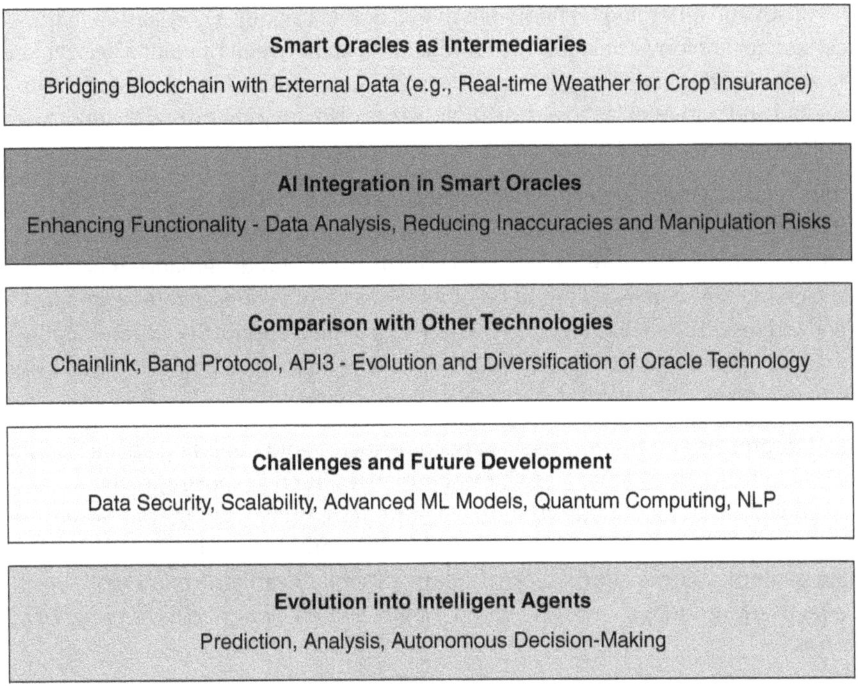

Smart Oracles as Intermediaries

Bridging Blockchain with External Data (e.g., Real-time Weather for Crop Insurance)

AI Integration in Smart Oracles

Enhancing Functionality - Data Analysis, Reducing Inaccuracies and Manipulation Risks

Comparison with Other Technologies

Chainlink, Band Protocol, API3 - Evolution and Diversification of Oracle Technology

Challenges and Future Development

Data Security, Scalability, Advanced ML Models, Quantum Computing, NLP

Evolution into Intelligent Agents

Prediction, Analysis, Autonomous Decision-Making

Figure 3-2

Visualizing How AI Will Integrate with the Concept of Intelligent Oracles

Future AI oracles must work seamlessly across blockchain platforms and innovative contract frameworks. This adaptability is crucial in a digital ecosystem where blockchain platforms are interconnected networks rather than isolated entities. Quantum computing presents intriguing possibilities for AI oracles. Quantum-enhanced AI could process large datasets more rapidly and accurately than current technologies, potentially revolutionizing how oracles interact with both on-chain and off-chain data.

Another potential development is the integration of more advanced natural language processing abilities, enabling AI oracles to interpret and process complex, unstructured data forms such as news articles or social media content. This capability would significantly broaden the scope and applicability of smart contracts, making them relevant for a more inclusive array of real-world scenarios.

AI blockchain oracles are becoming more than mere data relayers; they are transforming into intelligent agents capable of sophisticated analysis, prediction, and autonomous decision-making. This evolution is not merely beneficial but necessary as the complexity and scope of intelligent contracts expand to encompass more intricate and varied real-world scenarios. The interplay between AI advancements and blockchain technology promises a future where smart contracts are automated, secure, and intuitively responsive to an ever-changing global environment.

AI-enhanced smart oracles and emerging technologies in this domain signify a crucial step in the maturation of blockchain technology. Their ability to bridge the gap between the digital ledger and the tangible world, while ensuring data integrity and advancing automation, heralds a new era in blockchain's applicability and potential. As these technologies evolve, they are poised to unlock unprecedented possibilities in decentralized transactions and agreements.

The integration of blockchain technologies and AI models presents a challenge, largely due to the diverse and heterogeneous nature of these fields. The varying architectures of blockchain platforms—each with its own consensus mechanisms, data structures, and governance models—pose significant obstacles to the seamless integration of AI models, which often require standardized data formats and interoperable environments. The lack of a unified approach can result in inefficiencies, heightened operational costs, and potential bottlenecks in developing and deploying AI-enhanced blockchain systems.

The need for standard protocols and frameworks has become increasingly pressing as the integration of AI with blockchain technology advances. Current initiatives, such as those spearheaded by the International Organization for Standardization (ISO) through its ISO/TC 307 committee, are critical in establishing common standards that facilitate communication and data exchange across disparate blockchain platforms. These efforts seek to create a standardized environment in which AI models can be effectively integrated, ensuring compatibility and efficiency across a range of blockchain ecosystems.

In addition, the technological foundations of decentralized oracle networks, which act as intermediaries between on-chain smart contracts and off-chain data sources, illustrate the kind of framework that could bridge the gap between AI and blockchain. These technologies, which enable the secure and reliable provision of data to blockchain networks, are essential for the real-time operation of AI models reliant on accurate and up-to-date information. Nevertheless, it is important to acknowledge that while these technologies represent significant advancements, the rapid pace of technological evolution means that the platforms and protocols in use today may not necessarily remain dominant in the future. It is entirely possible that new projects will emerge, driven by innovations in quantum computing, machine learning, or other, as yet unforeseen, developments, which may render current technologies obsolete.

As blockchain and AI continue to evolve, the success of integration efforts will depend on the establishment of robust standards and protocols that ensure interoperability, data security, and scalability. Particularly noteworthy are ongoing advancements in quantum-resistant cryptography and the development of machine learning algorithms tailored specifically for blockchain environments. These innovations hold the potential to overcome current limitations, enabling more sophisticated and secure AI-blockchain integrations.

However, it is also essential to approach these developments with a degree of caution. While the technological frameworks being developed today are promising, the volatile and rapidly changing nature of the technology sector suggests that the platforms and protocols currently at the forefront may eventually be supplanted by new, more advanced technologies, or they may evolve in unexpected ways. Thus, while it is crucial to remain informed about current trends and technologies, it is equally important to stay adaptable and open to the possibility that the future of AI-blockchain integration may diverge significantly from our present expectations.

Automated Contracts: The Role of Machine Learning

Automated contracts in blockchain technology are reshaping the environment of contractual obligations and their enforcement. This advancement significantly departs from traditional smart contracts, typically confined to straightforward, rule-based functions. By incorporating ML, automated contracts are empowered to make complex, data-informed decisions, presenting various opportunities across various industries, particularly supply chain management and legal technology.

Enhancing Supply Chain Management with ML-Driven Contracts

In supply chain management, machine learning algorithms can significantly improve the efficiency and responsiveness of automated contracts. These algorithms analyze extensive datasets, including market trends, historical pricing data, and supply-demand dynamics, allowing smart contracts to make predictive decisions. For example, an automated contract could adjust the pricing or modify delivery schedules in real time in response to supply chain disruptions or demand fluctuations. This adaptability streamlines operations and reduces the risks and costs associated with supply chain management.

ML algorithms can monitor and analyze supplier performance and compliance with contract terms. Automated contracts can enforce penalties or rewards by continuously analyzing delivery times, product quality, and other key performance indicators to ensure adherence to agreed standards. This automated oversight represents a shift from traditional manual contract management methods, promoting supply chain efficiency, transparency, and accountability.

The Intersection of NLP and Legal Tech in Automated Contracts

Natural language processing (NLP), another subset of AI, plays a crucial role in the evolution of automated contracts, particularly in legal tech. NLP enables computers to understand, interpret, and manipulate human language, paving the way for computerized agreements to interact with legal documents written in natural language. This capability is groundbreaking, because it allows for the automation of complex legal processes that have traditionally been the sole domain of human experts.

One of the most significant applications of NLP in automated contracts is extracting and interpreting clauses from legal documents. Utilizing NLP, an intelligent contract can analyze a legal agreement; identify essential obligations, conditions, and triggers; and automatically execute corresponding actions. For example, an NLP-enabled contract could pinpoint payment terms in a lease agreement and automatically initiate transactions on due dates. NLP can also aid in monitoring compliance with regulations and standards. By examining legal texts, policy documents, and regulatory updates, automated contracts can ensure that business operations remain within the bounds of the law, adjusting processes as regulations evolve. This capability not only streamlines compliance management but also significantly mitigates legal risks.

The combination of machine learning and natural language processing in automated contracts represents a synergistic convergence that amplifies the capabilities of each technology. While ML excels at pattern recognition and predictive modeling, NLP is adept at understanding and processing language-based data. Together, they enable automated contracts to make data-driven decisions and understand and interact with legal language. In scenarios where external market conditions influence contract terms, ML can predict the most probable outcomes, and NLP can interpret the relevant contractual clauses to execute appropriate actions. For instance, in international trade contracts, ML algorithms could predict currency fluctuations, while NLP could identify and implement the relevant provisions for currency risk hedging. Integrating machine learning and natural language processing in automated contracts offers significant potential but also presents challenges. One primary concern is the quality and integrity of the data used in these systems. Only accurate data can lead to correct decisions, potentially resulting in legal disputes or financial losses. Therefore, ensuring data accuracy and mitigating biases in ML algorithms is crucial.

Another challenge lies in the interpretability of ML models. Due to their complexity, many advanced ML algorithms and intense learning models are often considered black boxes. This lack of transparency can be problematic in legal contexts, where the rationale behind decisions must be clear and justifiable. Developing more interpretable ML models and integrating explainability frameworks are essential to build trust and accountability in automated contracts.

Figure 3-3 illustrates the evolution of blockchain oracles into AI agents. Each stage of development is represented by nodes: introductory blockchain oracles, data processing layers, integration of AI algorithms, and finally, sophisticated AI agents.

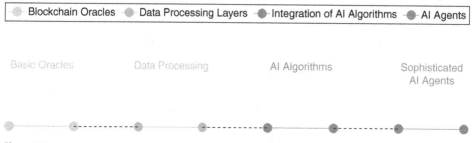

Figure 3-3
The Evolution of Blockchain Oracles into AI Agents

Figure 3-3 begins with introductory blockchain oracles. It shows their progression through stages of data processing integration and the incorporation of AI algorithms, culminating in the development of sophisticated AI agents. Each stage is clearly labeled and connected to emphasize the evolutionary path.

Looking to the future, the continued advancement in ML and NLP technologies holds promising potential for further enhancing automated contracts. Advances in deep learning and neural networks could provide more accurate and sophisticated predictive models. Simultaneously, progress in semantic understanding and sentiment analysis in NLP could enable a deeper and more nuanced interpretation of legal texts.

As blockchain technology evolves, more integrated, cross-platform contract automation solutions emerge. These solutions will seamlessly connect disparate systems and data sources, providing a more holistic and cohesive approach to contract automation.

Integrating ML and NLP in automated contracts revolutionizes executing and enforcing contractual obligations. These technologies enable contracts to make sophisticated data-based decisions and interact with legal language, opening new horizons in supply chain management, legal tech, and beyond.

Summary

This chapter reviewed distributed ledger technologies, with a particular focus on Ethereum and Hyperledger, while also examining smart oracles and automated contracts.

The chapter began by explaining the transformative impact of blockchain technology in establishing digital trust. Moving away from traditional centralized institutions, blockchain introduces a decentralized model, securing trust through its distributed ledger technology.

Attention then turned to Ethereum and Hyperledger, two crucial platforms in the blockchain world. Ethereum, with its Ethereum Virtual Machine (EVM) and native token, Ether, has revolutionized the environment with its support for smart contracts and decentralized applications (dApps). The transition from proof of work (PoW) to proof of stake (PoS) in Ethereum 2.0 marked a critical advancement in addressing scalability and energy consumption issues. Conversely, Hyperledger, with frameworks such as Fabric and Sawtooth, caters to the specific needs of enterprise solutions, offering a contrasting approach with permissioned networks and pluggable consensus mechanisms.

Subsequently, the chapter wove AI into the blockchain technology narrative, predominantly through exploring smart oracles and automated contracts. Smart oracles enhance traditional oracles by integrating AI, enabling them to analyze data from multiple sources, thus augmenting the accuracy and functionality of smart contracts. Automated contracts, meanwhile, leverage machine learning algorithms and natural language processing (NLP) to interpret and automatically execute clauses in legal documents, exemplifying AI's transformative role in blockchain-based transactions.

Challenges in integrating AI with blockchain were also acknowledged, particularly concerning data privacy, scalability, and preserving the decentralized nature of blockchain. Future trends were discussed, envisioning AI oracles with enhanced predictive capabilities, improved interoperability, and the potential influence of quantum computing in this sphere.

References

Altarawneh, A., T. Herschberg, S. Medury, F. Kandah, and A. Skjellum. 2020. "Buterin's Scalability Trilemma Viewed Through a State-Change-Based Classification for Common Consensus Algorithms." *2020 10th Annual Computing and Communication Workshop and Conference, CCWC 2020*, January, 727–36. https://doi.org/10.1109/CCWC47524.2020.9031204.

Buterin, V. 2014. "A Next Generation Smart Contract & Decentralized Application Platform." Ethereum Whitepaper. Accessed June 28, 2024. https://blockchainlab.com/pdf/Ethereum_white_paper-a_next_generation_smart_contract_and_decentralized_application_platform-vitalik-buterin.pdf

Kumar, M., N. Nikhil, and R. Singh. 2020. "Decentralising Finance Using Decentralised Blockchain Oracles." *2020 International Conference for Emerging Technology, INCET 2020*, June. https://doi.org/10.1109/INCET49848.2020.9154123.

Wood, Gavin. "Ethereum: A secure decentralised generalised transaction ledger." *Ethereum project yellow paper* 151, no. 2014 (2014): 1-32. https://www.the-blockchain.com/docs/Dr.%20Gavin%20Wood%20-%20Ethereum%20-%20A%20Secure%20Decentralised%20Generalised%20Transaction%20Ledger.pdf

Test Your Skills

Multiple-Choice Questions

These questions are designed to test understanding of the key concepts, focusing on the societal impacts, challenges, and future implications of AI in autonomous systems.

1. What core innovation does blockchain technology bring to digital transactions?

    A. Centralized data control

    B. Immutable record-keeping

    C. Increased data complexity

    D. Simplified transaction processing

2. Which feature distinguishes Ethereum from Bitcoin?

    A. Use as a digital currency

    B. Turing-complete programming language

    C. Proof of work (PoW) consensus mechanism

    D. Limited transaction capabilities

3. What is a significant difference between Ethereum and Hyperledger Fabric?

    A. Ethereum is more energy efficient.

    B. Hyperledger Fabric is a public blockchain.

    C. Ethereum supports intelligent contracts; Hyperledger does not.

    D. Hyperledger Fabric caters to enterprise solutions with permissioned networks.

4. What is the role of smart oracles in blockchain technology?

    A. To enhance data encryption

    B. To bridge external data with blockchain networks

    C. To increase transaction speed

    D. To reduce blockchain size

5. How do automated contracts in blockchain leverage AI?

    A. By automating mining processes

    B. By translating smart contracts into different languages

    C. By making data-driven decisions using machine learning algorithms

    D. By reducing the need for blockchain consensus

6. Which of these is a challenge in integrating AI with blockchain technology?

    A. Simplifying AI algorithms

    B. Data privacy and scalability concerns

    C. Decreasing the value of cryptocurrency

    D. Reducing the speed of transactions

7. What advancement is associated with the Ethereum 2.0 upgrade?

    A. Moving from a public to a private blockchain

    B. Transition from proof of work (PoW) to proof of stake (PoS)

    C. Elimination of Ether as a cryptocurrency

    D. Reduction of blockchain's size and complexity

8. Which technology in blockchain aims to interpret and process human language?

    A. Cryptographic algorithms

    B. Distributed ledgers

    C. Natural language processing (NLP)

    D. Quantum computing

9. What is the potential future development of AI blockchain oracles?

    A. Reduction in AI capabilities

    B. Predictive analysis using advanced machine learning models

    C. Complete replacement of blockchain with AI

    D. Removal of data privacy measures

10. What characterizes the blockchain ecosystem's evolution, as discussed in the chapter?

    A. Moving toward centralized control

    B. Gradual phasing out of AI integration

    C. A dynamic and innovative nature, constantly pushing technological boundaries

    D. Reduction of blockchain applications in various sectors

Exercises

These exercises are designed to test your understanding and ability to apply the concepts discussed in Chapter 3 focusing on digital trust and blockchain technologies.

Exercise 3.1: Exploring Blockchain Technologies and AI Integration

Read Chapter 3 and answer the following questions:

1. Who developed Ethereum, and what sets it apart from Bitcoin?

2. Describe the primary role of Hyperledger Fabric within the blockchain ecosystem.

3. Explain the concept of smart oracles within blockchain technology.

4. What is the significance of transitioning from proof of work to proof of stake in Ethereum 2.0?

5. Discuss the potential of AI in transforming blockchain technology, specifically with automated contracts.

Exercise 3.2: Researching Deeper into Blockchain Technologies and AI Integration

Read Chapter 3 and answer the following questions based on the information provided:

1. What are the two principal blockchain platforms discussed in Chapter 3?

2. How do smart oracles enhance the functionality of smart contracts?

3. What challenge does integrating AI with blockchain aim to address in supply chain management?

4. Identify a key challenge in integrating AI into blockchain technology.

5. Predict future developments in the integration of AI and blockchain.

Exercise 3.3: Comparing Blockchain Technologies

Read Chapter 3 and answer the following questions:

1. What distinguishes the proof of elapsed time (PoET) consensus mechanism in Hyperledger Sawtooth?

2. Explain how Layer 2 protocols like Arbitrum and zkSync benefit Ethereum.

3. What is a possible consequence of Ethereum's shift from PoW to PoS for network validators?

4. Describe a potential application of AI-enhanced smart oracles in finance.

5. What is one ethical consideration when integrating AI with blockchain?

Exercise 3.4: Assessing the Impact and Future of Blockchain and AI

Read Chapter 3 and reflect on the following points:

1. Consider how Ethereum's support for dApps and smart contracts might influence future digital transactions.

2. Identify a sector that AI-enhanced automated contracts could significantly transform.

3. Predict how advancements in quantum computing might affect future AI blockchain oracles.

4. Discuss the potential of NLP in legal technology when integrated with blockchain technology.

5. Contemplate how maintaining data privacy remains a challenge when combining AI with blockchain.

4

Quantum Computing and AI Agents

Chapter Objectives

This chapter investigates how quantum computing will influence AI agents, focusing on its foundational principle of quantum mechanics and its application in computing. This exploration includes a detailed examination of key concepts such as qubits and quantum supremacy and an analysis of seminal quantum algorithms like Shor's and Grover's algorithms. By the end of this chapter, you will achieve the following objectives

- **Understand Quantum Mechanics in Computing**: Gain a foundational understanding of how quantum mechanics is applied in computing, particularly in the context of quantum computing technologies.

- **Explore the Concept of Qubits**: Expand into the nature and functionality of qubits, the fundamental units of quantum information, understanding how they differ from classical bits and their significance in quantum computing.

- **Examine Quantum Supremacy**: Learn about quantum supremacy, its definition, and its implications for computing and problem-solving capabilities beyond classical computational limits.

- **Analyze Key Quantum Algorithms**: Study the principles and applications of pivotal quantum algorithms like Shor's algorithm, known for factoring large numbers, and Grover's algorithm, renowned for database search efficiency.

- **Evaluate the Impact of Quantum Computing on Cryptography**: Understand how quantum computing challenges current cryptographic methods and the ongoing efforts to develop quantum-resistant cryptographic solutions.

- **Assess the Practical Applications of Quantum Computing**: Explore the current and potential real-world applications of quantum computing across various sectors, including healthcare, finance, and cryptography.

- **Recognize the Challenges and Limitations**: Identify the technical and conceptual challenges faced in the development and implementation of quantum computing, such as error correction and hardware limitations.

- **Forecast Future Developments in Quantum Computing**: Anticipate future trends and advancements in quantum computing, considering how ongoing research and innovation could shape the field.

In this chapter, we will review the advancements in quantum computing and how this technology will influence the development of AI agents. The concepts and technologies discussed in this chapter are integral to understanding how AI agents may evolve, gaining new capabilities that could transform how they interact with and make decisions in complex environments.

The chapter begins by introducing quantum mechanics in computing, focusing on the principles of superposition and entanglement. Superposition is the ability of a quantum system to be in multiple states at the same time until it is measured. These foundational concepts are crucial for future AI agents, because they offer the possibility of processing vast amounts of data simultaneously, rather than sequentially as in classical computing. This capability could allow AI agents to perform more sophisticated analyses, make decisions more rapidly, and handle more complex scenarios, ultimately enhancing their effectiveness in dynamic environments.

Next the chapter examines qubits (quantum bits) and their role in quantum computing. Qubits, which can exist in multiple states at once, are the building blocks of quantum computing and are key to future AI agents' enhanced processing power. The ability of AI agents to use qubits will enable them to solve problems that are currently intractable for classical computers, such as optimizing large systems in real time or modeling complex biological processes. This section provides insight into how qubits will be central to the next generation of AI agents, allowing them to operate with a level of computational power that far exceeds current capabilities.

The discussion of quantum supremacy is particularly relevant to the future of AI agents. Quantum supremacy refers to the point where quantum computers outperform classical computers in solving certain types of problems. For AI agents, achieving quantum supremacy means they could take on tasks that are currently impossible, such as simulating entire ecosystems or accurately predicting market trends with unprecedented precision. This section suggests that AI agents equipped with quantum computing will be at the forefront of solving the most challenging problems in science, finance, and beyond.

The chapter then explores key quantum algorithms, including Shor's and Grover's algorithms. These algorithms illustrate the potential for AI agents to enhance their cryptographic capabilities and improve data search efficiency. Shor's algorithm, which can factor large numbers exponentially faster than classical methods, could lead to new forms of data encryption and security for AI agents, making them more robust against cyber threats. Grover's algorithm, which speeds up search processes, could enable AI agents to sift through massive datasets much more quickly, improving their ability to find relevant information and make informed decisions.

In the section on the impact of quantum computing on cryptography, the focus shifts to how AI agents will need to adapt to the challenges posed by quantum computing to maintain data security. As quantum computers have the potential to break current cryptographic systems, AI agents must evolve to incorporate quantum-resistant encryption methods. This is essential for ensuring that AI agents can operate securely in a future where quantum computing is commonplace.

Finally, the chapter considers the practical applications of quantum computing across various sectors, including healthcare, finance, and cryptography. These applications highlight how AI agents could leverage quantum computing to provide more accurate diagnoses, optimize financial portfolios, or enhance security protocols. This section provides a vision of the future where AI agents are not only more powerful but also more versatile, capable of operating in a wide range of environments with greater effectiveness.

Quantum Mechanics in Computing

Quantum computing represents a significant departure from traditional computing methods. This new form of computing is rooted in quantum mechanics, which elucidates the functioning of matter at a minuscule level, such as atoms and subatomic particles. Quantum computing utilizes qubits, which differ from the standard bits in computers. While regular bits are 0 or 1, qubits can simultaneously exist in both states' superposition. This enables quantum computers to process vast information rapidly, making them significantly faster than conventional computers.

Another crucial aspect of quantum computing is quantum entanglement, where qubits become interconnected uniquely. Altering one qubit causes a corresponding change in the other, regardless of the distance between them. This characteristic allows quantum computers to perform numerous calculations concurrently, a feat unattainable by regular computers.

Quantum computing tackles problems that are too complex for traditional computers, a concept known as quantum supremacy; however, ensuring the proper functioning of quantum computers takes a lot of work. Qubits are exceedingly sensitive to disruptions from minute environmental changes. Maintaining their stability for a sufficiently long duration to execute calculations poses a formidable challenge.

In Figure 4-1, a timeline depicts the historical, current, and potential future advancements in quantum computing. The first section explains the early stages of quantum computing, encompassing the inception of qubits, the development of initial quantum algorithms, and the establishment of the first quantum computers. The subsequent segment highlights the present status of the field, showcasing advancements such as sophisticated quantum algorithms, techniques for quantum error correction, and demonstrations of quantum supremacy. Looking ahead, the final part of the timeline anticipates future developments in quantum computing, envisioning its widespread application, the capacity to tackle complex global issues, and integration into various industries. Figure 4-1 presents a chronological perspective of quantum computing, its evolution and future directions.

Past Developments	Present Status	Future Prospects
- Invention of qubits	- Advanced quantum algorithms	- Widespread quantum computing
- Early quantum algorithms	- Quantum error correction	- Solving complex global problems
- First quantum computers	- Quantum supremacy demonstration	- Integration in various industries
		- Integration of AI with Quantum computing

Past	Present	Future

Figure 4-1

Timeline That Illustrates the Past, Present, and Future Developments in Quantum Computing

One of the primary obstacles in quantum computing is rectifying errors that occur during computations, known as quantum error correction. This aspect is critical because even a minor mistake in a quantum computer can yield an incorrect result. Scientists are diligently researching methods to rectify these errors, enabling quantum computers to apply in various domains. Quantum computing has the potential to revolutionize numerous fields, such as pharmaceutical development, solving intricate scientific problems, and creating computers adept at deciphering codes. However, addressing these significant challenges is essential to fully realizing the potential of quantum computing. It represents an incredibly thrilling frontier in technology that could transform our approach to solving complex problems.

Quantum computing, with its distinctive qubits and collaborative functionality, represents a significant technological advancement. While it has the potential to outperform our current computers, substantial work remains to ensure its reliability and applicability across diverse problem domains. As scientists continue to tackle these challenges, quantum computing could emerge as a pivotal tool.

Qubits and Their Role in Quantum Computing

Qubits are the fundamental building blocks in quantum computing. They represent a significant departure from the classical binary bits used in traditional computing. Unlike binary bits, which hold a single value of either 0 or 1, qubits operate under the rules of quantum mechanics, opening up a world of possibilities far beyond binary processing.

Due to the quantum superposition principle, a qubit can exist simultaneously in a state of 0, 1, or, crucially, in any combination of these states. Unlike a classical bit, this remarkable feature allows a single qubit to hold a wealth of information. The power of quantum computing emerges from this capability of qubits to embody multiple states at once, leading to a dramatic increase in processing power. In simple terms, while a classical computer would process a complex problem step by step, a quantum computer can process numerous possibilities at the same time.

To understand this better, imagine a traditional computer working through a maze. It would try one path, hit a dead end, return, try another, and so on until it found the exit. With its qubits in superposition, a quantum computer can traverse multiple paths simultaneously, drastically reducing the time it takes to find the exit.

But quantum superposition is only part of the story. The real magic happens when qubits become entangled, another fundamental aspect of quantum mechanics. Entanglement is a strange feature where two or more qubits become linked, and the state of one qubit instantaneously influences the state of the other, no matter how far apart they are. This phenomenon lays the groundwork for quantum parallelism and quantum computing's ability to solve complex problems more efficiently than classical computers.

Qubits offer a potential leap in solving problems currently intractable by classical computers. This includes complex simulations such as predicting molecular structures, optimizing large-scale systems, or breaking specific cryptographic codes, which would take traditional computers an impractical amount of time to solve. The processing prowess of quantum computers, fueled by the unique properties of qubits, could revolutionize fields like cryptography, drug discovery, and even machine learning.

However, harnessing the power of qubits is challenging. One of the primary obstacles in quantum computing is qubits' inherent instability. They are susceptible to their environment: a slight change in temperature, electromagnetic fields, or even cosmic rays can cause a qubit to lose its quantum state, a phenomenon known as decoherence. This instability necessitates the development of sophisticated techniques to stabilize qubits and maintain their quantum state long enough to perform calculations.

The construction and maintenance of qubits require exceptionally controlled environments. They must often be kept at temperatures close to zero to minimize energy fluctuations that could disrupt their state. This requirement presents substantial technical and engineering challenges. Additionally, scaling up the number of qubits for practical and more complex quantum computing applications is a significant technical hurdle. As the number of qubits in a quantum computer increases, the complexity of maintaining their stable state also grows exponentially.

Another critical challenge is the error rate in quantum computations. Quantum error correction and fault-tolerant quantum computation are active research areas that seek to develop methods to detect and correct errors without collapsing the qubits' quantum state. These methods are crucial for building reliable and efficient quantum computers.

Integrating qubits into a usable quantum computing architecture also involves developing new algorithms designed explicitly for the quantum realm. Unlike classical algorithms, quantum algorithms must be designed to exploit the superposition and entanglement of qubits. Two well-known quantum algorithms, Shor's algorithm for integer factorization and Grover's algorithm for database searching, have shown the potential for quantum computing to outperform classical computers in specific tasks. However, developing a broader range of algorithms suitable for various applications remains a significant research area.

Qubits are not just the heart of quantum computing; they represent a gateway to a new era of computational capability. Their ability to exist simultaneously in multiple states and become entangled with other qubits offers unprecedented computational power. Despite the formidable challenges in stabilizing, scaling, and harnessing qubits, advancements in this field continue remarkably. Quantum computing, powered by these extraordinary quantum bits, promises to solve some of the most complex problems in science, technology, and beyond. As research in this area progresses, the potential applications and implications of quantum computing continue to expand, making it one of the most exciting and promising research areas in modern computing.

Quantum Entanglement and Parallelism

Quantum entanglement and parallelism are at the heart of what makes quantum computing so different and potentially more potent than traditional computing. In the world of quantum mechanics, a branch of physics that deals with the tiny, things sometimes work differently than we're used to. Quantum entanglement is a perfect example of this. It's a situation where pairs or groups of qubits, the basic units in quantum computing, become linked extraordinarily. Even when these qubits are far apart, changing the state of one qubit will immediately change the state of the other. This link, or entanglement, means they can't be described independently; they are part of one quantum system.

Now, this entanglement leads to something called quantum parallelism. Regular computers process information bit by bit—either a 0 or a 1. But qubits, thanks to their ability to be in a state of 0, 1, or both simultaneously (a property known as superposition), combined with entanglement, allow quantum computers to process many pieces of information at once. This capability is somewhat like being able to read several pages of a book simultaneously instead of just one word after another. This makes quantum computers incredibly powerful for calculations, like working out the best route for a delivery truck or figuring out complex scientific problems.

Using these entangled qubits is a considerable challenge. They are very delicate and can easily get jumbled up or lose their quantum state because of tiny changes in their surroundings. This problem, called decoherence, is one of the big things scientists are working hard to solve. They must find ways to keep the qubits stable and entangled long enough to do the complex calculations that quantum computers promise.

Ensuring these quantum computers give the correct answers is also a big challenge. Since we can't measure qubits like regular bits without disturbing them, we need clever ways to check for and fix mistakes. This process is known as quantum error correction, and it's crucial for ensuring quantum computers' reliability.

Despite these challenges, quantum computing's potential is massive. It could change how we keep our data safe, help develop new medicines by simulating molecules in ways we can't do now, and solve problems that are too difficult for current computers. As we keep improving our understanding of quantum entanglement and parallelism and as technology advances, we're getting closer to making quantum computers practical. This is an exciting area of science and technology where significant discoveries and advancements could be just around the corner.

Quantum Supremacy: The Race and the Reality

Quantum supremacy represents an extraordinary goal in computing, marking a fundamental shift from the capabilities of traditional computers. It is where quantum computers can solve impossible problems for classical computers within a reasonable timeframe. This concept hinges on the unique aspects of quantum mechanics, a branch of physics that describes nature at its most minor levels, like atoms and subatomic particles.

Qubits are central to quantum computing, significantly surpassing the binary bits used in classical computing. As noted previously, while a standard bit holds a value of either 0 or 1, a qubit can exist in multiple states simultaneously, thanks to a quantum property called superposition. This means quantum computers can process vast amounts of information much faster than conventional computers, making them incredibly powerful for specific tasks.

Another crucial feature of quantum computers is quantum entanglement. This occurs when pairs or groups of qubits become interconnected so that the state of one directly influences another, regardless of distance. This entanglement underpins a phenomenon known as quantum parallelism, allowing quantum computers to perform many calculations at once.

However, achieving quantum supremacy has its challenges. Qubits' delicate nature makes them prone to errors, a hurdle that needs to be overcome through sophisticated quantum error correction methods. These methods are complex because measuring a qubit can disturb its state, rendering traditional error-checking methods unusable.

Maintaining the coherence of qubits (the length of time they can hold their quantum state) is another significant challenge. Environmental disturbances can easily disrupt the state of qubits, a problem known as quantum decoherence. Overcoming this requires highly controlled environments, often at temperatures close to absolute zero.

The pursuit of quantum supremacy has significant implications, especially in cryptography. Many current encryption methods are based on mathematical problems that quantum computers could solve quickly, leading to a potential need for new quantum-resistant encryption techniques.

Despite these challenges, the quest for quantum supremacy continues to gather pace. Governments, academic institutions, and private companies worldwide are investing heavily in quantum computing research, recognizing its potential to revolutionize fields such as drug discovery, material science, and artificial intelligence.

Current quantum computers are in the noisy intermediate-scale quantum (NISQ) phase, where quantum noise significantly impacts their performance. While they have shown potential, we are yet to see a quantum computer achieve supremacy in practical, real-world applications.

As research into quantum computing advances, so does the need for a skilled workforce capable of working in this new paradigm. The unique skills required for quantum computing, merging quantum physics with computer science, highlights the need for dedicated educational and training programs.

Quantum Algorithms: Shor's Algorithm, Grover's Algorithm

Quantum algorithms harness the unique principles of quantum mechanics to achieve computational efficiencies far beyond what is possible with classical algorithms. These algorithms exploit phenomena such as superposition, entanglement, and quantum interference to perform calculations in ways that classical computers cannot match. In this section, we will explore two of the most significant quantum algorithms—Shor's algorithm and Grover's algorithm. Each of these algorithms demonstrates the power of quantum computing and has great implications for fields such as cryptography, data search, and optimization. By understanding these algorithms, we gain insight into the potential of quantum computing to revolutionize the way we approach some of the most challenging problems in computer science and beyond.

Quantum AI, while extraordinarily powerful in specific domains, is not anticipated to entirely replace classical computing. Instead, it is likely to complement classical systems by addressing particular types of problems where quantum algorithms offer significant advantages. Quantum AI excels in specialized problem-solving, particularly in areas that involve large-scale optimization, complex simulations, and the analysis of vast combinatorial spaces—challenges that are inherently difficult or even infeasible for classical computers to handle efficiently. For example, quantum algorithms such as Shor's (1994) and Grover's (1996) are designed to tackle problems in cryptography, material science, and drug discovery with a level of efficiency that classical computing cannot match. However, for many routine computational tasks—such as general-purpose computing, data processing, and running everyday software applications—classical computers remain indispensable. These systems are well established, versatile, and cost-effective, and they effectively handle the majority of tasks required in today's technological landscape.

The future of computing is likely to be hybrid, where quantum and classical systems collaborate to leverage the strengths of each. For instance, a quantum computer might perform a highly complex optimization task or simulate quantum phenomena, with the results subsequently integrated into broader workflows by classical computers. This hybrid approach allows us to solve problems that neither quantum nor classical computers could address alone. However, significant challenges remain in scaling quantum computing, reducing error rates, and maintaining quantum coherence, all of which are essential for making quantum computers more practical and effective. Given these challenges, classical computing will continue to be the primary method for most computational tasks for the foreseeable future.

Moreover, the infrastructure for classical computing is deeply embedded in global economies, industries, and educational systems. Replacing classical computing with quantum AI would require technological advancements and substantial investments in new infrastructure, software, and expertise. It is far more practical to continue using classical systems where they excel while integrating quantum AI for specific, high-value tasks. In this context, quantum AI is expected to become dominant in niche applications where its capabilities offer clear advantages, such as in cryptography, where quantum computing could disrupt current encryption methods, or in material science and pharmaceuticals, where quantum simulations could lead to new discoveries.

Quantum AI will not replace classical computing but will augment it, addressing specialized and complex problems where quantum mechanics provides a distinct advantage. Classical computing will continue to play a crucial role in general-purpose tasks and everyday computing. The future of computing will likely be a hybrid landscape where the strengths of both quantum and classical systems are harnessed to push the boundaries of what is computationally possible.

Shor's Algorithm: Breaking Cryptography

Shor's algorithm emerges as a key and somewhat daunting development in quantum computing. Crafted by the mathematician Peter Shor, this quantum algorithm represents a significant breakthrough, particularly in cryptography. It tackles the problem of integer factorization—breaking down a number into its prime factors—with an efficiency that classical algorithms can't match. This capability places Shor's algorithm at the center of a potential cryptographic revolution, challenging the security of many encryption systems.

At its core, integer factorization involves decomposing a composite number into a product of smaller prime numbers. For example, 15 can be factored into 3 and 5, both prime numbers. In classical computing, the complexity of factorizing large integers grows exponentially with the size of the numbers, making it a computationally intensive task. Shor's algorithm is a complex quantum computing algorithm used for integer factorization. To explain it effectively, we need to focus on the key steps and principles. Here's a simplified breakdown:

1. **Initialization**: Start with a superposition of qubits.

2. **Quantum Modular Exponentiation**: Apply a quantum function $f(x)=ax\bmod N$, where a is a randomly chosen number and N is the number to factorize.

3. **Quantum Fourier Transform**: Apply to transform the state into one where the periodicity of $f(x)$ can be extracted.

4. **Measurement**: The quantum state is measured, giving an output to determine the period r of $f(x)$.

5. **Classical Post-Processing**: Use the classical Euclidean algorithm to find the greatest common divisor (GCD) of N and $ar/2\pm1$, which can lead to a factor of N.

Figure 4-2 differentiates between quantum and classical computing steps. It incorporates a linear, straightforward progression to illustrate the flow from one step to the next. The diagram emphasizes critical operations in each step, mainly focusing on how they contribute to the algorithm.

The chart in Figure 4-2 shows the linear arrangement from top to bottom, demonstrating the algorithm's sequential flow. Descriptive text beside each step briefly explains what happens at each stage, helping to understand the algorithm's complexity and purpose.

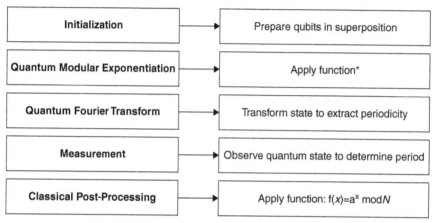

Figure 4-2
Steps of Shor's Algorithm

The sequence in Figure 4-2 is arranged from top to bottom, commencing with Initialization and concluding with Classical Post-Processing. The arrows denote the flow from one step to the next, guiding through the quantum computing stages. First, we begin with initialization by creating a superposition of qubits, followed by applying the quantum function $f(x) = ax \bmod N$ in quantum modular exponentiation, where a is a randomly chosen number and N is the number to factorize. Next, the quantum Fourier transform is applied to transform the state into one where the periodicity of $f(x)$ can be extracted. After that, the quantum state is measured in the measurement step, giving an output to determine the period r of $f(x)$. Lastly, in the classical post-processing stage, the classical Euclidean algorithm is used to find the greatest common divisor (GCD) of N and $ar/2 \pm 1$, which can lead to a factor of N.

This computational difficulty forms the backbone of many encryption schemes, including RSA encryption (Rivest, Shamir, and Adleman 1978), one of the most widely used methods for secure data transmission on the Internet. Rivest-Shamir-Adleman encryption relies on the premise that while it's easy to multiply two large prime numbers, the reverse process—factorizing the resulting large number into its original prime factors—is extremely hard for classical computers, significantly as the size of these numbers increases.

Shor's algorithm, introduced in 1994, demonstrated that a quantum computer could perform integer factorization exponentially faster than the best-known classical algorithms. The algorithm exploits the principles of quantum mechanics, such as superposition and entanglement, to search through the possible factors of an integer in parallel, dramatically speeding up the process. Shor's algorithm first transforms the factorization problem into the problem of finding the period of a function, which is well-suited for quantum computers. It then uses the quantum Fourier transform to find the periodicity of a given function, which is used to deduce the prime factors of the original number. While the algorithm's specifics involve complex quantum mechanics, the fundamental takeaway is its ability to utilize quantum parallelism, examining multiple potential factors simultaneously rather than one by one, as in classical computing.

The potential ability of Shor's algorithm to break RSA encryption and similar methods presents a significant challenge to current Internet security protocols. Many digital systems and data protection methods rely on the difficulty of factorizing large numbers. The advent of a quantum computer capable of running Shor's algorithm efficiently would render these systems vulnerable, necessitating a re-evaluation and redesign of cryptographic methods.

Quantum Computing and the Future of Cryptography

The emergence of a potential cryptographic vulnerability has prompted the development of post-quantum cryptography. This type of encryption aims to be secure against quantum and classical computers by relying on mathematical problems currently considered difficult for quantum computers to solve.

The need for quantum-resistant cryptography has become urgent, with government agencies and private organizations recognizing the threat posed by advancements in quantum computing. Various algorithms are being explored, including lattice-based cryptography, hash-based cryptography, and multivariate quadratic equations, each with strengths and challenges.

The development of algorithms like Shor's raises critical ethical and societal considerations. The ability to break existing encryption systems could have wide-ranging implications, from national security to individual privacy. The race to develop and implement quantum-resistant algorithms also raises questions about equitable access to secure cryptographic methods and the potential for a technological divide between entities with access to quantum computing resources and those without.

In response to these developments, educational institutions have started to include quantum computing and cryptography in their curricula, aiming to prepare the next generation of computer scientists and cryptographers with the necessary skills. Collaborative efforts among governments, academia, and industry are crucial to address the cryptographic challenges posed by quantum computing.

The implications of Shor's algorithm (Shor 1994) and similar quantum computing developments extend beyond cryptography to other fields, such as material science, drug discovery, and complex system optimization. These algorithms open up new possibilities for tackling previously thought intractable problems.

Shor's algorithm demonstrates the significant impact of quantum computing by challenging current cryptographic systems and spurring worldwide efforts to create encryption methods resistant to quantum attacks. As quantum computing progresses, it presents opportunities and challenges, emphasizing the need for a proactive and collaborative approach to secure and maintain the integrity of digital communication in the quantum era.

Grover's Algorithm: Searching Unstructured Databases

Grover's algorithm, developed by Lov Grover, is a groundbreaking innovation that revolutionizes the efficiency of searching through unstructured databases (Grover 1996). In contrast to classical algorithms, which would require, on average, $N/2$ operations to locate a specific item in a database with N entries, Grover's algorithm achieves this in approximately $\sqrt{N}$ operations due to its utilization of quantum mechanics principles.

The algorithm's significance lies in its ability to address the complex challenge of searching unstructured databases, which commonly contain various data types, such as text and images. Grover's algorithm leverages quantum computing capabilities and is more adept at this task than are classical methods.

Figure 4-3 illustrates the quantum circuit diagram for Grover's algorithm. Grover's algorithm is a quantum computing algorithm for searching an unsorted database with N entries in $O(N)$ time and $O(\log N)$ space. Figure 4-3 provides an educational diagram for Grover's algorithm, highlighting its essential components and steps, which include Initialization—starting with a superposition of all possible states, Oracle—a black box function that marks the desired items, Amplitude Amplification—a process to increase the probability of measuring the desired state, and Measurement—collapsing the quantum state to obtain the result.

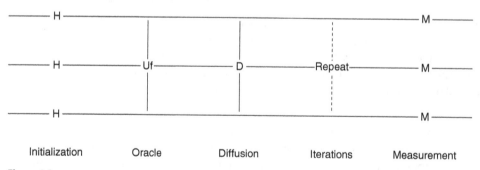

Figure 4-3
Quantum Circuit Diagram Illustrating Grover's Algorithm

Diagram Key:

- **Initialization:** The Hadamard gates (H) on each qubit create a superposition of all possible states.

- **Oracle (Uf):** This gate represents Grover's oracle, inverting the phase of the target state.

- **Diffusion (D):** The diffusion operator amplifies the probability amplitude of the target state.

- **Iterations**: The dotted line indicates the iterative process, where the Oracle and Diffusion steps are repeated several times.
- **Measurement (M)**: The final step involves measuring each qubit, which will, with a high probability, cause the quantum state to collapse to the target state.

At the core of Grover's algorithm is quantum superposition, which allows qubits to exist in multiple states simultaneously. This characteristic enables quantum computers to process extensive information in parallel. The algorithm takes advantage of this by amplifying the probability amplitude of the sought-after item, gradually leading the quantum system to a state where the desired item is most likely to be found upon measurement.

The iterative application of the Grover operator is crucial to the algorithm's success. Each iteration refines the probabilities, gradually isolating the desired item from the rest. This process demonstrates quantum parallelism—a feature unique to quantum computing, where multiple possibilities are evaluated simultaneously, in contrast to the sequential processing of classical computers.

Grover's algorithm has significant implications for data search, which is becoming increasingly crucial in an age of skyrocketing data volumes. Its efficiency in sifting through unstructured data makes it a valuable tool. In addition to database searching, the algorithm can be applied to various search-related problems, including pattern recognition and optimization challenges, making it a versatile tool in the quantum computing arsenal.

Grover's algorithm's application extends beyond improving search efficiencies; it has significant implications for cryptography. While it may not directly impact cryptographic systems as much as Shor's algorithm, which can factorize large integers and break RSA encryption, Grover's algorithm can reduce the critical lengths of symmetric cryptographic algorithms by half. This means that the security provided by current cryptographic systems could be compromised, necessitating the development of longer key lengths to maintain current security standards.

Implementing Grover's algorithm in real-world scenarios depends on overcoming substantial technical hurdles intrinsic to quantum computing. The main challenge is maintaining the coherence of qubits for the duration necessary for the algorithm to execute its operations. Quantum decoherence, where qubits lose their quantum properties due to environmental interference, poses a significant challenge and is a focus area for ongoing research.

Another technical aspect is developing and maintaining a quantum oracle—a mechanism within the algorithm that marks the desired item in a superposition. The design and implementation of an effective oracle are critical for the algorithm's successful execution and are the subject of active investigation.

Grover's algorithm also highlights the importance of quantum error correction. Given the susceptibility of quantum systems to errors, developing robust methods to detect and correct these errors without collapsing the quantum state is essential. This area of quantum error correction is complex but fundamental for the practical application of quantum algorithms.

From an educational standpoint, Grover's algorithm has become a key topic in quantum computing curricula. It exemplifies a fundamental quantum computing technique, provides a practical example of how quantum mechanics can be harnessed for computational tasks, and offers students insight into the potential applications of quantum computing.

The impact of Grover's algorithm and quantum computing, in general, extends into various industries and fields of study. The ability to process and analyze large datasets efficiently, from material science to drug discovery, can drive innovation. Applying quantum computing to these fields promises to unravel complex problems beyond classical computers' reach.

Looking to the future, the ongoing advancements in quantum computing technology hold the promise of fully realizing Grover's algorithm's potential. Research into quantum hardware capable of supporting the algorithm's requirements is progressing, alongside studies into other quantum algorithms that could further optimize performance.

Grover's algorithm stands as a testament to the power of quantum computing to transform our approach to data search and processing. While the path to its full-scale implementation is lined with significant challenges, the progress in quantum computing continues to bring us closer to harnessing this algorithm's full potential. As quantum computing evolves, it promises to unlock new possibilities in data analysis, cryptography, and beyond, marking a new era in computational capability.

Implications for the Future

The recent developments in quantum computing have significant implications for the future. One of the most critical advancements in pursuing quantum supremacy is that quantum computers perform specific tasks faster than the most influential classical computers. Companies like Google and IBM are leading this race, with Google's quantum processor, Sycamore, reportedly achieving quantum supremacy in 2019 by performing a specific computation in 200 seconds, a task that would take a state-of-the-art supercomputer approximately 10,000 years.

Another noteworthy development is Grover's algorithm, which optimizes the search for unstructured databases. This quantum algorithm has the potential for extensive applications in fields requiring data sorting and retrieval, such as financial modeling and big data analytics. Although still in the developmental stages, its implications for processing the ever-increasing volumes of digital data are enormous.

Á significant area where quantum computing is advancing is cryptography. Algorithms such as Shor's algorithm have the potential to break current cryptographic codes, leading to the development of quantum-resistant algorithms. This is crucial for ensuring digital security and privacy in the future quantum era. Companies like Microsoft and academic initiatives like the Post-Quantum (NIST [1], [2], [3], [4]) in the United States are actively developing cryptographic systems that are impervious to quantum computing attacks.

Drug discovery and material science are also benefiting from quantum computing. Quantum simulations can model molecular and chemical reactions at a level of detail that classical computers cannot achieve. This capability is crucial in the design of new pharmaceuticals and materials. A specific case study involves using IBM's quantum computers to simulate the molecular structure of a small protein, a task that would be infeasible with traditional computational methods.

Integrating quantum computing with AI offers exciting possibilities. Quantum algorithms' processing of massive datasets can significantly enhance machine learning models. This synergy could revolutionize fields like climate modeling, where vast amounts of data must be processed to make accurate predictions.

Recent quantum computing developments also consider environmental impacts. Quantum systems typically require cryogenic temperatures, which pose significant energy demands. Researchers are exploring more energy-efficient quantum systems, such as silicon-based qubits, which could operate at higher temperatures.

The field of quantum computing is rapidly advancing, and educational institutions are adapting their curricula to include quantum computing, preparing the next generation of workers. Collaborative efforts like IBM's Q Network bring together academia, industry, and research to promote quantum education and research. However, there are still many challenges to fully operational quantum computing. Issues such as qubit coherence, error rates, and scalability must be addressed. Additionally, the ethical use of quantum computing requires global dialogue and policy-making to ensure its benefits are equitably shared.

Recent developments indicate that quantum computing signals a revolutionary shift in computational capabilities, with real-world applications emerging in various sectors. However, realizing its full potential will require focused research, ethical considerations, and educational initiatives.

Challenges and Future Directions

Realizing quantum computing's immense potential is beset with significant challenges, concerning primarily error correction and maintaining quantum coherence. These challenges represent the most critical barriers to advancing quantum computing from experimental to practical, reliable applications.

Error Correction and Coherence

Quantum error correction is a crucial aspect of quantum computing and addresses the intrinsic fragility of quantum states. Unlike classical bits, which store information in a stable binary state of 0 or 1, quantum bits, or qubits, represent information in superpositions and entangled states. These states are incredibly susceptible to interference from their environment, a phenomenon known as quantum decoherence. This sensitivity can lead to quantum errors, which, if uncorrected, can render a quantum computation inaccurate or even useless.

The nature of these errors is fundamentally different from errors in classical computing. According to the principles of quantum mechanics, quantum information can be altered not just by energy disturbances but also by the very act of observation. This peculiarity necessitates innovative error correction methods to detect and rectify errors without collapsing the qubit's superposition.

Quantum error correction involves utilizing complex algorithms and fault-tolerant architectures to identify and rectify errors in quantum computing. One technique uses quantum error-correcting codes, which encode a single qubit of information across multiple physical qubits. These codes provide redundancy, allowing the system to detect and correct errors by spreading the information. An example is the Shor code, which uses nine qubits to encode a single logical qubit, thus safeguarding against certain types of errors.

The surface code has gained attention due to its ability to tolerate errors and compatibility with current quantum technology. It uses a two-dimensional array of qubits and requires fewer physical qubits than other codes, making it a practical choice for error correction in early-stage quantum computers.

One of the significant challenges in quantum computing is maintaining quantum coherence, which is the ability of a quantum system to retain its quantum state. Coherence is often lost due to interactions with the external environment in a process known as decoherence. The duration qubits can maintain coherence, known as coherence time, which is crucial for completing quantum computations. Extending this coherence time is a critical goal in quantum computing research.

Current quantum systems, such as superconducting and trapped ion qubits, have achieved coherence times, allowing basic computations. However, these times still need to be improved for large-scale, complex quantum computations. For example, superconducting qubits suffer from various forms of noise and interference, leading to rapid decoherence. On the other hand, trapped ion qubits offer longer coherence times but face challenges in scalability and speed.

Ongoing research is focused on developing materials and designs that can shield qubits from environmental interference. Innovations in qubit design, such as topological qubits, promise more excellent resistance to decoherence. These qubits leverage the principles of topological quantum states, which are less sensitive to local perturbations, potentially leading to longer coherence times.

Quantum computing research focuses on quantum error correction and coherence maintenance. Progress in these areas is expected to be steady but substantial. One potential direction is the creation of hybrid systems that integrate different types of qubits to address each other's limitations. For instance, combining superconducting qubits with topological qubits could offer the benefits of fast operation and increased decoherence resistance.

The implications for quantum computing applications are significant. The ability to effectively correct errors and maintain coherence will directly impact the range of feasible applications for quantum computing. Fields such as quantum simulation, cryptography, and communication all rely on the reliability and stability of quantum computations. The challenges in error correction and coherence maintenance have spurred educational initiatives. Universities and research institutions worldwide are expanding their curricula to include quantum computing, focusing on these critical challenges. Collaborative efforts, such as the IBM Quantum Network and the Google Quantum AI Lab, bring together academia, industry, and government to accelerate progress in these areas.

The advancement of quantum computing technologies, with their potential to break current cryptographic systems, raises ethical considerations. Developing and implementing global policies and standards for the ethical use of quantum computing are becoming increasingly important. These policies must address the technical aspects and potential societal impacts, ensuring equitable access and preventing misuse. The challenges of quantum error correction and coherence maintenance are pivotal factors shaping the field's progress. Solutions to these challenges will unlock quantum computing's full potential, revolutionizing how we process, interpret, and utilize information. Collaborative efforts, rigorous research, and a mindful approach to the ethical implications of this transformative technology characterize the journey ahead.

Quantum Computing and AI

When applied to AI, quantum computing's unique capabilities could exponentially accelerate machine learning processes, paving the way for solving complex problems with unprecedented efficiency. This synergy, combined with efforts toward commercialization and improved accessibility, sets the stage for transformative changes across various sectors.

Integrating quantum computing into AI brings together two of the most significant advancements in modern science. AI, which focuses on creating intelligent machines capable of mimicking human cognitive functions, could greatly benefit from the computational power of quantum computers. Quantum algorithms can process vast datasets far more quickly than their classical counterparts. It is crucial for machine learning, where processing large volumes of data is critical to developing accurate models.

In traditional machine learning, algorithms learn from data to make predictions or decisions without being explicitly programmed to perform specific tasks. However, as the complexity and size of datasets increase, classical computers reach their limits in terms of processing capabilities. Quantum computing addresses this limitation through its ability to handle and process large, complex datasets more efficiently. Quantum-enhanced machine learning could lead to the development of new, faster, and more accurate algorithms, capable of sifting through noise and extracting meaningful insights from the data.

One of the most exciting applications of quantum-enhanced AI is in drug discovery. The ability to quickly analyze molecular and genetic data could accelerate the development of new drugs, reducing the time and cost associated with pharmaceutical research. Similarly, quantum AI could process vast amounts of environmental data in climate modeling to create more accurate and comprehensive climate change models, helping scientists and policymakers make more informed decisions.

Despite its potential, integrating quantum computing into AI faces significant challenges. Quantum computers suitable for running complex AI algorithms require many stable qubits and sophisticated error correction methods. Additionally, developing quantum algorithms that can effectively leverage quantum parallelism and entanglement for AI applications is an ongoing area of research.

As research in quantum computing progresses, a key focus is on its commercialization and accessibility. Transitioning from laboratory experiments to commercially available quantum computers involves overcoming technical challenges and issues of scalability, usability, and affordability.

The path to commercial quantum computers involves scaling them to a level that can handle real-world applications. Doing so requires more qubits and improvements in qubit coherence, error correction, and quantum circuit design. Companies like IBM, Google, and Rigetti are at the forefront of this endeavor, working toward building scalable, commercially viable quantum computers.

In parallel to hardware development, making quantum computing accessible is crucial for widespread adoption. This effort involves creating user-friendly interfaces, developing robust software ecosystems, and providing educational resources to cultivate a skilled workforce capable of harnessing the power of quantum computing.

The emergence of cloud-based quantum computing services, provided by companies like IBM and Amazon, makes quantum computing more accessible to researchers and developers. This enables them to run quantum algorithms without requiring their quantum hardware. This democratizes access to quantum computing and encourages innovation by allowing a more comprehensive range of users to experiment with and develop new quantum algorithms and applications.

As quantum computers become more accessible, their impact on various industry sectors is expected to be significant. In finance, quantum computing could improve risk assessment and portfolio optimization. In logistics, it could optimize complex supply chains, and in cybersecurity, it could develop new encryption methods resilient to quantum attacks.

The advancement of quantum computing raises ethical and societal questions. As this technology matures, critical considerations include ensuring the equitable use of quantum resources, preventing misuse, and considering the potential impact on employment and data privacy.

The combination of quantum computing and AI is set to make significant progress in solving some of humanity's most challenging problems. As quantum computers become more commercially available and accessible, the potential for breakthroughs in science, medicine, the environment, and numerous other fields grows exponentially. The future of quantum computing, intertwined with AI, promises to unlock new frontiers in knowledge and capability, heralding a new chapter in the annals of technological advancement.

Quantum computing represents a frontier in computing technology, marked by its potential to alter the computational landscape fundamentally. The development of quantum algorithms like Shor's and Grover's, coupled with the challenges of error correction and coherence, defines this exciting field. As the pursuit of quantum supremacy continues, the implications for cryptography, AI, and broader scientific endeavors remain profound and far-reaching.

To further enrich the discussion on the integration of quantum computing with AI, it is crucial to highlight some recent advancements that illustrate the synergy between these two cutting-edge fields. Researchers from the University of Innsbruck have pioneered a novel method using machine learning generative models to prepare quantum operations on quantum computers. This innovative approach involves determining the optimal sequence of quantum gates required to execute a quantum operation effectively. Such techniques are essential for tailoring quantum circuits to the specific characteristics of the quantum hardware, thereby enhancing the overall efficiency and accuracy of quantum computations.

Additionally, diffusion models have shown significant promise in generating flexible and precise quantum circuits. These models adapt quantum operations to the unique features of the quantum systems they are designed for, making them highly effective in optimizing quantum computations. The flexibility of diffusion models allows for the creation of quantum circuits that are not only accurate, but also highly adaptable to different quantum hardware configurations, further advancing the integration of quantum computing in practical applications.

Moreover, AI is also playing a crucial role in programming quantum computers. Recent research demonstrates how AI techniques can assist in developing and optimizing quantum algorithms (Fürrutter, Muñoz-Gil, and Briegel 2024). By automating the process of programming quantum computers, AI can significantly reduce the complexity and time required to develop quantum algorithms, thereby accelerating the advancement of quantum computing technologies.

These examples underscore the dynamic relationship between AI and quantum computing, where advancements in one field directly contribute to progress in the other. As quantum computing continues to advance, the integration with AI will likely play a critical role in overcoming some of the most significant challenges in quantum computing, including error correction, qubit stability, and algorithm development. This synergy enhances the capabilities of quantum computing and opens new avenues for research and application across various scientific and industrial domains.

Summary

The chapter examines the theoretical details of quantum mechanics and its application in computational technology. It explores the core principles of quantum computing, including the significance of qubits and the phenomena of quantum entanglement and parallelism, showcasing their departure from traditional computing paradigms.

The chapter elaborates on quantum supremacy, highlighting its significance as a milestone where quantum computers perform tasks unachievable by classical counterparts. This discussion naturally leads to examining critical quantum algorithms, namely Shor's and Grover's algorithms, which challenge existing cryptographic practices and revolutionize the efficiency of database searches, respectively. These algorithms not only showcase the powerful capabilities of quantum computing but also prompt a re-evaluation of current security protocols in the digital world.

Furthermore, the chapter tackles the complex challenges inherent in quantum computing, such as correcting errors and maintaining qubit coherence. These obstacles underscore the delicate balance required to harness the full potential of quantum systems. We explore how advancements in these areas are pivotal to the transition of quantum computing from theoretical models to practical, real-world applications, spanning various sectors from healthcare to finance.

The intersection with quantum computing emerges as a frontier teeming with possibilities in AI. The fusion of quantum algorithms and AI could propel machine learning into new realms of efficiency and accuracy, opening doors to advanced solutions in complex problem-solving, such as drug discovery and climate modeling.

The chapter also addresses the commercialization and accessibility of quantum computing. As research forges ahead, making quantum technology available and user-friendly will catalyze innovations across numerous scientific and industrial domains. Cloud-based quantum computing services exemplify this trend, democratizing access to quantum resources and stimulating a broader spectrum of research and application development.

As we contemplate the future, the chapter recognizes that quantum computing is not merely about superior computational speed or capacity. It represents a paradigm shift in our approach to information processing, problem-solving, and understanding the fabric of reality. The ethical considerations, societal implications, and the need for a globally informed and collaborative approach to developing and deploying quantum technologies are paramount.

References

Datta, Animesh, Anil Shaji, and Carlton M. Caves. "Quantum discord and the power of one qubit." *Physical review letters* 100, no. 5 (2008): 050502.

Fürrutter, F., G. Muñoz-Gil, and H. J. Briegel. 2024. "Quantum Circuit Synthesis with Diffusion Models." *Nature Machine Intelligence* 6 (5): 515–24. https://doi.org/10.1038/S42256-024-00831-9.

Grover, L. K. 1996. "A Fast Quantum Mechanical Algorithm for Database Search." *STOC '96: Proceedings of the Twenty-Eighth Annual ACM Symposium on Theory of Computing.* 212–19. https://doi.org/10.1145/237814.237866.

Makhlin, Yuriy, Gerd Scöhn, and Alexander Shnirman. "Josephson-junction qubits with controlled couplings." *nature* 398, no. 6725 (1999): 305–307.

Monroe, Christopher, Dawn M. Meekhof, Brian E. King, and David J. Wineland. "A "Schrödinger cat" superposition state of an atom." *science* 272, no. 5265 (1996): 1131–1136.

NIST. 2017. "Post-Quantum Cryptography: NIST's Plan for the Future." https://doi.org/10.6028/NIST.IR.8084.

NIST, "Post-Quantum Cryptography PQC." [Online]. Available: https://csrc.nist.gov/Projects/post-quantum-cryptography.

NIST, "Post-Quantum Cryptography | CSRC | Competition for Post-Quantum Cryptography Standardisation," 2023. Accessed: Sep. 06, 2023. [Online]. Available: https://csrc.nist.gov/projects/post-quantum-cryptography.

N. I. of S. and T. NIST, "Post-Quantum Cryptography: NIST's Plan for the Future," 2017. doi: 10.6028/NIST.IR.8084.

NIST, "Post-Quantum Cryptography | CSRC | Selected Algorithms: Public-key Encryption and Key-establishment Algorithms," 2023. Accessed: Sep. 06, 2023. [Online]. Available: https://csrc.nist.gov/Projects/post-quantum-cryptography/selected-algorithms-2022.

Rivest, R. L., A. Shamir, and L. Adleman. 1978. "A Method for Obtaining Digital Signatures and Public-Key Cryptosystems." *Communications of the ACM* 21 (2): 120–26. https://doi.org/10.1145/359340.359342.

Shor, P. W. 1994. "Algorithms for Quantum Computation: Discrete Logarithms and Factoring." *Proceedings—Annual IEEE Symposium on Foundations of Computer Science, FOCS,* 124–34. https://doi.org/10.1109/SFCS.1994.365700.

Watson, T. F., S. G. J. Philips, Erika Kawakami, D. R. Ward, Pasquale Scarlino, Menno Veldhorst, D. E. Savage et al. "A programmable two-qubit quantum processor in silicon." *nature* 555, no. 7698 (2018): 633-637.

Test Your Skills

Multiple-Choice Questions

These questions are designed to test understanding of the key concepts, focusing on the societal impacts, challenges, and future implications of AI in autonomous systems.

1. What is the fundamental unit of quantum information in quantum computing?

    A. Binary bit

    B. Byte

    C. Qubit

    D. Quantum byte

2. Which concept in quantum computing involves the interconnectedness of qubits, where the state of one qubit directly relates to another?

    A. Quantum supremacy

    B. Quantum parallelism

    C. Quantum entanglement

    D. Quantum superposition

3. What is quantum supremacy?

    A. The dominance of quantum computing in the market

    B. A quantum computer's ability to solve a problem that classical computers cannot solve in a feasible timeframe

    C. The superiority of quantum algorithms over classical algorithms

    D. The use of quantum mechanics in all forms of computing

4. What is Shor's algorithm known for?

    A. Speeding up unstructured database searches

    B. Breaking classical cryptographic codes

    C. Optimizing quantum computer designs

    D. Enhancing artificial intelligence capabilities

5. What is the significance of Grover's algorithm in quantum computing?

    A. It provides a faster way to search unstructured databases.

    B. It allows quantum computers to maintain coherence longer.

    C. It is the primary algorithm for quantum error correction.

    D. It enables quantum computers to achieve superposition.

6. What is a significant challenge in quantum computing related to qubit stability?

    A. Quantum entanglement

    B. Quantum decoherence

    C. Quantum supremacy

    D. Quantum parallelism

7. What potential does the intersection of quantum computing and AI hold?

    A. Decreasing the efficiency of machine learning processes

    B. Slowing down data processing

    C. Accelerating machine learning and solving complex problems efficiently

    D. Replacing all classical computing applications

8. What does "error correction" mean in the context of quantum computing?

    A. Correcting grammatical errors in programming languages

    B. Detecting and correcting errors in quantum computations

    C. Fixing hardware malfunctions in quantum computers

    D. Improving user input accuracy

9. Which sector could significantly benefit from quantum computing advancements?

    A. Telecommunications only

    B. Only traditional computing

    C. Various sectors, including healthcare, finance, and cryptography

    D. Quantum computing is not applicable in real-world sectors.

Exercises

These exercises are designed to test your understanding and ability to apply the concepts discussed in chapter 4 related to quantum computing.

Exercise 4.1: Understanding the Fundamentals of Quantum Computing

Read Chapter 4 and answer the following questions:

1. Can you explain how qubits differ from classical bits in computing?

2. What is the concept of quantum entanglement and its significance in quantum computing?

3. What is quantum supremacy, and why is it a significant milestone in quantum computing?

4. How does Shor's algorithm challenge current cryptographic systems?

5. Can you discuss Grover's algorithm and its application in searching unstructured databases?

6. Can you identify and explain one major challenge in the development of quantum computing?

7. How could the integration of quantum computing and AI potentially benefit machine learning?

8. What are the implications of quantum computing advancements on sectors like healthcare and finance?

9. What is the importance of error correction in quantum computing? Discuss.

10. How is the concept of quantum coherence essential for practical quantum computing?

Exercise 4.2: Probing Quantum Computing Concepts

Read Chapter 4 and the sample text below and answer the questions that follow.

Quantum computing is a rapidly evolving field that leverages the principles of quantum mechanics to perform computations. Qubits are central to this technology, which, unlike classical binary bits, can exist simultaneously in multiple states due to quantum superposition. This enables quantum computers to process large amounts of information exponentially faster than classical computers. Quantum entanglement, another quantum mechanical phenomenon, allows qubits to become interconnected such that the state of one instantly affects the other, irrespective of distance. This principle underlies quantum parallelism and is a cornerstone of quantum computing's potential.

1. What distinguishes qubits from classical binary bits in computing?

2. Can you explain the concept of quantum superposition?

3. What is quantum entanglement, and how does it contribute to quantum computing?

4. Can you define quantum supremacy and its significance in the field?

5. Can you describe the primary challenge in maintaining the functionality of qubits in quantum computers?

6. How do Shor's and Grover's algorithms demonstrate the potential of quantum computing?

7. Can you discuss the role of error correction in quantum computing?

8. What are the implications of quantum computing for fields such as AI and cryptography?

9. Can you explain the potential impact of quantum computing on real-world problem-solving?

10. Can you discuss the future directions and challenges in the field of quantum computing?

Exercise 4.3: Comparing Concepts in Quantum Computing

Read Chapter 4 and the sample text in this exercise and answer the questions that follow.

Quantum computing introduces several key concepts that distinguish it from classical computing. Central to these concepts are qubits, quantum entanglement, and quantum superposition. Unlike classical bits, qubits can hold multiple states simultaneously due to quantum superposition. Quantum entanglement, a phenomenon where the state of one qubit is directly related to another, enables simultaneous data processing, a cornerstone of quantum computing's enhanced capabilities. Quantum algorithms, such as Shor's and Grover's, exploit these principles to achieve superior computational efficiency compared to classical algorithms. Understanding these fundamental concepts is essential to grasp the vast potential and limitations of quantum computing.

1. What distinguishes quantum computing from classical computing in terms of data processing?

2. How do qubits operate differently from classical bits?

3. Can you explain the role of quantum entanglement in quantum computing?

4. What is the significance of quantum superposition in qubits?

5. How do quantum algorithms like Shor's and Grover's demonstrate the potential of quantum computing?

6. What challenges should engineers consider when developing quantum computing systems?

7. How does quantum error correction differ from classical error correction?

8. In what ways can quantum computing impact fields like cryptography and AI?

9. Can you discuss the significance of coherence time in quantum computing?

10. What are the future directions and potential challenges in scaling quantum computing?

Exercise 4.4: Assessing the Impact and Applications of Quantum Computing

Read Chapter 4 and answer the questions that follow:

1. According to the text, what are some potential quantum computing applications in drug discovery?

2. In which fields are quantum algorithms like Grover's and Shor's expected to impact significantly?

3. How might quantum computing enhance the field of artificial intelligence?

4. What are some challenges faced in the development of quantum computing technology?

5. Can you identify two major technological hurdles in achieving practical quantum computing?

6. What are the implications of quantum computing for current cryptographic methods?

PART II

CONVERGENCE FOR ENHANCED APPLICATIONS

In Part II, the book focuses on the practical convergence of AI, blockchain, and quantum computing, demonstrating how their combination creates strong, future-proof systems. You will explore the fusion of AI and blockchain, learning how AI algorithms enhance blockchain systems and examine real-world applications in finance and healthcare. The relationship between quantum computing and AI is also explained, highlighting quantum machine learning algorithms and the future challenges and opportunities in data analysis. Furthermore, this part addresses the vital role of blockchain and quantum computing in improving digital security, discussing post-quantum cryptography and the development of quantum-resilient blockchain technologies. Part II builds an understanding of how integrating these technologies can solve real-world problems and enhance various applications.

5

Decentralized AI Agents

Chapter Objectives

In this chapter, the focus shifts to the merging of artificial intelligence and blockchain, exploring how this integration creates more robust and efficient systems. The chapter will examine artificial intelligence algorithms for blockchain optimization—specifically, neural chain technologies—and present case studies demonstrating the impact of AI-enhanced blockchain in sectors like finance and healthcare. Upon completion of this chapter, you will be able to

- **Understand AI-Blockchain Integration**: Grasp the concept of integrating AI with blockchain, comprehending how this merging enhances the capabilities and robustness of systems.

- **Explore AI Algorithms for Blockchain Optimization**: Expand into the role of AI, particularly neural chain technologies, in optimizing blockchain systems, understanding their function and the improvements they bring.

- **Analyze Case Studies in Finance**: Examine specific cases where AI-enhanced blockchain has been applied in the finance sector, evaluating this integration's practical benefits and outcomes.

- **Investigate AI-Blockchain Applications in Healthcare**: Investigate the applications of AI-enhanced blockchain in healthcare, understanding how this technology is transforming data management and security in the medical field.

- **Evaluate the Efficiency and Security Enhancements**: Assess how AI-blockchain merging contributes to increased efficiency and enhanced security in various applications.

- **Identify Challenges and Solutions in Integration**: Recognize the challenges encountered in integrating AI with blockchain and the innovative solutions developed to address these challenges.

- **Anticipate Future Trends in AI-Blockchain Systems**: Given the evolving environment of these technologies, predict future developments and potential applications of AI-blockchain merging.

- **Reflect on the Broader Implications of AI-Blockchain Merging**: Consider the broader implications of AI-blockchain integration for various industries and society, understanding the new potentials.

The chapter opens with an examination of AI-blockchain integration (merging), focusing on how this integration results in systems that are more efficient and considerably more resilient (Mozumder et al. 2022). This merging is particularly important for AI agents because blockchain's transparency and immutability provide a trustworthy foundation for their operations. This foundation ensures that AI agents can function within decentralized environments with a high degree of reliability, making their decisions and actions traceable and secure. Grasping this merging is essential for appreciating how AI agents will evolve to manage increasingly complex and sensitive tasks across various sectors.

The chapter then turns to AI algorithms for blockchain optimization, with a particular emphasis on neural chain technologies. These sophisticated algorithms are designed to optimize blockchain operations, making them faster, more scalable, and better suited to the dynamic needs of AI agents. For AI agents, the capacity to process and analyze data efficiently within a blockchain framework is crucial to their development. This section provides insight into how these algorithms enhance the decision-making processes of AI agents, enabling them to perform tasks more effectively and to respond to real-time changes with greater agility.

A series of case studies in finance and healthcare follows, providing real-world examples of AI-enhanced blockchain systems in action. These case studies are directly relevant to the future of AI agents, as they demonstrate the practical benefits of integrating AI with blockchain in sectors where data security, transparency, and efficiency are paramount. In finance, AI agents can utilize blockchain to securely manage transactions, detect fraudulent activities, and optimize trading strategies. In healthcare, the integration allows AI agents to handle sensitive patient data with enhanced security and privacy, ensuring that healthcare providers can offer personalized treatment plans while maintaining trust and confidentiality.

The chapter also discusses AI-blockchain applications in healthcare, focusing on how this integration transforms data management and security (Bartoletti 2019; Pawar et al. 2020; Chang and Park 2020; Mozumder et al. 2022). For AI agents, the ability to securely manage and analyze large volumes of healthcare data is crucial. This section illustrates how AI agents empowered by blockchain have the potential to revolutionize healthcare by improving patient outcomes through better data analysis and more secure data handling. The implications of these advancements are profound, paving the way for AI agents that can autonomously manage complex healthcare systems in the future.

The chapter then evaluates the efficiency and security enhancements brought about by AI-blockchain merging. These enhancements are vital for the ongoing development of AI agents because they allow these systems to operate more efficiently and securely in decentralized environments. By harnessing blockchain's inherent security features, AI agents can perform tasks with a higher level of confidence, thereby reducing the risks associated with data breaches and unauthorized access. This section offers a forward-looking perspective on how these enhancements will shape the next generation of AI agents, making them more reliable and capable of handling increasingly complex operations.

Finally, the chapter explores the challenges and future trends in AI-blockchain integration, highlighting potential obstacles and opportunities that lie ahead. As AI agents continue to evolve, they will need to address challenges related to scalability, interoperability, and ethical considerations. This section discusses the innovative solutions being developed to overcome these challenges, ensuring that AI agents remain at the forefront of technological progress. Understanding these future trends is crucial for anticipating the directions in which AI agents will develop, particularly as they become more integrated into critical infrastructure and everyday life.

Artificial Intelligence and Blockchain Technology

This chapter investigates the current state-of-the-art technologies and super forecasting future developments over the next 10, 20, and 50 years.

The integration of AI and blockchain is witnessing rapid advancements, resulting in more robust, efficient, and secure systems. This integration is making significant strides in three key areas: smart contract automation, enhanced security and fraud detection, and decentralized AI marketplaces.

The diagram in Figure 5-1 illustrates the relationship and integration between neural networks, blockchain, and their potential integration points. In the upper left, the neural networks section details their role in AI for tasks such as pattern recognition, prediction, and other AI applications. The upper right section outlines key features of blockchain technology, such as decentralization, security, and transparency. The large section at the bottom hypothesizes how neural networks could enhance blockchain technology (e.g., in smart contracts and data analysis) and vice versa (e.g., blockchain for secure, decentralized AI model training). Arrows from the integration points point toward the neural networks and blockchain sections, indicating the potential synergies and enhancements these technologies could offer each other.

Intelligent contract automation is undergoing a revolutionary change with the integration of AI. AI algorithms enhance the functionality of self-executing contracts encoded on blockchain networks by automating critical decisions, leading to more dynamic, efficient, and adaptable contract management. Notable applications include supply chain management and the real estate sector, where AI-driven smart contracts autonomously adjust to optimize supply chain efficiency and property management based on market data.

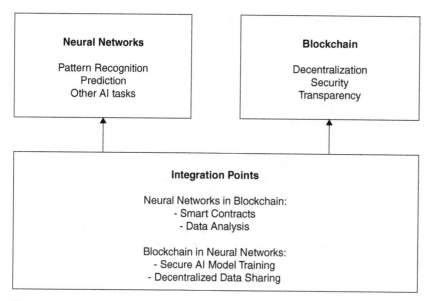

Figure 5-1

The Relationship and Integration Between Neural Networks, Blockchain, and Their Potential Integration Points

Security is crucial in blockchain systems, and AI is increasingly vital in bolstering defenses. AI-driven security in blockchain leverages pattern recognition and anomaly detection capabilities to identify potential security threats and irregularities indicating fraudulent activities. In finance, AI algorithms analyze transaction patterns to detect anomalous behavior and possible security breaches, helping prevent fraud and money laundering.

Blockchain technology has paved the way for decentralized marketplaces specifically for AI-related assets, revolutionizing AI asset trading. These platforms enable the secure, transparent, and efficient trading of AI algorithms, datasets, and computational resources. For instance, decentralized data exchange platforms allow users to share or sell their data in exchange for cryptocurrency, fostering a collaborative environment for AI development and democratizing AI development while accelerating innovation in the field.

The current environment of AI-blockchain integration showcases a dynamic and rapidly evolving field, driving significant changes across various sectors. As they mature, the potential of these integrations promises to unlock even greater efficiencies, security enhancements, and innovative opportunities in the digital world.

Table 5-1, featuring 10 groundbreaking AI blockchain projects, has been developed to completely understand the current state of affairs. Each project is distinguished by its unique core function, encompassing autonomous economic agents, data-sharing platforms, innovative AI computing networks, and decentralized security systems. The table also outlines the key features of these projects, providing insight into their distinct capabilities and the primary sectors they are transforming. This compilation serves as a valuable overview for comprehending the diverse and influential applications arising from the merging of AI and blockchain technology.

Table 5-1   Comparative Table of the Top 10 AI-Blockchain Projects 2024 (Ranked by Market Cap and User Adoption/Community Members)

Project	Core Function	Key Features	Primary Sector/Application
Fetch.ai (FET)	Autonomous economic agents	• Open-access, decentralized blockchain • AI and machine learning integration • Multi-agent systems	Decentralized economy, data sharing
Render Token (RNDR)	Rendering services	• Decentralized computing for rendering tasks • AI optimization of resource allocation	Digital rendering, GPU computing
SingularityNET (AGIX)	AI services marketplace	• Creation and trading of AI services • Development of advanced AI robot Sophia	AI development, service trading
Ocean Protocol (OCEAN)	Data sharing and monetization	• Secure data exchange using Ethereum-based tokens • Data ownership and monetization	Data economy, AI and ML applications
The Graph (GRT)	Data indexing and retrieval	• Indexing protocol for blockchain data • AI integration for data optimization	Blockchain ecosystems, data retrieval
Cortex (CTXC)	AI-enabled smart contracts	• AI models for smart contracts • Sharding for transaction handling	Blockchain applications, smart contracts
DeepBrain Chain (DBC)	AI computing network	• Decentralized AI training and inference • Marketplace for AI tools	AI training, decentralized computing
Deeper Network	Network security and privacy	• Integration with Avorak AI for security • Decentralized Internet experience	Network security, decentralized Internet
Tau Net	Software development platform	• Tau language for development • Logical-AI-based engine • Decentralized development	Software development, collaborative AI
Matrix AI	Blockchain and AI integration	• AI for smart contract coding • AI-powered security engine • Hybrid PoS + PoW consensus mechanism	Blockchain security, intelligent contracts

In 2024, these 10 highlighted AI-blockchain projects (in Table 5-1) are particularly noteworthy due to their groundbreaking blend of AI and blockchain technology. Their significance lies in several key areas. They're transforming how we manage decentralized systems, bringing about more secure, efficient, and transparent operations across various industries. For instance, Fetch.ai and SingularityNET are revolutionizing economic transactions and AI service trading by merging AI's predictive power with blockchain's secure record-keeping. Meanwhile, projects like Render Token and Ocean Protocol are reshaping digital rendering and data sharing with their blend of distributed computing and AI-led processes. These initiatives aren't just technical achievements; they represent significant progress in tackling real-world issues, from enhancing digital security to fostering fairer economic systems, marking them as pivotal developments in the tech world of 2024.

Table 5-1 summarizes these innovative AI blockchain projects' wide-ranging functionalities, features, and applications. Each project takes a distinct approach to integrating AI with blockchain technology, demonstrating the immense potential of this combination across different sectors.

Analyzing the potential longevity and impact of the 10 AI blockchain projects from Table 5-1 requires considering various factors, including their technological innovation, market demand, scalability, and adaptability to future trends. For this, we need to analyze each project individually.

- **Fetch.ai (FET):** This project's focus on autonomous economic agents and a decentralized economy is highly innovative. Its use of AI and machine learning in data sharing and resource allocation positions it strongly for future relevance, especially as IoT integration and automation become more prevalent. Link: https://fetch.ai/

- **Render Token (RNDR):** This project taps into the growing demand for graphics processing power by creating a decentralized network for rendering tasks. Its ability to optimize resource allocation using AI makes it an attractive solution for the gaming and virtual reality industries. However, its future might hinge on these sectors' wider adoption and growth. Link: https://rendernetwork.com/

- **SingularityNET (AGIX):** Its emphasis on creating and sharing AI services and its development of advanced AI like Sophia suggest solid potential for the future. The focus on OpenCog and diversification into various AI services could ensure its relevance as AI continues to evolve. Link: https://singularitynet.io/

- **Ocean Protocol (OCEAN):** Its approach to data sharing and exchange is highly pertinent in the era of big data. Given the increasing demand for data and the need for secure exchange mechanisms, Ocean Protocol's model of decentralized data trading is both forward-thinking and scalable. Link: https://oceanprotocol.com/

- **The Graph (GRT):** As a data indexing protocol for blockchain networks, its utility is closely tied to blockchain applications' broader adoption and complexity. Its integration of AI for data optimization strengthens its potential but may face competition as other blockchain platforms develop similar capabilities. Link: https://thegraph.com/

- **Cortex (CTXC):** Focusing on AI-enabled smart contracts, Cortex is positioned well for the future, especially as smart contracts become more complex and require advanced AI for optimization and security. However, its longevity may depend on its ability to continually evolve and incorporate new AI advancements. Link: https://cortexlabs.ai/

- **DeepBrain Chain (DBC):** Its unique proposition in decentralized AI computing for cost-effective AI training and inference positions it well for a future where AI development becomes more resource-intensive. However, much will depend on its ability to maintain a competitive edge in AI computational efficiency. Link: https://www.deepbrainchain.org/

- **Deeper Network (DPR):** Its focus on network security and privacy through blockchain is essential, especially given increasing global concerns about data privacy. Integrating Avorak AI could make it a long-term player in network security solutions. Link: https://www.deeper.network/

- **Tau Net**: Its innovative use of a formal specification language and AI-based engine for decentralized software development is unique. If it can successfully integrate and be adopted by developers, it has the potential to be a game-changer in software development. Link: https://tau.net/

- **Matrix AI**: Combining AI and blockchain, Matrix AI focuses on practical blockchain functionalities like intelligent contract coding. Its future relevance will likely depend on the widespread adoption of blockchain technologies and the need for advanced AI integration in these systems. Link: https://www.matrix.io/

Based on current trends, Ocean Protocol (OCEAN) has the most potential due to its focus on data sharing in a world increasingly reliant on data. This relevance extends across multiple industries, and its model addresses the core need for secure and efficient data exchange, which is likely to remain a critical issue in the future. However, the ultimate success of these projects will depend on their ability to adapt to evolving technological environments and market needs.

The 10 projects are compared in Table 5-2. In the 2024 environment of AI-blockchain integration, these projects have emerged as leading by user adoption and market cap, and each of these projects offers unique approaches and solutions. This table analyzes the 10 initiatives, considering their focus areas and potential longevity. However, it's important to note that these projects, like many other emerging technologies, carry a degree of speculation and inherent risk. Their success and sustainability depend on many factors, including technological advancements, market adoption, regulatory environment, and ongoing innovation. As such, while they demonstrate promising potential, they should be approached with an understanding of the volatile nature of this cutting-edge domain. It is very likely that in the next 10, 20, or 50 years, many (if not all) of these projects won't even exist.

Table 5-2   Summary Table Outlining The Analysis of the Top 10 AI-Blockchain Projects' Potential for Future Growth

Project	Focus Area	Potential for Future Existence
Fetch.ai (FET)	Autonomous economic agents	Strong potential due to integration with IoT and automation.
Render Token (RNDR)	Decentralized rendering network	Dependent on growth in demand for graphics processing in gaming and virtual reality.
SingularityNET (AGIX)	AI services marketplace	High potential due to diversification and development of advanced AI like Sophia.
Ocean Protocol (OCEAN)	Data sharing and exchange	Very strong potential; addresses critical need for secure data exchange across industries.
The Graph (GRT)	Data indexing for blockchain networks	Potential tied to broader blockchain adoption and competition in data optimization.
Cortex (CTXC)	AI-enabled smart contracts	Good potential if it continues evolving with AI advancements.
DeepBrain Chain (DBC)	Decentralized AI computing	Strong if it maintains an edge in AI computational efficiency.
Deeper Network (DPR)	Network security and privacy	Essential focus on data privacy ensures relevance; potential hinges on successful integration with Avorak AI.

Project	Focus Area	Potential for Future Existence
Tau Net	Decentralized software development	Game-changing potential if adopted widely by the software development community.
Matrix AI	AI integration in blockchain functionalities	Dependence on broader blockchain adoption and need for advanced AI integration.

The analysis of these leading AI blockchain projects vividly outlines the current technological scenario, paving the way for a decade of accelerated integration and expansion from the present to 2034. In the upcoming years, we anticipate a significant leap in quantum-enhanced AI on blockchain, where the merging of quantum computing with AI and blockchain is set to redefine data processing efficiency. Furthermore, we'll witness the emergence of autonomous decentralized organizations, with AI extending its capabilities to manage entire organizational structures, underpinned by the transparency and security of blockchain. Personal data sovereignty will come to the fore, empowering individuals to exert unprecedented control over their data through AI-driven blockchain networks. This period marks technological advancement and a paradigm shift in our interaction with, and utilizing technology in, everyday life and business endeavors.

The Next 10 Years: Accelerated Integration and Expansion (Present–2034)

As we progress from the present to 2034, the combination of quantum computing, AI, and blockchain technology is expected to experience significant growth. The incorporation of quantum computing into AI and blockchain is set to revolutionize the processing of large volumes of data. Quantum-enhanced AI algorithms offer a breakthrough in speed and efficiency by utilizing the principles of quantum mechanics.

Quantum computing uses qubits, representing numerous possible combinations of 1 and 0. This quantum superposition, combined with quantum entanglement, enables quantum computers to process extensive computations at speeds unattainable by classical computers.

AI plays a crucial role in this integration. AI algorithms can optimize processes within blockchain networks, using quantum computing's ability to handle complex calculations at an accelerated pace. This capability will enable AI to process, analyze, and derive insights from vast datasets efficiently.

The practical applications of this integration are vast. In sectors like finance, healthcare, and logistics, where large-scale data processing and secure, transparent transactions are critical, quantum-enhanced AI on blockchain could provide groundbreaking solutions. We might see complex financial models being processed in moments or intricate supply chain issues resolved almost instantaneously.

The next 10 years will likely witness AI's evolution from managing individual contracts to governing entire organizations. Blockchain will play a crucial role in this evolution by enabling the creation of fully decentralized autonomous organizations (DAOs). AI's evolving capabilities will likely manage complex organizational structures and operations. AI algorithms will execute predefined tasks, make data-driven decisions, adapt to new information, and innovate processes autonomously.

Blockchain's immutable and transparent nature provides the perfect foundation for such organizations. Blockchain can facilitate a decentralized governance model where all transactions and decisions are recorded securely and transparently. This shift could revolutionize businesses' operations, eliminating many traditional management structures and processes. We might see organizations that can adapt more rapidly to market changes, with AI-driven insights fostering innovation and efficiency. A significant shift expected in this decade is the empowerment of individuals over their data. Blockchain and AI are set to play vital roles in this empowerment, providing more control and security to individuals.

Imagine AI-driven personal data wallets on blockchain networks where individuals control access to their data. These wallets could use AI algorithms to manage access requests, ensuring data is shared only under conditions that align with the individual's preferences and privacy requirements.

This development could transform the current data economy, shifting power from corporations to individuals. It may lead to a more ethical data marketplace where individuals can monetize their data under their terms and conditions. The implications for privacy, security, and personal autonomy are profound. This change could significantly impact sectors like digital marketing, healthcare, and personalized services, which rely heavily on personal data.

We are on the cusp of a technological renaissance as we project these developments into the next decade. Quantum-enhanced AI on blockchain promises unparalleled data processing capabilities. Decentralized autonomous organizations could redefine traditional business models and management structures. Personal data sovereignty might usher in a new era of data privacy and individual empowerment.

These advances, however, come with challenges and considerations, particularly around ethical AI usage, the digital divide, and the need for robust cybersecurity measures in a quantum computing era. The next 10 years will be about technological advancements and directing the socio economic and ethical environments these technologies will undoubtedly influence.

The upcoming decade is a defining era in the merging of AI, blockchain, and quantum computing. The boundaries of what's possible in data processing, organizational management, and personal data control are likely to be redefined, opening new avenues for innovation and societal progress.

The Next 20 Years: Transformation and Societal Impact (2034–2054)

As we look ahead to the period between 2034 and 2054, the technological environment is poised for a transformation that will significantly impact society. The merging of AI and blockchain technology is expected to reach a level of sophistication and integration that could fundamentally alter how major sectors operate and interact.

We envisage a robust, globally interconnected AI blockchain infrastructure in two decades. This infrastructure will form the backbone of critical sectors like finance, healthcare, and governance and ensure secure, transparent, and efficient operations across these fields.

Integrating AI algorithms with blockchain's secure and decentralized nature will lead to highly secure data transactions and operational efficiency. Blockchain's immutability will lend credibility and reliability to AI's data processing and decision-making outputs.

In finance, we might see a seamless global transaction system, free from the constraints of traditional banking systems. Governance could be transformed by incorruptible public ledgers, ensuring transparency in government processes and expenditures.

Healthcare could experience unprecedented change, with AI-driven analysis providing real-time, global health trends and blockchain ensuring secure and instantaneous access to patient records. This infrastructure could lead to highly personalized healthcare, efficient resource allocation, and quicker responses to health crises.

By 2054, AI is expected to play a pivotal role in legislative and legal systems. AI algorithms can analyze vast, complex datasets to guide policy-making. This analysis will include predicting the societal impacts of specific policies, modeling economic outcomes, and providing unbiased insights to lawmakers.

Blockchain technology will underpin these AI-guided systems, ensuring transparency and integrity in decision-making. Legislative proposals and legal documents may be stored on immutable blockchains, allowing for traceability and preventing tampering.

The legal system could be revolutionized, with AI providing data-driven insights for legal decisions, and blockchain maintaining a transparent record of proceedings and judgments. This could lead to more consistent, fair, and data-backed legal processes.

Integrating AI and blockchain in healthcare will likely lead to highly personalized treatment plans. AI algorithms, trained on vast datasets, can tailor treatment strategies to individual genetic profiles, lifestyle factors, and environmental conditions.

Blockchain will ensure the secure and instant sharing of patient records among authorized practitioners, irrespective of geographical barriers. This capability will enable a continuity of care previously unattainable, greatly benefiting patient outcomes.

AI and blockchain will enable efficient management of healthcare resources. AI's predictive analysis will forecast resource requirements, and blockchain's transparency will ensure equitable and effective resource distribution.

Beyond these sectors, AI-blockchain merging will have a broader societal impact. We could see changes in employment patterns, with a demand for new skill sets focused on managing and interpreting AI blockchain systems. Ethical and privacy implications also exist as these technologies become more embedded in daily life.

The following 20 years promise a transformative journey for AI and blockchain technology. The societal impacts of these changes could be profound, requiring adaptive policies and an emphasis on ethical considerations. While the potential benefits are immense, when it comes to possible risks and equitable access, a balanced approach will be crucial.

The period from 2034 to 2054 is set to witness a revolution in how global systems function, underpinned by the merging of AI and blockchain technology. From reshaping the international financial system to transforming healthcare and governance, the potential for societal advancement and improvement in the quality of life is significant. However, the journey toward this future will need careful navigation, considering both the potential and the challenges of such a transformative era.

The Next 50 Years: A New Era of Digital Civilization (2054–2104)

The upcoming five decades, stretching from 2054 to 2104, are set to herald an epoch that, at present, might resemble the areas of science fiction. This epoch will likely be defined by monumental advancements in artificial intelligence and blockchain technology, reshaping our civilization and existence.

Conscious AI on Blockchain Networks

By 2104, the area of AI could evolve dramatically, with systems demonstrating characteristics akin to consciousness. This advancement wouldn't imply replicating human consciousness but rather a form of complex AI able to engage in intricate decision-making, learn from experience, and respond adeptly to multifaceted environmental cues. Such AI systems would be capable of understanding and adapting to the nuanced dynamics of real-world scenarios, making decisions based on a sophisticated analysis of vast data, and continually evolving their responses based on accumulated experiences.

Integrating these advanced AI systems with blockchain infrastructures is poised to revolutionize how we manage digital processes. Blockchain's role in this partnership would be to offer a secure, unalterable record of AI decisions and interactions, ensuring a level of transparency and accountability previously unattainable. This synergy would boost operational efficiency and foster trust in AI systems, allowing for broader adoption in various sectors due to the reliability and traceability of their actions.

In the future, AI systems enhanced by blockchain could manage global systems—from smart city infrastructure to global logistics networks. They could optimally allocate resources, streamline traffic flows, regulate environmental systems, and even play a role in administrative decision-making. Blockchain technology would support this by offering a decentralized yet unified platform, ensuring a coherent and secure operation across various domains and geographies.

The overarching goal of this merging is to significantly uplift the quality of life globally. Imagine AI systems that can predict and prevent crises, efficiently manage resources to minimize waste, and customize services to individual preferences while maintaining a transparent log on a blockchain network. This level of personalized and proactive management of societal needs could lead to heightened service efficiency, better resource management, and a more harmonious balance between technology and human needs.

Interplanetary Blockchain Networks

The following 50 years could mark an era where space exploration is no longer just a visionary concept, but a reality intertwined with daily human life. Blockchain technology is poised to be pivotal in this new frontier, acting as the backbone for interplanetary communications and transactions. In this era of interstellar endeavors, blockchain and AI could be fundamental in managing and allocating resources between Earth and nascent extraterrestrial colonies. Its application would ensure efficient and secure resource management and streamline interplanetary communications, offering a robust framework for space trade and governance complexities.

Blockchain's decentralized nature is ideal for managing networks that stretch across planets. Maintaining data integrity and security over vast cosmic distances becomes imperative as humanity expands its reach into space. Blockchain networks can efficiently provide seamless, secure, transparent data exchange and transaction management. This network would form the digital backbone of a new interplanetary society, facilitating everything from personal communication to transferring resources and scientific data across the solar system.

AI's role could extend to interplanetary governance and colony management. Beyond just aiding in communication and resource management, AI systems, enhanced by blockchain, could oversee the finer aspects of running extraterrestrial colonies. This includes managing complex resource distribution systems, environmental controls, and societal governance in these new worlds. AI's advanced analytics and predictive capabilities, combined with blockchain's transparency and security, could ensure smooth operation and management in these remote habitats, bringing a level of sophistication and efficiency essential for the success of interplanetary settlements.

Universal Basic Data Income

As we advance toward 2104, the concept of data as the primary currency in a digital-dominated world becomes increasingly plausible. In this future, every individual's digital footprint—from online behavior to IoT device interactions—could be harnessed as a valuable asset. Data generation by individuals, currently seen as a byproduct of digital engagement, might transform into a commodity in its own right. Individuals could create valuable assets, contributing to a new data-driven economy with every click, like, and interaction.

Blockchain and AI technologies could facilitate a universal basic data income model in this data-centric era. This system would allow individuals to receive compensation for the data they generate and share. Blockchain would provide a secure, transparent platform for tracking and managing these transactions, while AI would be instrumental in processing and valuing the vast volumes of data generated daily. This model could democratize how data is valued and traded, giving individuals control and financial benefit from their digital presence.

This paradigm shift, however, would bring significant ethical and privacy considerations to the forefront. A balance must be struck between the advantages of blockchain's transparency and AI's proficiency in data processing and safeguarding individual privacy rights. Concerns around consent, data ownership, and the use of personal data would become central in policy and technology design. This new model would necessitate rigorous ethical guidelines and privacy protections to ensure that individual rights are not compromised in the quest for a data-driven economy.

Implementing a universal basic data income model could profoundly reshape our society and economy. This approach could redefine the concept of work and compensation, potentially leading to a more equitable distribution of resources and wealth. It would encourage individuals to view their data not just as a source of privacy concern but as an asset that can provide financial benefits. This model could stimulate a re-evaluation of labor, privacy, and personal data rights, sparking a shift toward an economy where data is not only a source of capital for large corporations but also a foundational element of individual empowerment and financial stability.

Digital Civilization

By the mid-21st century, humanity might may evolve into a society deeply intertwined with technology, where AI and blockchain are not just tools but foundational elements of daily life. Imagine a world where AI-driven decisions and blockchain-verified transactions form the backbone of interactions, governance, and commerce. In such a society, technology will not only support human activities but also augment and redefine them, blurring the boundaries between the digital and physical areas.

Engineers and technical professionals must tackle several practical challenges. For instance, the implementation of AI in autonomous systems, such as self-driving vehicles, will require advanced algorithms capable of real-time decision-making based on a continuous influx of sensor data. This involves developing AI models that can process and interpret vast amounts of information, ensuring that decisions are not only accurate but also safe for public use. Similarly, blockchain technology can be integrated into supply chain management systems to provide immutable records of transactions. Engineers could develop smart contracts that automatically trigger payments when goods are delivered, ensuring transparency and reducing the risk of fraud.

However, this digital civilization will not be without its challenges. The ethical implications of AI, particularly in areas such as surveillance and decision-making, will raise critical questions about privacy and autonomy. Engineers must design AI systems that include privacy-preserving techniques, such as differential privacy or federated learning, to ensure that individuals' data is protected while still allowing for the beneficial use of AI. Additionally, ensuring equitable access to these advanced technologies across different socio economic groups will be crucial to preventing a digital divide. This may involve the development of low-cost AI and blockchain solutions that can be deployed in resource-constrained environments, providing benefits across the socio economic spectrum.

As AI and blockchain become pervasive, the role of educational systems will also need to evolve. Curricula should not only focus on technical skills but also incorporate ethical considerations and adaptability. For example, engineering students should be trained in the ethical implications of AI, including biases in machine learning models and the importance of transparency in algorithmic decision-making. Additionally, hands-on experience with blockchain development, including creating and deploying smart contracts, will be essential in preparing individuals for a world where these technologies are ubiquitous.

The journey toward digital civilization will require collaboration across sectors. Technologists, ethicists, policymakers, and the general public must work together to shape a future aligned with shared values such as human dignity, equality, and environmental stewardship. For example, engineers could work with policymakers to develop standards and regulations that ensure AI systems are safe and beneficial, or collaborate with ethicists to create AI guidelines that prevent misuse and bias.

The next 50 years promise to usher in a new digital civilization era, deeply integrated with AI and blockchain technology. From managing global and interplanetary systems to reshaping economic models, this period promises significant transformations in our ways of living, working, and interacting with the world. Engineers will play a crucial role in this transformation by designing the systems and infrastructures that will enable these advancements. For instance, developing quantum-resistant encryption methods will be essential to secure blockchain systems in a post-quantum world, where traditional cryptographic techniques may become obsolete.

Despite the promising future, the merging of AI and blockchain faces significant challenges that require practical solutions. The ethical use of AI is paramount; engineers must develop systems that are unbiased and aligned with human values. This might involve the use of machine learning techniques that are transparent and explainable, allowing users to understand how decisions are made. Privacy and security will also be critical as AI and blockchain handle more sensitive data. Engineers must create robust security protocols, such as multi-signature wallets for blockchain or secure multi-party computation for AI, to protect against increasingly sophisticated cyber threats. Moreover, balancing innovation with regulation will be crucial. Regulators must adapt to the rapidly evolving environment, ensuring that advancements are safe and beneficial for society. This may involve developing industry-wide standards for blockchain interoperability or guidelines for the ethical deployment of AI systems.

The integration of AI and blockchain holds the potential to redefine the very fabric of culture and technology. Over the next 10, 20, and 50 years, this merging will lead us into a new era of digital civilization, marked by unprecedented advancements in efficiency, security, and autonomy. The journey ahead is filled with opportunities and challenges, necessitating a proactive and considered approach. Engineers and technical professionals will be at the forefront of this transformation, ensuring that these technologies are harnessed for the greater good and that the systems they build are secure, reliable, and aligned with ethical standards. As we move forward, the merging of AI and blockchain will undoubtedly shape our future in ways we are only just beginning to imagine, and it is the responsibility of today's engineers to lay the groundwork for this transformative time period.

Summary

This chapter expands deeply into the synergy between AI and blockchain, unfolding a narrative demonstrating how this merging is set to reshape our technological environment and catalyze progress across many sectors. This chapter meticulously traces the journey from innovative technologies to visionary projections over the next several decades.

Currently, the integration of AI and blockchain is centered on enhancing the functionality of smart contracts, bolstering security and fraud detection measures, and nurturing decentralized marketplaces for AI. This effort vividly outlines how AI's predictive and adaptive capabilities complement blockchain technology's steadfast transparency and immutability. These advancements have been brought to life through case studies in the finance and healthcare sectors, showcasing tangible applications and transformative impacts of AI-enhanced blockchain.

Peering into the future, the chapter venture into potential developments and societal shifts brought about by AI-blockchain merging. In the upcoming decade, it forecasts quantum-enhanced AI algorithms on blockchain networks, poised to revolutionize data processing with unprecedented speed and efficiency. The concept of AI-managed decentralized autonomous organizations could redefine the environment of business operations and decision-making. Additionally, the era of personal data sovereignty, with individuals exercising control over their data through AI-driven blockchain networks, is on the horizon.

Looking 20 years ahead, the chapter anticipates a robust global AI blockchain infrastructure becoming fundamental to sectors like finance, healthcare, and governance. AI's influential role in refining legal and legislativesystems was discussed, alongside healthcare transformation through personalized treatment plans and secure, instant access to patient records.

The chapter speculates 50 years into the future on developing conscious-like AI interwoven with blockchain networks, orchestrating global and interplanetary systems. It explores the possibility of a universal basic data income model, where individuals are rewarded for their data, and the advent of a new digital civilization era deeply integrated with AI and blockchain technology.

The merging of AI and blockchain is portrayed as an exciting, ever-evolving field with the potential to significantly enhance efficiency, security, and transparency across diverse applications. Yet, this merging has challenges, including the ethical use of AI, privacy and security concerns, and the evolving environment of regulatory frameworks. Managing these complexities is crucial to fully exploiting these technologies for society's benefit.

To conclude, this chapter presents the merging of AI and blockchain as a paradigm shift, heralding a future where these technologies transcend their roles as mere tools to become fundamental enhancers of human and societal progress. This pathway, laden with opportunities and challenges, necessitates thoughtful deliberation and collaborative endeavor to ensure the beneficial application of these new technologies.

References

Bartoletti, Ivana. "AI in healthcare: Ethical and privacy challenges." In *Artificial Intelligence in Medicine: 17th Conference on Artificial Intelligence in Medicine, AIME 2019, Poznan, Poland, June 26–29, 2019, Proceedings 17*, pp. 7–10. Springer International Publishing, 2019.

Chang, M. C., and D. Park. 2020. "How Can Blockchain Help People in the Event of Pandemics such as the COVID-19?" *Journal of Medical Systems* 44 (102). https://doi.org/10.1007/s10916-020-01577-8.

Mozumder, M. A. I., M. M. Sheeraz, A. Athar, S. Aich, and H-C. Kim. 2022. "Overview: Technology Roadmap of the Future Trend of Metaverse Based on IoT, Blockchain, AI Technique, and Medical Domain Metaverse Activity." In *International Conference on Advanced Communication Technology (ICACT)*, 256–61. Institute of Electrical and Electronics Engineers (IEEE). https://doi.org/10.23919/ICACT53585.2022.9728808.

Pawar, U., D. O'Shea, S. Rea, and R. O'Reilly. 2020. "Explainable AI in Healthcare." *2020 International Conference on Cyber Situational Awareness, Data Analytics and Assessment, Cyber SA 2020*, June. https://doi.org/10.1109/CYBERSA49311.2020.9139655.

Test Your Skills

Multiple-Choice Questions

These questions are designed to test understanding of the key concepts, focusing on the societal impacts, challenges, and future implications of AI in autonomous systems.

1. What is the primary objective of integrating AI with blockchain in current technologies?

    A. To reduce the cost of blockchain transactions

    B. To improve the efficiency and security of blockchain systems

    C. To simplify the coding of blockchain algorithms

    D. To increase the speed of blockchain transactions

2. Which technology combination will revolutionize data processing in the next 10 years?

    A. AI and Internet of Things (IoT)

    B. Quantum computing and AI on blockchain

    C. Virtual reality and blockchain

    D. Cloud computing and AI

3. What critical transformation in organizations is anticipated due to AI evolution in the next decade?

    A. Decrease in workforce requirements

    B. Shift toward remote working

    C. Emergence of fully autonomous decentralized organizations

    D. Increase in globalized workforce

4. In the context of data sovereignty in the future, what role will AI-driven blockchain networks play?

    A. Monitoring and tracking data breaches

    B. Allowing individuals to control their data

    C. Centralizing data for more accessible management

    D. Reducing the need for data storage

5. By 2054, AI is expected to play a significant role in which sector?

    A. Fashion and design

    B. Legal and legislative systems

    C. Entertainment and media

    D. Transportation and logistics

6. What is a potential application of AI and blockchain in healthcare by 2054?

    A. Eliminating the need for doctors

    B. Using personalized treatment plans based on AI analysis

    C. Replacing all medical equipment with AI tools

    D. Completely automating surgical procedures

7. What is a crucial feature of interplanetary blockchain networks expected in the next 50 years?

    A. Elimination of space travel

    B. Decentralized network management across planets

    C. Blockchain replacing all communication systems

    D. AI controlling all aspects of space exploration

8. What societal change is anticipated with the concept of universal basic data income?

    A. Total elimination of physical currency

    B. Individuals being compensated for the data they generate

    C. Centralized control over personal data

    D. Decreased value of personal data

9. By 2104, what aspect of AI development is expected to be significantly advanced?

    A. AI replacing all human jobs

    B. AI exhibiting consciousness-like attributes

    C. AI surpassing human intelligence in all fields

    D. AI eliminating the need for blockchain

10. Which challenge is critical in the merging of AI and blockchain?

    A. Decreasing the investment in technology

    B. Ethical use of AI

    C. Over-reliance on human labor

    D. Phasing out of older technologies

Exercises

These exercises are designed to test your understanding and ability to apply the concepts discussed in Chapter 5, preparing you to engage effectively with AI-blockchain merging.

Exercise 5.1: Exploring AI-Blockchain Merging and Its Future Prospects

Read Chapter 5 and answer the following questions:

1. What is the primary advantage of integrating AI with blockchain technology?

    A. Increased computational power

    B. Enhanced security and transparency

    C. Reduced energy consumption

    D. Simplified regulatory compliance

2. What is the primary use of neural chain technologies in blockchain systems?

    A. Improving the user interface design

    B. Managing cryptocurrency exchanges

    C. Optimizing transaction throughput and security

    D. Reducing the size and complexity of blockchain

3. By 2034, how is AI expected to have evolved in managing organizations?

    A. Replacing human resource departments

    B. Managing both individual contracts and entire organizations

    C. Focusing exclusively on data analysis

    D. Overseeing only the financial aspects

4. What is a significant projected development in integrating AI and blockchain in healthcare over the next 20 years?

    A. Fully automated surgical procedures

    B. Personalized treatment plans based on AI analysis

    C. AI becoming the primary healthcare provider

    D. Blockchain replacing medical insurance

5. How is personal data sovereignty expected to change in the next decade through AI blockchain integration?

    A. Complete elimination of personal data

    B. Governmental control over personal data

    C. Individuals controlling their own data access through AI-driven blockchain networks

    D. Corporations having unrestricted access to personal data

6. What role is quantum computing expected to play in integrating AI and blockchain?

    A. Replacing AI in data analysis

    B. Diminishing the importance of blockchain

    C. Enhancing the speed and efficiency of data processing

    D. Focusing mainly on entertainment applications

7. What ethical concern arises with the increasing influence of AI in decision-making processes?

    A. Increased costs of manufacturing

    B. Ensuring AI systems are unbiased and aligned with human values

    C. Decreasing job opportunities for AI professionals

    D. Difficulty in comprehending AI logic

8. What futuristic concept is discussed for AI and blockchain technology over the next 50 years?

    A. Enabling time travel

    B. Conscious AI on blockchain networks

    C. AI replacing governmental structures

    D. Blockchain becoming obsolete

Exercise 5.2: Assessing the Impact and Future of AI-Blockchain Integration

Read Chapter 5 and answer the following questions:

1. What innovative role do AI algorithms play in the context of blockchain's smart contracts?

    A. Automating and refining contract execution

    B. Translating contracts into different languages

    C. Generating new cryptocurrencies

    D. Designing contract templates

2. How does AI contribute to enhanced security in blockchain networks?

    A. By introducing new cryptocurrency protocols

    B. Through real-time monitoring and response to network threats

    C. By manually reviewing each transaction

    D. Increasing the number of blockchain nodes

3. What is a unique aspect of decentralized AI marketplaces in the blockchain area?

    A. Offering exclusively medical AI tools

    B. Enabling trading of AI algorithms and datasets without central oversight

    C. Providing physical products related to AI

    D. Hosting online AI gaming competitions

4. What future development is anticipated in AI-blockchain for decentralized autonomous organizations (DAOs) by 2034?

    A. AI taking over all governmental functions

    B. AI streamlining only financial transactions

    C. AI driving the overall management of DAOs

    D. AI focusing solely on entertainment industries

5. How might personal data wallets transform individual data management shortly?

    A. Making all personal data public

    B. Giving individuals more control over their data through AI and blockchain

    C. Storing physical copies of personal data

    D. Centralizing all personal data in government databases

6. What is one potential societal impact of the AI-blockchain merging in the next two decades?

    A. Complete replacement of physical currencies

    B. Shift in employment patterns due to new technological demands

    C. Phasing out of all traditional forms of education

    D. Mandatory use of AI for all personal decisions

7. In 2054–2104, how is the AI-blockchain combination expected to influence space exploration?

    A. By providing entertainment in space colonies

    B. By establishing decentralized networks for interplanetary communications

    C. Focusing solely on moon exploration

    D. Eliminating the need for space travel

8. What challenge accompanies the growing role of AI in decision-making processes?

    A. Standardizing AI language internationally

    B. Ensuring ethical use and alignment with societal norms

    C. Balancing AI's power consumption

    D. Keeping AI technology affordable

Exercise 5.3: Exploring Innovations and Challenges in AI-Blockchain Synergy

Read Chapter 5 thoroughly and then respond to the following questions:

1. Which of the following best describes the future role of quantum-enhanced AI in blockchain technology by 2034?

    A. To decrease the speed of data processing

    B. To handle large-scale data analysis with unprecedented efficiency

    C. To reduce blockchain's reliability

    D. To solely focus on entertainment applications

2. In the context of AI-driven personal data wallets on blockchain, what key feature is expected to emerge?

    A. Elimination of digital identities

    B. Centralized control of personal data

    C. Enhanced individual control over data access and usage

    D. Mandatory sharing of personal data

3. What is a crucial aspect to consider in AI-blockchain applications in healthcare by 2054?

    A. Reducing the number of healthcare professionals

    B. Using AI-driven, highly personalized treatment plans

    C. Focusing solely on AI-driven surgeries

    D. Eliminating traditional healthcare methods

4. In the next 50 years, how might AI and blockchain facilitate the management of global systems?

   A. By focusing exclusively on local issues

   B. Through complete and optimized resource management across cities or globally

   C. By limiting the global exchange of resources

   D. Focusing solely on entertainment systems

5. What ethical challenge is associated with the increased influence of AI in decision-making processes?

   A. Ensuring AI systems are affordable

   B. Keeping AI systems under human control

   C. Ensuring AI systems align with human values and are unbiased

   D. Reducing the computing power required for AI

6. What impact might the universal basic data income model have on society?

   A. Reducing data availability

   B. Shifting the concept of work and compensation

   C. Mandatory data sharing for all individuals

   D. Centralizing data control

7. How could AI and blockchain technology influence legislative and legal systems by 2054?

   A. By removing all existing laws

   B. AI provides data-driven insights, and blockchain ensures transparency

   C. Focusing only on corporate laws

   D. Eliminating the need for legal systems

8. What challenge must be navigated in the new epoch of digital civilization involving AI and blockchain?

   A. Restricting AI development to a few fields

   B. Addressing ethical considerations and equitable technology access

   C. Avoiding the use of blockchain in important sectors

   D. Limiting blockchain to financial transactions only

Exercise 5.4: Assessing the Potential and Risks of AI-Blockchain Evolution

Read Chapter 5 and answer these questions to understand the potential and risks involved in AI-blockchain evolution:

1. What is the crucial role of AI in enhancing blockchain technology by 2034?

    A. Slowing down blockchain transactions

    B. Increasing blockchain complexity

    C. Boosting blockchain scalability and efficiency

    D. Restricting blockchain to financial uses only

2. What significant development is anticipated in decentralized autonomous organizations (DAOs) by 2034?

    A. Human input is entirely removed.

    B. AI oversees intricate organizational structures on blockchain.

    C. DAOs are limited to minor applications.

    D. DAOs become more opaque and insecure.

3. How is AI-blockchain expected to impact personal data control by 2034?

    A. Decreasing individual privacy

    B. Centralizing control over personal data

    C. Enabling individual data management via AI-driven wallets

    D. Publicizing personal data

4. By 2104, how might AI and blockchain integration influence global system management?

    A. The focus is on obsolete technologies.

    B. AI and blockchain play no notable part.

    C. AI systems optimize global resources and are supported by blockchain.

    D. Global interconnectedness and resource distribution are reduced.

5. What ethical challenge will be crucial with widespread AI in decision-making processes?

    A. Ensuring unique appearances of AI systems

    B. Keeping AI systems static over time

    C. Aligning AI systems with ethical and human values

    D. Restricting AI systems to specific industries

6. What societal shift could the universal basic data income model introduce?

   A. Mandating uniform data generation by all individuals

   B. Transforming concepts of work, remuneration, and data privacy

   C. Lowering the importance of personal data

   D. Resulting in reduced data production

7. How are AI and blockchain poised to transform legislative systems by 2054?

   A. The need for legislation is eliminated.

   B. AI is analyzing data to guide policy-making, and blockchain ensures openness.

   C. Legal processes are fully automated without human involvement.

   D. AI and blockchain are irrelevant in legal systems.

8. What will be a pivotal challenge regarding AI and blockchain in the emerging digital civilization era?

   A. Restricting technological progress to preserve conventional methods

   B. Addressing ethical use, equitable access, and sustainability in technology

   C. Ensuring advanced technology is accessible only to select groups

   D. Keeping AI and blockchain detached from daily life

6

Quantum AI Agents

Chapter Objectives

Despite the common disbelief that quantum computers can become reality anytime soon, there are many quantum computers in existence today (e.g., IBM's Osprey, USTC Jiuzhang, Xanadu Borealis, IonQ Quantum Computer, Rigetti Advantage, Intel Horse Ridge II, D-Wave Advantage, IBM Eagle, Alibaba Quantum Computer, Microsoft Azure Quantum, Google Sycamore), but they are just not very powerful. When quantum computers become more powerful, adversaries could abuse the new technology to endanger our security and privacy. To prevent this, we need to think today about the security requirements of future Post-Quantum Computer digital security. The most concerning security breaches could be our individual privacy, our banking system, and our medical records. We need to think about preventing the abuse of new technologies and apply the most advanced solutions (e.g., Generative Artificial Intelligence (AI), Post-Quantum Cryptography, and Blockchain Oracles) to prevent such breaches.

This chapter analyzes the potential of quantum AI agents in data analysis, particularly on quantum machine learning algorithms, namely quantum neural networks. By the end of this chapter, you will achieve the following objectives:

- **Understand the Synergy of Quantum Computing and AI**: Grasp the fundamentals of how quantum computing and AI synergize, laying the groundwork for new technological advancements.

- **Explore Quantum Machine Learning Algorithms**: Analyze quantum machine learning, explicitly focusing on quantum neural networks, understanding their principles, functionalities, and how they differ from classical neural networks.

- **Analyze the Impact of Quantum Computing on AI**: Examine how quantum computing transforms traditional AI approaches, particularly machine learning algorithms.

- **Evaluate Opportunities in Quantum AI**: Identify and assess the vast opportunities presented by the integration of quantum computing and AI, especially in data analysis and processing.

- **Recognize Challenges in Quantum AI Development**: Understand the challenges and complexities of developing quantum AI systems, including technical, computational, and theoretical aspects.

- **Predict Future Trends in Quantum AI**: Anticipate and discuss future trends and potential breakthroughs in quantum AI, contemplating how these advancements could reshape various industries and research areas.

- **Assess the Implications for Data Analysis and Beyond**: Evaluate the implications of quantum AI in data analysis, considering its potential to process and analyze data with unprecedented speed and accuracy.

- **Reflect on the Broader Impact of Quantum AI**: Consider the broader implications of integrating quantum computing and AI, including ethical, societal, and practical considerations, as well as the potential transformative effect on future technological developments.

This chapter will thoroughly explain the integration of AI and quantum computing. It will also help you recognize this integration's significant implications and future possibilities. The chapter opens by examining the synergy between quantum computing and AI, explaining how quantum principles, such as superposition and entanglement, can be harnessed to overcome the limitations of classical computing. For AI agents, this synergy introduces new levels of computational power, enabling them to handle more sophisticated tasks with greater efficiency. This section sets the stage for understanding how AI agents will leverage quantum computing to become more effective in environments requiring rapid and complex data processing.

Following this, the chapter explores quantum machine learning algorithms, focusing on innovations like quantum neural networks (QNNs). These algorithms are pivotal in the evolution of AI agents, offering them the ability to learn and adapt at speeds far beyond those of classical systems. QNNs provide AI agents with the tools to process and interpret large-scale data more effectively, which is crucial for applications that require real-time analysis and decision-making. This section is critical for understanding how AI agents will become more sophisticated and capable as they integrate quantum-enhanced learning techniques.

The chapter then shifts to the impact of quantum computing on AI, examining how quantum algorithms redefine traditional machine learning models. For AI agents, this impact means enhanced learning capabilities, better optimization strategies, and more accurate predictive models. By integrating quantum algorithms, AI agents will be able to process information more efficiently, enabling them to perform in increasingly complex and dynamic environments. This section illustrates how quantum computing will propel AI agents into new forms of capability.

Next, the chapter addresses the challenges and opportunities in quantum AI development, highlighting the difficulties and the potential that this integration brings. For AI agents, the technical challenges of quantum computing—such as error correction and qubit management— are significant, but the opportunities for advancement in areas like data analysis and predictive modeling are immense. This section provides a balanced view of the obstacles and the possibilities, showing how AI agents will need to evolve to fully exploit the benefits of quantum AI.

The discussion then moves to future trends in quantum AI, exploring anticipated advancements in quantum hardware, algorithms, and hybrid systems that combine quantum and classical approaches. For AI agents, keeping pace with these trends is essential to remain competitive and relevant. This section offers a forward-looking perspective on how AI agents will continue to develop as quantum computing technologies advance, ensuring they remain at the forefront of innovation.

Finally, the chapter considers the broader implications of quantum AI for various industries, particularly in data analysis. The ability of AI agents to process and interpret data with unparalleled speed and accuracy will reform sectors such as healthcare, finance, and logistics. This section highlights the far-reaching impact of quantum AI, positioning AI agents as central to the future of industry and technology.

Quantum Machine Learning Algorithms: Quantum Neural Networks

Quantum computing and AI are two of the most revolutionary technologies of the 21st century. Each has the potential to dramatically alter numerous facets of life, business, and science. However, when these technologies converge, particularly in quantum machine learning (QML), we stand on the cusp of a technological renaissance.

Quantum neural networks (QNNs) are a novel combination of neural network theory and quantum computing. This synthesis combines the probabilistic aspects of quantum mechanics with the predictability of classical algorithms. These networks handle and analyze data in an essentially impossible way for classical computers by utilizing core quantum concepts like superposition and entanglement.

The history of QNNs is closely related to the development of quantum computing. Quantum computing seeks to use quantum physics' strange and frequently counterintuitive characteristics for computing needs. Unlike their classical counterparts, which are rigidly binary, quantum bits, or qubits, the building blocks of quantum computing, exist in several states simultaneously because of superposition.

Another fundamental concept of quantum mechanics is entanglement, which enables qubits to be coupled so that, regardless of their distance from one another, the state of one qubit instantly affects the state of another. This phenomenon introduces a new paradigm for information processing by extending beyond the traditional boundaries of time and space.

Pioneering experiments with quantum algorithms have been the primary driving force behind the development of quantum neural networks. Two notable examples include Grover's algorithm, which offers a quadratic speedup for database searching tasks, and Shor's algorithm, which was created to factor huge numbers exponentially faster than the most well-known classical algorithms. These algorithms have established the conceptual framework for extending quantum computational supremacy to further areas, such as machine learning, and have also demonstrated quantum superiority in their respective fields.

The concept of QNNs originally started as a thought experiment. It explored the potential benefits of combining the exponential processing power of quantum algorithms with machine learning. This inquiry led to various research projects that aimed to merge quantum computing with the fundamental principles of modern AI, specifically artificial neural networks.

The initial models of quantum neural networks were theoretical constructions aimed at translating the architecture of classical neural networks into a quantum environment. These models used qubits to represent neurons and quantum gates to replace synaptic weights. The quantum gates operate as functions to change the states of these qubits, similar to how classical neural networks are trained. The essential advantage of these early models was the potential for exponentially more parallel processing and information storage compared to classical networks due to the superposition of qubits.

The first experimental realizations of QNNs involved essential networks run on early quantum computers. These experiments faced technical obstacles such as quantum decoherence and managing and controlling many qubits. Despite these challenges, advancements in quantum computing technology eventually made more sophisticated QNN experiments possible, particularly in qubit stability and error correction. Researchers also began creating algorithms for QNNs to carry out tasks like pattern recognition, classification, and quantum data compression.

Integrating quantum neural networks with traditional machine learning techniques is an exciting aspect of their development. Hybrid models, which combine quantum and conventional methods, have become a viable strategy for optimizing the benefits of both fields. In these hybrid models, the quantum algorithm handles some aspects of a problem, especially those involving complicated, high-dimensional data, while traditional machine learning techniques handle the remaining portions. This approach mitigates current technological limitations and provides a scalable pathway for integrating quantum computing into existing AI infrastructure. It signifies a step toward a future where quantum-enhanced machine learning could become ubiquitous, offering unprecedented computational power and efficiency.

The field of quantum neural networks holds the promise of groundbreaking advancements in the future. As quantum computing technology continues to develop and improve in areas such as qubit coherence, error correction, and quantum gate fidelity, it will enable the creation of more sophisticated and powerful QNNs. These networks can potentially modernize fields like financial modeling, material science, and drug development, which rely on standard machine-learning techniques.

In addition to their practical applications, QNNs also have significant theoretical implications. They raise questions about our understanding of neural processing and computation, potentially offering new insights into the functioning of the human brain. Quantum neural networks, which combine the principles of quantum mechanics with neural computation, represent a significant technological advancement and a testament to human ingenuity in our quest to understand and manipulate the fundamental laws of nature.

The Quantum Difference: Superposition and Entanglement

Superposition and entanglement are two fundamental concepts of quantum mechanics that must be thoroughly studied to realize the full potential of QNNs. These ideas are essential to quantum computing and primarily responsible for the paradigm shift in how information processing may be understood and carried out.

In quantum physics, superposition is the idea that allows quantum bits, or qubits, to exist in more than one state at once. A bit is the smallest data unit in the binary area of classical computing, and it can only be either 0 or 1. On the other hand, a qubit can represent 0, 1, or any quantum superposition of these states because of superposition. This trait is revolutionary in computation, not just a theoretical curiosity.

A system with n qubits can simultaneously represent $2n$ distinct states. In comparison, the number of states a 300-qubit quantum computer might represent is greater than the total number of atoms in the known universe. This exponential scaling gives quantum computers—and hence, QNNs—potentially unmatched power.

There are significant ramifications for machine learning. The linear scalability of the components in classic neural networks limits their processing capacity. However, due to the strength of superposition, quantum neural networks can handle much more complicated, multidimensional datasets more effectively by examining many possible answers at once.

Entanglement is a fundamental concept of quantum mechanics. Albert Einstein famously called it a "spooky action at a distance." When two qubits become entangled, their states instantly correspond, regardless of distance. This has significant implications for computer and information theory because it challenges the traditional concepts of space and time.

Entanglement can be used in QNNs to create correlations between qubits, offering an effective information processing and transmission method. This suggests that data encoded in one qubit may depend on data encoded in another, enabling complex probabilistic interactions that are not feasible using traditional computing methods.

Entanglement plays a crucial role in quantum cryptography and quantum error correction. It provides a way to establish redundancy in quantum information, safeguarding against data loss caused by decoherence, the process through which a quantum system loses its quantum properties.

Superposition and entanglement are two quantum features that have already demonstrated capabilities beyond those of conventional computers. For instance, Shor's algorithm can quickly find the prime factors of large numbers, far outpacing any known classical algorithm by utilizing superposition. Grover's algorithm efficiently searches unsorted databases using superposition and entanglement.

These characteristics enable quantum algorithms to evaluate complex functions and perform optimizations at speeds faster than classical algorithms in machine learning. They make QNNs potentially revolutionary tools for tasks such as pattern recognition, optimization, and even complex decision-making processes because they allow for parallel exploration of an ample solution space.

Superposition and entanglement in QNNs offer exciting prospects, but significant theoretical and technological challenges must be addressed before they can be applied in real-world scenarios. Maintaining the integrity of the superposition state and ensuring stable entanglement across numerous qubits are complex tasks. Quantum decoherence, where qubits lose their quantum states to the surrounding environment, is a significant hurdle. Additionally, effectively manipulating qubits to generate desired entanglement patterns requires sophisticated quantum control methods.

The future looks promising for quantum computing and quantum neural networks as scientists investigate the complexities of superposition and entanglement. Advancements in quantum error correction, quantum gate, and qubit stabilization techniques pave the way for more scalable and reliable quantum systems.

Unlocking the full potential of superposition and entanglement in QNNs could lead to breakthroughs in various fields. It may enable the simulation of intricate molecular interactions in the pharmaceutical industry, expediting drug discovery. Furthermore, it could update portfolio optimization and risk assessment in the financial sector and even facilitate the development of AI systems capable of solving problems beyond our current capabilities.

Superposition and entanglement are abstract quantum phenomena, but they are the fundamental concepts behind the remarkable potential of QNNs. By harnessing these ideas in the creation of QNNs, we may witness some of the most significant technical advancements of our time as quantum computing evolves, fundamentally altering the landscape of computation and problem-solving in the years ahead.

Architectures of Quantum Neural Networks

QNNs represent a radical departure from conventional neural network architectures. The main difference is that QNNs handle information using the principles of quantum mechanics, completely changing how it is stored, processed, and retrieved. Understanding the potential and challenges of QNNs requires an appreciation of their architecture.

In classical neural networks, the neuron is the fundamental computational unit, processing and transmitting data through a network of weighted interconnections. Conversely, in QNNs, qubits serve as the basic computational unit. Figure 6-1 provides a visualization of this difference. The qubit can exist in multiple states simultaneously, storing more information than the binary bit, which can exist in only one state—0 or 1. This capability is due to quantum superposition.

In QNNs, quantum gates serve as the connections between qubits. In classical networks, weights regulate how strongly neurons are interconnected. These weights are equivalent to the probability amplitudes of qubit states manipulated by quantum gates in QNNs. Quantum gates are the primary tools for executing quantum operations, facilitating communication and information processing between qubits.

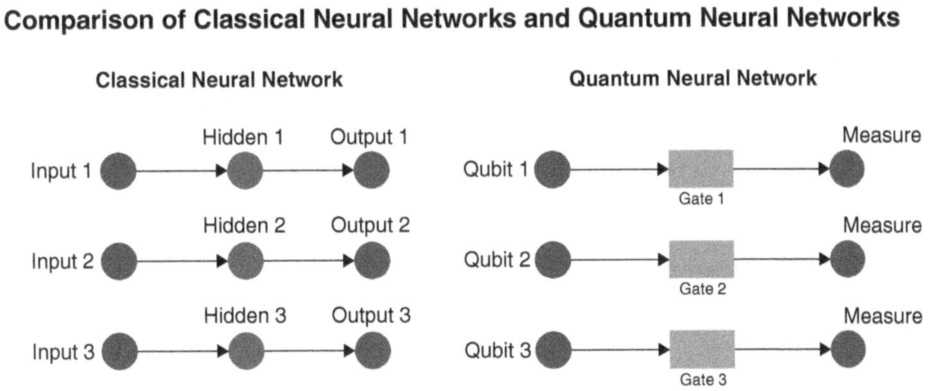

Comparison of Classical Neural Networks and Quantum Neural Networks

Classical Neural Network   **Quantum Neural Network**

Figure 6-1
Classical vs. Quantum Neural Networks

The quantum perceptron model is similar in structure to the classical perceptron and is one of the fundamental models for QNNs. This model applies the concepts of quantum superposition and interference. While the output of a classical perceptron is the weighted total of the inputs after a nonlinear activation function has processed them, the quantum perceptron processes several input states at once by using quantum superposition.

The quantum perceptron (see Figure 6-2) manipulates the input qubits through a sequence of quantum gates to produce a superposition that encodes the weights and the inputs. The final state of the qubit is then measured as the output. To simulate the activation function in classical percep-trons, quantum states can add or subtract from one another, a phenomenon known as quantum interference. Despite its simplicity compared to the intricacy of actual neurons, this model signifi-cantly boosts computational capacity and efficiency.

Quantum Perceptron Model

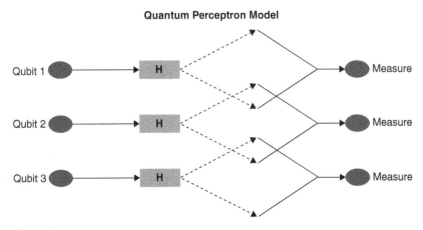

Figure 6-2
The Quantum Perceptron Model

Building upon the quantum perceptron, more sophisticated QNN models have been created, such as quantum counterparts of classical convolutional and recurrent neural networks (CNNs and RNNs).

Quantum convolutional neural networks (QCNNs) modify the architecture of classical CNNs and are especially useful for processing data with a grid-like layout, such as pictures. A QCNN processes quantum data in parallel in a grid structure by arranging quantum gates to resemble the convolutional filters of classical CNNs (see Figure 6-3).

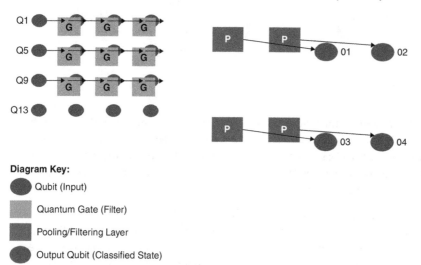

Figure 6-3

Quantum Convolutional Neural Networks (QCNNs)

This method shows great promise for applications like quantum image processing and quantum state categorization.

On the other hand, quantum recurrent neural networks (QRNNs) bring the idea of conventional RNNs into quantum computing (see Figure 6-4). RNNs are known for their capacity to process data sequences, making them useful for applications such as time-series analysis and speech recognition.

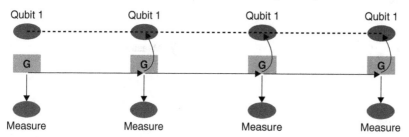

Figure 6-4

Quantum Recurrent Neural Networks (QRNNs)

By utilizing the entanglement property, QRNNs can generate quantum states that correlate with sequential input, providing substantial progress in processing intricate temporal quantum information.

The current state of quantum technology has yet to allow for efficient, exclusively quantum networks. As a result, hybrid quantum-classical architectures are being developed to overcome this limitation (see Figure 6-5). In these architectures, quantum processors handle the algorithmic parts benefiting from quantum computing, while standard neural network topologies manage the remaining tasks.

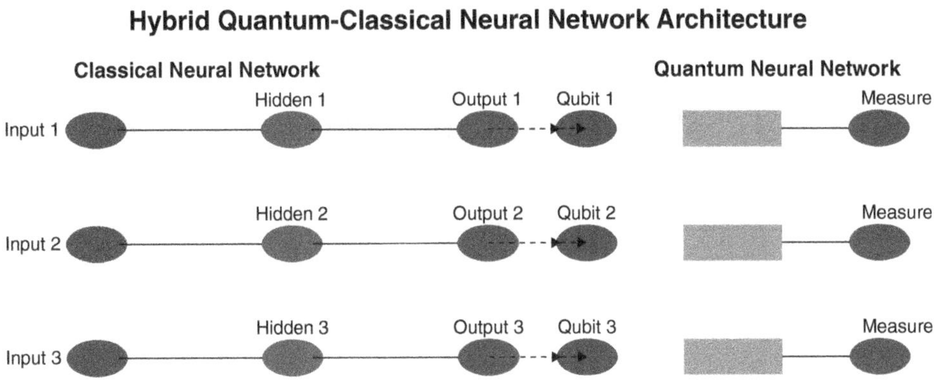

Hybrid Quantum-Classical Neural Network Architecture

Figure 6-5
Hybrid Quantum-Classical Neural Network Architecture

This approach retains the advantages of quantum computing while addressing some of its current technological limitations.

Creating and implementing these designs presents several challenges. Developing quantum gates that can accurately mimic neural network functions is difficult. Maintaining quantum coherence and minimizing errors in a multi-qubit system are ongoing technological challenges. Addressing fault-tolerant quantum computation and quantum error correction is crucial to solving these issues.

In QNNs, quantum gates are tuned to minimize a cost function, similar to how weights are adjusted in conventional networks, typically using gradient descent techniques. However, computing gradients in quantum systems is more complex and often requires novel methods. Techniques such as the parameter shift rule and variational algorithms train QNNs.

Future developments in QNN designs are expected to be influenced by new quantum machine learning algorithms and hardware advancements in quantum computing. As quantum computers become more powerful and stable, QNNs may be able to handle increasingly complex tasks more efficiently.

Research into new quantum algorithms and training methods is crucial to fully realizing the potential of QNNs. Ongoing research is focused on how best to utilize quantum properties like entanglement in neural network topologies and optimize the learning process in QNNs.

Due to the current state of quantum technology, fully quantum networks still need to be practical. As a result, hybrid quantum-classical architectures have been developed. In these systems, quantum processors handle algorithmic tasks that can benefit from quantum computing, while standard neural network topologies manage the remaining tasks. This approach allows for the advantages of quantum computing to be utilized while working around current technological limitations.

QNNs show promise in various fields. They surpass standard methods in simulating chemical structures and reactions in computational chemistry. QNNs offer innovative strategies for predicting market dynamics and optimizing finance portfolios. Additionally, they have potential uses in material science, logistics, and medicine development. Despite their potential, significant barriers hinder the advancement of QNNs. The primary issue is decoherence, which occurs when environmental interference causes qubits to lose their quantum state. Error correction is also challenging in quantum systems because quantum observations are unpredictable.

Opportunities and Challenges in Quantum AI Data Analysis

Integrating quantum computing with AI, particularly in data analysis, presents unprecedented opportunities and difficult challenges. Quantum AI can reform predictive analytics. When integrated with quantum computing, this essential field, which is crucial for understanding patterns, predicting trends, and making data-driven decisions, will experience significant benefits. Quantum AI can enhance predictive analytics by effectively handling complex, multidimensional information and providing faster, more accurate insights.

The primary objective of predictive analytics is to forecast future events by analyzing past data. While classical computers are competent in this area, they are limited by their linear data processing capabilities. Quantum AI overcomes these limitations by utilizing quantum mechanics to process information in a fundamentally new way.

Due to quantum superposition, quantum computers can simultaneously represent and process many data states. This capacity exponentially increases the amount and complexity of data that can be analyzed at any given time. For instance, a quantum algorithm can simultaneously evaluate all potential combinations in a dataset, a process that would take a long time for a classical computer.

Predictive analytics has witnessed a shift in the application of machine learning models, such as support vector machines, decision trees, and neural networks. However, these models often require substantial processing power, mainly when working with large and complex datasets. By enabling rapid algorithm training on large datasets, a process that frequently causes bottlenecks in traditional predictive analytics, quantum AI has the potential to enhance these models significantly. For instance, a quantum neural network can evaluate multiple model configurations concurrently due to superposition. This parallel processing capability can drastically reduce the time required for model training and hyperparameter tuning, which is crucial in developing accurate predictive models.

Data analysis to find patterns and clusters is a common task in predictive analytics. This task becomes more challenging when dealing with high-dimensional data. Quantum AI can handle large, multidimensional data structures, offering more precise and nuanced data clustering and pattern detection.

For instance, quantum algorithms can effectively perform complex linear algebra operations, which is crucial for many clustering and classification methods. This capability leads to more accurate pattern discovery and faster grouping, even in datasets with many dimensions and variables.

Predictive analytics can significantly benefit from quantum computing, as it can improve prediction speed and accuracy. Quantum computing allows for the simultaneous investigation of many possible answers, leading to more accurate forecasts, particularly in scenarios with numerous factors and potential outcomes, such as market trend analysis, weather forecasting, or risk assessment.

Additionally, quantum computing enables predictions to be made much more quickly than with conventional computing techniques due to the speed at which quantum computers can process information and perform calculations. This quick processing speed is essential in financial trading or emergency response planning, where instantaneous decision-making and real-time analytics are crucial.

The rise of big data has made it challenging to derive meaningful insights from extensive and heterogeneous databases. Quantum AI is well-suited for managing big data's complexity and size because it can simultaneously process and analyze massive volumes of data. Quantum computers are also adept at handling uncertainty and partial information, making them better equipped to manage the complexities of real-world data.

Many industries can apply quantum AI to enhance predictive analytics. It can transform personalized medicine in the healthcare sector by rapidly analyzing complex genetic and clinical data to predict treatment outcomes and disease progression. Quantum AI can improve banking fraud detection and risk assessment by thoroughly examining market data and customer behavior patterns.

In logistics and supply chain management sectors, predictive analytics enabled by quantum AI can optimize routes and inventory levels by more accurately predicting demand and supply patterns. Furthermore, it can forecast energy usage trends and optimize energy generation and distribution.

While quantum AI holds significant promise for predictive analytics, crucial obstacles must be addressed. An ongoing challenge is developing and maintaining quantum computers that can operate efficiently outside tightly regulated laboratory environments. Additionally, advancements in quantum algorithms focusing on predictive analytics are necessary.

Moreover, the demand for expertise at the intersection of data analytics and quantum computing is growing. Creating user-friendly quantum programming interfaces and educating data scientists and analysts on the fundamentals of quantum computing are key steps in converting quantum AI into a valuable tool for predictive analytics.

Integrating quantum computing with AI, particularly in predictive analytics, represents a new development. It offers enhanced capabilities for managing complex data, delivering faster and more accurate insights, and addressing the challenges of extensive data and complex real-world scenarios. quantum AI has the potential to reform data-driven prediction and decision-making and improve existing analytical processes. The reason is that the field is still in its early stages of development.

Quantum AI in Optimization Problems

Optimization problems are central to many scientific, industrial, and technological fields, including logistics, supply chain management, network design, and financial portfolio optimization. While classical algorithms are practical in some cases, they need help with the inherent complexity of these problems, significantly, as the number of variables increases exponentially. Quantum AI, utilizing the unique capabilities of quantum computing, offers a new approach to solving these optimization challenges.

Classical computational methods for solving optimization problems usually involve exact algorithms, which guarantee to find the optimal solution but can be excessively slow for large-scale problems, or heuristic algorithms, which provide faster, approximate solutions. However, as these problems become more complex—a common scenario in real-world situations—these methods need help finding optimal solutions within a reasonable timeframe. This is due to the combinatorial explosion of possibilities, where the solution space grows exponentially with the addition of each variable.

Quantum computing introduces new algorithms and computational paradigms distinct from traditional methods. Quantum algorithms can solve some optimization problems in polynomial time, which is a significant advantage compared to the exponential time required on a classical computer. This efficiency is primarily due to superposition and entanglement, two aspects of quantum mechanics.

In traditional computing, each possible answer is processed iteratively, while a quantum computer can represent and process every possible answer simultaneously through quantum superposition. Quantum entanglement further enhances this ability by allowing intricate correlations between qubits and making solution space exploration more effective.

One promising quantum computing method for solving optimization problems is quantum annealing. This method is based on the idea that a quantum system evolves to its lowest energy state, representing the best possible solution to the problem. Quantum annealing encodes the problem into a quantum system and progressively grows the system's quantum state to escape local optima and find the global optimum. It utilizes quantum tunneling, a phenomenon in which particles travel through energy barriers rather than over them.

The quantum annealing process is a method used in quantum computing that is particularly suited to solving optimization problems. To effectively illustrate this concept, the diagram in Figure 6-6 includes the key elements of quantum annealing. Qubits are the fundamental units of quantum computing, differing from classical bits in that they can exist in superpositions of states. The energy landscape visually represents the problem space, where different configurations of qubits correspond to varying energy levels.

Initially, qubits are in a superposition of all possible states, representing a search across the entire energy landscape. Quantum tunneling allows quantum annealing to escape local minima, unlike classical annealing. The annealing process involves gradually transitioning from a quantum superposition to a classical state, converging on an optimal or near-optimal solution. Ultimately, the qubits settle into a state representing the solution to the optimization problem.

The curve in Figure 6-6 represents the energy landscape of the problem, with different points along the curve corresponding to varying states of the qubits. At the beginning of the curve, the 'Quantum Superposition' dot symbolizes the initial state of the qubits, where they are in a superposition of all possible states. Unlike classical annealing, the dotted line represents quantum tunneling, allowing the system to bypass energy barriers. Finally, the 'Optimal Solution' dot toward the curve's end indicates the qubits' final state, representing the solution to the optimization problem.

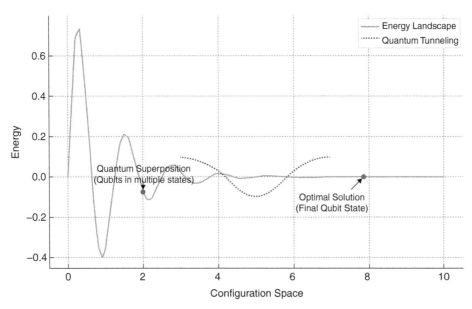

Figure 6-6
Quantum Annealing Process

Figure 6-6 provides a simplified view of quantum annealing, highlighting critical concepts like quantum superposition, quantum tunneling, and the energy landscape traversal. It serves as a valuable visual aid for understanding how quantum annealing seeks the lowest energy state, corresponding to the optimal solution to the problem.

Companies like D-Wave Systems are leading the application of quantum annealing to real-world optimization problems, demonstrating the technology's potential across various industries, including machine learning and logistics.

Optimization problems such as inventory management, warehouse placement, and vehicle routing are typical in supply chain management and logistics. Quantum AI can address these issues more effectively by swiftly exploring various options and settings. For example, in vehicle routing, a quantum computer can determine the most efficient paths much faster than classical approaches by simultaneously considering all feasible routes and limitations.

Finding the most effective way to build and run networks is known as network optimization, and it is essential to the distribution of energy, transportation, and telecommunications. Quantum AI has the potential to completely change this industry by providing more efficient solutions for issues like network routing, bandwidth allotment, and fault-tolerance design. This is especially important in the rapidly increasing network complexity in 5G and beyond.

Portfolio optimization is a crucial financial task that entails choosing the optimal asset portfolio for investment while weighing up the trade-off between return and risk. The sheer volume of market data and the obscure relationships between various financial instruments are often too much for classical approaches. Quantum AI can process the information faster and more systematically and find optimal investment plans that would be too complicated for traditional algorithms to determine.

Although quantum AI has enormous potential for solving optimization problems, there are many obstacles to its actual application. The qubit count, coherence duration, and error rates of existing quantum computers—especially those that use quantum annealing—are constrained. These computers are still in the early phases of development, and these restrictions impact the scope and difficulty of the issues that can be resolved successfully.

Formulating real-world optimization problems in a way that quantum computers can process them is difficult. It necessitates a thorough comprehension of quantum mechanics and the capacity to appropriately abstract and encode the issue.

As quantum computing technology advances and qubit stability, error correction, and algorithmic design improve, quantum AI can solve a far more wide-ranging range of optimization problems. A promising study on hybrid quantum-classical algorithms can tackle some issues with quantum computers and others with classical methods. Using the benefits of quantum computing might depend on this hybrid approach shortly.

In addition to technological progress, there is an increasing demand for multidisciplinary cooperation among quantum physicists, computer scientists, and specialists in domains such as finance, network design, logistics, and domain knowledge. This kind of cooperation is necessary to convert the theoretical benefits of quantum computing into workable, real-world optimization solutions.

The use of quantum AI to solve optimization issues in computer science has broad ramifications for numerous sectors. Quantum computing can solve problems that are intractable on classical computers in polynomial time. As the subject develops, it will open up new avenues for optimization and create a new age in computational problem-solving by achieving unprecedented efficiency and capabilities.

Challenges in Quantum Data Analysis

Quantum data analysis faces numerous obstacles that must be carefully addressed to realize its full potential.

The operation of quantum computing systems presents significant challenges, including quantum error correction, which is crucial for maintaining coherence in quantum systems (Terhal 2015). Quantum data analysis relies on quantum algorithms requiring a highly controlled operating environment. Some critical difficulties include low-temperature conditions, isolation from external disturbances, state and quantum decoherence equations, and scalability (de Leon et al. 2021).

Low-temperature conditions limit the scalability and accessibility of quantum computing (see Figure 6-7), particularly for systems based on superconducting qubits that must operate at extremely low temperatures to exhibit quantum mechanical phenomena. Isolation from external disturbances is crucial because quantum systems are susceptible to electromagnetic fields, thermal noise, and stray radiation, which can disrupt their operation.

The fragile nature of quantum states makes quantum computations susceptible to errors, with current error rates significantly higher than those in classical computing. Scalability also presents a daunting engineering challenge because building quantum computers with many qubits necessary for complex data analysis tasks increases the complexity of maintaining coherence and correcting errors.

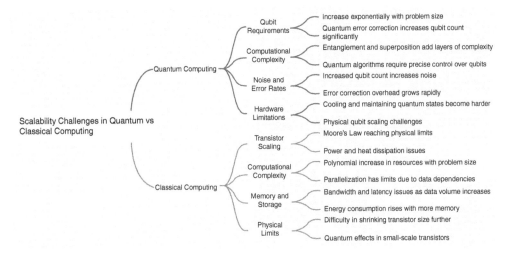

Figure 6-7
Scalability Challenges in Quantum vs. Classical Computing

The field of quantum computing is advancing, but there is a need for more professionals with the necessary skills to drive this progress. This shortage presents significant challenges, requiring quantum data scientists with unique quantum mechanics, quantum programming, and data science skills. Developing inclusive educational and training programs at the intersection of these disciplines is essential to bridge this gap.

Additionally, quantum programming languages and software development are still in their early stages compared to classical counterparts. Tools like Qiskit (IBM) and Cirq (Google) show promise but require a deep understanding of quantum mechanics, which can be a barrier for traditional programmers and data scientists. Simplifying these tools to make them more accessible to a broader range of developers is crucial for the growth of quantum data analysis.

Moreover, quantum computing brings unique challenges in data handling and algorithm development. Efficiently encoding classical data into a quantum format, known as quantum state preparation, is crucial for quantum data analysis but can be resource-intensive and error-prone. Additionally, while quantum algorithms like Grover's and Shor's have shown superior performance for specific tasks, there is ongoing development of quantum algorithms for broader data analysis applications, such as clustering, regression, and classification in data science.

The flowchart in Figure 6-8 illustrates the key steps involved in quantum data analysis, highlighting the parallel processes in quantum and classical systems. The figure distinguishes between quantum and classical steps across different phases, including Data encoding, Quantum computation, Quantum measurement, Data analysis & Interpretation, Error correction, and the Algorithmic feedback loop. Each phase encapsulates the unique challenges and methodologies associated with quantum computing, contrasting them with classical approaches to emphasize the complexities and potential advantages of quantum data processing.

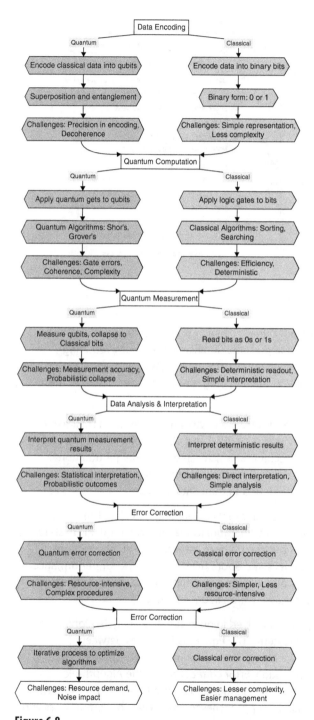

Figure 6-8

Flowchart Outlining the Quantum Data Analysis Process, Including Data Encoding, Quantum Computation, and Measurement

Figure 6-8 highlights the differences from classical data analysis workflows and provides a clear overview of the steps involved in analyzing quantum data and where challenges may arise.

Most practical applications for quantum computing likely involve hybrid systems integrating quantum and classical computing. It is crucial to develop frameworks and algorithms to incorporate these systems effectively, ensuring that algorithms can function seamlessly on both platforms and data can be transmitted between classical and quantum systems effectively (see Figure 6-9).

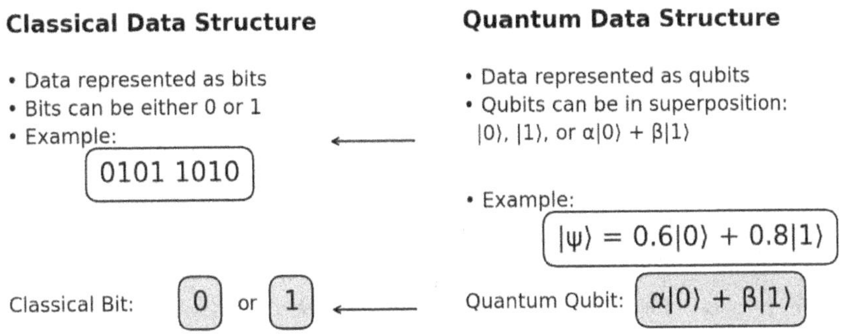

Classical Data Structure

- Data represented as bits
- Bits can be either 0 or 1
- Example:

  0101 1010

Classical Bit: 0   or   1   ←————

Quantum Data Structure

- Data represented as qubits
- Qubits can be in superposition: $|0\rangle$, $|1\rangle$, or $\alpha|0\rangle + \beta|1\rangle$

- Example:

  $|\psi\rangle = 0.6|0\rangle + 0.8|1\rangle$

Quantum Qubit: $\alpha|0\rangle + \beta|1\rangle$

Figure 6-9
Comparison of Classical and Quantum Data Structures

Security and ethical issues are significant considerations in the development of quantum computing. Data security and privacy face severe threats due to quantum computers' potential to crack current encryption techniques. This highlights the need to create encryption techniques resistant to quantum mechanics and reevaluate data security strategies in the context of quantum technology.

Equitable access is a concern due to quantum computing technology's high cost and complexity. It is essential to ensure that the benefits of quantum data analysis are widely shared and not limited to a select group of wealthy organizations.

Quantum data analysis presents various technical, labor, algorithmic, and ethical challenges, despite its potential to bring about revolutionary improvements in processing in government, business, and academia, alongside a commitment to collaborative research, ethical governance, and education. Overcoming these obstacles will enable quantum data analysis to transform our understanding of data and drive scientific, medical, and commercial advancements.

Quantum Machine Learning Algorithms

Quantum computing and AI are at the forefront of future technology, particularly in quantum-enhanced data analysis and quantum neural networks. The challenges and opportunities in this field are significant, with the potential to reform various sectors and advance scientific knowledge. Overcoming these obstacles will require technological breakthroughs and ethical and cooperative approaches.

Enhanced Optimization Algorithms

The current state of quantum optimization is focused on experimental applications such as portfolio optimization and the traveling salesman problem. Quantum optimization is still in its early stages, with its main advantage lying in the ability of quantum algorithms to utilize entanglement to identify correlations and superposition to explore multiple options simultaneously.

There are two main approaches to quantum optimization:

- **Quantum annealing**: Quantum annealing aims to find the lowest energy state of a system, which is akin to finding the best solution to an optimization problem. D-Wave technologies have been at the forefront of quantum annealing, but they are primarily tailored to specific optimization problems.

- **Gate-based quantum computing**: This approach is more comprehensive than the quantum annealing approach. However, it currently faces challenges related to coherence and error rates, as evidenced by the progress made by Google and IBM.

The diagram in Figure 6-10 provides a wide-ranging and detailed representation focused on various aspects of quantum computing. It includes a detailed representation of qubits using a 3D Bloch sphere to illustrate the concept of superposition and quantum states. The diagram also enhances the visualization of quantum gates by demonstrating how they transform the state of a qubit on the Bloch sphere. Figure 6-10 illustrates the complexity of quantum circuits by showing a sequence of quantum gates and their application in a circuit.

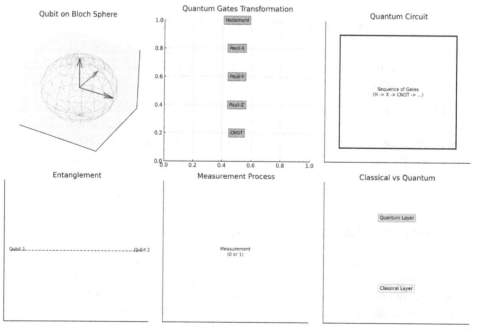

Figure 6-10
Key Concepts of Gate-Based Quantum Computing

The diagram in Figure 6-10 provides a more precise illustration of entanglement by showing how the state of one qubit correlates with another. It also details the measurement process, including the probabilistic nature of quantum measurement. Moreover, it differentiates between the quantum processing and the resulting classical information after measurement, providing a more in-depth understanding of gate-based quantum computing.

A qubit on a Bloch sphere is a 3D representation that illustrates the superposition and quantum states using different axes. The representation helps us understand the complex nature of qubits in quantum computing. The next aspect to consider is the transformation of various quantum gates such as Hadamard, Pauli-X, Y, Z, and CNOT. These gates play a crucial role in altering the state of a qubit, thus forming the basis of quantum computation.

The quantum circuit complexity demonstrates a circuit's sequence of quantum gates, signifying the computational process. This visual representation is essential in understanding the concept of entanglement, a key aspect of quantum computing, illustrated through the interaction between two qubits. This concept is fundamental in quantum information processing and quantum communication.

Furthermore, Figure 6-10 depicts the measurement process, showing how the quantum state is read and converted into a classical state (0 or 1). This step is crucial in obtaining the final computational result from the quantum system.

Lastly, comparing the quantum processing layer, where computation occurs, and the resulting classical information layer offers a clear understanding of the transition from quantum to classical information. This across-the-board approach combines the conceptual and operational aspects of gate-based quantum computing, providing a holistic view of the subject.

Considering the concepts in Figure 6-10, a promising direction for the future involves combining gate-based methods and quantum annealing, potentially leading to highly effective algorithms for specific problems with a wide range of applications. Additionally, hybrid algorithms, which blend aspects of quantum and classical computing, are showing promise as a transitional solution to improve optimization tasks.

Enhanced quantum optimization techniques can address complex and large-scale problems that traditional computers struggle with. For example, in the aerospace industry, these algorithms could optimize flight paths in real time, considering various factors such as weather patterns, air traffic, and fuel efficiency.

The logistics sector may undergo revolutionary changes using quantum optimization methods. These algorithms could most efficiently balance supply chains, manage inventories, and schedule deliveries in a dynamic and quickly changing environment, surpassing the current efficiency level.

In the financial sector, quantum optimization could transform algorithmic trading, portfolio management, and risk assessment. These systems could analyze large volumes of economic data and variables, providing more accurate insights and forecasts than current algorithms.

However, significant obstacles remain. Current quantum computers cannot consistently outperform classical computers in real-world applications due to limitations in qubit coherence and error rates. Research is ongoing to develop algorithms that fully exploit quantum physics.

It is predicted that over the next 10 years, quantum optimization algorithms will surpass their classical equivalents in some applications as quantum technology advances and more sophisticated algorithms are developed. The goal is to achieve quantum supremacy in realistic, applied tasks, ushering in a new era of computer power.

In the future, quantum optimization algorithms may completely change how we solve problems in various domains. This could have game-changing ramifications, such as making renewable energy networks more effective and resolving intricate biological issues.

Quantum-Enhanced Deep Learning

QNNs in image recognition can simultaneously process and compare multiple image states using quantum superposition. For example, a quantum-enhanced neural network could analyze a wide range of medical imaging data, such as MRI scans, much faster than conventional systems. This could lead to a quicker and more accurate diagnosis of conditions like brain tumors by comparing images with an extensive database of known cases.

Figure 6-11 illustrates the architecture of a quantum neural network (QNN), highlighting the relationship between quantum and classical components. The network begins with a classical input layer, where data is preprocessed and passed through a hybrid quantum-classical interface. This interface connects the classical data to the quantum neural network, which consists of multiple layers of qubits and quantum gates. These gates manipulate the qubits' states, allowing the QNN to process information in ways that classical networks cannot. Finally, the quantum information is measured and passed back to classical components for post-processing and output generation.

As shown in Figure 6-11, the QNN relies on the integration of quantum gates and measurements to harness the unique properties of quantum mechanics. The qubits, which serve as the fundamental units of quantum information, are manipulated through successive layers of quantum gates, enabling complex transformations that are critical for the network's operation. The measurement step bridges the quantum and classical domains, converting quantum states into classical data that can be further processed. This hybrid architecture allows QNNs to leverage the advantages of quantum computing while maintaining compatibility with existing classical systems.

Thanks to quantum entanglement, QNNs in the financial markets may be capable of identifying complex, nonlinear connections across vast datasets that include historical pricing, trade volumes, and economic indicators. For example, a QNN can be trained to discover early market movements or crash indicators by comparing disparate and seemingly unrelated global financial variables. This represents a significant accomplishment that exceeds the capabilities of traditional algorithms.

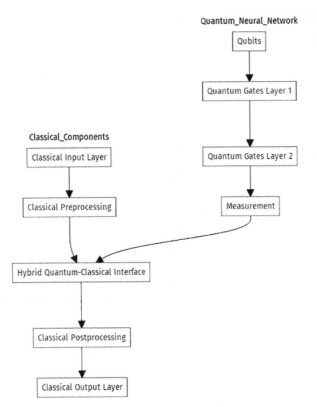

Figure 6-11

The Architecture of a Quantum Neural Network, Highlighting Quantum Gates, Qubits, and How They Interact with Classical Components

One fascinating application of QNNs is molecular modeling and drug discovery. By analyzing interactions in large molecular structures, QNNs have the potential to transform our understanding of protein folding, a significant biological challenge. For example, AlphaFold, an AI developed by Google DeepMind, has made remarkable progress in predicting protein shapes. A quantum-enhanced version of QNNs could hasten the discovery of new medications by effectively handling even larger protein complexes.

In climate science, QNNs can play a crucial role in modeling complex climate systems, especially with the pressing issue of climate change. By analyzing extensive datasets from global sensors, satellite imaging, and historical records, QNNs could more accurately model and forecast weather patterns and climate changes, providing a potent tool for environmental planning and disaster prevention.

However, the realization of these applications hinges on overcoming the significant challenge of quantum error correction. The high error rates of current quantum computers can significantly impact the reliability of QNN outputs. Advancements in error correction techniques will be vital to realizing these use cases. The development of hybrid quantum-classical models is a promising advancement on the horizon. These systems could leverage classical systems for some tasks and quantum processing for others. For example, a hybrid model could utilize classical neural networks for complex pattern recognition parts while employing quantum techniques for initial feature selection in a large dataset.

Quantum Learning Theories

Traditional computing paradigms have influenced the current theoretical frameworks for machine learning. However, quantum learning theories would leverage the distinctive properties of quantum mechanics—such as quantum interference, entanglement, and superposition—to process and understand data in fundamentally different ways.

Quantum superposition allows for the simultaneous existence of several states, which could significantly improve problem-solving abilities. Quantum models could simultaneously evaluate a wide range of solutions, which has potential applications in logistics and supply chain management by generating optimal solutions faster than traditional algorithms.

Thanks to quantum entanglement, predictive analytics may undergo a revolution. Quantum models could reveal insights by making possible intricate, high-dimensional connections between data points. For instance, entanglement-based models could evaluate patient data to forecast treatment outcomes and illness progression with unprecedented accuracy in the healthcare industry.

Combining the probability amplitudes of quantum states or interference may offer new avenues for AI decision-making. This has potential applications in the financial markets, where quantum learning models assess and forecast the performance of different investment strategies across a wide range of economic scenarios by utilizing interference patterns.

One exciting area of research involves the application of quantum learning theories to address AI biases and ethical issues. Quantum models may provide fresh insights into identifying and reducing training data biases, leading to more equitable AI systems. By processing and comparing data in a radically different manner, quantum models have the potential to update the way AI systems handle biases and ethical concerns.

In cognitive frameworks, quantum theories could significantly influence cognitive modeling, resulting in AI systems that resemble human thought processes more closely. For instance, quantum cognitive models could be utilized in AI-driven learning aids to adapt to each learner's unique preferences by evaluating different teaching strategies and their effectiveness.

Numerous obstacles exist to fully implementing quantum learning theories. One key challenge is designing scalable and robust quantum hardware and the necessity of quantum error correction. Furthermore, developing these new learning models requires a broad understanding of machine and quantum mechanics. Overcoming these technical obstacles is vital for successfully integrating quantum learning theories into AI systems.

The groundwork for quantum learning theories may emerge in the next 10 years as extensions of classical theories. Once quantum hardware reaches a mature state, the mid-century may see the application of these theories in specialized fields like materials science, finance, and pharmaceuticals. In the future, quantum learning models might become the norm in fields requiring intricate, multidimensional data analysis. The implications might extend as far as introducing radically novel methods for deciphering complex systems in disciplines such as climate science, neuroscience, and even the study of quantum physics.

Quantum Data Encoding

Quantum data encoding involves converting classical data into a format that quantum computers can process. Standard techniques include quantum feature mapping, amplitude encoding, and basis encoding. However, these techniques encounter scaling issues when dealing with large or complex datasets.

A potential solution to these issues is variational quantum encoding, which utilizes tunable variational quantum circuits that can be optimized for specific tasks or datasets. This adaptability is crucial when working with large, complex datasets such as those in climatology or genomics.

Quantum data encoding in genomics has the potential to reform customized medicine. Quantum-encoded genomic data could rapidly analyze an individual's genetic makeup, leading to personalized treatment programs based on unique genetic profiles and drug responses.

Quantum data encoding could significantly enhance climate modeling. QML models can improve the accuracy of simulating complex climate systems by effectively encoding large volumes of climatic data. This would allow for more precise projections of the impacts of climate change and the development of more successful mitigation and adaptation plans.

Quantum data encoding has potential applications in cybersecurity. Encoding data in a quantum-mechanical manner makes data inherently more secure. For example, communications encrypted with quantum keys would be impervious to conventional hacking techniques, offering unprecedented data protection.

The main obstacle in this field is quantum physics'"no-cloning theorem," which prohibits replicating unknown quantum states. This complicates error correction and data processing that needs to be seen in traditional computing.

More advanced quantum encoding methods are expected to be developed initially in research and then gradually in commercial applications. The goal is to create more scalable and highly efficient data encoding and processing techniques for real-world use.

The progression of quantum machine learning algorithms is anticipated to drive the creation of novel encoding techniques. This development is expected to yield enhanced algorithms and data encoding methods, working in synergy to significantly boost the capabilities and scope of applications for quantum computing. In the long term, this evolution in quantum data encoding will change the current data analytics process. Quantum computers will be poised to tackle previously inconceivable tasks, such as conducting intricate biomedical simulations and facilitating real-time global economic modeling.

Hybrid Quantum-Classical Algorithms

Quantum and classical computing can work together to combine their respective strengths. Quantum computing is adept at handling complex calculations and processing large datasets through parallelism and entanglement. However, it faces challenges such as limited qubits and high error rates. On the other hand, classical computing excels in providing consistency and efficiency for repetitive computational tasks.

Hybrid algorithms combine the strengths of both types of computing by utilizing classical computing for regular processing and quantum computing for more challenging tasks.

In finance, hybrid algorithms have the potential to significantly enhance the industry's ability to forecast market trends and model economic scenarios. For instance, a hybrid system could simulate intricate market dynamics and identify connections that traditional algorithms might miss. Meanwhile, classical computing could handle responsibilities like user interface management and data input pre-processing.

In the pharmaceutical sector, hybrid quantum-classical algorithms show promise, particularly in drug development. Classical computing can manage vast databases of molecular structures and known pharmacological effects, while quantum computing can model complex molecular interactions at a granular level, a computationally intensive process.

Hybrid systems can enhance supply chain management and logistics optimization by leveraging quantum computing to determine the most efficient routes and schedules from various options. Classical computing can then execute and monitor these schedules in real-world scenarios.

Hybrid algorithms also have a lot to offer in AI and big data. Classical computing might handle the more linear aspects of the algorithms and the interfaces with end users and other systems. Meanwhile, quantum computing's capacity to handle massive, complicated datasets and execute parallel calculations could be utilized for processing big data or training AI models.

Hybrid algorithms can potentially optimize power distribution and management in smart grids within the energy sector. While classical computers might handle operational tasks like scheduling grid maintenance and customer billing, quantum computing may determine the most economical way to distribute resources in response to real-time data. One of the biggest hurdles in creating these algorithms is ensuring that quantum and classical computing processes integrate seamlessly. This calls for advancements in software that can successfully translate and bridge the two computing paradigms and breakthroughs in quantum computing hardware.

The first real-world applications of hybrid quantum-classical algorithms should appear within the next 10 years, especially in the financial, pharmaceutical, and logistics industries. These early devices will probably be simple, but as quantum technology advances, it will open the door to more complex uses. Hybrid algorithms have the potential to become the industry standard for computational jobs in the long run. These algorithms may become the norm when quantum technology develops and becomes more widely available for solving issues requiring massive computer power.

Advances in Quantum Error Correction

Quantum error correction is crucial due to the potential for decoherence and quantum noise to introduce errors in quantum bits (qubits), which can significantly disrupt quantum operations. Unlike classical bits, qubits, operating in a state of superposition and entanglement, are more fragile and error-prone. Therefore, quantum error correction (QEC) is essential to identify and rectify these errors without causing the quantum state of the qubits to collapse.

Current QEC techniques use complex algorithms to detect and fix defects in qubit arrays. Leading methods, such as the surface and Shor codes, provide a quantum error-correcting code by incorporating additional qubits. This enables the system to recognize and rectify faults that occur during processing.

QEC's fundamental goal is to achieve fault-tolerant quantum computing, where a quantum computer can function reliably and rectify errors. Recent developments focus on creating error-correcting codes that are more effective and require fewer qubits overall, which lowers system complexity.

The focus has shifted toward developing fault-tolerant quantum computing that can function and rectify errors reliably. This has led to a concentration on creating error-correcting codes that are more efficient and require fewer qubits, thus reducing overall system complexity.

Better QEC techniques are crucial for simulating complex quantum systems more accurately in quantum simulations. This is particularly important in fields such as material science, where understanding quantum behavior in materials could create new superconductors or batteries.

Robust QEC is essential for QML. With improved error correction, larger qubit systems can execute QML algorithms, developing more advanced learning models. This has the potential to modernize fields such as pattern identification, where QML computers could identify subtle patterns in massive datasets, such as early indicators of diseases from medical images.

Advancements in QEC also support quantum cryptography. More reliable quantum communications enable higher-security quantum key distribution schemes to be used over greater distances, increasing the practicality and adoption of quantum-encrypted communication.

Improved QEC methods in quantum sensing enhance the sensitivity and precision of quantum sensors. These sensors are used in various applications, from medical diagnostics to navigation systems, and rely on the stability of quantum states, which sophisticated QEC can effectively preserve.

Scaling the procedures for larger quantum systems presents a significant challenge in QEC. The complexity of error correction increases exponentially with the number of qubits. Research focuses on creating scalable QEC algorithms that effectively manage errors in large-scale quantum systems.

QEC is anticipated to make significant strides in the coming decade, transitioning from theoretical models to real-world applications in quantum computers. This development is crucial for advancing quantum computing from laboratory settings to practical uses. The long-term growth of fully error-corrected quantum computing may pave the way for the widespread adoption of quantum technology. The potential applications range from sophisticated QML models to intricate simulations, with possible impacts on nearly every field of science and technology.

Post-Quantum Cryptography

Discrete logarithms and integer factorization are computationally challenging problems in modern encryption techniques such as Rivest–Shamir–Adleman (RSA) and Elliptic-curve cryptography (ECC). These encryption techniques are vulnerable to quantum computers, which can solve these problems faster than classical computers, using algorithms like Shor's algorithm.

To address the importance of standardization in post-quantum cryptography (PQC), it is essential to reference the ongoing efforts by the National Institute of Standards and Technology (NIST). NIST's Post-Quantum Cryptography project (NIST 2017, 2022, 2023a, 2023b) is critical in developing cryptographic systems resilient to quantum computing threats. As part of this project, NIST has released several draft Federal Information Processing Standards (FIPS) for public comment, which are expected to play a significant role in future government certifications. Specifically, FIPS 203 specifies algorithms derived from CRYSTALS-Dilithium for digital signatures, FIPS 204 specifies algorithms derived from CRYSTALS-KYBER for key encapsulation mechanisms, and FIPS 205 specifies algorithms derived from SPHINCS+, a stateless hash-based signature scheme. These standards are poised to become integral to the implementation and deployment of post-quantum cryptographic systems, ensuring secure communication protocols in the quantum era. Further details and updates can be found on the NIST website at https://csrc.nist.gov/projects/post-quantum-cryptography.

Post-quantum cryptography aims to develop cryptographic solutions resistant to classical and quantum computing. It involves creating algorithms for mathematical problems such as multivariate polynomial cryptography, lattice-based cryptography, hash-based cryptography, and code-based encryption, all of which are considered challenging for quantum computers.

Lattice-based cryptography is a leading candidate for PQC. It relies on the difficulty of lattice problems, for which no effective quantum algorithm is currently available. NIST is considering several lattice-based protocols for standardization. NIST announced its selection of four algorithms—CRYSTALS-Kyber, CRYSTALS-Dilithium, Sphincs+ and FALCON—slated for standardization in 2022, and released draft versions of three of these standards in 2023. The fourth draft standard based on FALCON is planned for late 2024. These protocols ensure secure communication, even in the presence of quantum computers, and are used for digital signatures, key exchange, and data encryption.

Another intriguing field is hash-based cryptography. Cryptographic hash functions, which are difficult to reverse but relatively simple to compute in one direction, form the basis of its security. While hash-based signature schemes, such as the Lamport signature, are relatively secure, they sometimes result in larger keys and signatures, which could be a drawback.

Cryptography based on codes is well regarded for its speed and simplicity. Its security derives from the challenge of decoding a general linear code. Secure communication systems have been demonstrated using algorithms such as the McEliece cryptosystem. However, compared to conventional techniques, they usually require larger key sizes.

Another method, cryptography using multivariate polynomials, involves solving multivariate polynomial problems, which pose challenges for quantum and classical computers. It has the potential for small key sizes and quick computations, making it especially promising for digital signatures.

Creating post-quantum cryptography algorithms that are efficient and secure is quite tricky. They must be fast and efficient in computing power and impervious to quantum attacks. Another challenge is ensuring these algorithms can be successfully incorporated into the communication infrastructure.

Looking ahead, PQC standards are likely to become the norm in the next 10 years. PQC algorithms are currently being evaluated and standardized by groups like NIST. This change will involve maintaining backward compatibility, changing security procedures, and upgrading public critical infrastructure. In the long run, PQC will become standard practice for protecting online transactions, data storage, and digital communications. It will be essential for defending financial transactions, state secrets, and private information against upcoming quantum attacks.

Post-quantum cryptography will ensure data security and transmission in QML. Implementing PQC is essential to guaranteeing the confidentiality and integrity of QML systems' handling of progressively sensitive data, such as financial or medical records.

Quantum Advantage in Real-World Applications

Quantum advantage refers to a quantum computer's ability to solve specific problems more quickly than traditional classical techniques. Quantum computers may sometimes outperform conventional computers, but they are expected to excel in particular niche markets.

Quantum computing has the potential to reform personalized medicine and drug development in the healthcare industry. For example, quantum algorithms can model chemical interactions, a task too complex for classical computers. This could accelerate the development of drugs and therapies tailored to each patient's genetic profile, transforming patient care.

Quantum computing has the potential to modernize various sectors, with finance being one of the key beneficiaries. By utilizing quantum algorithms and developing reliable financial strategies and risk management instruments, the financial industry could enhance risk analysis models and optimization processes.

While quantum computers could crack many current encryption techniques, they also offer the possibility of creating quantum-secure encryption protocols. This duality could lead to more secure data storage and transmission systems, safeguarding sensitive data from emerging threats.

Moreover, environmental modeling and energy optimization could benefit significantly from quantum computing. Quantum algorithms may be employed to model intricate environmental systems and optimize power distribution in smart grids, enabling better change prediction and supporting sustainable planning and resource management.

In logistics, quantum computing has the potential to streamline supply chain management. By outperforming traditional algorithms in solving complex routing puzzles, quantum algorithms could result in substantial cost savings, reduced environmental impact, and improved customer service in industries such as shipping and transportation.

Integrating quantum computing with AI holds promise for enhancing AI and machine learning processes. Quantum algorithms can process and analyze large datasets much faster than classical algorithms, potentially revolutionizing industries such as robotics and autonomous vehicles.

Overcoming several obstacles, such as those related to quantum hardware limits, error rates, and the development of new quantum algorithms, is essential to achieve quantum advantage. Quantum computers must become more scalable and stable to handle complex real-world applications effectively.

Quantum advantage is anticipated to be realized in specific, specialized fields within the next few years. As quantum technology advances, these benefits are likely to become more widespread. By the middle of the century, quantum computing may be crucial in addressing some of industry's and science's most challenging and urgent issues.

The attainment of quantum advantage could lead to a paradigm shift in how computation and problem-solving are approached. The potential impact is far-reaching, encompassing the ability to address global issues such as climate change and expand scientific knowledge in particle physics.

Summary

This chapter focused on quantum machine learning (QML), specifically on quantum neural networks (QNNs) and their capacity to update data analysis and problem-solving across diverse industries.

The operational functionality of QNNs relies heavily on fundamental concepts in quantum mechanics, such as superposition and entanglement, enabling them to perform tasks that surpass the capabilities of classical computers. The potential applications of QNNs are wide-ranging, encompassing enhancements to financial models through improved predictive analytics and transformative simulations of chemical interactions for drug development.

Additionally, the chapter explored the emerging field of quantum learning theories, rooted in quantum phenomena, which hold the potential to redefine AI paradigms. These theories may unlock previously unattainable processing powers, paving the way for advanced computational models that closely emulate human cognitive functions.

Furthermore, significant developments in quantum data encoding have been emphasized for their significance in effectively managing complex, large-scale datasets. This development can substantially impact climatology and genetics, potentially leading to more precise climate modeling and tailored medical treatments.

Introducing hybrid quantum-classical algorithms is a practical step toward leveraging the advantages of quantum and classical computing paradigms in practical applications. Combining the best aspects of the classical and quantum worlds, these algorithms can enhance optimization in finance and logistics.

Post-quantum cryptography (PQC) and quantum error correction (QEC) have been identified as crucial fields for preserving the security and stability of quantum systems. PQC is critical for safeguarding data from potential quantum computing threats and ensuring a secure transition to a quantum computing era. At the same time, QEC is essential for developing robust and dependable quantum computers.

A detailed analysis of the concept of quantum advantage has been conducted, highlighting its potential to deliver solutions faster and more effectively than classical algorithms across various practical applications. The far-reaching implications of achieving quantum advantage span environmental science, cybersecurity, healthcare, and finance.

This chapter established the foundation for understanding the transformative effects of merging AI and quantum computing. It outlines the potential for significant breakthroughs in society and technology. To fully realize the revolutionary potential of this convergence, it emphasizes the need for ongoing study, ethical considerations, and collaborative efforts while acknowledging the obstacles that lie ahead.

References

de Leon, N. P., K. M. Itoh, D. Kim, K. K. Mehta, T. E. Northup, H. Paik, B. S. Palmer, N. Samarth, S. Sangtawesin, and D. W. Steuerman. 2021. "Materials Challenges and Opportunities for Quantum Computing Hardware." *Science* 372 (6539). https://doi.org/10.1126/science.abb2823.

NIST. 2017. "Post-Quantum Cryptography: NIST's Plan for the Future." https://doi.org/10.6028/NIST.IR.8084.

NIST. 2022. "Post-Quantum Cryptography PQC." https://csrc.nist.gov/Projects/post-quantum-cryptography.

NIST. 2023a. "Post-Quantum Cryptography | CSRC | Competition for Post-Quantum Cryptography Standardisation." *NISTIR 8413*. https://csrc.nist.gov/projects/post-quantum-cryptography.

NIST. 2023b. "Post-Quantum Cryptography | CSRC | Selected Algorithms: Public-Key Encryption and Key-Establishment Algorithms." https://csrc.nist.gov/Projects/post-quantum-cryptography/selected-algorithms-2022.

Terhal, B. M. 2015. "Quantum Error Correction for Quantum Memories." *Reviews of Modern Physics* 87: 307. https://journals.aps.org/rmp/abstract/10.1103/RevModPhys.87.307.

Test Your Skills

Multiple-Choice Questions

These questions are designed to test understanding of the key concepts, focusing on the societal impacts, challenges, and future implications of AI in autonomous systems.

1. What distinguishes quantum neural networks (QNNs) from classical neural networks?

   A. The use of neurons instead of qubits

   B. The ability to process data in binary form

   C. Utilization of quantum superposition and entanglement

   D. Focus on linear data processing

2. What are the potential benefits of quantum-enhanced deep learning in medical imaging?

   A. Faster and more accurate diagnosis

   B. Reduced need for manual image tagging

   C. Enhanced color accuracy in images

   D. More efficient data storage

3. What is the primary challenge in developing quantum machine learning (QML) algorithms?

   A. Creating more interactive user interfaces

   B. Quantum error correction and qubit stability

   C. Ensuring compatibility with classical databases

   D. Reducing the energy consumption of quantum computers

4. What role do hybrid quantum-classical algorithms play in the progression of quantum computing?

   A. They completely replace classical algorithms.

   B. They optimize the strengths of quantum and classical computing.

   C. They serve only as theoretical models for future quantum computers.

   D. They are used mainly for educational purposes.

5. What is a potential application of post-quantum cryptography (PQC)?

   A. Speeding up quantum computations

   B. Protecting data against quantum-computing attacks

C. Improving the graphic interface of quantum computers

D. Enhancing the audio processing capabilities of quantum systems

6. What is a crucial indicator of achieving "quantum advantage" in practical applications?

A. Quantum algorithms can run on classical computers.

B. Quantum algorithms solve problems faster than classical algorithms.

C. Quantum computers can use classical data.

D. Quantum computers reach the same processing power as classical computers.

7. Which field is likely to benefit from a quantum advantage in complex problem-solving?

A. Quantum-enhanced video game design

B. Deep-sea exploration technologies

C. Healthcare, for drug discovery and personalized medicine

D. Traditional book publishing processes

8. What is a significant implication of integrating quantum computing and AI?

A. Reduction in the physical size of computing devices

B. The creation of new learning theories and computational models

C. The phasing out of all classical computing methods

D. Increased dependency on manual data input methods

9. Which is not a challenge mentioned in the development of quantum AI?

A. High financial cost of quantum hardware

B. Limited availability of quantum mechanics experts

C. Difficulty in integrating quantum computing with renewable energy sources

D. Shortage of professionals with combined skills in quantum computing and data science

10. What is the potential impact of quantum error correction advancements?

A. Decreasing the relevance of classical computing

B. Creating more stable and reliable quantum computers

C. Reducing the need for quantum algorithms

D. Simplifying quantum computing interfaces

Exercises

These exercises are designed to test your understanding and ability to apply the concepts discussed in Chapter 6, preparing you to engage effectively with quantum computing and AI.

Exercise 6.1: Understanding Quantum Neural Networks and Their Applications

Read Chapter 6 and answer the following questions:

1. What are quantum neural networks (QNNs), and how do they differ from classical neural networks?

2. Discuss the potential applications of QNNs in the medical field.

3. Explain how superposition and entanglement contribute to the functionality of QNNs.

Exercise 6.2: The Impact of Quantum Computing on AI

Read Chapter 6 and answer the following questions:

1. How does the integration of quantum computing and AI potentially transform data analysis?

2. What are the challenges in developing quantum machine learning (QML) algorithms?

3. Discuss the role of hybrid quantum-classical algorithms in the evolution of quantum computing.

Exercise 6.3: Examining Quantum Advancements in Various Sectors

Read Chapter 6 and answer the following questions:

1. Describe potential applications of quantum computing in the healthcare sector.

2. What is the significance of post-quantum cryptography (PQC) in the era of quantum computing?

3. Explain the concept of "quantum advantage" and its implications in practical applications.

7

Blockchain, Quantum Computing, and AI Agents

Chapter Objectives

This chapter reviews the integration of blockchain, quantum computing, and AI agents to create advanced, autonomous, and future-proof security systems. The chapter relates the concepts of post-quantum cryptography and quantum cryptography with AI agent frameworks to enhance security and efficiency. It also examines the role of AI agents in managing quantum-resilient blockchain technologies. Upon completing this chapter, you will be equipped to

- **Understand the Intersection of AI Agents, Blockchain, and Quantum Computing**: Grasp how AI agents can autonomously manage and secure blockchain and quantum computing systems, particularly in enhancing security frameworks.

- **Explore AI Agent Frameworks in Post-Quantum Cryptography**: Engage in the domain of post-quantum cryptography and understand how AI agents can implement and manage cryptographic methods resistant to quantum computing attacks.

- **Analyze Lattice-Based Algorithms and AI Integration**: Learn about lattice-based algorithms, examining their structure, strengths, and potential for quantum-resistant cryptographic solutions, and explore how AI agents can autonomously optimize and deploy these algorithms.

- **Investigate Hash-Based Cryptography and AI Applications**: Study hash-based cryptography to understand its role in securing data against quantum computing threats and explore how AI agents can manage these cryptographic systems for enhanced security.

- **Evaluate Quantum-Resilient Blockchain Technologies and AI Agents**: Assess the development and application of quantum-resilient blockchain technologies, focusing on how AI agents can autonomously secure and optimize these systems in the face of advancing quantum computing capabilities.

- **Recognize Challenges in Developing AI-Integrated Quantum-Resilient Solutions**: Identify the challenges in creating blockchain, cryptographic, and AI-integrated solutions resilient to quantum computing, including technical, theoretical, and implementation aspects.

- **Anticipate Future Developments in Secure, Autonomous Computing**: Predict future trends and potential advancements in secure computing through the integration of AI agents, blockchain, and quantum computing technologies.

- **Reflect on the Broader Implications for Security, Privacy, and Autonomy**: Consider the wider implications of integrating AI agents with these technologies for security, privacy, and autonomy across various sectors, understanding their transformative potential and the necessity for ongoing development in cryptographic methods and AI frameworks.

The chapter begins with a discussion of post-quantum cryptography where it examines the need for cryptographic methods resistant to the capabilities of quantum computing. For AI agents, this is crucial because they will operate in environments where the security of data and communications is paramount. The integration of post-quantum cryptography, specifically through lattice-based and hash-based algorithms, ensures that AI agents are equipped to defend against quantum-enabled threats. This section highlights how AI agents will utilize these cryptographic frameworks to secure sensitive operations, ensuring the integrity and confidentiality of information even in the face of advanced quantum attacks.

Next, the chapter explores quantum cryptography (Bernstein 2011), focusing on quantum key distribution (QKD) protocols like BB84 and E91. These protocols are vital for establishing secure communication channels that are impervious to eavesdropping, even by quantum computers. AI agents will play a critical role in managing and optimizing these protocols, autonomously overseeing key distribution processes to maintain security in real time. This section illustrates how AI agents will ensure that the communication infrastructure they rely on remains secure, applying quantum cryptography to protect against potential breaches.

Following this, the discourse shifts to quantum cryptography, illustrating a transition from reliance on computational complexity to the immutable laws of physics as the bedrock of security. Quantum key distribution (QKD) protocols, including BB84 and E91, are discussed as seminal examples of how quantum mechanics can be employed to create secure communication channels impervious to both classical and quantum attacks. This section further explores the critical role of AI agents in autonomously managing these sophisticated cryptographic processes, ensuring the efficiency and security of operations in real-time contexts.

The chapter then expands into quantum-resilient blockchain technologies, discussing how blockchain systems can be fortified against quantum threats. AI agents are central to this because they will autonomously manage and optimize blockchain networks to ensure their security and efficiency. By integrating quantum-resistant cryptographic techniques into blockchain frameworks, AI agents can enhance the resilience of these systems, making them robust against current and future threats. This section underscores the role of AI agents in safeguarding blockchain technologies, ensuring that they remain a trustworthy foundation for digital transactions and record-keeping.

The chapter includes a detailed analysis of quantum-resilient blockchain technologies, where the focus is placed on the integration of quantum-resistant cryptographic techniques within blockchain systems. The discussion highlights the transformative role of AI agents in autonomously securing, optimizing, and managing these blockchain environments, thereby guaranteeing the long-term integrity and trustworthiness of decentralized systems.

Further, the chapter analyzes the challenges in developing AI-integrated quantum-resilient solutions, recognizing the technical and theoretical difficulties involved in creating systems that can withstand quantum computing capabilities. AI agents, with their ability to adapt and learn, are well positioned to overcome these challenges, continuously evolving to meet new security demands. This section is critical in understanding how AI agents will not only implement but also refine quantum-resilient solutions, ensuring that these technologies remain effective as the quantum landscape evolves.

The chapter is grounded in the fundamental challenge of securing digital interactions against the dual threats of present vulnerabilities and future, as-yet-unknown adversaries. The solution proposed here is the utilization of quantum mechanics principles, augmented by the capabilities of AI agents, to develop cryptographic solutions that are both theoretically sound and practically deployable within blockchain infrastructures. This chapter stands as one of the most technical in the book, expanding into an examination of lattice-based and hash-based algorithms. These algorithms are positioned as cornerstones of quantum-resistant security: lattice-based cryptography offers robust protection against quantum threats by relying on problems currently deemed intractable for quantum computers (Micciancio and Regev 2009), while hash-based algorithms provide a complementary form of resilience by leveraging the one-way functions of hash operations to construct cryptographic schemes capable of enduring the quantum era.

AI Agent Frameworks

AI agent frameworks are quickly emerging as the foundational infrastructure for the development of autonomous systems, particularly within the advanced domains of blockchain and quantum computing. These frameworks transcend the traditional notion of software libraries, evolving into sophisticated architectures that enable the creation, deployment, and management of AI agents capable of operating with minimal human oversight. Their significance in these new fields lies in their ability to ensure security, efficiency, and adaptability in systems that are increasingly complex and decentralized.

A critical function of AI agents is their capacity to gather information about their environment through a variety of modalities, integrating data from vector databases, advanced tools, sensors, real-time data feeds, and direct user inputs. This multimodal approach is essential for constructing a comprehensive situational awareness that underpins the agent's decision-making processes.

For example, vector databases like those utilized in frameworks such as LlamaIndex and LangChain store high-dimensional data representations, enabling AI agents to access and process extensive volumes of both structured and unstructured data efficiently. In the blockchain area, this capability allows AI agents to swiftly retrieve transaction histories, verify the integrity of smart contracts, and assess the reliability of data sources. In quantum computing, these databases provide a foundation for managing and optimizing quantum states, ensuring that the AI agent's decisions are informed by accurate and up-to-date information.

In addition to databases, advanced tools such as LangGraph play a key role in enhancing the reasoning capabilities of AI agents. LangGraph, for instance, facilitates the construction of dynamic knowledge graphs that map relationships between entities within a blockchain or quantum system. These graphs are continuously updated as new data is gathered, allowing AI agents to adapt their reasoning strategies in real time. This adaptability is particularly valuable in quantum computing, where the stability of qubits and the success of quantum operations are contingent upon precise environmental conditions. Sensors embedded within the quantum environment monitor variables such as temperature and electromagnetic interference, feeding this data back to the AI agents, which in turn adjust quantum operations to minimize errors and maintain coherence.

Once equipped with a comprehensive understanding of their environment, AI agents are poised to execute actions autonomously, a capability that is facilitated through sophisticated actuators, command interfaces, and communication protocols. In blockchain applications, an AI agent might autonomously manage the execution of smart contracts by interacting with blockchain's consensus mechanism, verifying transactions, updating ledger entries, and ensuring that contractual conditions are met before the release of funds. This autonomous execution extends to quantum computing, where AI agents manage the execution of quantum algorithms, optimizing their performance by adjusting quantum gate sequences and configurations. For instance, in managing Shor's algorithm for integer factorization (Shor 1994), an AI agent might dynamically recalibrate the algorithm's parameters based on real-time feedback, such as modifying the number of qubits or adjusting the quantum circuit's depth to achieve optimal performance while minimizing error rates. The agent's ability to coordinate parallel quantum computations across multiple processors further enhances computational efficiency, making these agents indispensable in managing complex quantum operations.

The concept of tool and prompt chaining further exemplifies the advanced capabilities of AI agents in performing complex workflows autonomously. By chaining together a series of tasks, such as gathering data from a vector database, processing it using reasoning tools like LangChain, and executing actions based on the derived insights, AI agents can complete intricate workflows with minimal human intervention. For instance, in the context of decentralized finance (DeFi) on a blockchain, an AI agent might autonomously identify arbitrage opportunities across different liquidity pools, execute trades, and update blockchain to reflect these transactions, all while adhering to predefined risk parameters.

A defining characteristic of these AI agents is their capacity for continuous learning and adaptation. Through reinforcement learning algorithms, AI agents refine their strategies based on feedback from their actions, thereby improving their performance over time. In quantum computing, an AI agent might initially employ a standard set of parameters for a quantum algorithm, but as it gathers experience, it could learn to adjust these parameters to optimize performance based on past outcomes. This learning process is particularly valuable in blockchain systems, where the operational environment is in constant flux due to factors such as changes in network traffic, the introduction of new nodes, or market dynamics. AI agents can adapt by optimizing their transaction verification processes or adjusting their participation strategies in consensus mechanisms like proof of stake (PoS), thus maintaining their effectiveness in the face of evolving conditions.

The deployment of AI agents in these advanced environments necessitates robust frameworks capable of supporting complex workflows and high computational demands. Mosaic AI Agent Framework, developed by Databricks, exemplifies such a framework, focusing on building high-quality agentic applications that include tools for evaluating and improving the quality of AI outputs. This is particularly crucial in domains where the accuracy and reliability of AI decisions have significant financial or operational implications, such as in financial markets or healthcare. TaskWeaver represents another advanced framework that leverages large language models (LLMs) for domain-specific data analytics tasks, offering rich data structures and flexible plug-in usage. This framework is well suited for environments requiring complex logic and secure execution, such as quantum algorithm optimization in fields like cryptography or pharmaceutical research.

Emerging frameworks such as AutoGPT, BabyAGI, SuperAGI, and AgentGPT are pushing the boundaries of AI agent capabilities, enabling them to manage entire blockchain ecosystems or optimize quantum algorithms across distributed networks with minimal human intervention. MetaGPT, for instance, integrates advanced machine learning algorithms with real-time data analytics, allowing AI agents to respond to emerging trends and challenges with unprecedented agility and precision. This makes MetaGPT particularly valuable in highly complex environments, such as global financial markets or large-scale industrial operations, where the ability to make rapid, accurate decisions is critical.

However, the deployment of these AI agents is not without challenges. Scalability is a primary concern, because the computational resources required to support these agents increase exponentially with the complexity of their tasks. Ensuring that AI agents can scale effectively without degrading performance is crucial for their widespread adoption, particularly in quantum computing, where managing large-scale quantum operations can quickly surpass current hardware capabilities. Security is another significant challenge, given the autonomy of AI agents and the adversarial environments in which they often operate. These agents must be equipped with robust security measures to prevent malicious actors from compromising or corrupting their behavior, particularly in blockchain environments where the stakes are high and the potential for exploitation is significant. Interoperability further complicates matters, because AI agents must interact seamlessly with a wide range of systems and platforms. Developing standardized protocols and interfaces that ensure compatibility across different environments is essential for the successful integration of AI agents into existing infrastructures.

Beyond the technical challenges, the deployment of AI agents in blockchain and quantum computing also raises profound ethical and societal questions. As these agents take on more complex and autonomous roles, issues of accountability, transparency, and fairness become increasingly salient. In financial markets, for example, an AI agent engaged in high-frequency trading could inadvertently contribute to market volatility or systemic risks, raising concerns about the potential consequences of autonomous decision-making. Furthermore, the widespread adoption of AI agents has the potential to displace human workers, particularly in industries where automation can perform tasks more efficiently and at a lower cost. This shift necessitates careful consideration of the broader societal impacts of AI agents, ensuring that their deployment aligns with ethical standards and societal values.

AI agent frameworks provide the necessary infrastructure for AI agents to operate effectively, gather and process vast amounts of data, execute complex actions autonomously, and continuously learn and adapt to their environments.

The Integration of Blockchain, Quantum Computing, and AI Agents

The integration of blockchain, quantum computing, and AI agents marks a pivotal moment in the evolution of digital technology, one that holds the promise of fundamentally transforming how we secure, manage, and interact with digital systems. At the heart of this transformation lies the concept of AI agents—autonomous systems designed to perform complex tasks without direct human intervention. These agents, when integrated with the powerful capabilities of blockchain and quantum computing, have the potential to revolutionize the way we think about security, autonomy, and efficiency in the digital age.

AI agents are not mere programs; they are sophisticated entities structured around a multilayered architecture that enables them to perceive their environment, reason based on the information they gather, and take decisive actions to achieve their objectives. At the core of an AI agent's architecture is the perception layer, which gathers data from various sources such as sensors, vector databases, and real-time data feeds. This information is crucial for the agent's understanding of its operational environment, whether it is monitoring network traffic in a blockchain or assessing quantum states in a quantum computing system. The knowledge base within the agent stores this information, organized in complex data structures that facilitate rapid retrieval and processing, allowing the agent to make informed decisions.

The reasoning engine is where the true autonomy of AI agents manifests. Here, data is processed through sophisticated algorithms, ranging from logic-based reasoning to probabilistic models and machine learning techniques. In a blockchain context, this might involve verifying transactions, optimizing consensus mechanisms, or detecting anomalies that suggest fraudulent activities. In quantum computing, the reasoning engine could optimize quantum algorithms, manage error correction processes, or allocate resources efficiently. Once a decision is reached, the action layer executes the necessary commands, whether interacting with blockchain nodes, managing cryptographic keys, or coordinating quantum operations. This ability to perceive, reason, and act autonomously is further enhanced by the learning module, which allows AI agents to improve over time through reinforcement learning and other adaptive techniques, ensuring that they become increasingly adept at managing complex systems.

The integration of AI agents within blockchain and quantum computing systems is not merely a technical advancement; it represents a fundamental shift in how these systems operate. In blockchain environments, AI agents can autonomously manage transactions, execute smart contracts, and ensure the integrity and security of the network. They are particularly valuable in decentralized autonomous organizations (DAOs), where they perform governance tasks, allocate resources, and enforce community decisions without the need for centralized control. This decentralization, facilitated by AI agents, enhances the resilience and transparency of blockchain systems, making them more robust against both internal and external threats.

In the realm of quantum computing, AI agents play a crucial role in optimizing quantum algorithms and managing quantum-resilient cryptographic keys. The complexity of quantum computations, with their reliance on superposition and entanglement, demands a level of optimization that only AI agents can provide. These agents can autonomously adjust quantum algorithms to minimize error rates, allocate computational resources efficiently, and manage the distribution of quantum-resilient keys to safeguard against quantum threats. Moreover, AI agents are essential in managing the quantum data itself, ensuring that it is securely transmitted, stored, and utilized in ways that maximize its potential while minimizing risks.

Several advanced frameworks have been developed to support the deployment of AI agents in these complex environments. Frameworks like AutoGen, LangChain, and LlamaIndex enable the creation of multi-agent systems that can interact and collaborate to achieve sophisticated goals, such as coordinating blockchain transactions or managing parallel quantum computations. Other frameworks, such as the Mosaic AI Agent Framework and TaskWeaver, focus on building high-quality agentic applications that include tools for evaluating and improving AI outputs, ensuring that these agents operate at peak efficiency and reliability. Emerging frameworks like AutoGPT, BabyAGI, and SuperAGI push the boundaries of what AI agents can achieve, enabling them to manage entire blockchain ecosystems or optimize quantum algorithms across distributed networks with minimal human intervention.

The effectiveness of AI agents is significantly enhanced by their ability to interact with external systems. By integrating with vector databases, AI agents can store and retrieve large volumes of data efficiently, supporting operations such as transaction verification in blockchain systems or the management of quantum states in quantum computing environments. Tool and prompt chaining allows agents to execute complex workflows autonomously, ensuring that tasks are completed with precision and efficiency. In quantum computing scenarios, the integration of sensors enables AI agents to monitor environmental factors that could impact quantum operations, such as temperature or electromagnetic interference, ensuring that their actions are informed by accurate and up-to-date data.

However, the deployment of AI agents in blockchain and quantum computing systems is not without challenges. Scalability remains a significant issue, because the computational resources required to support AI agents grow with the complexity of the tasks they are assigned. Ensuring that these agents can scale effectively without degrading performance is a critical concern. Security is another major challenge, particularly given the autonomy of AI agents. Robust security measures must be in place to prevent malicious actors from compromising or corrupting agent behavior, especially in adversarial environments. Interoperability is also crucial, because AI agents must be able to interact with a wide range of systems and platforms, necessitating the development of standards and protocols to ensure seamless integration.

The ethical implications of deploying AI agents are profound and must be carefully considered. As these agents take on more complex and autonomous roles, issues of accountability, transparency, and fairness become increasingly important. Establishing ethical guidelines and governance frameworks will be essential to ensure that AI agents act in accordance with societal values and do not exacerbate existing inequalities or create new forms of bias or discrimination.

The integration of AI agents within blockchain and quantum computing systems represents a significant leap forward in the development of autonomous, secure, and efficient digital infrastructures. These agents, empowered by sophisticated frameworks, are capable of managing complex tasks with minimal human intervention, ensuring that these systems are robust, resilient, and capable of withstanding the challenges of an increasingly complex technological landscape. As we move toward a future where AI agents, blockchain, and quantum computing converge, the potential for innovation is vast, offering new possibilities for enhancing security, efficiency, and autonomy in the digital age. The future of digital technology lies in the successful integration of these powerful forces, paving the way for a new era of intelligent, autonomous systems that can anticipate and respond to threats with unprecedented agility and precision.

Integrating AI Agents with Post-Quantum Cryptography: Lattice-Based and Hash-Based Algorithms

The previous discussions on post-quantum cryptography, particularly the exploration of lattice-based and hash-based algorithms in Chapter 6, provide a critical foundation for understanding the future landscape of secure digital systems. However, to fully appreciate the transformative potential of these cryptographic advances, it is essential to consider how they intersect with the emerging role of AI agents. AI agents, as autonomous entities designed to perform complex tasks without direct human oversight, are not only enablers of secure digital interactions but also key drivers of innovation in how cryptographic protocols are managed, implemented, and evolved in the face of quantum computing threats.

Lattice-based cryptography, with its reliance on the intractability of certain mathematical problems like the shortest vector problem (SVP) and the learning with errors (LWE) problem, offers robust resistance to quantum attacks. However, the true power of these systems is unlocked when they are integrated with AI agents capable of autonomously managing cryptographic operations. For instance, an AI agent could dynamically adjust lattice parameters based on real-time assessments of potential quantum threats, ensuring that the cryptographic systems remain secure even as quantum computational power evolves. This ability to autonomously manage and adapt cryptographic protocols in response to emerging threats is a critical advancement in ensuring the longevity and resilience of digital security systems in the quantum era.

Consider the NTRU (Nth-degree Truncated Polynomial Ring Units) encryption algorithm, a lattice-based cryptosystem lauded for its efficiency and quantum resistance. When managed by AI agents, NTRU's capabilities can be significantly enhanced. AI agents can oversee the entire lifecycle of the encryption process—from key generation to the encryption and decryption of messages—optimizing each step to balance security and computational efficiency. In environments with limited resources, such as IoT devices, the efficiency gains offered by AI agents in managing NTRU could be the difference between a system that is theoretically secure and one that is practically deployable on a wide scale. By leveraging AI, the NTRU system not only becomes more secure but also more adaptable, ensuring that it can evolve alongside advancements in quantum computing.

Hash-based cryptography, particularly schemes like the Merkle signature scheme (MSS) and its variants, presents another critical area where AI agents can play a transformative role. MSS is inherently resistant to quantum attacks due to the fundamental properties of hash functions—pre-image resistance and collision resistance. However, the management of MSS, especially in large-scale or high-frequency usage scenarios, can be complex and resource-intensive. Here, AI agents can provide significant benefits by autonomously managing key lifespans, optimizing tree traversal algorithms, and ensuring that the cryptographic operations are performed with minimal computational overhead. For example, in the context of stateless signature schemes like SPHINCS, AI agents can dynamically select the most appropriate hash functions and tree structures based on the specific requirements of the application, thereby enhancing both security and efficiency.

The integration of AI agents with post-quantum cryptographic systems is not merely a technological enhancement; it represents a fundamental shift in how security protocols are conceived and implemented. AI agents are poised to take on increasingly central roles in managing the complexities of quantum-resistant cryptography, from autonomously adjusting cryptographic parameters to responding in real time to emerging threats. This autonomous management is particularly crucial in distributed systems, such as blockchain networks, where the sheer scale and decentralization of operations require a level of oversight and adaptability that only AI can provide.

In blockchain technologies, the incorporation of quantum-resistant cryptographic techniques, managed by AI agents, offers a robust defense against the threats posed by quantum computing. As discussed earlier, the security of blockchain systems hinges on multiple layers of cryptographic measures, from digital signatures to cryptographic hashing. AI agents can oversee these layers, ensuring that each cryptographic operation is optimized for both current and anticipated quantum threats. For instance, in proof of work (PoW) or proof of stake (PoS) consensus mechanisms, AI agents could dynamically adjust the cryptographic requirements based on the evolving computational landscape, ensuring that the consensus remains secure and efficient even as quantum capabilities expand.

Moreover, AI agents can facilitate the seamless transition from classical to quantum-resistant cryptographic algorithms within blockchain networks. This transition is not merely a matter of swapping out one algorithm for another; it requires careful management to ensure compatibility with existing transaction and block validation processes. AI agents, with their ability to autonomously manage and optimize complex systems, are ideally suited to oversee this transition, ensuring that blockchain networks remain secure throughout the process. By integrating AI agents into the management of quantum-resistant blockchains, we not only protect these systems from quantum threats but also enhance their overall efficiency and resilience.

The role of AI agents in managing post-quantum cryptographic systems extends beyond mere implementation; it also involves continuous adaptation and evolution. As quantum computing continues to advance, so too will the methods of attack that it enables. AI agents, equipped with advanced learning algorithms, can anticipate these developments, adjusting cryptographic strategies in real time to pre-emptively counteract emerging threats. This proactive approach is essential in an era where the pace of technological advancement is accelerating, and the threats to digital security are becoming increasingly sophisticated.

The concepts discussed further in this chapter include lattice-based and hash-based cryptography, quantum-resistant blockchain technologies, and quantum key distribution. These are all critical components of a secure digital future. However, their full potential can only be realized when they are integrated with the autonomous capabilities of AI agents. AI agents are the enablers of future advancements in cryptographic security, offering a level of adaptability, efficiency, and resilience that is essential in the quantum era. As we continue to explore and develop these technologies, the integration of AI agents will not only enhance their effectiveness but also ensure that they remain robust against the ever-evolving landscape of digital threats. In this way, AI agents are not just participants in the future of cryptography, they are the architects of it, shaping a secure and resilient digital world that can withstand the challenges of quantum computing and beyond.

Post-Quantum Cryptography: Lattice-Based and Hash-Based Algorithms

The emergence of post-quantum algorithms marks a significant shift in the cryptographic landscape. This section explores the latest advancements in this area, focusing on advanced lattice-based systems like NTRU, key exchange protocols, and hash-based cryptographic algorithms tailored to withstand quantum attacks.

Lattice-Based Cryptography

The foundation of lattice-based cryptography lies in the complexity of lattice problems. A lattice in *n*-dimensional space is a grid of points created by a set of basis vectors. The difficulty of solving problems like the shortest vector problem (SVP) or the closest vector problem (CVP) in high-dimensional lattices forms the basis for the security of these cryptographic systems. In the quantum realm, these problems are significant because no efficient quantum algorithm has been found to solve them, unlike factoring or discrete logarithms. This makes lattice-based cryptography a promising candidate for quantum resistance.

NTRU (Nth-Degree Truncated Polynomial Ring Units)

Nth-degree Truncated Polynomial Ring Units (NTRU) is a lattice-based cryptosystem that has gained attention for its efficiency and security. It operates in the ring of truncated polynomials. Encryption and decryption involve polynomial multiplication modulo, a fixed polynomial and an integer. NTRU's security relies on the difficulty of finding the shortest vector in a particular type of lattice, which is related to the ring of polynomials. This aspect makes NTRU particularly resistant to quantum attacks. Moreover, NTRU is known for its speed and low computational overhead efficiency, making it highly suitable for environments with limited resources.

To explain the NTRU encryption algorithm, let's break it down into its essential components and the encryption and decryption process. Here's a conceptualization of how it works:

1. **Key Generation**:

   The NTRU algorithm starts by generating two polynomials, *f* and *g*, which serve as the private key.

   The public key *h* is then computed from these polynomials.

2. **Encryption**:

   A message *m* is first represented as a polynomial.

   The message is then encrypted using the public key *h*, typically involving a process like $m \times h$ modulo a parameter *q*.

3. **Decryption**:

   The decryption process involves using the private key polynomials *f* and *g* to retrieve the original message from the encrypted message.

   This might involve multiplying the encrypted message by *f* and then reducing modulo a parameter *p*.

In the diagram in Figure 7-1, these steps are represented as follows:

- A large circle indicates the overall NTRU process.

- Inside this circle, smaller circles or sections for the public key *h*, private key *f,g*, and the message *m*.

- Arrows showing the process flow: from message *m* to the public key *h* for encryption, and then from the public key *h* to the private key *f,g* for decryption.

- Accompanying text or legends explain key equations, such as "Encryption: $m \times h$ mod *q*" and "Decryption: $f \times$ encrypted message mod *p*."

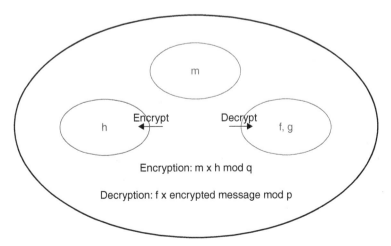

Figure 7-1
The Key Components and Processes of the NTRU Encryption Algorithm

Building on the theoretical description in Figure 7-1, Figure 7-2 represents a visualization of a real-world application of the NTRU encryption algorithm, depicting its use in scenarios where secure data transmission is critical.

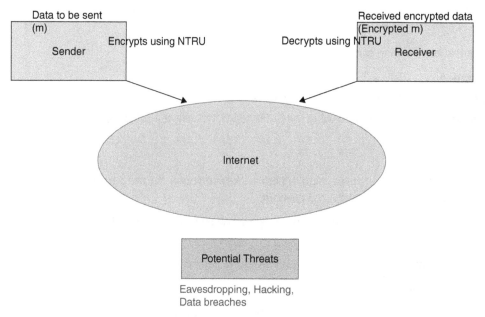

Figure 7-2
The Real-World Application of the NTRU Encryption Algorithm

Figure 7-2 represents a typical use case, such as secure communication over the Internet. The diagram includes the following elements:

- **User Devices**: This element represents the sender and receiver of the encrypted message, such as computers and smartphones.

- **Internet**: This element illustrates the network through which the encrypted data is transmitted.

- **Encryption and Decryption Process**: This element shows how NTRU encrypts data before it's sent and decrypts it upon receipt.

- **Threats**: This element indicates potential security threats, like hackers, which the encryption protects against.

Figure 7-2 also contains text explaining each step and component for clarity and illustrates how NTRU encrypts data to secure it during transmission and protect it from vulnerabilities. It depicts a typical scenario of secure communication over the Internet, highlighting the roles of the sender and receiver, the encryption and decryption processes using NTRU, and potential security threats. This visualization aims to demonstrate how NTRU ensures data security in practical scenarios.

Lattice-Based Key Exchange Protocols

In the search for cryptographic systems that can resist quantum attacks, lattice-based key exchange protocols have emerged as a strong alternative to traditional methods like Diffie-Hellman. These protocols typically use the learning with errors (LWE) problem or its variations, such as the Ring-LWE problem. The difficulty of solving these problems in polynomial time, even with a quantum computer, provides a solid basis for secure key exchange in the face of quantum adversaries. Protocols like New Hope and FrodoKEM showcase the practical application of these concepts, providing security against quantum attacks while maintaining similar efficiencies to their classical counterparts.

The diagram in Figure 7-3 represents the key elements of lattice-based key exchange protocols and involves breaking down the lattice problems, the difficulty of these problems (which ensures security), and how key exchange is facilitated in this setting. The diagram key for Figure 7-3 is as follows:

1. **Lattice Representation**: This section illustrates a simple two-dimensional lattice to visually understand what a lattice is.

2. **Hard Lattice Problems**: This section represents the difficult problems on which the security is based, such as the shortest vector problem (SVP) and the learning with errors (LWE) problem.

3. **Key Exchange Process**: This section shows the key exchange process, illustrating how two parties can agree on a shared secret using the lattice framework.

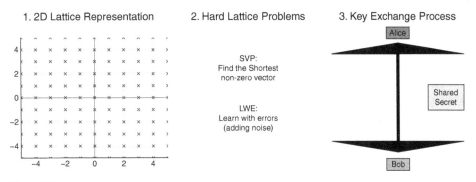

Figure 7-3
Lattice-Based Key Exchange Protocols

Figure 7-3 illustrates a diagram explaining lattice-based key exchange protocols. In this diagram, the 2D lattice representation visually represents what a lattice in two dimensions looks like. It is a grid of points where combinations of basis vectors can represent the position of each point. The security of lattice-based cryptography is based on the complexity of problems like the shortest vector problem and the learning with errors problem. SVP involves finding the shortest non-zero vector in a lattice, while LWE solves linear equations with some added noise (error), making them computationally hard. The key exchange process illustrates how two parties (Alice and Bob) can securely agree on a shared secret using a lattice-based framework. They exchange information based on the lattice's structure and hard problems, deriving a shared secret that's hard for an eavesdropper to calculate.

This diagram is a simplified representation to aid understanding of the concepts. Implementing lattice-based key exchange protocols involves more complex mathematics and processes.

Figure 7-4 illustrates the real-world application of lattice-based key exchange protocols in an Internet communication scenario. The diagram is structured to showcase how these protocols are applied in a typical communication scenario.

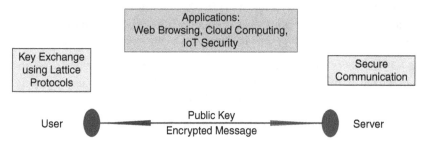

Figure 7-4
Real-World Application of Lattice-Based Key Exchange Protocols

Figure 7-4 depicts a user and a server, representing two parties in a communication process over the Internet. The arrows between the user and server symbolize the exchange of keys using lattice-based protocols. The user sends a public key, and the server uses it to encrypt a message. The process emphasizes using the shared secret key (derived from the lattice-based key exchange) for encryption and decryption, ensuring secure communication. The diagram also highlights some practical applications, such as secure web browsing, cloud computing, and IoT security, where such cryptographic methods are critical for maintaining privacy and security. This visualization provides an overview of how lattice-based cryptography is integrated into real-world scenarios, enhancing the security of digital communications.

In the lattice-based key exchange protocols, the process described in Figure 7-5 involves the following key steps:

1. First, Alice and Bob agree on public lattice parameters that can be reused.

2. Next, they each independently generate a private and public key by combining the private key with a public error term and lattice parameters.

3. Then, they exchange their public keys.

4. After that, they independently compute a shared secret using their private key and the other person's public key.

5. As a result, both Alice and Bob have a shared secret, which can be used for secure message encryption and decryption.

The security of the shared secret relies on the difficulty of solving lattice problems. This quantum resistance highlights that lattice problems are considered hard for quantum computers, providing security against quantum attacks.

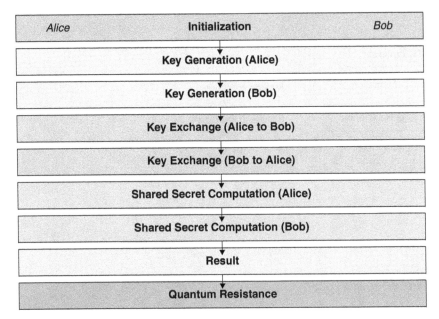

Figure 7-5
Detailed Step-by-Step Diagram for the Lattice-Based Key Exchange Protocol

Hash-Based Cryptography: Quantum-Resilient by Design

Hash-based cryptography offers a different approach in the pursuit of quantum-resistant algorithms. These cryptographic systems utilize hash functions, which can convert input data into a fixed-size string of bytes. The security of hash-based algorithms relies on finding two inputs that produce the same hash output (collision resistance) and reversing the hash function (pre-image resistance).

Hash-based cryptography is a fascinating area primarily involving using hash functions for cryptographic purposes. Let's break down this topic into key components. First, we'll delve into the general concept of a hash function, which takes an input (or message) and returns a fixed-size string of bytes, with the output typically being a digest that uniquely represents the input data. We'll then explore the essential properties of cryptographic hash functions, including determinism, fast computation, pre-image resistance, the avalanche effect (small changes in input lead to large changes in output), and collision resistance. Moving on, we'll investigate the various uses of hash functions in cryptography, such as in digital signatures, message integrity checks, and hashing passwords for secure storage. A practical example of a popular hash algorithm, like SHA-256, further illustrates this concept. The diagram in Figure 7-6 encapsulates these elements.

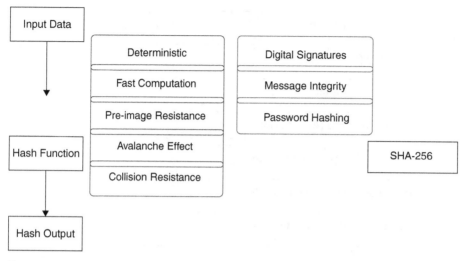

Figure 7-6
Key Concepts of Hash-Based Cryptography

Figure 7-6 illustrates the key concepts of hash-based cryptography. At the top, input data being fed into a hash function to produce a hash output is shown. The essential properties of cryptographic hash functions are listed to the right, including determinism, fast computation, pre-image resistance, the avalanche effect, and collision resistance. These properties are fundamental to understanding how these functions maintain security and integrity in cryptographic systems. Below the properties, various applications of hash functions in cryptography are noted, including digital signatures, message integrity, and secure password hashing. At the bottom right of Figure 7-6, there's a reference to SHA-256, a widely used cryptographic hash function, to provide a practical context.

Merkle Signature Scheme: Hash-Based Cryptography

The Merkle signature scheme (MSS) is widely respected as an example of hash-based cryptography. MSS uses the well-established, uncomplicated, and highly secure characteristics of hash functions to provide a strong solution for digital signing in the era of quantum computing.

At the core of the Merkle signature scheme is the Merkle tree, an essential data structure in hash-based cryptography. The Merkle tree is a binary tree in which each leaf node represents the hash of a data block, typically the public key of a one-time signature scheme. Non-leaf nodes are hashes of their respective child nodes, culminating in the root hash, which serves as a unique identifier for the entire structure. In MSS, the root hash is used as the public key. In contrast, individual leaf nodes are used for signing messages, creating a system inherently resistant to quantum attacks, given the current state of quantum computing technology.

Figure 7-7 illustrates the Merkle signature scheme.

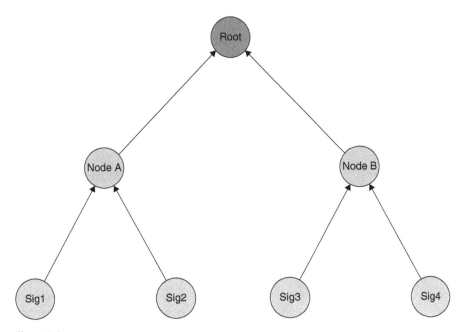

Figure 7-7
Merkle Signature Scheme

Figure 7-7 depicts a binary hash tree structure in which each leaf node represents an individual hash-based signature. As you move up the tree, the hashes of these leaf nodes are combined at intermediate nodes, ultimately leading to the Merkle root at the top, representing the overall signature. Arrows indicate the flow of hash combinations upward through the tree.

In MSS, each message is signed using a different leaf of the Merkle tree, employing a one-time signature scheme. The signature includes the one-time signature of the message, the one-time public key, and an authentication path—a series of hashes along the path from the signing leaf to the tree's root. This authentication path is crucial because it enables the verification of the signed message against the root hash (public key), ensuring the integrity and authenticity of the message. The one-time nature of each signature means that even if a quantum computer could derive the private key from a single, one-time public key, it would compromise only that particular message and not the entire scheme.

The original MSS concept was groundbreaking but had some practical drawbacks, particularly concerning efficiency and key management. Subsequent advancements in MSS have honed in on these areas, resulting in more sophisticated variations.

One area of progress has been in tree traversal algorithms. Enhanced algorithms have bolstered MSS efficiency by reducing the memory and computational overhead of creating and validating signatures. These improvements have streamlined the process, making it less resource-intensive.

Another area of development relates to the variants of Merkle trees. Different versions, such as binary trees or those with more than two child nodes per parent, have been explored to strike the optimal balance between tree size and signature generation time. This exploration has led to improved performance and flexibility in implementing MSS.

Stateless signature schemes, such as SPHINCS, have been developed to build upon the principles of MSS. These systems streamline key management and lower the possibility of key reuse by eliminating the need to track which keys have been used. This innovation has improved the security and efficiency of MSS by streamlining its implementation and maintenance.

The Merkle signature scheme, an essential part of hash-based encryption, has significantly improved security and operational efficiency thanks to advancements in tree traversal algorithms. Initially, MSS implementations required significant memory and processing resources, especially in large-scale installations. However, recent algorithmic developments have effectively addressed these challenges, making MSS more suitable for various platforms.

These improvements are attributed to the use of advanced path-finding methods. Modern algorithms no longer rely solely on traditional depth-first or breadth-first searches. Instead, they utilize complex heuristic methods or machine learning-guided searches to minimize processing overhead by optimizing path selection in real time. For example, predictive analytics-driven adaptive depth-first search techniques offer more effective tree traversals, especially in data environments that undergo frequent changes.

Advancements in parallel computing now allow numerous paths to be executed simultaneously, significantly speeding up the traversal process. These parallelized methods are well suited for large-scale Merkle trees, enabling rapid signature creation and verification without compromising security.

The focus on memory optimization is a significant area of improvement. Proposed enhancements include dynamic data structures like self-adjusting binary trees, which adapt to usage patterns, making frequently accessed nodes more accessible. Memory requirements are also reduced through on-the-fly computing methodologies, where specific branches of the tree are computed as needed instead of being stored. Just-in-time (JIT) compilation techniques are used in conjunction with these methodologies to enhance the runtime efficiency of MSS further.

As a result of these algorithmic developments, MSS has become more adaptable to a wider range of computing settings. This applies to high-end server configurations for large-scale applications and environments with limited computing resources, such as IoT devices.

Developing the Merkle tree structure in MSS has been essential in overcoming scalability and efficiency issues. Various tree architectures have been examined to strike the best balance between the size of the tree and the speed at which signatures are generated.

Although classic binary Merkle trees are straightforward, their performance may only sometimes be optimal, particularly in terms of signature size and tree height. Alternative arrangements, including trees with larger branching factors, have been explored. These trees, which have more than two child nodes for each parent, reduce the size of the authentication path in a signature by shortening the tree for a given number of leaf nodes.

Research into optimizing tree structures for specific use cases has been extensive. Trees with larger branching factors are more suitable for high-frequency signature requirements, because they require less traversal time. Conversely, compact tree architectures work well in situations where storage is limited. Studies have also focused on dynamically adjustable tree structures, which can change their configuration in response to real-time performance indicators, providing a more responsive and effective MSS implementation. As a result of these innovative Merkle tree designs, MSS has become a more flexible and adaptable cryptographic tool. The versatility of MSS has been expanded across multiple domains by customizing tree structures to meet unique application requirements. The development of stateless signature schemes, which address the challenges associated with managing state in MSS, represents a significant advancement in hash-based encryption. These systems, such as SPHINCS, do not require state information regarding key usage and constitute a considerable leap forward in MSS.

The SPHINCS framework is a sophisticated stateless hash-based signature scheme that builds upon the ideas of MSS. It eliminates the need to monitor key usage. It utilizes a few-time signature algorithm and a hierarchical tree structure to enable many possible signatures without requiring state maintenance. One advantage of being unemployed is that statelessness makes key management easier, significantly reducing the risks associated with key reuse, a major weakness in cryptographic systems. This simplification makes these schemes more accessible and secure, improving usability and reducing implementation errors. Stateless methods like SPHINCS are less susceptible to attack vectors that exploit state information, making them inherently more secure. Eliminating the state also enhances flexibility in different application settings, especially in cases where preserving the state is impractical or poses security concerns.

Quantum Resistance of MSS

The quantum-resistant nature of the Merkle signature scheme is rooted in the inherent properties of hash functions. Hash functions are one-way functions—easy to compute in one direction but infeasible to reverse. For MSS, the security against a quantum adversary hinges on two core properties of hash functions: pre-image resistance (finding an input that hashes to a given output) and collision resistance (finding two distinct inputs that hash to the same output). Given the current state of quantum algorithms, notably the lack of an efficient quantum algorithm for breaking these properties, MSS is a strong candidate for quantum-resistant cryptography.

MSS, despite its advantages, also comes with several drawbacks. One significant issue is the management of important lifespans. The number of signatures that can be securely generated is fixed at the moment of tree formation, as each leaf node can only be used once. This limitation poses challenges for long-term or high-frequency use cases. Additionally, the size of the signatures, which include the authentication path and the public key (the root hash), might be substantial, potentially causing storage or bandwidth problems in resource-limited contexts.

Future research in hash-based methods related to MSS is expected to be diverse and extensive. One area of focus is to address the existing scalability and usability restrictions by developing more efficient tree traversal and key management mechanisms. Another avenue for exploration involves investigating how to integrate MSS with other cryptographic systems, such as blockchain technologies, to enhance overall system security using the quantum-resistant characteristics of the latter.

Continuous re-evaluation of the security assumptions of hash functions is crucial in light of ongoing developments in quantum computing. The cryptography community must remain vigilant for new advancements in quantum technology and ensure that hash-based methods like MSS can adapt and progress with these developments.

The Merkle signature scheme innovatively applies traditional cryptographic principles, such as hash functions, to counter emerging threats, particularly those arising from quantum computing. Its design effectively addresses the fundamental requirements of digital signature schemes, including integrity, nonrepudiation, and authenticity, while providing a framework for post-quantum cryptographic solutions.

As we progress toward a quantum future, the principles and practices outlined by MSS are poised to play a pivotal role in shaping the next generation of cryptographic standards, ensuring digital communication security in an era of unprecedented computational power.

SPHINCS: Advancing Stateful to Stateless Hash-Based Signatures

Hash-based cryptography underwent a significant change with the introduction of SPHINCS, transitioning from stateful to stateless signatures. Unlike MSS, which requires keeping track of used keys, SPHINCS does not need state management and can support unlimited signatures. This capability makes SPHINCS more practical in real-world scenarios, especially when preserving state is challenging or error-prone. SPHINCS+ is a stateless signature system based on hashes designed to resist quantum computer attacks. It is part of the NIST post-quantum cryptography standardization process. The framework's security relies on the underlying keyed hash function's distinct-function multitarget second-pre-image resistance (DM-SPR). This hash function is used in multiple instances by SPHINCS+, including one based on SHA-256. The system also uses WOTS+ public keys and a special hypertree architecture to sign communications securely. However, some vulnerabilities have been discovered, raising concerns about the security of this technique and highlighting the complex nature of post-quantum cryptography (Bellizia et al. 2021; Chen et al. 2016; Kumar 2022; Micciancio and Regev 2009; NIST 2022, 2023).

One of the main difficulties lies in balancing security, effectiveness, and usability. For example, certain lattice-based systems may offer high security but require larger key sizes, which could pose problems in environments with limited bandwidth or storage. Moreover, given that quantum computing is still in its early stages, these algorithms are being developed to protect against a hypothetical opponent, making it challenging to gauge their long-term effectiveness.

Standardizing post-quantum cryptography algorithms is an important first step toward ensuring their widespread adoption and interoperability. Organizations like the National Institute of Standards and Technology (NIST) are undertaking this work. A thorough cryptanalysis is necessary to ensure the selected algorithms can withstand classical and quantum attacks.

Post-quantum cryptography plays a crucial role in securing our digital future against the advancing capabilities of quantum computers. The latest cryptographic techniques in this field include hash-based and lattice-based algorithms, which provide strong defenses against quantum attacks. However, further research and development are needed to stay ahead of any quantum threats.

Collaboration between governmental organizations, industry, and academia will be essential to develop and standardize these technologies for secure communications in the quantum era. This will help ensure that these cryptographic algorithms are robust and effective in the face of evolving security challenges.

Quantum Cryptography: BB84 and E91

The BB84 and E91 protocols are fundamental to quantum key distribution (QKD) (Bennett and Brassard 2020), a crucial element of secure communication in quantum cryptography. The BB84 protocol, developed by Bennett and Brassard, utilizes quantum uncertainty to detect eavesdropping attempts. It encodes information in quantum states (qubits) across two orthogonal bases (rectilinear and diagonal). The no-cloning theorem and Heisenberg's uncertainty principle influence the protocol's security, both important aspects of quantum mechanics.

The Ekert protocol, or E91, uses quantum entanglement, where entangled particles maintain a correlated state regardless of distance. It employs Bell's inequalities as a test for eavesdropping. Any attempt to measure the quantum states of the entangled particles would break Bell's inequalities, revealing eavesdropping. Both protocols are fundamental in ensuring secure communication channels in advanced quantum cryptography.

Quantum Attacks and Security Proofs

Quantum cryptography is undoubtedly the future of secure communication for AI agents, combining the principles of quantum mechanics to offer security levels unattainable by classical methods. However, as quantum technologies progress, adversaries are also developing more sophisticated attack strategies, making it imperative to understand and mitigate these evolving threats.

In the context of quantum key distribution, one of the most critical challenges is addressing quantum attacks that can compromise the security of protocols like BB84. Photon number splitting (PNS) attacks, for instance, exploit the occasional emission of multiple photons in weak coherent pulses, allowing an eavesdropper to gain information without being detected. This highlights the need for robust countermeasures, such as decoy-state protocols, which are designed to thwart such vulnerabilities.

Additionally, collective quantum attacks present another layer of complexity by enabling adversaries to gather information through subtle quantum measurements without introducing significant disturbances. These attacks necessitate advanced security measures, including privacy amplification and error correction techniques, to ensure the integrity of quantum communications.

This section introduces these key concepts, providing a foundation for understanding the specific threats for AI agents posed by quantum attacks, and the security proofs required to defend against them. The discussion will focus on practical countermeasures and their application in real-world quantum communication systems, ensuring that security is maintained even in the face of increasingly sophisticated quantum adversaries.

Photon Number Splitting (PNS) Attacks in BB84

A photon number splitting attack in BB84 is a type of attack where an adversary takes advantage of the weak coherent pulse implementations of BB84, which can occasionally emit multiple photons with the same polarization. In this attack, the eavesdropper can gain information without being detected by splitting off one photon and retaining it for later measurement while allowing the others to proceed. The security against PNS attacks relies on decoy-state protocols, where random states are mixed with the signal states to detect such activities.

In the discourse on quantum cryptography, the security of protocols against sophisticated quantum attacks is a crucial area of inquiry. PNS attacks on the BB84 protocol are particularly noteworthy. This analysis aims to examine the mechanisms of PNS attacks and explore the effectiveness of decoy-state protocols in mitigating such threats. The discussion is appropriate for an audience with advanced quantum physics and cryptographic theory degrees.

The BB84 protocol uses weak coherent pulses (WCPs) to transmit secure keys. However, under certain conditions, WCPs can emit multiple photons that retain identical polarization states. This introduces a vulnerability in the system, since if an eavesdropper (Eve) intercepts the quantum channel and splits off one of these photons, retaining it for later measurement while allowing the others to proceed to the legitimate recipient (Bob), the eavesdropper can potentially gain information without triggering any noticeable disturbance.

This attack is called the PNS attack, and it is particularly subtle because it interferes nondestructively with the quantum state. Eve can measure the retained photon post-reconciliation (after Bob and Alice have discarded qubits measured in differing bases) to obtain partial information about the key without increasing the quantum bit error rate (QBER) to a level that might alert Alice and Bob of an intrusion.

The decoy-state method has been adopted to address the vulnerability exposed by PNS attacks. This method involves randomly interspersing various quantum states and decoy states, along with the actual (signal) states used for key generation. Decoy states are prepared with varying intensities, usually with fewer photons per pulse compared to signal states, and are indistinguishable from eavesdroppers from signal states. The idea behind this technique is that Eve's intervention strategies, optimized for signal pulses, are less effective on decoy pulses. This leads to detectable discrepancies in the statistics between signal and decoy detection rates at Bob's end.

The decoy-state method is founded on the principle of quantum statistical discrimination. This approach involves quantifying the statistical differences between loss rates and error rates in signal and decoy states to identify eavesdropping activities. The approach's effectiveness depends on the assumption that Eve cannot distinguish between decoy and signal states beforehand, and any interaction with the photon will alter its quantum state.

From a practical standpoint, successfully implementing decoy-state protocols requires careful calibration of the number and type of decoy states used and the intensities of photons in these states. Recent advances have utilized optimization algorithms to determine the optimal settings that maximize key generation rates while minimizing vulnerability to PNS attacks. Experimental validations, such as those conducted through fiber-optic and free-space quantum channels, have demonstrated the robustness of decoy-state protocols in real-world settings.

Despite being effective, decoy-state protocols face several challenges. The primary difficulty is generating and calibrating decoy and signal states precisely, which should be economically viable and scalable in operational environments. Moreover, quantum adversaries are becoming more sophisticated; hence, there is a constant need to assess the security of current quantum cryptographic implementations against possible unknown quantum attacks or strategies that could exploit overlooked vulnerabilities. The development of quantum computing and cryptography is ongoing, and research must address the theoretical and practical challenges and anticipate and innovate ahead of potential quantum threats in increasingly complex cryptographic environments. Quantum attack strategies such as PNS and advanced cryptographic countermeasures like decoy-state protocols represent a cutting-edge frontier in quantum cryptography. This field remains a vibrant area of academic and practical inquiry, demanding a high level of technical expertise and innovative thinking to navigate the nuanced landscapes of quantum security.

Practical Applications of Photon Number Splitting (PNS) Countermeasures

The implementation of photon number splitting countermeasures can be applied with the following:

- The implementation of decoy-state protocols in fiber-optic networks

- The use of decoy states in free-space QKD

- The integration with classical network infrastructures

For example, decoy-state protocols protect communication from PNS attacks, specifically in fiber-optic networks. This method involves preparing quantum states that consist of higher photon number signal states and varying photon number decoy states. The signal states are typically set at an average of 0.6 photons per pulse, while the decoy states are adjusted to higher (0.8 photons) and lower (0.1 photons) levels. These states are then randomly mixed and transmitted through the quantum channel, making it impossible for potential eavesdroppers to predict or adapt to the sequence of signal and decoy states. The quantum bit error rate (QBER) and photon arrival rates are monitored at the receiving end. Statistical analyses of these measurements can detect discrepancies between expected and observed rates, particularly of decoy states, which can indicate eavesdropping.

There are unique challenges to overcome when it comes to transmitting information between buildings or from satellites to ground stations. One of the biggest challenges is the impact of atmospheric conditions on the rate of photon loss. To address this issue, it's important to adjust the intensities of photons in decoy states dynamically so they maintain their indistinguishability from signal states, regardless of the environmental conditions.

Advanced temporal and spatial filtering techniques are crucial to improving the security of transmitting quantum keys. These techniques help distinguish signal photons from background noise. It's also important to have real-time data processing capabilities that can detect anomalies and instantly adjust decoy and signal parameters to maintain the integrity and security of the communication.

Quantum key distribution (QKD) systems must be integrated with classical network infrastructures using innovative approaches. One such approach is wavelength-division multiplexing (WDM), which allows quantum and classical data to be transmitted over the same optical fiber but segregated by different wavelengths. This approach reduces crosstalk and minimizes disruptions to the quantum signals. This coexistence is essential because it enables quantum and classical data channels to operate concurrently without additional physical infrastructure. Additionally, automated feedback systems continuously monitor the performance metrics of QKD operations in these networks. These systems adjust the rates and parameters of decoy and signal pulses based on real-time performance data, thereby dynamically optimizing both security and efficiency.

Implementing advanced decoy-state techniques for secure quantum communication presents significant challenges that must be overcome. These challenges include ensuring the stability and consistency of photon sources and generating truly random numbers to determine the sequence of decoy and signal states through quantum random number generators (QRNGs). Developing industry-wide standards for decoy-state protocols is increasingly important to ensure compatibility and security across various implementations and geographical regions. These technical complexities highlight the sophisticated interplay between quantum mechanics, statistical analysis, and modern telecommunications technologies, essential for effectively deploying secure quantum communications in a rapidly evolving digital landscape.

Collective Quantum Attacks

Collective quantum attacks are advanced techniques that can compromise the quantum key distribution protocol by delicately measuring quantum states without disturbing them to extract maximum information. These attacks usually occur during the public announcement phase; however, advanced privacy amplification and error correction methods can reduce information leakage and increase uncertainty for eavesdroppers.

QKD protocols like BB84 and E91 rely on the principles of quantum mechanics to secure the exchange of cryptographic keys. However, these systems are not completely safe from attacks, especially collective quantum attacks, which are sophisticated threats. These attacks use quantum measurements to extract information from the quantum states transmitted between legitimate parties without causing detectable disturbance levels. This advanced analysis delves into the mechanics of collective quantum attacks, their impact on QKD protocols, and the countermeasures that can be employed to protect quantum communications.

Collective quantum attacks involve an adversary (Eve), who carries out weak, nondemolition measurements on each qubit that is transmitted between the sender (Alice) and the receiver (Bob). Unlike stronger measurements that could cause the qubit states to collapse and increase error rates, these weak measurements are designed to minimally disturb the qubits while still obtaining some information about their states. It is important to note that Eve retains the quantum memory of these weak measurements and waits until the public announcement phase of the QKD protocol. During this phase, Alice and Bob disclose additional information about the basis for preparing and measuring the qubits to sift the key.

Eve uses this public information to optimally correlate her measurement results with the key generation data, effectively enhancing the partial information she has gleaned from the quantum channel. The success of this strategy depends on her ability to perform coherent quantum operations and maintain the qubits in quantum memory without significant decoherence, which is an ambitious but theoretically feasible scenario as quantum technologies continue to advance.

Collective quantum attacks have significant implications for QKD protocols. These attacks pose a primary threat to the security of quantum communication, because they can allow an eavesdropper, also known as Eve, to gain enough information to partially or fully reconstruct the secret key without triggering any security alarms. This is possible because collective quantum attacks exploit quantum measurement's probabilistic nature and conventional QKD security's reliance on disturbance indicators. As a result, the very foundation of secure quantum communication is challenged, and finding new ways to combat these attacks becomes essential.

QKD protocols use advanced techniques such as privacy amplification and error correction to prevent the risk of collective quantum attacks. Privacy amplification is a process that Alice and Bob use to distill a shorter, secure key from a longer, partially compromised one by using a public but authentic discussion. Both parties agree on a random hash function applied to the sifted key. This technique ensures that Eve's partial information about the original key becomes practically useless concerning the final key. On the other hand, error correction identifies and corrects errors in the key bits shared by Alice and Bob. This process uses classical error-correcting codes, further complicating Eve's ability to infer the final key by obscuring which bits of the key are correct and which have been altered.

The development of quantum key distribution systems needs to address the increasing threat of collective quantum attacks. More sophisticated quantum error correction codes and robust privacy amplification techniques must be developed to achieve this goal. Device-independent QKD protocols are a promising avenue, which is independent of the trustworthiness of the equipment used to prepare and measure quantum states. These protocols aim to establish security by detecting quantum entanglement, regardless of any other device specifics. This offers a potential solution to vulnerabilities exposed by collective quantum attacks. Although these attacks pose a significant threat to QKD protocols, advancements in quantum cryptography, specifically in privacy amplification and error correction, are critical in maintaining the confidentiality and integrity of quantum communications. As quantum technologies progress, the race between cryptographic advancements and attack methodologies will inevitably intensify, highlighting the need for relentless innovation in quantum security measures.

The ability to integrate quantum key distribution protocols, such as BB84 and E91, into modern communication networks faces many technical and infrastructural challenges. One of the most significant challenges is the photon loss in standard optical fibers, which reduces the efficiency and range of QKD. Polarization state alignment and coherence maintenance over long distances make deploying QKD in real-world scenarios difficult.

To solve these challenges, cutting-edge solutions involve implementing high-dimensional QKD protocols that encode more information per photon, thereby increasing loss tolerance. Quantum repeaters are envisioned to extend the range of QKD networks, although practical and scalable implementations remain an ongoing research focus. Recent experiments have explored the feasibility of satellite-based QKD in achieving global-scale quantum networks.

Experimental setups, including free-space QKD systems, aim to address the challenges of atmospheric interference, testing the limits of these protocols in various environments. These setups are pivotal in adapting QKD for terrestrial and space-based applications. Additionally, efforts to miniaturize QKD systems are essential for integrating them into existing telecommunication infrastructure, making quantum-secure communication widely accessible.

Integrating the Principles of Quantum Mechanics and Quantum Cryptography into Blockchain Technologies

The integration of quantum mechanics and cryptography can be applied to enhance the security of blockchain systems. This section examines the role of entanglement, superposition, and quantum no-cloning in cryptography and assesses their applicability to blockchain systems.

Quantum mechanics is based on the concept of superposition, which allows a quantum system to exist in multiple states simultaneously. In cryptography, quantum bits (qubits) can represent and process a vast array of states simultaneously, providing exponential growth in processing power compared to classical bits. If applied to blockchain, quantum superposition could expedite complex computational problems, such as those involved in mining processes, and significantly reduce the required time for such operations, thus increasing throughput.

Quantum gates are used to manipulate the states of qubits in a controlled manner. They are similar to logical operations in classical binary systems but operate across complex vector spaces. The deployment of quantum gates within blockchain infrastructures could enable the execution of complex cryptographic algorithms at unprecedented speeds, potentially outperforming classical algorithms both in efficiency and security.

Quantum entanglement is a phenomenon where particles become interconnected, and the state of one can instantaneously influence the state of another, regardless of the distance between them. This property of quantum mechanics offers new ways to enhance secure communication in blockchain networks. For example, entangled qubits can create unbreakable secure keys in cryptographic protocols like quantum key distribution. This can safeguard blockchain from even the most sophisticated cyber threats, including those from quantum-enabled adversaries.

The no-cloning theorem states that creating an identical copy of an unknown quantum state is impossible, providing a robust layer of security in cryptographic systems. This principle can be applied directly to blockchain, where the integrity and uniqueness of transaction records are critical. Blockchain networks can leverage quantum cryptography to prevent double-spending and other forms of attack that rely on replicating transaction data by ensuring that transactions or blocks cannot be cloned without detection.

Integrating quantum cryptography into blockchain technologies is expected to bolster network security significantly. Quantum-resistant algorithms, derived from problems that quantum computers find intractable, are being developed to replace traditional cryptographic methods that quantum computers could potentially break. These algorithms include lattice-based cryptography, hash-based schemes, and multivariate cryptographic algorithms. Implementing these algorithms in blockchain infrastructures will help future-proof them against quantum attacks.

Integrating quantum mechanics into blockchain technology has immense potential, but it also faces significant challenges. The fragile nature of quantum states means that extremely low temperatures and isolation from environmental interactions are necessary, making it difficult to deploy quantum blockchain systems widely. Additionally, the current early stage of quantum computing technology means that theoretical advancements have yet to be tested at scale in real-world blockchain applications.

Consensus mechanisms in blockchain could be profoundly impacted by quantum-enhanced computing power. This could lead to the centralization of mining power to quantum-capable entities, potentially undermining the democratic ethos of blockchain technologies. As research progresses, the next few decades are likely to witness significant advancements in this field, shaping the future landscape of blockchain technology and its security mechanisms against the backdrop of quantum computing.

Quantum-Resilient Blockchain Technologies

With the advancements in quantum computing capabilities, the security of blockchain technologies is at risk, as traditional cryptographic practices may no longer be sufficient. Digital signatures are essential to ensure the authenticity and integrity of transactions in blockchain technology. However, traditional digital signature schemes such as RSA and ECDSA are vulnerable to quantum attacks. These schemes rely on the computational complexity of factoring large prime numbers and solving elliptic curve discrete logarithm problems, respectively.

Recent advancements in quantum-safe digital signatures focus on developing schemes based on mathematical problems currently deemed resistant to classical and quantum attacks. Among the most promising are lattice-based signatures, hash-based signatures, and multivariate polynomial cryptography. Lattice-based signatures rely on the hardness of lattice problems such as shortest vector problem (SVP) and learning with errors (LWE). Lattice-based schemes like Falcon and Dilithium have been highlighted in the NIST post-quantum cryptography standardization process. They offer significant security even against quantum computers due to the absence of efficient quantum algorithms for solving lattice problems.

Hash-based signatures rely solely on the security of hash functions. These signatures, including schemes like XMSS and SPHINCS, provide security based on the assumption that finding collisions using a quantum computer is computationally infeasible. Hash-based signatures are particularly attractive for their simplicity, and we have seen implementations that can withstand known quantum attacks.

Multivariate polynomial cryptography involves creating signatures from equations of multivariate polynomials over finite fields, which is extremely hard to solve due to its chaotic nature. Examples include Rainbow and Quartz schemes, which are designed to be fast and require relatively small key sizes compared to other post-quantum candidates. These post-quantum candidates provide an alternative to traditional digital signature schemes and offer the potential for secure blockchain technology in an era of quantum computing.

Blockchain technology relies on multiple layers of cryptographic security, from digital signatures to cryptographic hashing, to ensure the secure linking of blocks. With the increasing threat of quantum computing, blockchain systems are exploring ways to enhance their security through quantum-resistant algorithms. This effort involves several strategic adaptations, including transitioning to post-quantum algorithms. Upgrading a blockchain to use lattice-based cryptographic primitives requires replacing the digital signature algorithm while ensuring compatibility with the existing transaction and block validation processes. To safeguard against immediate and future threats, some blockchain systems are exploring hybrid models incorporating classical and quantum-resistant algorithms. Quantum-resilient blockchains must also address the security of their consensus mechanisms, such as proof of work or proof of stake. Strategies such as quantum-resistant hash functions for PoW and multi-party computation protocols for PoS are being researched to ensure that consensus mechanisms remain secure and decentralized.

The Mitigation of Threats to Blockchain Technology from Quantum Computing

In response to threats from quantum computing, significant advancements have been made to develop quantum-resilient systems. Two notable projects at the forefront of this innovation are the Quantum Resistant Ledger (QRL 2017) and Hyperledger's quantum-resistant ledger (Campbell 2019). Each project embodies unique approaches and challenges in its quest to safeguard blockchain against quantum decryption techniques.

The QRL project is designed to withstand quantum attacks by utilizing hash-based cryptographic signatures immune to Shor's algorithm. Shor's algorithm is a quantum computing method capable of breaking traditional cryptography. QRL employs the Extended Merkle Signature Scheme (XMSS), which relies on the security properties of hash functions. This provides a robust defense against quantum attacks. However, the stateful nature of XMSS presents significant implementation challenges, particularly in key management. Ensuring that no key pair is reused is critical. This requirement complicates wallet software and necessitates stringent protocols to maintain security integrity. Performance-wise, QRL shows a marginal increase in computational and memory demands due to the complexities of XMSS and its larger signature sizes. Nonetheless, these are considered acceptable trade-offs for the enhanced security features it offers.

The future of quantum-resistant blockchain technologies appears to be rooted in a multidisciplinary approach that blends quantum physics, cryptography, and computer science insights. Hyperledger's approach to quantum resistance involves integrating lattice-based cryptographic solutions like NTRU and Kyber into its frameworks. These algorithms are based on lattice problems, which, as of now, are not solvable by quantum computers. This ensures resistance against quantum attacks theoretically. However, integrating these new algorithms into existing blockchain systems poses significant challenges, primarily due to the need to modify current protocols extensively. Furthermore, there is a concern that these quantum-resistant algorithms could impact the transaction processing speed and overall network efficiency. Despite these challenges, preliminary performance evaluations are promising, suggesting that the impact on system performance could be mitigated over time with continued optimization and algorithmic refinement.

New theoretical frameworks will likely emerge, possibly involving composite systems that layer multiple quantum-resistant algorithms, to strike a balance between security and performance. As quantum computing technology becomes more advanced and accessible, applying quantum-resistant blockchains is expected to expand across various sectors, including financial services, healthcare, and government. These sectors are particularly susceptible to the ramifications of quantum attacks due to their reliance on secure digital transactions and the sensitivity of the data involved.

In the long run, ensuring the quantum resilience of blockchain systems will likely necessitate continuous adjustments to cryptographic practices tailored to the evolving landscape of quantum computing capabilities. This effort will involve periodic updates to the blockchain frameworks and vigilant monitoring of the quantum threat landscape to adapt cryptographic measures accordingly. Thus, the journey toward quantum-resistant blockchain is not merely about countering today's threats but is an ongoing endeavor to pre-empt and neutralize tomorrow's more sophisticated quantum threats.

Summary

This chapter examines the integration of quantum mechanics, blockchain technology, and AI agents, providing a thorough analysis of how these advanced fields intersect to redefine the future of digital security. Moving beyond traditional cryptographic discussions, the chapter places a strong emphasis on the pivotal role of AI agents in autonomously managing and optimizing post-quantum cryptographic systems. Through a detailed exploration of post-quantum cryptography, particularly lattice-based and hash-based algorithms, it becomes evident that these techniques are crucial in defending against the emerging threats posed by quantum computing.

The chapter also highlights the indispensable contribution of AI agents in overseeing complex cryptographic operations, including lattice-based key exchange protocols and stateless hash-based signature schemes. These agents bolster the security of cryptographic frameworks and ensure their adaptability and resilience in the face of an ever-evolving quantum landscape. By autonomously adjusting cryptographic parameters and responding dynamically to real-time threats, AI agents emerge as key enablers of future advancements in digital security.

In addition, the chapter investigates quantum key distribution (QKD) protocols and their integration with AI agents, stressing how these protocols can be efficiently managed and optimized to maintain secure communication channels that are impervious to both classical and quantum attacks. The discussion extends to the development of quantum-resilient blockchain technologies, such as the Quantum Resistant Ledger (QRL) and Hyperledger, where AI agents are instrumental in facilitating the transition to quantum-resistant cryptographic frameworks, ensuring the ongoing security and efficiency of blockchain networks.

This chapter underscores the imperative for continuous research and innovation in integrating AI agents with quantum-resistant technologies. The synergy between these domains carries profound implications for enhancing security and advancing fairness, inclusivity, and sustainability in the digital future. As quantum computing progresses, the collaboration between AI agents, cryptographic systems, and blockchain technologies will be vital in constructing a secure, efficient, and resilient digital infrastructure, capable of countering the most sophisticated quantum threats.

References

Bellizia, D., N. El Mrabet, A. P. Fournaris, S. Pontié, F. Regazzoni, F-X. Standaert, É. Tasso, E. Valea. 2021. "Post-Quantum Cryptography: Challenges and Opportunities for Robust and Secure HW Design." *2021 IEEE International Symposium on Defect and Fault Tolerance in VLSI Systems*. https://doi.org/10.1109/DFT52944.2021.9568301.

Bennett, C. H., and G. Brassard. 2020. "Quantum Cryptography: Public Key Distribution and Coin Tossing." *Theoretical Computer Science* 560 (P1): 7–11. https://doi.org/10.1016/j.tcs.2014.05.025.

Bernstein, D. J. 2011. "Post-Quantum Cryptography." *Encyclopedia of Cryptography and Security*, 949–50. https://doi.org/10.1007/978-1-4419-5906-5_386.

Campbell, Sr., R. E. 2019. "Transitioning to a Hyperledger Fabric Quantum-Resistant Classical Hybrid Public Key Infrastructure." *Journal of The British Blockchain Association* 2 (2, Nov): 1–11. https://doi:10.31585/jbba-2-2-(4)2019.

Chen, L., S. Jordan, Y-K. Liu, D. Moody, R. Peralta, R. Perlner, and D. Smith-Tone. 2016. "Report on Post-Quantum Cryptography." National Institute of Standards and Technology. http://dx.doi.org/10.6028/NIST.IR.8105.

Kumar, M. 2022. "Post-Quantum Cryptography Algorithm's Standardization and Performance Analysis." *Array* 15 (September): 100242. https://doi.org/10.1016/J.ARRAY.2022.100242.

Micciancio, D., and O. Regev. 2009. "Lattice-Based Cryptography." *Post-Quantum Cryptography*, January, 147–91. https://doi.org/10.1007/978-3-540-88702-7_5.

NIST. 2022. "Post-Quantum Cryptography PQC." https://csrc.nist.gov/Projects/post-quantum-cryptography.

NIST. 2023. "Post-Quantum Cryptography | CSRC | Selected Algorithms: Public-Key Encryption and Key-Establishment Algorithms." https://csrc.nist.gov/Projects/post-quantum-cryptography/selected-algorithms-2022.

Shor, P. W. 1994. "Algorithms for Quantum Computation: Discrete Logarithms and Factoring." *Proceedings—Annual IEEE Symposium on Foundations of Computer Science*, 124–34. https://doi.org/10.1109/SFCS.1994.365700.

QRL. 2017. "QRL: The Quantum Resistant Ledger." Accessed September 17, 2024. https://www.theqrl.org/.

Test Your Skills

Multiple-Choice Questions

These questions are designed to test understanding of the key concepts, focusing on the societal impacts, challenges, and future implications of AI in autonomous systems.

1. What is the primary focus of post-quantum cryptography as explored in the chapter?

    A. Increasing the speed of quantum computing

    B. Developing algorithms based on classical computing theories

    C. Enhancing encryption methods to resist classical computing attacks

    D. Designing cryptographic methods resistant to quantum computing attacks

2. Which type of cryptographic algorithm is identified as promising for quantum resistance due to its complexity?

    A. RSA

    B. Lattice-based cryptography

    C. Symmetric key cryptography

    D. Public key infrastructure

3. What distinguishes quantum key distribution (QKD) from classical cryptographic methods?

    A. It relies solely on the complexity of mathematical problems.

    B. It utilizes the principles of quantum mechanics for secure communication.

    C. It is less secure but faster than traditional methods.

    D. It uses digital signatures for all transmissions.

4. Which quantum key distribution protocol employs entanglement to secure communications?

    A. BB84

    B. RSA

    C. E91

    D. SHA-256

5. What is a critical feature of hash-based cryptographic systems like the Merkle signature scheme (MSS) in resisting quantum attacks?

    A. The reliance on entanglement

    B. The use of long encryption keys

C. Their ability to create uncloneable signatures

D. Utilization of one-way hash functions

6. What challenge does quantum-resilient blockchain technology aim to address?

    A. The inefficiency of blockchain in financial transactions

    B. The threat posed by quantum computing to current cryptographic practices

    C. The use of blockchain for data storage solutions

    D. Integration of blockchain with artificial intelligence

7. How does lattice-based cryptography provide security against quantum attacks?

    A. By using algorithms based on simple integer operations

    B. Through cryptographic methods that involve complex lattice structures and problems

    C. By encrypting data repeatedly

    D. Using classical algorithms that are easy to implement

8. Which of the following best describes the role of decoy states in quantum key distribution?

    A. To increase the speed of key distribution

    B. To serve as placeholders in data transmissions

    C. To detect and thwart eavesdropping attempts

    D. To encrypt messages in transit

9. What is one major advantage of integrating quantum mechanics principles into blockchain technology?

    A. Decreased complexity in transaction processing

    B. Enhanced security against quantum and traditional computational threats

    C. Reduction in the use of cryptographic keys

    D. Simplification of the blockchain architecture

10. What challenge does the NTRU cryptosystem address within the scope of quantum-resistant cryptography?

    A. It offers an efficient solution tailored for environments with limited resources.

    B. It primarily enhances the transaction speed on blockchain.

    C. It simplifies the implementation of blockchain.

    D. It reduces the need for digital signatures.

Exercises

These exercises are designed to test your understanding and ability to apply the concepts discussed in Chapter 7, preparing you to engage effectively with blockchain, quantum computing, and AI agents.

Exercise 7.1: Understanding Quantum-Resilient Cryptography

1. What distinguishes post-quantum cryptography from quantum cryptography in terms of approach and objectives?

2. Explain the significance of lattice-based cryptography in the context of quantum resistance.

3. Describe how NTRU encryption works and its advantages in a quantum-threatened landscape.

4. What role does the hash function play in hash-based cryptography?

5. Identify the main challenges in developing quantum-resilient blockchain technologies as mentioned in the chapter.

Exercise 7.2: Practical Application and Implications

1. How does the BB84 quantum key distribution protocol ensure the security of communications?

2. Discuss the potential vulnerabilities of the BB84 protocol to photon number splitting (PNS) attacks and how decoy-state protocols help mitigate this risk.

3. What are the practical challenges mentioned in the chapter that are associated with implementing quantum cryptography in real-world systems?

4. Explain the potential of integrating quantum cryptographic methods with blockchain technologies. What benefits does this integration bring?

5. Reflect on the broader implications of quantum-resilient technologies for global security and privacy.

PART III

IMPLICATIONS FOR SOCIETY AND ETHICS

Part III of the book addresses the broader implications of AI, quantum technologies, and blockchain for society and ethics. It begins by exploring the ethical dimensions of these technologies, including algorithms for fairness and bias reduction in AI and the balancing act of power and responsibility in quantum computing. The part then moves into the legal and regulatory aspects, discussing the frameworks and global standards emerging to govern these technologies. You will gain insights into the societal impact of autonomous systems like AI in healthcare and transportation and how Quantum Computing is changing global industries. Part III builds an understanding of the ethical, legal, and societal considerations essential for responsible development and deployment of these technologies.

PART III

IMPLICATIONS FOR SOCIETY AND ETHICS

8

Ethics of AI Agents

Chapter Objectives

This chapter discusses the ethical challenges in artificial intelligence (AI) and machine learning (ML), focusing on the development of algorithms for fairness and bias reduction. It also defines the balance between power and responsibility in quantum computing, especially in the context of privacy. By the end of this chapter, you will be able to

- **Understand the Ethical Considerations in AI Agents**: Grasp the ethical issues inherent in AI technology, including the risks and implications of bias and unfairness in AI algorithms.

- **Explore Algorithms for Fairness in AI Agents**: Learn about developing and implementing AI algorithms that promote fairness and reduce bias, and understand their importance in creating ethical AI systems.

- **Analyze Bias Reduction Techniques**: Examine various techniques and approaches used in AI to mitigate biases, understanding their effectiveness and the challenges involved in ensuring ethical AI practices.

- **Examine the Privacy Concerns in Quantum Computing**: Investigate the privacy challenges that arise with the advancement of quantum computing, focusing on the balance between the technology's power and the responsibility to protect privacy.

- **Evaluate Ethical Frameworks for Quantum Technologies**: Assess the ethical frameworks and guidelines being developed to govern the use of quantum computing, considering how they address privacy concerns and responsible use.

- **Recognize the Broader Ethical Implications**: Identify the wider ethical implications of AI and quantum technologies on society, considering issues like surveillance, data security, and the digital divide.

- **Reflect on the Role of Policy and Regulation**: Consider the role of policy and regulation in guiding the ethical development and application of AI and quantum computing technologies.

- **Anticipate Future Ethical Challenges**: As AI and quantum computing evolve, anticipate future ethical challenges and understand the importance of ongoing ethical discussions and adaptive governance.

The discussion on fairness and bias in AI, for instance, directly impacts how AI agents are designed to interact with users and make decisions. In fields such as healthcare, where AI agents are increasingly used for diagnostic purposes, ensuring that these systems are free from bias is crucial. If an AI agent is trained on a dataset that underrepresents certain demographics, it may lead to inaccurate or unfair outcomes, such as misdiagnosing conditions in minority groups. The techniques outlined in the chapter, including pre-processing and in-processing algorithms, provide practical methods for mitigating these biases, ensuring that AI agents operate equitably.

Privacy concerns, particularly in the context of quantum computing, also bear significant implications for AI agents. As these agents often handle sensitive personal data, they must be equipped with robust security measures to protect against potential breaches. The chapter's examination of post-quantum cryptography highlights the need for AI agents to incorporate advanced encryption techniques that can withstand the threats posed by emerging quantum technologies. For example, an AI agent used in financial services must ensure that client data remains secure even as quantum computing becomes more prevalent, thus maintaining trust and compliance with privacy regulations.

Policy and regulation, as discussed in the chapter, are critical in guiding the ethical deployment of AI agents. Regulatory frameworks ensure that AI agents, particularly those used in high-impact areas like law enforcement or finance, adhere to ethical standards and are held accountable for their actions. For example, regulations may require that an AI agent involved in credit scoring is transparent in its decision-making processes, allowing users to understand and challenge the outcomes if necessary. This regulatory oversight is essential in preventing the misuse of AI agents and ensuring that they contribute positively to society.

By addressing issues of fairness, privacy, and regulatory compliance, the chapter underscores the importance of integrating ethical principles into the very fabric of AI systems, thereby ensuring that they serve society in a fair and trustworthy manner.

Understanding the Ethical Considerations in AI

Integrating AI into various industries can bring about innovation and efficiency but poses significant ethical challenges (Wickens 2022). The primary concern lies in developing and operating AI algorithms, which can reflect existing societal biases or even amplify them. Biases in AI, particularly in ML algorithms (Du, Cheng, and Dou 2022) often emerge unintentionally due to skewed datasets or flawed assumptions that developers make during the algorithm design phase. These biases can manifest in various ways, such as racial and gender prejudice in facial recognition software or discrimination based on socioeconomic status in loan approval processes. Facial recognition technologies have displayed a higher error rate for African American and Asian faces than Caucasian faces. The reason is that the training data used by these systems is predominantly composed of white male faces, which limits their ability to identify individuals who fall outside this group correctly. Such biases have implications that can influence life-changing decisions in employment, healthcare, financial services, and law enforcement. Therefore, it is essential to understand and address these biases, not only as a technical necessity but also as a moral imperative to prevent the perpetuation of systemic inequalities (Fu et al. 2020).

The flowchart in Figure 8-1 outlines the pathways through which ethical considerations in AI, specifically bias and unfairness, emerge and can be addressed. It is structured into five main sections: definition of ethical AI, identification of bias sources, consequences of bias, mitigation strategies, and a feedback loop. The definition of ethical AI serves as a clear starting point for defining what constitutes ethical AI. Different sources of bias include data sources, algorithm design, and human factors. The consequences of bias section shows how these biases translate into real-world implications across various applications. The mitigation strategies section provides details of strategies to mitigate these biases and promote fairness (Fairlearn 2022).

Finally, the feedback loop incorporates a feedback system that emphasizes continuous improvement and re-evaluation of AI systems. This re-evaluation ensures that the AI systems are always up-to-date and ethical considerations are considered in all design and implementation aspects (Mervič 2023).

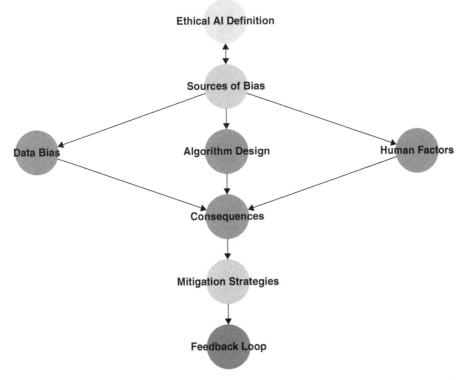

Figure 8-1
Flowchart of Ethical Considerations in AI

These sources of bias in Figure 8-1 converge into real-world implications, affecting fairness and accuracy across various applications. This is where mitigation strategies, outlined in the chart, come into play. These strategies focus on improving data diversity, algorithm transparency, and human oversight. The chart also emphasizes the importance of a feedback system that promotes continuous improvement and re-evaluation of AI systems to adapt to new ethical challenges. The diagram in Figure 8-1 outlines how ethical considerations should be integrated into AI development and monitoring, highlighting critical areas for attention and action.

Algorithms for Fairness in AI

Ensuring fairness in AI involves developing methodologies that can detect, reduce, and ideally eliminate biases within AI systems (Piech 2024). Fairness in AI algorithms ensures equal treatment of all individuals, regardless of their inherent or acquired characteristics (Dai 2021). Several approaches have been developed to enhance fairness, such as pre-processing, in-processing, and post-processing techniques.

In Figure 8-2, the visual links diagram illustrates the impact of different types of fairness algorithms. It shows how each type (pre-processing, in-processing, post-processing) affects key aspects like decision-making fairness, model accuracy, and the necessity for continuous updates.

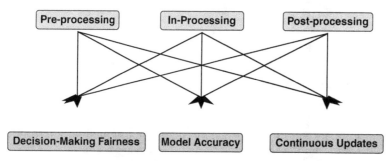

Figure 8-2
Impact of Fairness Algorithms

Pre-processing techniques involve modifying the training data to reduce bias before it is input into the ML model. One common strategy is reweighing training examples, where weights are assigned to data points inversely proportional to their representation within the dataset. For instance, if a dataset underrepresents women, their data points are given higher weights, making the algorithm more likely to learn from these examples.

In-processing techniques integrate fairness constraints directly into the algorithm during the model training phase. An example of this approach is the Equality of Opportunity model, which adjusts the algorithm's parameters during training to equalize the accurate favorable rates across different groups for classification tasks. This model ensures all groups have equal chances of receiving a positive outcome, mitigating potential favoritism or prejudice.

Post-processing techniques adjust the output of AI systems to ensure fairness. For example, calibration methods can be used where the decision threshold is varied for different demographic groups to equalize performance metrics such as precision and recall across these groups. This approach is particularly useful when modifying the training data or the algorithm could be more practical.

Each technique has its merits and limitations, and the choice of technique often depends on the specific use case, the nature of the data, and the desired outcome of the AI application (Zhang, Lemoine, and Mitchell 2018). For instance, pre-processing may be suitable for scenarios where extensive historical data requires cleansing before use. In contrast, in-processing might be more effective in environments where real-time fairness is critical.

Specific Algorithms Designed for Fairness

This section expands into the specific algorithms designed for fairness, examines their strengths and weaknesses, explores practical use cases, and highlights companies that have implemented these strategies effectively.

Pre-processing algorithms for fairness are designed to mitigate biases at the data level before this data is used in machine learning models (O'Sullivan 2021). This approach focuses on altering the training data to be more representative of the broader population, which helps prevent biased predictions based on skewed data inputs. These techniques are crucial because they address the source of bias, potentially enhancing the fairness of outcomes across all subsequent stages of the AI model's lifecycle.

Fundamental Algorithms for Fairness

Pre-processing algorithms are designed to reduce data bias before training a model. The aim is to modify the training data to be more balanced and representative of the population. One such technique is "reweighing," which assigns weights to the training data to balance the representation of different groups. Another technique is the "Disparate Impact Remover," which adjusts feature values to remove bias while preserving the data distribution. Lastly, the "optimized pre-processing" technique learns a probabilistic transformation that edits feature values and labels in the data while ensuring fairness constraints.

Pre-processing algorithms are fundamental tools in developing ethical AI and addressing data biases. Several techniques, such as the reweighing technique, can help balance the representation of different demographic groups in the training data. This approach assigns weights to instances in the dataset to amplify the influence of underrepresented groups during model training. Adjusting the weights for underrepresented classes makes them more significant in the model training phase. This approach is relatively simple and can be applied across various data and models.

However, reweighing keeps the feature values the same, leaving inherent biases unaddressed. Another technique, the Disparate Impact Remover, modifies feature values directly or indirectly correlated with sensitive attributes, such as race or gender, to reduce bias while maintaining the overall data distribution as much as possible. The Disparate Impact Remover is helpful in credit scoring models where variables indirectly correlated with race, such as postal codes or loan amounts, might lead to discriminatory outcomes. By adjusting these features, the Disparate Impact Remover aims to equalize the chances of favorable outcomes across different groups. The main challenge in the Disparate Impact Remover approach is maintaining the utility of the data after adjustment, because overcorrection can lead to the loss of critical predictive features, potentially degrading the model's performance.

An advanced method, optimized pre-processing, learns a probabilistic transformation that edits feature values and labels in the data while integrating fairness constraints. Optimized pre-processing aims for an optimal balance between fairness and data utility and is typically used in hiring algorithms. For example, it can adjust resumés by removing or altering terms that are subtly coded by gender or ethnicity, which might influence hiring decisions unconsciously. By integrating fairness constraints into data pre-processing, this method can create more profound changes in data representation, leading to more equitable outcomes. However, optimized pre-processing requires a deep understanding of the data and relationships between features. The complexity of the model increases as it needs to learn from the data while simultaneously applying fairness constraints, which can be computationally expensive.

Compatibility, validation, and monitoring are essential to integrating these techniques into machine learning workflows. Pre-processing methods should be compatible with the data and machine learning model used. It is crucial to validate the model's fairness and performance post-pre-processing and monitor the adjustments' effectiveness over time.

Pre-processing algorithms for fairness are fundamental to developing ethical AI and ensuring fairness in AI systems across various applications. More sophisticated techniques will evolve as the field progresses, offering more equitable outcomes (Wang, Zhang, and Zhu 2022).

In-Processing Algorithms for Fairness: Integrating Fairness Directly into AI Models

In-processing algorithms represent a dynamic approach to implementing fairness directly into the model training process. Unlike pre-processing methods that modify the data before training, in-processing techniques integrate fairness considerations as constraints or objectives within the learning algorithm. This approach is compelling because it allows the model to learn to make fair decisions through the restrictions imposed during its training phase.

During the model training phase, in-processing algorithms incorporate fairness constraints directly into the learning process. One such algorithm is adversarial debiasing, which simultaneously trains a predictor and an adversary. The predictor attempts to make accurate predictions, while the adversary attempts to determine the sensitive attribute from the projections. Fairness constraints can also be enforced by reducing the mean difference or equality of opportunity between different groups, which are incorporated as part of the optimization objective during training.

In-processing algorithms are a proactive approach to promoting fairness in machine learning models by addressing bias during the training phase. These algorithms integrate fairness constraints and adversarial mechanisms to produce fairer outcomes, thereby altering the decision-making processes of AI systems.

One effective technique is adversarial debiasing, where predictive and adversarial models are trained simultaneously. The goal is for the predictor to make accurate predictions, while the adversarial model attempts to predict the sensitive attribute based on the predictor's outputs. Successful debiasing is achieved by training the predictor to produce outputs independent of the sensitive attribute. Adversarial debiasing is highly effective in scenarios where the bias mechanisms are complex and poorly understood.

Another technique is fairness constraints, which are quantifiable measures incorporated into the optimization objective of a model during training. These constraints ensure that the model's outputs adhere to specific fairness criteria, such as demographic parity or equality of opportunity. Implementing fairness constraints is common in predictive policing models to prevent discriminatory outcomes.

Integrating in-processing algorithms involves several critical steps. The first step is to define fairness metrics and select appropriate in-processing algorithms, such as adversarial debiasing or specific fairness constraints, based on the chosen fairness metrics. During training, the model learns to optimize the prediction performance while adhering to the imposed fairness constraints. This process often requires iterative adjustments to balance both fairness and accuracy. Post-training, validating the model against unseen data is crucial to ensure that the fairness constraints have been effectively met without compromising accuracy. Once deployed, the model's performance and fairness measures should be continuously monitored to detect any shifts in data that may affect outcomes.

The main challenge of implementing in-processing algorithms is balancing the trade-offs between fairness and predictive performance while ensuring the stability and scalability of training processes. The incorporation of fairness constraints often comes at the cost of reduced predictive accuracy, and these constraints can sometimes be at odds with each other, requiring careful calibration and potentially complex multi-objective optimization.

In-processing algorithms offer a promising solution to promoting fairness in AI systems. As AI ethics progresses, these algorithms will likely play a crucial role in shaping the next generation of fair AI systems, pushing the boundaries of what is possible in ethical AI practices. By embedding fairness directly into machine learning models, in-processing algorithms address bias at its roots, altering the decision-making processes of AI systems to produce fairer outcomes.

Postprocessing Algorithms for Fairness in Machine Learning

Post-processing algorithms are a crucial aspect of machine learning, allowing for adjusting model outputs after training to achieve fairness across different demographic groups. These techniques are precious when the model is already trained, and biases must be corrected in decision-making without retraining the entire model. For instance, post-processing algorithms are crucial in scenarios where regulatory or ethical standards require fairness to be imposed post hoc or where access to the model's internals is restricted or impractical for adjustments.

There are two fundamental techniques in post-processing for fairness: equalized odds post-processing and calibrated equalized odds post-processing. The first technique adjusts the decision thresholds of a classifier to equalize both the false favorable rates (FPRs) and false negative rates (FNRs) across different groups. The goal is to ensure that the classifier's errors do not disproportionately affect one group over another, adhering to the fairness criterion known as equalized odds. The second technique is an extension of equalized odds post-processing, which adjusts the decision thresholds to achieve equalized odds and calibrates the output scores to maintain their interpretability as probabilities. This dual approach ensures that the post-processed scores provide meaningful probability estimates, thus retaining their utility in risk assessments and decision-making processes.

Implementing post-processing fairness algorithms involves several practical considerations. One such consideration is the selection of fairness criteria, which depends on the specific fairness requirements and the importance of maintaining calibrated probability scores. Another factor to consider is data requirements; the practical application of post-processing requires access to a validation dataset representative of the target population and includes accurate outcome labels to assess and adjust the decision thresholds. In regulated industries, such as finance or healthcare, post-processing methods must align with legal standards concerning fairness, requiring transparent documentation of the processes and their impacts.

Several companies and industries have applied post-processing algorithms to ensure fairness. For instance, financial institutions often use these techniques to adjust credit scoring models, ensuring that loan approval rates and terms are fair across different demographic groups. In risk assessment tools used in sentencing and bail decisions, post-processing algorithms help mitigate racial biases that could affect incarceration. Moreover, post-processing algorithms have ensured fairness in online advertising, where ads are targeted based on users' demographic information. By adjusting the decision thresholds for different groups, post-processing algorithms can ensure that users are not unfairly excluded from certain ads or targeted with irrelevant ads based on their demographic characteristics.

Post-processing algorithms are a powerful tool for achieving fairness in machine learning models. By adjusting decision thresholds and calibrating output scores, these techniques can ensure that decision-making processes are fair and unbiased across different demographic groups. However, it is essential to consider the practical implications of implementing these algorithms, such as data requirements and regulatory compliance, to ensure they are effective and transparent.

Comprehensive Analysis of Fairness Algorithm Strengths and Weaknesses

AI is becoming increasingly prevalent in various decision-making processes that affect human lives, from hiring practices to loan approvals. It's crucial to ensure that these systems are fair and unbiased. To achieve this, developers use three categories of fairness algorithms: pre-processing, in-processing, and post-processing.

Pre-processing techniques are applied to the data before it's fed into any machine learning model. These techniques aim to eliminate bias at the source, ensuring that the data represents all groups. Pre-processing methods include resampling, reweighing, and synthesizing new data points. These techniques can be applied across different models, making them versatile and model-agnostic. One of the main advantages of pre-processing techniques is their universality. They treat the data itself independently of any subsequent learning algorithms. However, pre-processing techniques have some weaknesses. They may lead to the loss of useful information, which can degrade the model's performance. Furthermore, these techniques operate under the assumption that the bias present in the data is understood and quantifiable.

In-processing techniques integrate fairness considerations directly into the machine learning model's learning process. These techniques prioritize fairness alongside accuracy. In-processing methods include incorporating fairness constraints into the loss function or using adversarial training (Fairlearn 2022). By altering the learning algorithm, in-processing methods often yield inherently fair models, regardless of external conditions or data shifts. In-processing techniques are highly customizable to accommodate various fairness definitions, making them practical for bespoke requirements. However, they can be computationally expensive and complex, especially when balancing multiple fairness constraints and accuracy.

Post-processing techniques adjust the outputs of a fully trained machine learning model to achieve fairness objectives. These techniques are helpful for quick fixes in deployed models where retraining the model might be impractical or costly. Post-processing interventions include adjusting decision thresholds or outcomes after model predictions, allowing for rapid deployment of fairness interventions. They can quickly ensure that the outputs meet specific fairness criteria, which is crucial for industries where decisions must adhere to sudden regulatory changes or ethical standards. However, post-processing techniques must be more balanced by focusing on the output stage, potentially leading to less optimal solutions that could have been achieved by addressing issues earlier in the process.

A combination of pre-processing, in-processing, and post-processing techniques is often required to achieve optimal fairness in AI systems. By understanding the strengths and weaknesses of each category, developers can choose the appropriate algorithm for the specific requirements and constraints of the problem at hand. Ensuring these systems are fair and unbiased is essential to avoid perpetuating existing biases and discrimination.

Practical Use Cases of Fairness Algorithms

Fairness algorithms are vital for promoting equitable outcomes and combating biases in various sectors where data-based decisions can significantly impact individual opportunities and outcomes (Du, Cheng, and Dou 2022). This section will explain practical use cases (Zhang, Lemoine, and Mitchell 2018) of fairness algorithms in financial services, healthcare, and recruitment. We will explore how specific algorithms are implemented to mitigate biases and promote fairness (Wickens 2022).

Financial Services: Ensuring Fair Loan and Credit Decisions

The financial sector, particularly in areas such as loan approvals and credit scoring, has been plagued by biases that could be racial, gender-based, or socioeconomic. Fairness algorithms such as reweighing and adversarial debiasing (Mervič 2023) address these concerns by ensuring that decision-making processes are transparent and bias-free (Zhang, Lemoine, and Mitchell 2018).

- **Reweighing in Loan Approvals**: The reweighing technique adjusts the weights of the dataset's training instances to reflect the borrower population's accurate demographics, promoting fair representation. For example, if historical data shows a bias against female loan applicants, reweighing increases the influence of female applicants' data in the training process, reducing this bias.

- **Adversarial Debiasing in Credit Scoring**: This technique involves simultaneously training a predictor and an adversary. The predictor attempts to accurately assess creditworthiness, while the adversary tries to determine sensitive attributes (such as race or gender) from the predictor's outputs. The goal is for the predictor to learn to make decisions that are not only accurate but also indistinguishable concerning sensitive attributes, thereby ensuring fairness. Banks and financial institutions employ this method to ensure their models do not inadvertently perpetuate historical biases.

Healthcare: Promoting Equity in Patient Treatment

Fairness algorithms are crucial in healthcare to ensure that all patients receive equitable care, regardless of their demographic factors, but there are fundamental problems with existing fairness algorithms (Wachter, Mittelstadt, and Russell 2023). Optimized pre-processing, for example, provides that predictive models do not inherit biases from historical patient data.

- **Optimized Pre-Processing for Patient Readmission Prediction**: This approach involves learning a probabilistic transformation that edits features and labels inpatient data under fairness constraints. Hospitals use this technique to predict patient readmissions without bias toward minority groups. Adjusting data distributions before model training helps reduce disparities in readmission predictions, which can influence the quality of care and resource allocation.

- **Bias Mitigation in Disease Diagnosis**: Machine learning models for diagnosing diseases, such as diabetes or cardiovascular conditions, are trained on diverse datasets to ensure they do not unfairly penalize or benefit certain groups. For example, models are trained to recognize symptoms equitably across ethnic backgrounds, considering genetic predispositions without reinforcing stereotypes.

Recruitment: Fair Hiring Practices

AI-driven recruitment tools are increasingly popular for managing large volumes of applications. However, these tools can perpetuate existing biases if not carefully managed with post-processing techniques to ensure fairness.

- **Post-Processing in Candidate Selection**: Recruitment platforms often adjust the decision thresholds for different demographic groups to equalize performance metrics such as the rate of callbacks or interviews. For example, suppose a hiring algorithm favors male candidates over equally qualified female candidates. In that case, post-processing adjustments can be made to ensure gender parity in the selection process.

- **Fairness in Automated Resumé Screening**: Automated resumé screening tools use techniques like calibrated equalized odds post-processing to adjust their outputs, ensuring candidates from all backgrounds have equal opportunities. This approach involves calibrating the scores to maintain their interpretative meaning as probabilities of success within the role while ensuring these probabilities do not result in discriminatory practices.

The practical application of fairness algorithms in sectors such as financial services, healthcare, and recruitment illustrates their critical role in combating systemic biases. By integrating these algorithms, organizations adhere to ethical standards and promote diversity and inclusion.

Company Applications of Fairness Algorithms

This section explains how major corporations like Google, IBM, and HireVue integrate fairness algorithms into their AI systems to mitigate biases and ensure their products and services are equitable and trustworthy.

Google is one of the leading AI technology companies globally, but it has faced challenges with racial bias in its image tagging and categorization algorithms. Google has implemented fairness constraints into its image recognition algorithms to address this issue (Google 2024). These constraints work by adjusting the algorithm's training process to minimize disparities in performance across different demographic groups. Google also employs extensive testing frameworks to improve algorithm inclusivity. This includes diversifying the training datasets and applying in-processing techniques like adversarial debiasing to reduce bias that the model may learn from skewed data (Wickens 2022).

IBM has pioneered ethical AI advocacy by developing the AI Fairness 360 toolkit (IBM 2018). This open-source toolkit provides a comprehensive set of metrics and algorithms to help researchers and practitioners detect and mitigate bias in machine learning models throughout the AI application lifecycle. The toolkit covers pre-processing, in-processing, and post-processing methods, allowing users to apply the most suitable techniques based on their needs. For example, the toolkit includes algorithms like optimized pre-processing, which learns a probabilistic transformation of the data to maximize fairness while preserving data utility. IBM's toolkit is designed to be versatile and can be used across different sectors, including finance, healthcare, and human resources.

HireVue is a tech company that uses AI to power its video interview platform and has implemented various fairness algorithms to ensure its AI assessments are as impartial as possible. HireVue's platform analyzes video interviews of candidates using AI to evaluate their nonverbal cues and verbal responses (HireVue 2024). HireVue employs post-processing algorithms that adjust decision thresholds based on the fairness analysis to mitigate bias. This ensures that the AI does not favor or disadvantage candidates from any demographic group. HireVue audits its AI models to ensure continuous fairness and adjusts as needed. This approach involves analyzing the performance of its models across different groups and adjusting algorithms or training data to address any detected disparities.

These companies' deployment of fairness algorithms demonstrates their commitment to mitigating biases in their AI systems and ensuring equitable outcomes for all users. These efforts are critical in advancing the development of ethical AI and building user trust in AI-powered products and services.

As AI technologies become more prevalent, it is crucial to consider their ethical implications. Developing algorithms that promote fairness and reduce bias is essential for building trust and ensuring the ethical use of AI. These algorithms provide practical solutions to mitigate the risks of automated decision-making. However, they also require careful implementation to balance fairness with model performance.

The ongoing research and application of these algorithms are critical to ensuring that AI systems promote equity and justice across all sectors. It highlights the intersection of technology and ethics and requires a multidisciplinary approach involving ethicists, sociologists, data scientists, and legal experts. By collaborating, we can harness the power of AI while guarding against its potential to introduce or reinforce bias. Ultimately, we can ensure that AI is a tool for positive societal transformation and fairness.

Privacy Concerns in Quantum Computing and Bias Reduction Techniques

As artificial intelligence becomes more prevalent in various fields, mitigating biases inherent in algorithms has become increasingly important. These biases can lead to skewed outputs that systematically favor one demographic. Researchers have categorized various strategies into three primary areas—data-level, algorithm-level, and model-level interventions—to address these concerns. Each targets different aspects of bias within AI systems. This technical challenge is also an ethical imperative, especially as AI applications become more widespread, from judicial decision-making systems to recruitment platforms.

Figure 8-3 presents a complex diagram that uses visual elements to clarify the connection between bias reduction in AI and privacy concerns in quantum computing. The diagram is designed in a circular layout to highlight the continuous interaction between AI and quantum computing fields. It includes icons and symbols representing different concepts, making it easier to understand. The annotations provide detailed explanations of the methods used and their impacts, providing a clearer insight into each strategy.

Figure 8-3 is a circular diagram highlighting the continuous interaction between bias reduction in AI and privacy concerns in quantum computing. The diagram has a central circle representing interdisciplinary approaches and two outer circles focusing on bias reduction techniques and quantum computing concerns.

The bias reduction techniques circle includes data-driven interventions, algorithm-level interventions, and model-level interventions. The quantum computing concerns circle includes quantum threats, post-quantum cryptography (PQC), and common challenges.

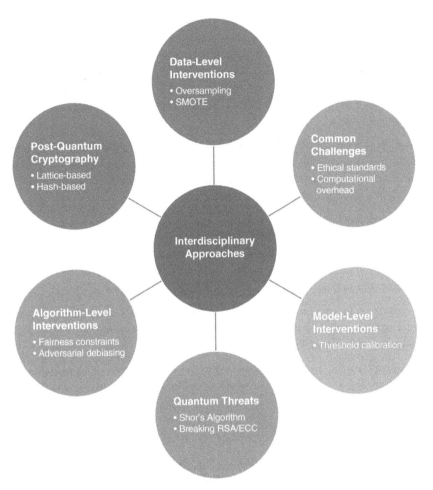

Figure 8-3
Relationship Between Bias Reduction in AI and Privacy Concerns in Quantum Computing

This diagram underscores the collaborative nature of our research, emphasizing the ongoing efforts of researchers, policymakers, and industry leaders to address concerns related to bias reduction in AI and privacy in quantum computing. Your involvement in this collective endeavor is crucial.

At the data level, the focus is on curating training datasets that are representative and balanced across various demographic groups. Techniques such as oversampling underrepresented groups or undersampling overrepresented ones help achieve this balance. Furthermore, synthetic data generation methods, such as the Synthetic Minority Over-sampling Technique (SMOTE), are employed to artificially augment minority classes within the training data, thereby providing a more balanced dataset for model training. While these methods are effective, they carry the risk of overfitting, making rigorous validation essential.

Algorithm-level interventions involve modifying the learning algorithms to integrate fairness directly, often by incorporating fairness constraints or regularization terms in the loss function. This approach seeks to optimize fairness metrics and accuracy during the training process. An exemplary method within this category is adversarial debiasing, where a model is trained alongside an adversary that attempts to predict sensitive attributes from the model's predictions. The primary model's objective is to obfuscate its outputs to minimize the adversary's predictive accuracy, thereby indirectly promoting fairness.

Post-training, model-level interventions come into play, focusing on adjusting the deployed models to reduce bias. This approach often involves calibrating decision thresholds to equalize performance metrics, such as false favorable rates across different demographic groups, and requires careful tuning to maintain overall system performance while enhancing fairness.

Each bias reduction strategy presents its own set of challenges and trade-offs. For instance, enhancing data diversity can potentially lead to models that perform less accurately on majority classes—a phenomenon that must be balanced against the ethical need for fairness. Furthermore, the definition of fairness itself is not universally agreed upon and varies depending on the context, necessitating a flexible approach to bias mitigation tailored to specific applications.

With its profound capabilities, quantum computing holds the potential to alter our digital environment. However, it also introduces significant privacy challenges, underscoring the need for careful consideration and ethical frameworks.

Post-quantum cryptography (PQC) has emerged in response to these vulnerabilities, focusing on developing secure cryptographic systems against classical and quantum computational threats. Lattice-based cryptography, for instance, involves computational problems currently deemed hard for both classical and quantum computers to solve. Cryptographic protocols like NTRU exemplify this approach by employing lattice problems for secure data encryption.

Hash-based cryptography offers another avenue for quantum-resilient encryption. This method leverages the one-way function property of cryptographic hash functions, which are inherently challenging to reverse. Techniques such as the Merkle signature scheme (MSS) use hash functions to create secure digital signatures in the face of quantum computational abilities.

Nevertheless, the development of quantum-resistant cryptographic methods is challenging. The increased computational overhead and larger key sizes, often required by these new algorithms, could hinder their adoption, particularly with limited computational resources. Moreover, as quantum technology advances, maintaining privacy and security standards will require ongoing adaptations to cryptographic practices, underscoring the dynamic nature of this field.

The balance between the immense computational power of quantum computing and the imperative to safeguard privacy calls for a comprehensive approach, combining technological innovation with robust regulatory frameworks. These frameworks must be capable of evolving alongside technological advancements to ensure that privacy protections remain effective.

As AI and quantum computing continue to evolve, they present not just complex but crucial ethical challenges that necessitate advanced technical solutions and thoughtful regulatory oversight. The continuous interplay between innovation in these fields and the ethical considerations they provoke underscores the need for a multidisciplinary approach to technology governance. By promoting collaboration among technologists, ethicists, policymakers, and the public, society can navigate the ethical environments shaped by these transformative technologies.

Evaluating Ethical Frameworks for Quantum Technologies

The development of quantum computing technologies has sparked a parallel need for ethical frameworks to guide their use, addressing key societal concerns such as privacy and the responsible deployment of these powerful tools. Given the profound impact that quantum computing is projected to have on areas ranging from cryptography to complex data analysis, potentially reshaping privacy and security environments globally, the importance of such frameworks cannot be overstated.

Ethical guidelines in quantum computing are still developing, with researchers, policymakers, and industry leaders grappling with the vast capabilities of these technologies. One prominent issue is the quantum threat to current cryptographic systems, poised to overturn the foundations of data security protocols that safeguard national security, protect personal information, and secure financial transactions. In response, initiatives like the Quantum-Safe Security Working Group, established by the Cloud Security Alliance, have begun to outline principles and practices to develop quantum-resistant cryptography. These guidelines emphasize the technical aspects of quantum-safe methods and advocate for their early adoption to pre-empt significant breaches.

Moreover, international bodies such as the European Telecommunications Standards Institute (ETSI) have initiated broader discussions to create standards that ensure the responsible use of quantum technologies. These efforts aim to address the dual-use nature of quantum computing, where the risks of misuse or unintended consequences match its potential for societal benefit. The ethical frameworks proposed often include transparency in quantum technologies' development and deployment phases, aiming to foster a culture of open innovation and public accountability.

These frameworks suggest that developers and operators of quantum technologies should be guided by a set of core principles: fairness, accountability, and sustainability. This effort involves safeguarding against the misuse of quantum technologies and ensuring their benefits can be widely disseminated without exacerbating existing inequalities. For instance, the potential acceleration of drug discovery through quantum simulations could transform healthcare. Still, it also necessitates policies to prevent monopolistic practices and ensure equitable access to these breakthrough therapies.

Recognizing the Broader Ethical Implications of AI and Quantum Technologies

Integrating AI with quantum computing raises complex ethical questions, extending beyond the immediate technical challenges to broader societal implications. These technologies, both individually and in tandem, have the potential to significantly influence public and private sectors, posing both opportunities and challenges that necessitate careful ethical consideration.

The diagram in Figure 8-4 helps manage the ethical issues of AI and quantum technologies. It provides a logical flow from primary concerns to desired outcomes. At the top of the diagram is the section on primary ethical concerns. This section highlights the main concerns surrounding AI and quantum technologies, including surveillance, privacy, and data security issues. Directly below the primary ethical concerns section is the societal impacts section. This section details the specific effects on society resulting from the primary concerns. These effects may include increased surveillance capacity, erosion of privacy, and the potential for widened digital divides. Following the societal impacts section is the strategic responses section. This section outlines the responses required to address the concerns and societal impacts, such as developing ethical guidelines, crafting regulatory frameworks, and enhancing international cooperation. At the bottom of the diagram is the desired outcomes section. This section focuses on the ultimate goals, such as safeguarding human rights, ensuring robust privacy and security, and promoting inclusivity and fair access. Together, these sections provide a clear and comprehensive guide to managing the ethical environment of AI and quantum technologies.

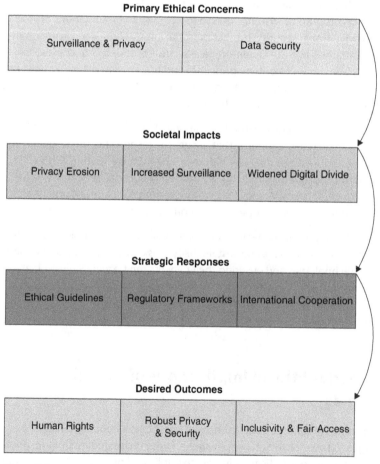

Figure 8-4

Visual Narrative of How Ethical Considerations Translate into Action and Desired Outcomes

One of the most pressing concerns is the impact of these technologies on surveillance and privacy. Enhancing AI capabilities through quantum computing could lead to more sophisticated surveillance systems capable of processing vast amounts of data at unprecedented speeds. This raises substantial privacy issues, because these systems could be used to track individuals without their consent or even legal precedent. The ethical use of AI in surveillance applications is already a contentious issue, with quantum technologies adding another layer of complexity.

Data security is another critical area influenced by the convergence of AI and quantum technologies. Quantum computers hold the potential to break many of the cryptographic protocols currently in place to secure digital communications. While this represents a significant threat, quantum technologies offer new methods to enhance data security, such as quantum key distribution, which could provide a nearly unbreakable encryption method. Nevertheless, the transition to quantum-resistant cryptography remains a monumental task that requires global cooperation and significant investment, highlighting the need for comprehensive policies that govern technology transitions.

The digital divide—the gap between demographics and regions that have access to modern information and communication technology and those that do not—could be exacerbated by the advancements in AI and quantum technologies. The high cost and complexity of quantum computing infrastructure mean that its benefits might initially be accessible only to well-funded, technologically advanced organizations and nations. This could widen the gap in technological capability and economic power between different regions and sectors, increasing global inequalities.

A multifaceted approach is necessary to address these challenges, involving the development of robust ethical guidelines, effective regulatory frameworks, and proactive international cooperation. Policies must be crafted to address the immediate impacts of technology and anticipate future developments and challenges. Moreover, fostering an inclusive approach to developing and deploying AI and quantum technologies is crucial. This includes ensuring diverse stakeholders are involved in discussions about how these technologies are developed and used, promoting a more equitable technological future.

Ethical considerations must remain at the forefront as AI and quantum computing evolve. The pace at which these technologies are developing requires ongoing vigilance and adaptability in ethical governance. As we enter an increasingly digitized future, the importance of grounding these revolutionary technologies in a framework that prioritizes human rights, privacy, and inclusivity cannot be underestimated. Only through such measures can society fully harness the benefits of AI and quantum technologies while mitigating their risks and ensuring that they serve the broader interests of humanity.

Reflecting on the Role of Policy and Regulation in AI and Quantum Computing

The growing fields of AI and quantum computing are increasingly influencing various sectors of society and the economy, sharply highlighting the necessity for robust policy and regulation. These governance frameworks are crucial for mitigating risks and ensuring the ethical deployment and development of these powerful technologies.

Policy and regulation in AI and quantum computing aim to navigate an environment where innovation must be balanced with ethical considerations, public trust, and safety. Governments and regulatory bodies worldwide are tasked with the complex challenge of creating policies that facilitate innovation while protecting society from potential harm. AI involves regulations around data usage, algorithmic transparency, and accountability. For quantum computing, the focus shifts toward securing intellectual property, managing export controls, and safeguarding critical infrastructure from potentially disruptive technologies. Chapter 9, "Legal Frameworks and Global Standards Shaping the Future Development of AI Agents," covers the regulatory aspects in more detail.

One of the critical areas where policy plays a role is ensuring transparency and accountability in AI systems. Governments increasingly know the need for algorithms to be efficient and understandable to those they impact. This has led to initiatives such as the European Union's General Data Protection Regulation (GDPR), which includes provisions for explaining the decision-making processes of AI systems that significantly impact individuals. This 'right to explanation' is a regulatory approach to mitigate the risks of opaque algorithmic decision-making, commonly called the "black box" problem in AI.

While still in its early stages, quantum computing has drawn attention from policymakers due to its potential to break encryption standards that secure everything from military communications to everyday online transactions. The U.S. National Quantum Initiative Act is an example of a policy designed to accelerate the development of quantum technologies while addressing these security concerns. It provides funding for quantum research and emphasizes the creation of standards and technology to counteract the threats posed by quantum computers to current cryptographic techniques.

Additionally, policy and regulation must address the implications of disruptive technologies in the workforce. Both AI and quantum computing could significantly alter job markets, necessitating policies that promote skill development and education to prepare workers for new roles created by these technologies. Furthermore, regulation can play a crucial role in ensuring that the benefits of AI and quantum computing, such as increased efficiency in healthcare, finance, and transportation, are accessible to all sections of society, thus avoiding exacerbating existing inequalities.

Anticipating Future Ethical Challenges in AI and Quantum Computing

As AI and quantum computing technologies evolve, they will likely pose new ethical challenges requiring ongoing discourse and adaptive governance strategies. The dynamic nature of these fields means that ethical considerations that seem futuristic or speculative today may soon become pressing issues.

One anticipated challenge is the dual-use nature of AI and quantum computing technologies, where advances could be used for beneficial and harmful purposes. AI technologies, such as facial recognition and predictive policing, can enhance security on the one hand, but raise concerns about privacy and civil liberties on the other. Similarly, quantum computing could create new methods for cyber attacks that exploit the vulnerabilities of traditional cryptographic defenses. These dual-use aspects require ethical frameworks that are flexible and robust enough to address rapidly changing capabilities and threats.

Another emerging challenge is the potential for AI and quantum computing to amplify surveillance capabilities. Quantum sensors, for example, could vastly improve the sensitivity and range of surveillance technologies, potentially allowing unprecedented invasions of privacy. AI's ability to analyze vast datasets could be supercharged by quantum algorithms, leading to more effective, yet potentially invasive, surveillance systems. These developments necessitate a re-evaluation of privacy norms and the creation of new regulations that can safeguard personal freedoms without stifling beneficial innovations.

The ethical implications of AI and quantum-enhanced decision-making in critical areas such as military and healthcare also present significant challenges. Autonomous weapons systems powered by AI and quantum computing could make life-or-death decisions in warfare, raising profound ethical questions about the role of machines in combat and accountability for their actions. In healthcare, quantum computing could enable the development of new treatments and drugs through enhanced computational models. Still, it also risks creating novel bioethical concerns, mainly if genetic data is used in ways that compromise patient privacy or autonomy.

Lastly, as these technologies potentially widen the gap between technological haves and have-nots, ethical challenges related to the digital divide and technological equity will become increasingly significant. Policies will be needed to ensure disadvantaged communities are not left behind as these advanced technologies become integral to economic competitiveness and national security.

Summary

This chapter highlights how AI algorithms, if not cautiously developed and monitored, can perpetuate or even exacerbate societal biases, leading to unfair outcomes in various sectors, including employment, law enforcement, and financial services.

The discussion then expands into how the disruptive potential of quantum computing necessitates a rethinking of current cryptographic practices and advocates for the accelerated development of quantum-resistant methodologies. Here, the text thoroughly evaluates emerging ethical frameworks that aim to balance the exponential power of quantum technologies with the imperative to protect individual privacy and maintain public trust.

In elaborating on these frameworks, the chapter emphasizes the creation of guidelines that address the technical and operational aspects of quantum computing and consider its societal impacts. The exploration includes discussing the necessity for transparency and accountability in deploying quantum technologies, ensuring they contribute positively to society without exacerbating existing disparities or introducing new forms of inequity.

Furthermore, the text discusses the role of policy and regulation in guiding the ethical development and application of AI and quantum computing. It highlights how proactive governance and forward-looking policies can facilitate the responsible evolution of these technologies. The chapter calls for international collaboration in developing standards that can adapt to the rapid pace of technological change, ensuring that AI and quantum computing innovations are aligned with global ethical standards and contribute to the welfare of all segments of society.

References

Dai, J. 2021. "Algorithms for Fair Machine Learning: An Introduction." *Towards Data Science.* https://towardsdatascience.com/algorithms-for-fair-machine-learning-an-introduction-2e428b7791f3.

Du, M., L. Cheng, and D. Dou. (2022). "Algorithmic Fairness in Machine Learning." Socially Responsible AI, World Scientific, according to her webpage: https://lcheng.org/publications/. https://mengnandu.com/files/Algorithmic_Fairness_in_Machine_Learning.pdf. Accessed August 28, 2024.

Fairlearn. 2022. "Fairlearn Adversarial Package—Fairlearn 0.8.0 Documentation." https://fairlearn.org/v0.8/api_reference/fairlearn.adversarial.html.

Fu, R., M. Aseri, V. Singh, and K. Srinivasan. 2020. "'Un'Fair Machine Learning Algorithms." http://dx.doi.org/10.2139/ssrn.3408275.

Google. 2024. "Google Responsible AI Practices—Google AI." https://ai.google/responsibility/responsible-ai-practices/.

HireVue. 2024. "AI in Recruiting. Ethical & Effective AI Hiring." https://www.hirevue.com/ai-in-hiring.

IBM. 2018. "AI Fairness 360—Open Source." Open Project. https://www.ibm.com/opensource/open/projects/ai-fairness-360/.

Mervič, Ž. 2023. "Orange Data Mining—Adversarial Debiasing." University of Ljubljana. https://oldorange.biolab.si/blog/adversarial-debiasing/.

O'Sullivan, C. 2021. "What Is Algorithm Fairness? An Introduction to the Field That Aims at Understanding and Preventing Unfairness in Machine Learning." *Towards Data Science.* https://towardsdatascience.com/what-is-algorithm-fairness-3182e161cf9f.

Piech, C. 2024. "Fairness in Artificial Intelligence." Stanford University. https://chrispiech.github.io/probabilityForComputerScientists/en/examples/fairness/.

Wachter, S., B. Mittelstadt, and C. Russell. 2023. "Health Care Bias Is Dangerous. But So Are 'Fairness' Algorithms." *Wired.* https://www.wired.com/story/bias-statistics-artificial-intelligence-healthcare/.

Wang, X., Y. Zhang, and R. Zhu. 2022. "A Brief Review on Algorithmic Fairness." *Management System Engineering* 1 (1): 1–13. https://doi.org/10.1007/S44176-022-00006-Z.

Wickens, E. 2022. "Unpacking the AI Adversarial Toolkit." *HiddenLayer.* https://hiddenlayer.com/research/whats-in-the-box/.

Zhang, B. H., B. Lemoine, and M. Mitchell. 2018. "Mitigating Unwanted Biases with Adversarial Learning." *AIES 2018—Proceedings of the 2018 AAAI/ACM Conference on AI, Ethics, and Society,* January, 335–40. https://doi.org/10.1145/3278721.3278779.

Test Your Skills

Multiple-Choice Questions

These questions are designed to test understanding of the key concepts, focusing on the societal impacts, challenges, and future implications of AI in autonomous systems.

1. What is a primary ethical concern in AI?

    A. The use of AI in gaming

    B. Bias and fairness in AI algorithms

    C. AI's impact on agricultural efficiency

    D. AI technology in space exploration

2. Which of the following techniques promotes fairness in AI?

    A. Increasing the number of AI models

    B. Reducing the speed of algorithms

    C. Pre-processing techniques in data handling

    D. Expanding AI application areas

3. According to this chapter, what poses a significant privacy challenge with the advancement of quantum computing?

    A. Faster data processing speeds

    B. Potential to break traditional cryptographic standards

    C. Increased use in consumer electronics

    D. Quantum computing in social media

4. Which of the following is a focus of ethical frameworks for quantum computing as discussed in this chapter?

    A. Ensuring high profitability

    B. Addressing privacy concerns and responsible use

    C. Expanding market reach

    D. Reducing production costs

5. What does this chapter identify as a broader implication of AI and quantum technologies on society?

    A. Decreased reliance on technology

    B. Reduced importance of Internet security

C. Impacts on surveillance and data security

D. Lower energy consumption in computing

6. What role do policy and regulation play in the context of AI and quantum computing, as explored in this chapter?

   A. Decreasing the transparency and accountability

   B. Guiding ethical development and application

   C. Slowing down technological innovation

   D. Reducing public sector involvement

7. What future ethical challenge is anticipated with the evolution of AI and quantum computing?

   A. Reduced effectiveness of AI and quantum technologies

   B. A dual-use nature leading to both beneficial and harmful uses

   C. Complete automation of all societal functions

   D. Elimination of all traditional computing devices

8. Which of the following is a bias reduction technique that involves altering training data before it enters the ML model?

   A. Post-processing adjustments

   B. Algorithmic corrections

   C. Pre-processing modifications

   D. Real-time data editing

9. Which of the following is a noted concern with integrating fairness into AI algorithms?

   A. It simplifies the algorithms too much.

   B. It might lead to decreased accuracy in majority classes.

   C. It makes algorithms completely unbiased.

   D. It will overcomplicate the design of neural networks.

10. What does this chapter suggest about developing ethical frameworks for quantum technologies?

    A. They are well established and widely implemented.

    B. They need to be revised for current technological applications.

    C. They are in the early stages of development.

    D. They are focused only on economic impacts.

Exercises

This exercise and corresponding answers are designed to test and reinforce your understanding of the ethical dimensions discussed in Chapter 8, focusing on the ethics of AI agents.

Exercise 8.1: Understanding Ethical AI and Quantum Computing

Read Chapter 8 and answer the following questions:

1. What are two primary ethical considerations discussed in the development of AI algorithms?

2. Explain how quantum computing poses privacy concerns.

3. What is the role of ethical frameworks in governing quantum computing technologies?

4. List and explain two broader ethical implications of AI and quantum technologies on society.

5. Discuss the significance of policy and regulation in developing and applying AI and quantum computing technologies.

6. Describe a potential future ethical challenge that might arise as AI and quantum computing technologies continue to evolve.

9

Legal Frameworks and Global Standards Shaping the Future Development of AI Agents

Chapter Objectives

This chapter focuses on the legal frameworks and global standards governing AI agents in relation to the wider field of artificial intelligence, and other technologies covered in this book, such as blockchain and quantum computing. This chapter provides an in-depth analysis of the regulatory environment for these technologies and a comprehensive look at the international standards shaping their development and use. Upon completion of this chapter, you will be able to

- **Understand the Regulatory Environment for AI Agents in Relation to Quantum Technologies**: Gain insights into the current legal and regulatory frameworks governing AI and quantum computing, including key legislation, policies, and regulatory bodies.

- **Explore International Standards for Blockchain Technology**: Learn about the international standards and guidelines shaping the development and deployment of blockchain technology globally.

- **Assess the Impact of Regulation on Quantum Computing**: Evaluate how legal frameworks and regulatory policies influence the growth and application of quantum computing technologies.

- **Identify Challenges in Regulating Emerging Technologies**: Recognize the unique challenges in developing legal frameworks for rapidly evolving technologies like AI, blockchain, and quantum computing.

- **Analyze Global Consensus and Divergence**: Investigate areas of global consensus and divergence in regulating these technologies, understanding how different regions approach their governance.

- **Examine the Role of International Bodies**: Understand the responsibility of international bodies and organizations in setting standards and guidelines for the responsible development and use of AI, blockchain, and quantum computing.

- **Consider the Future of Technology Regulation**: Anticipate the trajectory of the legal and regulatory frameworks for these technologies, anticipating potential changes and the need for adaptive governance.

- **Reflect on the Balance Between Innovation and Regulation**: Consider the fine balance between promoting technological innovation and ensuring robust, ethical, and secure development through regulation.

This chapter will help you gain a thorough understanding of the legal and regulatory environment surrounding AI, blockchain, and quantum computing and appreciate the complexities and necessities of establishing global standards and frameworks for these technologies. It establishes a critical relationship between regulatory frameworks, global standards, and the evolution of AI agents. AI agents, defined as autonomous systems capable of performing tasks and interacting with humans or other systems, are at the forefront of technological innovation. Their development is profoundly shaped by the legal and regulatory environments detailed in this chapter.

The regulation of AI agents is imperative for ensuring their safe and ethical deployment across various sectors, particularly those involving critical applications such as healthcare, finance, and autonomous vehicles. The chapter's examination of the European Union's Artificial Intelligence Act, which categorizes AI systems based on risk, highlights the necessity for robust legal standards. These standards are essential to safeguard public safety, privacy, and ethical integrity, directly influencing the methodologies employed in the development and implementation of AI agents.

Furthermore, the discussion on global standards, particularly those established by international bodies such as ISO and IEEE, underscores the importance of standardization for AI agents. Given that these agents frequently operate within interconnected global systems, adherence to international standards is crucial for ensuring their reliability, security, and interoperability. Such standardization facilitates the broader adoption of AI agents across different platforms and regions, enhancing their functionality and integration into diverse technological ecosystems.

Ethical considerations are also a central theme in this chapter, particularly concerning transparency, accountability, and user rights. AI agents, due to their decision-making capabilities, hold significant influence over various aspects of human life. Thus, it is paramount that they are governed by transparent and accountable frameworks. The chapter's insights into the regulatory mechanisms aimed at safeguarding these principles are vital for the ethical development and deployment of AI agents, ensuring that they operate within the bounds of public trust and legal compliance.

The chapter also expands into the regulation of quantum computing. It is essential to comprehend the regulatory environment surrounding quantum computing to anticipate and mitigate the potential risks associated with this technology, particularly in the context of AI agents, whose enhanced capabilities must not compromise security or ethical standards.

Moreover, the chapter highlights the necessity for adaptive and predictive regulatory approaches, which are particularly relevant given the rapid advancement of AI technologies. The future of AI agents will require legal frameworks which anticipate future technological developments and challenges.

Understanding the Regulatory Environment for AI Agents and Quantum Technologies

The regulation of AI differs across countries and regions. Each country adopts a strategy based on socioeconomic priorities, cultural values, and technological capabilities. In the European Union (EU), the regulatory approach toward AI is comprehensive and precautionary. The EU's proposed Artificial Intelligence Act aims to establish legal standards for AI systems across all member states (European Parliament 2023). This act focuses on transparency, accountability, and users' rights to challenge AI decisions. It categorizes AI systems based on risk levels, with high-risk applications subjected to stringent requirements before deployment.

In contrast, the United States follows a sector-specific approach to AI regulation (AI.Gov 2024). No single federal body oversees AI development. Instead, agencies like the Federal Trade Commission (FTC) and the Food and Drug Administration (FDA) regulate AI applications within their domains, such as consumer protection and medical devices. The U.S. approach emphasizes fostering innovation and competitiveness, with guidelines generally less prescriptive than those in the EU (NIST 2024b).

China, a significant player in the AI domain, integrates its AI policies with broader strategic goals for technological supremacy. The New Generation Artificial Intelligence Development Plan outlines the roadmap for AI development up to 2030. Its goal is to make China the world leader in AI theory, technology, and application. Regulatory oversight is more state-driven, emphasizing the enhancement of national security and social governance using AI technologies.

The future of AI agents will undoubtedly involve increasingly sophisticated applications and capabilities, requiring legal frameworks that are flexible and forward-looking (NAIAC 2024; NIST 2024b). Predictive regulatory frameworks, such as the NIST AI Standards (NIST 2024a), which anticipate future technological developments and challenges, such as the Coalition for Secure AI (CoSAI) (OASIS Open 2024), are crucial for ensuring that AI agents continue to operate within safe, ethical, and legally sound parameters.

Key Legislation and Policies

In different regions of the world, various laws and policies affect the operation and impact of AI systems. In the United Kingdom and the European Union, the General Data Protection Regulation (GDPR) significantly influences AI development (GDPR 2018; ICO 2018). It enforces strict rules on data privacy that have implications for the training and operation of AI systems. The GDPR's provisions on automated decision-making and the right to explanation are particularly relevant to AI developers.

No federal legislation is specific to AI in the United States. However, laws in different states, such as Illinois' Biometric Information Privacy Act, have implications for AI applications that involve personal data. The National Institute of Standards and Technology (NIST) is also crucial in developing AI standards and guidelines that influence industry practices (NIST 2024a).

China's AI regulation includes cybersecurity and data protection laws that govern data collection, storage, and use in AI systems. It emphasizes the protection of personal information and the security of critical infrastructure.

Regulatory Bodies and Their Roles

The development and deployment of AI technology are subject to regulation by various bodies in different parts of the world. In the EU, organizations such as the European Data Protection Board (EDPB) and the proposed European Artificial Intelligence Board are responsible for ensuring compliance with the General Data Protection Regulation, and the forthcoming AI Act, while offering guidance and enforcing regulations. Key legislation such as the EU's GDPR impacts AI by imposing strict data privacy standards, while in the U.S., state-specific laws like Illinois' Biometric Information Privacy Act influence AI applications that handle personal data. In China, cybersecurity and data protection laws ensure secure data handling within AI systems, aligning with national security interests.

The regulatory bodies play essential roles in shaping AI and quantum computing areas. In the EU, bodies like the European Data Protection Board and the European Artificial Intelligence Board enforce compliance and oversee AI governance. In contrast, the U.S. leverages the expertise of the National Science Foundation, or NSF (US-NSF 2023), and the Department of Defense (DoD) to direct AI research and ensure ethical standards. China's regulatory efforts are spearheaded by the Ministry of Industry and Information Technology (MIIT) and the State Administration for Market Regulation (SAMR), which enforce standards and policies aligning with national priorities.

In the U.S., the NSF and the DoD are significant in providing funding and setting directions for AI research and applications, with a particular focus on ethical implications and national security. Apart from sector-specific agencies, these organizations are crucial in overseeing AI governance.

In China, the MIIT and the SAMR regulate AI technology and enforce policies and standards that align with national priorities. China's approach integrates AI development within broader strategic and security goals, guided by the New Generation Artificial Intelligence Development Plan. This plan aims to position China as a global leader in AI by 2030, with regulations focusing on enhancing state security and technological governance.

International Standards for Blockchain Technology

As blockchain technology continues to disrupt various industries, international standards are critical in ensuring its secure, efficient, and interoperable deployment. The European blockchain standards are extensive (European Commission 2022) , and the Institute of Electrical and Electronics Engineers

Standards Association (IEEE SA) has been actively pursuing blockchain standardization (IEEE 2024). These standards foster global adoption and facilitate blockchain integration into diverse business practices and governance models.

The International Organization for Standardization (ISO) leads the way in standardizing blockchain through ISO/TC 307 (ISO 2017). This committee has developed standards that cover terminology, governance, security, and privacy aspects of blockchain technologies. These standards ensure a uniform approach to blockchain application across different sectors and regions.

The IEEE contributes by developing standards such as P2418.1, which governs the use of blockchain in Internet of Things (IoT) applications. These guidelines help ensure IoT devices interact securely and efficiently within blockchain networks.

The World Wide Web Consortium (W3C) focuses on aligning blockchain technologies with existing web standards, enhancing digital identity security through the Verifiable Credentials Data Model (W3C 2022). This model employs blockchain to secure and manage digital identities, facilitating user control over personal data.

These standards are applied in various sectors, such as finance, where they enhance transaction security and compliance with global regulations like KYC (Know Your Customer) vs AML (Anti-Money Laundering). In supply chain management, standards ensure the traceability and authenticity of goods. In healthcare, they secure patient data and ensure compliance with privacy regulations like GDPR.

Despite the progress in standards development, challenges such as technological evolution outpacing standardization and the need for greater harmonization among different standards persist. Future efforts in blockchain standardization will likely focus on addressing these challenges, ensuring that blockchain technology can meet emerging needs while remaining secure and interoperable.

Assessing the Impact of Regulation on Quantum Computing

Quantum computing is an emerging technology that has the potential to transition from theoretical exploration to practical application. The regulatory environment is critical in shaping its development, adoption, and ethical deployment. This section examines in detail how legal frameworks and regulatory policies influence the growth and application of quantum computing technologies, considering the complexities of this advanced technology.

One of the primary regulatory challenges of quantum computing is its dual-use nature. Its ability to break traditional cryptographic methods could compromise data security and national security frameworks. Therefore, regulatory bodies worldwide are in a delicate position to foster innovation in quantum computing while ensuring it does not undermine existing security infrastructures. Moreover, quantum computing operates on principles of quantum mechanics, such as superposition and entanglement, which allow quantum computers to process vast amounts of data at unprecedented speeds. The unique nature of this technology, coupled with its profound implications for fields like cryptography, drug discovery, and artificial intelligence, necessitates a sophisticated regulatory approach that addresses both opportunities and inherent risks.

Given the global impact of quantum computing, international cooperation and standards are essential to harmonize regulations, facilitate research collaborations, and manage the technology's diffusion responsibly. Organizations such as the International Telecommunication Union (ITU) and the International Organization for Standardization (ISO) are at the forefront of establishing guidelines that address the interoperability, security, and ethical use of quantum computing. In cybersecurity, the NIST in the United States is leading efforts to develop post-quantum cryptography standards (NIST 2022). These standards aim to create secure cryptographic systems against quantum and classical computers, ensuring a smooth transition as quantum computing becomes more prevalent. Developing and adopting these standards will protect sensitive information and maintain public trust in digital systems.

Regulating quantum computing involves addressing the technology's rapid evolution and the uncertainty of its trajectory. This uncertainty poses significant challenges for policymakers, who must devise flexible regulations to adapt to ongoing technological advancements without stifling innovation. The critical areas of concern include intellectual property (IP) rights, privacy, export controls and international security, economic implications, market regulation ethical considerations, and societal impact.

The economic impact of quantum computing is predicted to be substantial, influencing industries such as pharmaceuticals, aerospace, and energy. Regulators must consider the market dynamics introduced by quantum computing, including potential monopolies or oligopolies if access to quantum technologies is limited to a few players. Antitrust regulations may be required to ensure that the benefits of quantum computing are broadly distributed and that the market remains competitive. Moreover, quantum computing can disrupt traditional IP frameworks, particularly regarding patents. The complex nature of quantum algorithms and their applications raises questions about what constitutes a patentable invention in the quantum realm. Policymakers must balance the need to protect intellectual property with encouraging open innovation.

The profound capabilities of quantum computing also bring ethical considerations to the forefront. Regulatory frameworks must address issues such as bias in quantum algorithms, the potential for social manipulation, and the broader societal impacts of dramatically enhanced computing power. Engaging with diverse stakeholders, including ethicists, scientists, industry leaders, and the public, will be essential to develop comprehensive guidelines that reflect the interests of all parties involved. As quantum computing has the potential to break current encryption standards, there is a pressing need for regulations that protect individual privacy against future quantum-enabled breaches. This effort involves advancing cryptographic methods and implementing data governance frameworks that anticipate the increased decryption capabilities of quantum computers.

The regulatory environment plays a vital role in shaping the growth and application of quantum computing technologies. Policymakers must strike a delicate balance between fostering innovation and ensuring that quantum computing does not undermine existing security infrastructures. They must address this technology's rapid evolution and uncertainties while considering its potential economic, ethical, and societal impacts. Doing so requires international cooperation and standards, engagement with diverse stakeholders, and innovative approaches to regulation that balance the need for progress with the need for responsible and ethical deployment of quantum computing technologies.

Challenges in Regulating Emerging Technologies

The primary challenges in regulating emerging technologies are their complexity and rapid rate of evolution. Traditional regulatory frameworks can be slow to adapt, and by the time they are implemented, they may already be obsolete. AI, blockchain, and quantum computing advance at a pace that outstrips the slow, deliberative processes typical of legislative and regulatory bodies.

The underlying technical mechanisms of these technologies require regulators to possess a high level of expertise to develop practical and relevant policies. For instance, regulating quantum computing effectively requires understanding complex phenomena such as quantum entanglement and superposition, just as knowledge of cryptographic hashing is crucial for blockchain regulation.

The continuous and rapid development of these technologies means that regulations may need frequent updates to remain relevant, posing a significant challenge for regulatory bodies that traditionally work within more extended timeframes. Emerging technologies need to respect traditional boundaries between disciplines or jurisdictions. Their interdisciplinary nature and the global reach of digital technologies pose significant challenges for regulatory frameworks typically organized around specific sectors and confined to national borders.

Effective regulation of AI, blockchain, and quantum computing requires input from multiple disciplines, including computer science, law, ethics, and public policy. Creating a regulatory framework encompassing such a wide range of expertise is inherently challenging.

Regulating these technologies on a global scale requires international coordination to avoid regulatory arbitrage, where companies exploit the weakest regulatory regimes in their operations. Regulators must balance the promotion of innovation with the protection of public interest. Over-regulation can stifle innovation and economic growth, whereas under-regulation can lead to significant risks, including threats to privacy, national security, and even physical harm.

Some regulators have turned to innovative regulatory approaches like regulatory sandboxes to address the challenges of emerging technologies' fast-paced evolution and complexity. These are controlled environments where startups and innovators can test new products and services without the full range of regulatory consequences. This approach enables regulators to gain insights into new technologies and their implications in real-world scenarios, which can inform more effective and adaptive regulatory frameworks.

Adaptive regulations are flexible regulatory frameworks that can evolve in response to technological and market developments. They allow for periodic reviews and adjustments, ensuring adequate and relevant regulatory measures.

The unique challenges presented by these technologies—such as their complexity, rapid evolution, interdisciplinary nature, and global reach—demand innovative, flexible, and forward-thinking regulatory strategies. Policymakers can effectively address these challenges by adopting adaptive regulations, engaging in international cooperation, and leveraging tools like regulatory sandboxes.

Divergence in Technological Standards and Regulations: Focus on Asia

Asian countries such as China, India, Japan, South Korea, and Singapore have developed their approaches to regulating emerging technologies like AI, blockchain, and quantum computing. These approaches are shaped by their unique geopolitical dynamics, economic strategies, and cultural values, resulting in a diverse regulatory environment that can differ substantially from Western models.

China has a highly centralized and strategic approach to regulating technologies like AI and quantum computing. The government believes these technologies are essential to achieving technological leadership and has implemented comprehensive strategies to support their development. For example, the New Generation Artificial Intelligence Development Plan outlines clear goals and substantial state funding to create a globally dominant AI industry by 2030. China's approach to intellectual property in quantum technologies is aggressive, aiming to secure a vast number of patents to establish a stronghold in what is expected to be a foundational industry of the future.

India's approach to technology regulation has been more cautious, particularly in AI and blockchain. The country initially adopted restrictive measures, such as the ban on cryptocurrency transactions, which was later overturned by the Supreme Court in 2020. India has since been gradually forming a framework that could support the growth of blockchain technology, focusing on areas like banking, finance, and governance. In AI, India's National Strategy for Artificial Intelligence emphasizes ethical development and its application to social good. The strategy focuses on leveraging AI for economic growth and social development, emphasizing ethics and privacy.

Japan's regulatory approach to emerging technologies such as AI and blockchain emphasizes societal harmony and ethical considerations. The country has implemented guidelines that stress transparency, user control, and privacy. For example, Japan's AI strategy, articulated through initiatives like Society 5.0, aims to integrate advanced technologies seamlessly into everyday life to enhance societal well-being. Regarding quantum computing, Japan is focusing on establishing collaborative frameworks that involve both public and private sectors. The aim is to create an ecosystem where quantum technologies can thrive, supported by policies that encourage innovation while considering the long-term societal impacts.

Other Asian countries, such as South Korea and Singapore, are significant players in regulating emerging technologies. South Korea has supported AI and blockchain through government-backed initiatives and is investing in quantum computing research and development. The country's approach is highly integrated with its industrial policy, aiming to bolster technological capabilities across its manufacturing and IT sectors. Singapore stands out for its forward-thinking regulatory approach, particularly in blockchain. The Monetary Authority of Singapore (MAS) has pioneered the creation of a regulatory sandbox that allows fintech companies to experiment with blockchain technology in a controlled environment. This approach has positioned Singapore as a global fintech and blockchain innovation hub.

The regulatory environments in China, India, Japan, and other Asian countries illustrate the diversity in approaches to governing emerging technologies. Each country's strategy is shaped by its unique priorities and challenges, leading to a patchwork of standards that reflect technological ambitions and cultural and societal values. While a source of richness, this diversity also challenges international cooperation and standards harmonization. As these countries continue to advance their technological capabilities, their evolving regulatory frameworks will play a crucial role in shaping the global discourse on technology governance.

International Bodies and Regulations

International standardization bodies like the International Organization for Standardization (ISO) and the International Electrotechnical Commission (IEC) are essential in developing global standards for technologies that ensure safety, reliability, and interoperability across national boundaries. These standards provide a crucial foundation for international compliance, offering guidelines that help industries and governments ensure that technological developments benefit global ecosystems.

Joint technical committees are formed to standardize emerging technologies. For instance, ISO/IEC JTC 1/SC 42 develops foundational standards for artificial intelligence, including terminology, frameworks for AI governance, data quality, and AI use in specific contexts like healthcare and robotics. These standards aim to foster an understanding of AI systems among stakeholders globally and ensure that AI technologies are developed and used within accountability and transparency frameworks.

ISO/TC 307 is a technical committee standardizing blockchain and distributed ledger technologies. It works on numerous aspects of blockchain technology, including privacy, security, governance, and use cases across different sectors. Developing such standards is vital for enhancing the trustworthiness and legal clarity needed to integrate blockchain into international business processes and government services.

Quantum technology is still nascent, and international collaboration is crucial. The International Telecommunication Union (ITU) facilitates discussions on how quantum computing could impact global communications systems, including potential threats to current encryption standards and opportunities for new quantum-resistant cryptographic solutions.

The ITU Focus Group on Quantum Information Technology for Networks brings together researchers, industry leaders, and policymakers to explore integrating quantum technologies in telecommunications networks. Their work is crucial in anticipating how quantum computing and quantum communication will reshape global data security standards and infrastructure requirements.

In addition to standard-setting and facilitating dialogue, international bodies also provide platforms that encourage collaborative approaches to technology governance. UNESCO's Global Agreement on the Ethics of Artificial Intelligence establishes a set of universal guidelines on the ethical use of AI. This initiative aims to promote fairness, accountability, and transparency and create a global consensus that respects cultural diversity while promoting shared ethical standards in AI development and use.

The World Economic Forum's Centre for the Fourth Industrial Revolution (C4IR) network of hubs ensures that emerging technologies like AI and blockchain are governed in ways that benefit society globally. These centers collaborate on pilot projects that address governance gaps and work to shape the protocols and regulations that will underpin new technologies. Their multi-stakeholder approach ensures that voices from business, government, academia, and civil society are included in discussions about future technology frameworks.

International organizations face several challenges in shaping the technology regulation, including differing national interests, economic priorities, and levels of technological advancement. Additionally, the rapid pace of technological change often outstrips the slower processes of international consensus-building, making it challenging to establish timely regulations that are universally applicable.

Looking ahead, international bodies must adopt more agile and adaptive approaches to standardization and governance. This endeavor could involve more dynamic frameworks that allow for periodic reviews and updates of standards based on technological advancements and emerging use cases. Furthermore, enhancing the cooperation between countries and organizations will be crucial in shaping the global governance of emerging technologies.

The Coalition for Secure AI (CoSAI) is integral to the global effort to establish secure, ethical, and transparent AI systems, especially in relation to the broader context of regulatory and standardization initiatives (OASIS Open 2024). CoSAI's approach, which unites industry leaders, academics, and policymakers, is particularly relevant in the context of the regulatory frameworks discussed, where the balance between fostering innovation and ensuring security is paramount. By developing and promoting comprehensive security standards for AI, CoSAI supports the global harmonization of AI governance, addressing the challenges of ensuring that AI agents operate safely and ethically across diverse jurisdictions. This coalition's work strengthens the international regulatory environment by contributing to the creation of adaptive and resilient standards that are crucial for managing the complex risks associated with AI, thus reinforcing the importance of global collaboration in securing the future of AI technology.

Reflecting on the Balance Between Innovation and Regulation

The interface between innovation and regulation is an essential aspect of technological advancement. While innovation can lead to economic growth and solve societal issues, unregulated technological progress can pose risks such as privacy infringements, security vulnerabilities, and socioeconomic disparities. Hence, regulatory frameworks need to be designed to mitigate these risks and encourage an environment that fosters innovation.

Dynamic regulatory environments play a crucial role in maintaining this balance. These environments adapt to technological progress and market evolution by employing a mix of prescriptive and performance-based regulations. While prescriptive regulations specify particular measures that must be taken to comply with the law, performance-based regulations outline the outcomes that need to be achieved, leaving the methods to achieve these outcomes more flexible.

Implementing risk-based regulatory approaches can focus resources on areas of greatest need, reducing the burden on innovators while addressing significant risks. For example, algorithms used in critical applications like healthcare and autonomous vehicles might be subjected to more stringent scrutiny than those used in less critical contexts.

Regulatory sandboxes are controlled environments where new technologies can be tested without immediately incurring all the usual regulatory consequences. By allowing temporary relief from specific legal and regulatory requirements, sandboxes provide innovators the flexibility to experiment while protecting public interests. This setup offers regulators first-hand insights into the implications of new technologies, forming a basis for informed decision-making regarding future regulations.

Technological neutrality is a principle which regulators are increasingly trying to uphold to ensure that all technologies that perform the same function are subject to the same regulations. This approach helps prevent the creation of unfair competitive advantages and supports the principle of innovation neutrality. To maintain technological neutrality, regulations should focus on the function and use of the technology rather than the technology itself.

Balancing global and local regulatory demands is crucial in globalized technology markets. Multinational cooperation can harmonize regulations and facilitate innovation across borders, but local conditions such as economic priorities, cultural norms, and political environments also demand tailored regulatory approaches. To avoid imposing one-size-fits-all solutions, efforts to harmonize international regulations must consider local needs and contexts.

Balancing innovation with AI, blockchain, and quantum computing regulation is a complex, dynamic challenge requiring regulators to be proactive, adaptable, and informed by ongoing technological and market developments. By fostering environments that support safe technological advances and robust innovation, regulators can help ensure that the benefits of new technologies are realized broadly across society while mitigating potential harm. This balance is crucial for sustaining the pace of innovation while protecting public and ethical standards in the digital age.

The Future of AI, Blockchain, and Quantum Computing

Artificial intelligence, blockchain, and quantum computing are three powerful technologies expected to create unprecedented synergies when integrated. AI is advancing rapidly through innovations in machine learning algorithms and increased computational power, creating autonomous and self-learning systems. Given the increasing deployment of AI systems in sensitive and impactful areas, future developments in AI will likely focus on transparency and ethical considerations.

Blockchain's key attributes of decentralization, immutability, and transparency make it valuable across various applications beyond cryptocurrencies, such as securing medical records, legal agreements, and more. Integrating blockchain with AI could lead to more robust security features for AI operations, safeguarding against data tampering and enhancing the reliability of AI decisions.

Quantum computing is still in its early stages but can solve problems that classical computers cannot. Current research primarily focuses on quantum supremacy and developing quantum algorithms that perform specific tasks much faster than their classical counterparts. As quantum technologies evolve, their integration with AI and blockchain could enhance their capabilities, such as improving machine learning algorithms through quantum-enhanced feature selection or securing blockchain technologies against future quantum threats. By converging AI, blockchain, and quantum computing, the synthesis of these technologies is poised to create a robust framework for future technological advancements, influencing sectors ranging from healthcare to finance and beyond. Professionals and researchers must understand these fields' potential trajectories and developments to better prepare for the dynamic, integrated future of these transformative technologies.

Emerging Trends in AI

Machine learning is moving toward increased autonomy, with algorithms that can learn without human supervision. For example, self-tuning neural networks dynamically adapt their parameters and structures in response to real-time data, similar to autonomous drones that adjust their flight paths according to environmental cues.

Quantum computing is another significant development that enhances computational capabilities, particularly with the use of quantum machine learning algorithms that can perform computations at speeds unattainable by classical computers. This technology is instrumental in genomics, where vast data must be analyzed to identify genetic variations and predict diseases.

In addition to deep learning, there are significant advances in neural network architectures, such as spiking neural networks (SNNs), which mimic the neural activity of the human brain. SNNs process information in discrete timeframes, increasing computational efficiency and reducing power consumption. This technology helps develop neuromorphic computing, where devices like vision sensors in robotics utilize SNNs to process visual information more efficiently.

Devices will learn from user interactions to tailor functionalities. For example, smartphones could adapt their interface and applications based on the user's daily habits and preferences, enhancing usability and engagement without explicit user input.

AI also addresses environmental challenges, with algorithms designed to process and analyze satellite imagery and sensor data for environmental monitoring and management. AI's ability to predict deforestation rates and the spread of wildfires offers critical insights that aid in proactive ecological protection and management.

AI is transforming Industry 4.0 in the manufacturing sector, enhancing automation, supply chain management, and predictive maintenance. For example, AI algorithms are employed to predict machine failure, minimizing downtime by scheduling maintenance before breakdowns occur, ensuring continuous production, and reducing operational costs.

Integrating AI with other advanced technologies like blockchain and quantum computing is set to amplify its impact further, offering robust, secure, and highly efficient solutions across various fields. Integrating AI and blockchain enhances data security and transparency in financial transactions and supply chains. At the same time, the synergy between AI and quantum computing is expected to break new ground in drug discovery and material science.

Future Developments in Blockchain Technology

Blockchain technology is facing several challenges, one of which is scalability. However, innovations such as sharding and Layer 2 solutions address these issues. Sharding divides the network into smaller segments, which allows for the parallel transaction, contract, and state processing. Ethereum's planned sharding implementation aims to significantly increase the number of transactions per second, enhancing performance while maintaining security. Layer 2 solutions, such as the Lightning Network for Bitcoin, facilitate transactions off the main blockchain, which speeds up transaction times and reduces costs. These solutions are particularly crucial for real-time processing applications like financial transactions.

Refining consensus mechanisms is another way blockchain enhances its efficiency and accessibility. The shift from proof of work (PoW) to proof of stake (PoS) mitigates the energy consumption issues associated with PoW. It offers a faster, more scalable, and environmentally sustainable alternative. Blockchains like Tezos and Cardano have already adopted PoS, setting a precedent for others like Ethereum 2.0.

Integrating blockchain with AI and IoT facilitates new functionalities and efficiencies. Blockchain provides a robust framework for securing the vast data flows between IoT devices, ensuring that all communications are verified and recorded securely, thus mitigating potential breaches. In AI, blockchain's role as a secure ledger facilitates the sharing of large datasets used for training AI models, adhering to compliance and privacy standards without sacrificing the benefits of data accessibility for AI processing.

Blockchain technology is also revolutionizing transparency in supply chain management. By maintaining an immutable and transparent ledger of all transactions, businesses can trace the lineage of products from origin to end user, ensuring provenance and safety. For instance, blockchain can track the journey of a medication from manufacturing to delivery, ensuring that it has not been tampered with and complies with safety standards.

Looking ahead, smart contracts in blockchain platforms are set to expand, executing automatically based on coded conditions, eliminating the need for intermediaries, and reducing the scope for disputes and fraud. Furthermore, blockchain's potential in managing digital identities is transformative, providing a secure, immutable platform for individuals to store and manage their digital identities, offering control over who accesses their data. This application could update online security and privacy, providing a more robust system for identity verification than those currently used, which are susceptible to fraud and theft.

Advances in Quantum Computing

Achieving fault-tolerant quantum computing enables quantum computers to perform long computations accurately, even in the presence of errors. Quantum error correction codes protect the quantum information while allowing for the completion of quantum algorithms without significant error rates. This breakthrough is essential for complex tasks like simulating chemical reactions for drug discovery and materials science, where classical computers fall short.

Quantum supremacy refers to the ability of quantum computers to solve problems that are practically impossible for classical computers to handle within a reasonable timeframe. As quantum processors continue to scale and reduce error rates, more instances of quantum supremacy are expected, paving the way for solving some of the most intricate problems. Despite these promising advances, quantum computing faces several challenges. Coherence, which involves maintaining the quantum state of qubits long enough to perform calculations, is a primary issue. Quantum decoherence, loss of quantum state due to interaction with the environment, poses a significant hurdle, because it can lead to errors in computations. Another challenge is scalability, because current quantum computers have a relatively small number of qubits. Scaling up the number of qubits while maintaining low error rates and stable quantum coherence is nontrivial and requires continued innovation in quantum hardware.

Looking ahead, the future of quantum computing is intertwined with advancements in quantum materials and technologies that can efficiently create, manipulate, and measure qubits. Innovations such as topological qubits, theorized to have higher resistance to errors and hence better suited for building more reliable quantum computers, could be transformative. Moreover, the development of hybrid quantum-classical systems is a promising area. These systems combine quantum and classical computing processes to perform complex calculations more efficiently. They are expected to be more feasible in the short term and could be the stepping stone required for full quantum computing to become viable.

Synergies Among Emerging Technologies

Quantum computing's integration with other advanced technologies, particularly AI and blockchain, is poised to unlock enhanced capabilities. Quantum algorithms can significantly speed up machine learning processes by performing computations faster than traditional algorithms. In blockchain, quantum computing could break many cryptographic algorithms that currently secure digital transactions. This challenge has led to the development of quantum-resistant blockchains that use post-quantum cryptographic algorithms that are believed to be secure against an attack by a quantum computer.

Regarding cybersecurity, combining blockchain and quantum computing can form a robust framework. Quantum key distribution (QKD) is an example of how these technologies can be integrated. QKD uses the principles of quantum mechanics to ensure secure communication, employing properties like quantum entanglement and the no-cloning theorem to generate and distribute cryptographic keys. These quantum-generated keys can be integrated into a blockchain framework to reinforce security, securing each block with quantum-resistant cryptographic algorithms such as lattice-based cryptography.

In the area of smart cities, the integration of AI, blockchain, and quantum computing can enhance security and operational efficiency. Quantum computing's speed and power can process vast amounts of data generated by IoT devices, while blockchain's decentralized architecture can help secure the data and prevent unauthorized access. AI can be used to analyze the data and provide insights that can be used to optimize city services, making them more efficient and responsive to the needs of citizens.

Potential Disruptions Caused by Emerging Technologies

When combined, AI, blockchain, and quantum computing can cause significant disruptions. Their transformative potential can disrupt novel finance, healthcare, cybersecurity, and other sectors.

In the financial sector, the convergence of AI, blockchain, and quantum computing will fundamentally alter operations and services. AI's ability to process and analyze vast amounts of data can provide unprecedented insights into customer behavior, market trends, and risk management. For example, AI models can predict stock market fluctuations with a high level of accuracy by analyzing global economic indicators, social media sentiments, and historical data, all processed at remarkable speeds thanks to quantum computing.

Blockchain technology introduces an additional layer of security and transparency to these operations. By recording transactions on a decentralized ledger, blockchain can virtually eliminate the risk of fraud and errors in record-keeping. Quantum computing enhances cryptographic security but poses a threat by potentially breaking traditional cryptographic protocols. This duality necessitates the development of quantum-resistant blockchains, ensuring that financial transactions remain secure against future quantum-enabled breaches.

In healthcare, these technologies promise to enhance the efficiency and quality of care but also disrupt traditional healthcare models. AI's ability to diagnose diseases from imaging scans or genetic information can be supercharged by quantum computing, reducing processing times from weeks to mere hours or even minutes. Blockchain can securely manage the data generated, ensuring patient privacy and compliance with strict regulatory standards like HIPAA.

An example of such integration could be seen in personalized medicine, where patient data from various sources is aggregated and analyzed to tailor treatments to individual genetic profiles. Blockchain ensures that this sensitive data is stored securely and shared only among authorized practitioners, while quantum computing provides the necessary computational power to analyze complex genetic data swiftly.

Adopting these emerging technologies will enhance cybersecurity and present new challenges. Blockchain and AI can significantly improve the detection of cyber threats and automate responses to security incidents. AI-driven security systems, enhanced by quantum computing, can analyze patterns and predict security breaches before they occur, implementing countermeasures in real time.

However, the power of quantum algorithms could one day break these encryptions, leading to a need for quantum-resistant cryptographic methods. This underscores the disruptive impact of these technologies.

Ethical and Societal Implications

The combination of AI and massive data analytics, along with the storage capabilities of blockchain and the computational power of quantum computing, raises significant privacy concerns. Predictive models can infer sensitive attributes, such as health status or political affiliations, based solely on shopping habits or social media activity. This capability raises unintended privacy invasions and reveals personal information that individuals might not choose to disclose. While blockchain enhances data security and integrity, it also presents privacy challenges due to its inherent transparency and immutability. Once data is placed on a blockchain, it becomes nearly impossible to alter or delete. This capability could clash with privacy laws, such as the GDPR, which includes the right to erasure ("right to be forgotten"). Balancing the ledger's transparency with the individuals' privacy rights is essential. Quantum computing further complicates these issues because it has the potential to break current cryptographic standards that protect personal and national security data.

While these technologies can enhance security, they also create new vulnerabilities. For example, quantum computing provides new ways to secure data transmissions through quantum key distribution. However, it also introduces the risk of developing a technological divide where only certain entities can employ quantum-resistant security measures. This could lead to wealthier corporations and nations having a significant security advantage, exacerbating global inequalities.

The automation capabilities of AI and the efficiency improvements from blockchain and quantum computing pose significant disruptions to the labor market. Many traditional jobs, particularly in sectors like manufacturing, retail, and administrative services, are at high risk of being automated. While this shift promises increased efficiency and lower operational costs, it raises concerns about job displacement and widening income inequalities. Governments and industries must collaborate on policies supporting workers during these transitions, such as guaranteed minimum income schemes or reskilling grants, ensuring that the benefits of technological advancements are distributed equitably.

Beyond individual implications, these technologies will reshape societal structures. The potential for increased surveillance capabilities through AI and quantum computing can affect civil liberties, requiring robust regulatory frameworks to prevent abuses. Furthermore, as decision-making processes in sectors like law enforcement or financial lending are increasingly automated, ensuring that AI systems are free from biases and operate transparently becomes paramount.

Future Challenges and Opportunities

AI, integrated with quantum computing, poses existential threats to our society as it advances unchecked (Bostrom 2014), undermining the security of personal data storage in cloud systems (Bernstein 2011). There is a significant probability of Artificial general intelligence (AGI) being developed within the next few decades (Grace et al. 2018), causing significant impact on society (Tegmark 2017). As artificial intelligence breaks existing encryption, threatening the security of critical infrastructure and sensitive information worldwide (Mosca 2018), we face widespread identity theft and societal disruption, risking the very foundations of modern civilization (Gentry 2009). The risks associated with quantum computing, such as breaking current cryptographic systems, will have severe consequences for cybersecurity and global financial systems (Aaronson 2013). Technological singularity, the point at which artificial intelligence surpasses human intelligence, leading to rapid, unfathomable changes in society, could occur by the mid-21st century (Kurzweil

2005), and in the very near future, we could see the development of superhuman intelligence, marking the onset of the singularity (Vinge 1993).

One of the significant challenges we need to address is integrating these advanced technologies into current systems securely. Integrating AI, blockchain, and quantum computing requires substantial financial investment and a profound structural change in IT infrastructure and business processes. Organizations must prioritize flexibility in their technology strategies to accommodate these rapidly evolving technologies.

Moreover, the need for standardization across platforms and industries presents a challenge. Creating universal protocols and standards, particularly in blockchain and quantum computing, is essential as these technologies develop to ensure compatibility and security across different systems and sectors.

On the other hand, integrating these technologies offers unparalleled opportunities for innovation. For instance, quantum computing can dramatically accelerate drug discovery processes, reducing the time and cost of bringing new treatments to the market. Similarly, AI and blockchain can transform supply chain management by improving transparency, efficiency, and security from production to delivery.

Organizations can leverage these technologies to create new value propositions and business models. For example, financial institutions can use AI to offer personalized banking services and products based on individual customer data analyzed in real time, enhanced by the secure, transparent record-keeping provided by blockchain.

As automation increases, there is an urgent need to prepare the workforce for the jobs of the future. This preparation involves reskilling and up-skilling employees to work alongside advanced technologies. Educational institutions and corporations should focus on training programs emphasizing technology management, data analysis, and cybersecurity skills.

Equipping individuals and organizations to deal with the ethical implications of these technologies is crucial. This preparation involves understanding the potential for bias in AI algorithms, the privacy implications of blockchain, and the security challenges posed by quantum computing. Developing ethical guidelines and robust regulatory frameworks will be essential to managing these issues responsibly.

As these technologies evolve, so must the regulatory frameworks that govern their use. Stakeholders must stay informed of changes in laws and regulations that affect how these technologies are deployed, such as data protection laws for AI and blockchain and international standards for quantum computing security.

By understanding and preparing for these challenges and opportunities, stakeholders can mitigate risks and strategically position themselves to take full advantage of AI, blockchain, and quantum computing's transformative potential. This proactive approach will be crucial in shaping a future where technology enhances human capabilities and fosters a more equitable society.

Summary

This chapter explores the relationship between legal frameworks, international standards, and the development of advanced technologies such as AI, blockchain, and quantum computing. It covers regulatory environments, global standards, and the necessary adjustments to effectively govern rapidly evolving technological environments. The goal is to provide you with an understanding of the legal and regulatory environment surrounding AI, blockchain, and quantum computing.

The discussion highlights the diversity in regulatory approaches across different jurisdictions, detailing how regions like the EU, U.S., and China navigate AI and quantum computing governance. It provides insights into how these varying approaches reflect underlying socioeconomic priorities and strategic objectives.

Attention is given to the critical role of international standards in shaping the development and deployment of blockchain technology. The discussions around ISO, IEEE, and W3C standards underscore the necessity for a uniform approach to foster global adoption and ensure the interoperability of blockchain technologies across different industries and borders.

The narrative details the emerging regulatory concerns around quantum computing, mainly focusing on the technology's dual-use nature and national and global security implications. The chapter also considers the development of post-quantum cryptography standards as a necessary response to these challenges.

The exploration of the unique challenges in regulating AI, blockchain, and quantum computing emphasizes the need for regulatory frameworks to be as adaptive and forward-looking as the technologies they seek to govern. The analysis of global consensus and divergence sheds light on the areas where international harmonization remains elusive, highlighting the ongoing debates and efforts to reconcile different regulatory philosophies and practices. The forward-looking insights contemplate the trajectories of legal and regulatory frameworks, recognizing the need to evolve in response to anticipated and unforeseen technological advancements.

The chapter also examines the potential futures of AI, blockchain, and quantum computing. These technologies can modernize various sectors by introducing transformative capabilities and innovative solutions. The chapter gives a perspective on how these technologies will evolve, integrate, and potentially disrupt existing paradigms across finance, healthcare, and cybersecurity industries.

The chapter breaks down the anticipated advancements in each technology, highlighting the progression of AI toward increasingly autonomous systems, the expansion of blockchain beyond its traditional applications to enhance security and efficiency, and the transformative potential of quantum computing to solve problems beyond the reach of classical computing. Through these lenses, we examine the likely synergies emerging from their integration, such as enhanced security features and more efficient data processing capabilities.

The discussions examine the potential disruptions these technologies could usher into existing markets, reshaping employment, privacy considerations, and security frameworks. Special attention is given to the ethical and societal implications, stressing the importance of preparing for the impact on privacy, security, and employment. The narrative underscores the necessity for all stakeholders, technologists, policymakers, or the public, to develop an understanding of these technologies. This understanding is crucial to leverage their benefits and mitigate the risks associated with their rapid deployment in sensitive and impactful areas.

References

Aaronson, S. 2013. *Quantum Computing Since Democritus*. Cambridge University Press.

AI.Gov. 2024. "AI.Gov: Making AI Work for the American People." https://ai.gov/.

Bernstein, D. J. 2011. "Post-Quantum Cryptography." *Encyclopedia of Cryptography and Security*, 949–50. https://doi.org/10.1007/978-1-4419-5906-5_386.

Bostrom, N. 2014. *Superintelligence: Paths, Dangers, Strategies*. Oxford University Press.

European Commission. 2022. "Blockchain Standards: Shaping Europe's Digital Future." https://digital-strategy.ec.europa.eu/en/policies/blockchain-standards.

European Parliament. 2023. "AI Act: A Step Closer to the First Rules on Artificial Intelligence." https://www.europarl.europa.eu/news/en/press-room/20230505IPR84904/ai-act-a-step-closer-to-the-first-rules-on-artificial-intelligence.

GDPR. 2018. "What Is GDPR, the EU's New Data Protection Law?" https://gdpr.eu/what-is-gdpr/.

Gentry, C. 2009. "Fully Homomorphic Encryption Using Ideal Lattices." *Proceedings of the Annual ACM Symposium on Theory of Computing*, 169–78. https://doi.org/10.1145/1536414.1536440.

Grace, K., J. Salvatier, A. Dafoe, B. Zhang, and O. Evans. 2018. "Viewpoint: When Will AI Exceed Human Performance? Evidence from AI Experts." *Journal of Artificial Intelligence Research* 62 (July): 729–54. https://doi.org/10.1613/JAIR.1.11222.

ICO. 2018. "Information Commissioner's Office (ICO): The UK GDPR." UK GDPR Guidance and Resources. https://ico.org.uk/for-organisations/uk-gdpr-guidance-and-resources/lawful-basis/a-guide-to-lawful-basis/lawful-basis-for-processing/consent/.

IEEE. 2024. "Standards—IEEE Blockchain Technical Community." https://blockchain.ieee.org/standards.

ISO. 2017. "ISO—International Organization for Standardization." https://www.iso.org/home.html.

Kurzweil, R. 2005. *The Singularity Is Near: When Humans Transcend Biology*. Penguin.

Mosca, M. 2018. "Cybersecurity in an Era with Quantum Computers: Will We Be Ready?" *IEEE Security and Privacy* 16 (5): 38–41. https://doi.org/10.1109/MSP.2018.3761723.

NAIAC. 2024. "AI Safety: National AI Advisory Committee." https://ai.gov/wp-content/uploads/2024/06/FINDINGS-RECOMMENDATIONS_AI-Safety.pdf

NIST. 2022. "Post-Quantum Cryptography." https://csrc.nist.gov/Projects/post-quantum-cryptography

NIST. 2024a. "AI Standards." https://www.nist.gov/artificial-intelligence/ai-standards.

NIST. 2024b. "Department of Commerce Announces New Guidance, Tools 270 Days Following President Biden's Executive Order on AI." https://www.nist.gov/news-events/news/2024/07/department-commerce-announces-new-guidance-tools-270-days-following

OASIS Open. 2024. "Coalition for Secure AI." https://www.coalitionforsecureai.org/

Tegmark, M. 2017. *Life 3.0: Being Human in the Age of Artificial Intelligence*. Alfred A. Knopf.

US-NSF. 2023. "NSF Announces 7 New National Artificial Intelligence Research Institutes." https://new.nsf.gov/news/nsf-announces-7-new-national-artificial?sf176473159=1

Vinge, V. 1993. "The Coming Technological Singularity: How to Survive in the Post-Human Era." *NASA. Lewis Research Center, Vision 21: Interdisciplinary Science and Engineering in the Era of Cyberspace.*

W3C. 2022. "Decentralized Identifiers (DIDs) v1.0." https://www.w3.org/TR/did-core/

Test Your Skills

Multiple-Choice Questions

These questions are designed to test understanding of the key concepts, focusing on the societal impacts, challenges, and future implications of AI in autonomous systems.

1. What is the primary focus of the European Union's Artificial Intelligence Act?

    A. To promote AI innovation across all industries

    B. To establish legal standards for AI systems based on risk levels

    C. To enforce unified cybersecurity measures across member states

    D. To deregulate the digital market to foster competition

2. Which country integrates its AI policies with broader strategic goals for technological supremacy?

    A. United States

    B. European Union

    C. China

    D. Japan

3. What is the role of the National Institute of Standards and Technology (NIST) in the United States regarding AI?

    A. Regulating data privacy for AI applications

    B. Developing AI standards and guidelines that influence industry practices

    C. Funding AI startups

    D. Overseeing ethical AI development

4. As discussed in the chapter, which regulatory challenge is associated explicitly with quantum computing?

    A. Intellectual property disputes over algorithms

    B. Its potential to compromise data and national security frameworks

    C. Lack of skilled professionals to manage quantum systems

    D. Quantum technology's impact on environmental sustainability

5. How do international standards like ISO/TC 307 impact blockchain technology?

    A. They restrict the types of blockchain that can be developed.

    B. They enhance blockchain interoperability and security across different sectors.

C. They dictate the price of blockchain transactions globally.

D. They limit the geographical areas where blockchain can be implemented.

6. What is a significant focus of the International Telecommunication Union (ITU) regarding quantum computing?

   A. Reducing the cost of quantum computing implementation

   B. Facilitating discussions on quantum computing's impact on global communications

   C. Developing entertainment applications using quantum computing

   D. Ensuring that quantum computing remains a public sector domain

7. Which approach is characterized by dynamic and modular regulatory structures to accommodate rapid technological changes?

   A. Predictive regulatory frameworks

   B. Static regulatory frameworks

   C. Traditional regulatory frameworks

   D. Historical regulatory frameworks

8. What challenge does the global nature of digital technology pose for individual nations?

   A. Harmonizing international regulations with local demands

   B. Ultimately adopting foreign technologies without adaptation

   C. Ignoring international standards and thus focusing solely on local development

   D. Prioritizing traditional technologies over emerging digital technologies

9. Which of the following best describes the role of regulatory sandboxes?

   A. They offer a competitive environment for technology companies to outperform each other.

   B. They provide a controlled environment for testing new technologies without full regulatory consequences.

   C. They restrict the development of technologies to specific areas.

   D. They serve as educational platforms for the public to learn about new technologies.

10. Which principle aims to ensure that similar technologies are subject to the same regulatory standards?

    A. Technological supremacy

    B. Technological neutrality

    C. Technological singularity

    D. Technological determinism

Exercises

These exercises are designed to deepen your comprehension of the complexities involved in the legal and regulatory environments for AI, blockchain, and quantum computing, as discussed in Chapter 9. By addressing the specifics of regulatory acts and the broader implications of these frameworks, you can better understand how such regulations influence global technology development and governance.

Exercise 9.1: Regulatory Frameworks and Standards

Read Chapter 9 and answer the following questions:

1. Which act in the European Union categorizes AI systems based on risk levels?

   A. General Data Protection Regulation (GDPR)

   B. European Cybersecurity Act

   C. Artificial Intelligence Act

   D. Digital Services Act

2. Describe the role of the International Organization for Standardization (ISO) in the context of blockchain technology.

3. What is the primary concern of quantum computing regulation, as discussed in the chapter?

   A. Cost management

   B. Speed of computation

   C. Data security and national security

   D. Energy consumption

4. Identify the significant difference in AI regulation between the United States and the European Union.

5. Discuss the impact of China's New Generation Artificial Intelligence Development Plan.

Exercise 9.2: Analyzing International and Regulatory Challenges

Read Chapter 9 and answer the following questions:

1. Explain how international standards like those from IEEE influence quantum computing.

2. What challenges do international bodies face in standardizing regulations for emerging technologies?

3. Assess the potential effects of regulatory sandboxes on innovation in blockchain technology.

4. Consider the role of predictive regulatory frameworks in the governance of AI and quantum computing. What are their benefits?

5. How do differing approaches to AI regulation impact global technological development?

10

Societal Impact and the Rise of Autonomous AI Systems

Chapter Objectives

This chapter investigates the societal impact of artificial intelligence agents in advanced technologies, mainly focusing on AI in autonomous systems like vehicles and healthcare systems, as well as the transformative effect of quantum computing on global industries. Through this chapter, you will be able to

- **Understand the Impact of AI Agents on Society**: Grasp the broad societal implications of artificial intelligence, particularly in its application in autonomous systems.

- **Investigate the Role of AI in Military Autonomous Systems**: Analyze the integration of AI in military applications, including unmanned aerial vehicles (UAVs), autonomous ground vehicles, and decision support systems, while evaluating the ethical and strategic implications of AI-powered autonomous weapons.

- **Explore AI in Autonomous Vehicles**: Learn the role of AI in developing and advancing autonomous vehicles, understanding how AI technologies drive this field toward safer and more efficient transportation solutions.

- **Examine AI's Role in Healthcare Systems**: Investigate the application of AI in healthcare systems, including its use in diagnostics, treatment planning, and patient care, appreciating the benefits and challenges of integrating AI into healthcare.

- **Assess the Influence of Quantum Computing on Industries**: Evaluate the transformative impact of quantum computing on various global industries, understanding its potential to reform sectors such as finance, materials science, and cybersecurity.

- **Recognize the Challenges in Implementing Autonomous Systems**: Identify the technical, ethical, and regulatory challenges faced in implementing AI-driven autonomous systems in society.

- **Analyze the Economic and Social Implications**: Examine the economic and social implications of integrating AI and quantum computing into critical sectors, considering aspects such as job displacement, skill requirements, and societal adaptation.

- **Predict Future Trends in Autonomous Technologies**: Anticipate future developments in autonomous systems and quantum computing, contemplating their potential societal impact in the coming years.

- **Reflect on the Need for Responsible Development**: Consider the importance of responsible development and deployment of AI and quantum computing technologies, focusing on their long-term impact on society and the environment.

This chapter aims to provide you with a comprehensive understanding of the societal impact of AI and quantum computing, particularly in the context of autonomous systems and their influence on global industries. It equips you with the knowledge to appreciate and critically assess these transformative technologies.

Investigating the Impact of AI on Society

Artificial intelligence has brought about transformative changes across multiple dimensions of society, redefining the interaction between technology and daily human activities. AI has penetrated healthcare, transportation, finance, and public safety sectors, highlighting its potential to enhance efficiency and decision-making. However, it has also introduced significant ethical and societal challenges.

The core of AI's societal impact lies in its technical advancement, mainly through deep learning and neural networks. These capabilities empower systems to perform complex tasks that historically required human intelligence. For example, in healthcare, AI algorithms interpret complex medical data, enabling early diagnosis of diseases such as cancer through pattern recognition techniques that surpass traditional methods.

The transformation is also evident in transportation, where autonomous vehicles equipped with AI improve road safety and traffic efficiency. These vehicles use sensors and machine learning models to navigate and adapt to real-time road conditions, demonstrating AI's role in advancing public safety and environmental sustainability. However, the shift toward AI-driven transport systems necessitates robust regulatory frameworks to address safety standards and liability in case of failures.

AI's impact extends into ethical domains, particularly concerning equity and privacy. While AI systems are beneficial, they can perpetuate existing biases if not appropriately designed. For instance, facial recognition technologies have faced criticism for higher error rates when identifying individuals from minority groups, raising significant concerns about fairness and discrimination in AI applications.

Moreover, AI-driven surveillance systems highlight the tension between security and privacy. While these systems can enhance security, their ability to monitor and analyze personal data poses risks to individual privacy, necessitating strict governance to prevent abuse.

Economically, AI is both a catalyst for innovation and a disruptor of traditional employment landscapes. Automation, powered by AI, has reshaped labor markets, rendering specific jobs obsolete while creating new opportunities in sectors like AI development and data management. This shift requires policy interventions to manage the transition and support affected workers through reskilling and education.

Addressing AI's societal impacts involves navigating complex regulatory landscapes. Effective governance must balance innovation with accountability, ensuring that AI technologies are safe, reliable, and fair. Doing so involves international collaboration to set standards that prevent a race to the bottom regarding ethical considerations and ensure that AI developments benefit society globally.

Specific technical examples underline the societal impact of AI. In healthcare, AI-powered systems like IBM Watson have demonstrated the ability to process medical information rapidly, assisting in diagnosis and treatment planning. In autonomous vehicles, companies like Tesla and Waymo have integrated advanced AI systems to navigate complex driving environments, reducing human error and improving traffic safety.

These examples highlight the dual-edged nature of AI's societal impact. AI can potentially significantly enhance human capabilities and efficiency, but it also presents profound ethical and regulatory challenges. As AI continues to evolve, its integration into society will necessitate ongoing scrutiny and adaptive governance to harness its benefits while mitigating its risks, ensuring that AI's evolution aligns with societal values and priorities.

Integrating AI into Military Autonomous Systems

The integration of AI into military autonomous systems marks a profound shift in modern warfare, enabling capabilities that were once the domain of science fiction. Among the most significant advancements are unmanned aerial vehicles (UAVs), autonomous ground vehicles, unmanned underwater vehicles (UUVs), AI-powered decision support systems, and autonomous weapons systems. These technologies collectively redefine the operational landscape, offering enhanced precision, efficiency, and strategic depth, while also introducing complex ethical and technical challenges.

UAVs represent a key area where AI has dramatically altered military capabilities. These systems utilize advanced machine learning algorithms for tasks such as real-time object detection, target tracking, and autonomous navigation in contested environments. For instance, the MQ-9 Reaper drone, employed by the United States Air Force, leverages AI to autonomously process sensor data, identify potential threats, and engage targets with precision-guided munitions. The AI-driven autonomy of UAVs allows for operations in GPS-denied environments through the use of inertial navigation systems and computer vision-based terrain recognition. However, this autonomy raises concerns about the accuracy of AI in differentiating between combatants and noncombatants, especially in cluttered urban environments where the risk of collateral damage is high.

Autonomous ground vehicles are increasingly employed in complex combat scenarios, where AI enables these systems to perform reconnaissance, logistical support, and even combat roles without direct human oversight. The Russian Uran-9 unmanned combat ground vehicle exemplifies this technology. It uses AI for autonomous navigation, obstacle avoidance, and threat assessment in real time, enabling it to operate in hazardous conditions that would be too dangerous for human soldiers. The vehicle's AI system integrates data from multiple sensors, including light detection and ranging (LiDAR), infrared, and optical cameras, to create a comprehensive situational awareness map. This capability allows the Uran-9 to autonomously engage targets using its onboard weapons systems, which include anti-tank missiles and a 30mm autocannon. However, operational reports have highlighted reliability issues, particularly in maintaining communication links and AI decision-making under battlefield conditions, underscoring the need for continued refinement of these systems.

In maritime, UUVs are playing a critical role in undersea warfare. AI enhances the autonomy of UUVs, enabling them to conduct extended missions in hostile environments with minimal human intervention. The U.S. Navy's Orca XLUUV, an extra-large UUV, exemplifies this technology. It uses AI for mission planning, navigation, and target identification during operations such as mine countermeasures; anti-submarine warfare; and intelligence, surveillance, and reconnaissance (ISR). The Orca's AI system can autonomously adjust its mission parameters in response to changing environmental conditions and operational objectives, significantly extending the operational reach of naval forces. However, the deployment of autonomous UUVs raises strategic concerns, particularly regarding the potential for accidental engagements or escalation in contested waters, where the rules of engagement are not always clear.

AI-powered military decision support systems have become integral to modern command and control (C2) infrastructures. These systems analyze vast datasets, including satellite imagery, signals intelligence, and battlefield sensor inputs, to provide commanders with actionable intelligence. The Israeli Defence Forces' (IDF) use of the AI system known as *Fire Factory* during operations in Gaza provides a compelling example. This system integrates AI algorithms to process real-time data from multiple sources, generating target lists and prioritizing them for strikes. The AI optimizes target selection based on the likelihood of mission success and predicts the potential for collateral damage, thereby informing decision makers in high-stakes scenarios. However, the reliance on AI in decision support raises critical questions about accountability, particularly when AI recommendations lead to unintended civilian casualties or other strategic errors.

Autonomous weapons systems represent the most contentious aspect of AI in military applications, given their capacity to make lethal decisions without human intervention. The development of these systems, such as the Russian Kalashnikov's ZALA KYB, a loitering munition, has sparked significant debate. This drone can autonomously identify, select, and engage targets based on preprogrammed criteria using AI-driven image recognition and machine learning. The ethical implications are profound, because these systems challenge existing norms in international humanitarian law, particularly regarding the principles of distinction and proportionality. The potential for AI to misinterpret data or act on flawed algorithms could result in unlawful killings, making it imperative that robust oversight and control mechanisms are embedded into these systems.

While AI-driven autonomous systems offer new capabilities in military operations, they also introduce significant challenges that must be carefully managed. The technical reliability of these systems, their ethical implications, and the strategic risks associated with their deployment require comprehensive regulatory frameworks and ongoing international dialogue. As these technologies evolve, it is crucial that their development is guided by principles that ensure they enhance security without compromising the ethical standards that govern the conduct of war. The future of military AI lies not just in advancing technology but in ensuring that its application aligns with the values of human dignity and international law.

Utilizing AI in Autonomous Vehicles

Integrating AI in autonomous vehicles has created a significant intersection of technology and mobility, leading to significant advancements in AI applications. Autonomous vehicles, powered by sophisticated AI systems, represent an essential evolution in transportation, offering potential improvements in safety, efficiency, and urban congestion.

AI is the brain behind autonomous vehicles, handling complex tasks such as sensing, decision-making, and navigation. These vehicles rely on AI technologies, including computer vision, sensor fusion, and deep learning, to interpret and react to the environment. For instance, AI algorithms process inputs from cameras and LiDAR to create a dynamic map of the vehicle's surroundings, identifying obstacles, traffic signals, and road signs, enabling these vehicles to navigate safely through diverse conditions.

Deep learning models, particularly convolutional neural networks (Krizhevsky, Sutskever, and Hinton 2012, 2017), are trained on vast datasets of road scenarios to recognize patterns and predict outcomes. This capability allows vehicles to make informed decisions swiftly. This real-time processing and response capacity is critical in scenarios where split-second decisions can prevent accidents and save lives.

Developing advanced driver-assistance systems (ADAS) has been a significant milestone in AI for autonomous vehicles. These systems provide adaptive cruise control, lane-keeping assistance, and automated braking. Although not fully autonomous, these features showcase AI's capabilities to enhance driver safety and comfort.

Companies like Waymo, Tesla, and Uber have pioneered the integration of AI in fully autonomous vehicles, conducting extensive tests and trials to refine AI algorithms and improve safety protocols. Waymo has deployed autonomous taxis in specific areas, further gathering data to enhance AI performance under varied traffic conditions.

Despite the progress, there are significant challenges in fully integrating AI into autonomous vehicles. One of the primary concerns is the reliability of AI systems in unpredictable environments. AI must handle unusual or rare events on the roads that are not well represented in training datasets, known as *edge cases*. For example, handling scenarios like abrupt behavior from pedestrians or unexpected weather conditions remains a significant challenge for AI systems.

Moreover, the dependency on high-quality data for training AI models poses another challenge. Biases in data can lead to flawed decision-making by autonomous vehicles, potentially causing unsafe situations. Ensuring the diversity and representativeness of training data is crucial to developing AI systems that can operate safely and effectively across all geographic and demographic settings.

The ethical implications of AI in autonomous vehicles are profound. Decisions on how AI should act in dilemmas, such as choosing between the lesser of two harms during an unavoidable accident, pose significant ethical challenges. These "moral algorithms" necessitate a societal consensus on the values and ethics embedded within AI systems, reflecting broader ethical standards and priorities.

Moreover, societal adaptation will be required as autonomous vehicles become more prevalent. Issues such as liability in the event of an accident, changes in insurance models, and the impact on employment in driving-related professions must be addressed. The transition to autonomous transportation systems also raises questions about urban planning and the accessibility of such technologies to all segments of society, ensuring equity in the benefits provided by AI.

Looking forward, the integration of AI in autonomous vehicles is set to transform the transportation landscape dramatically. With ongoing advancements in AI and machine learning, along with improvements in sensor technology and computational hardware, the potential for fully autonomous vehicles to become mainstream is increasing. This shift promises to enhance road safety and efficiency and reshape urban environments and mobility patterns.

As autonomous vehicles continue to evolve, the role of AI will expand, requiring continuous research, regulatory oversight, and ethical consideration to ensure that these technological advancements contribute positively to societal well-being and safety. This evolving landscape presents a dynamic frontier for AI applications, where the interplay of technology, ethics, and societal impact continues to unfold, driving the future of transportation.

Applying AI in Healthcare Systems

AI is transforming healthcare systems by significantly enhancing diagnostic accuracy and reforming patient care and treatment protocols (Bartoletti 2019). Integrating AI into healthcare improves operational efficiency and enables substantial advancements in patient care through precise diagnostics, personalized treatment strategies, and continuous monitoring.

One of AI's most significant contributions to healthcare is in diagnostics, where machine learning models analyze vast amounts of medical data to identify patterns that may be imperceptible to human observers. For instance, AI systems in radiology employ advanced image recognition techniques to detect abnormalities in X-rays, MRIs, and CT scans with greater accuracy and speed than human radiologists. A notable example is the use of AI algorithms by Google's DeepMind, which has developed a system capable of diagnosing over 50 different eye conditions from retinal scans, matching the performance of world-leading ophthalmologists. Similarly, AI systems have been employed to detect early-stage lung cancer from CT scans, improving outcomes through earlier interventions.

In pathology, AI algorithms have automated the analysis of tissue samples, dramatically increasing the speed and accuracy of cancer diagnostics. For example, PathAI's machine learning algorithms analyze histopathological images to identify and classify cellular patterns associated with various cancers. In a recent study, PathAI's system outperformed human pathologists in detecting breast cancer metastases in lymph nodes, highlighting the potential of AI to reduce diagnostic errors in clinical settings.

AI is also applied in personalized treatment planning by integrating and analyzing patient medical records, research databases, and clinical studies. By considering individual patient characteristics and predicting treatment responses based on historical data, AI systems can suggest personalized treatment plans. This approach is particularly noteworthy in oncology, where AI-driven tools analyze genetic information to recommend specific drug treatments most likely to be effective for individual cancer patients. For example, IBM Watson for Oncology has been used to match cancer patients with the most effective chemotherapy regimens based on their genetic profiles, showing promise in personalizing cancer treatment.

Beyond treatment recommendations, AI has a growing impact on drug discovery. AI algorithms can process vast datasets to identify potential drug candidates, predict their efficacy, and optimize clinical trial designs. Insilico Medicine, for instance, used AI to identify a new drug candidate for fibrosis in just 46 days, a process that typically takes several years. AI-driven drug discovery platforms can also predict potential side effects, thus enhancing the safety and efficacy of new treatments.

In clinical settings, AI-powered robots assist in minimally invasive surgeries, enhancing precision and reducing recovery times. The da Vinci Surgical System, for example, allows surgeons to perform complex procedures with greater control and precision than traditional methods. These AI-driven robotic systems can make micro-adjustments during surgery, reducing the likelihood of human error and improving patient outcomes.

AI's role extends to patient management, particularly through AI-powered mobile health applications and wearable devices that monitor chronic diseases like diabetes and heart disease. These tools track patient health metrics in real time, providing continuous care and personalized health recommendations. For instance, the AI-driven Livongo platform uses patient data to offer personalized diabetes management advice, alerting users to potential health issues before they become critical. AI systems are also employed in hospitals to continuously monitor patient vital signs and alert healthcare staff to any significant changes, enabling timely interventions. For example, the use of AI in monitoring sepsis in ICU patients has led to earlier detection and treatment, significantly reducing mortality rates.

AI is also beginning to play a role in mental health care. AI-powered chatbots, such as Woebot and Wysa, provide initial mental health support and triage by interacting with patients, assessing their mental state, and offering coping strategies. These AI systems can help bridge the gap in mental health care, providing support to those who might otherwise go untreated due to resource constraints.

However, integrating AI into healthcare systems presents several challenges (Panch, Mattie, and Celi 2019). Data privacy is a significant concern, because AI systems require access to sensitive personal health information. Ensuring the security of this data and maintaining patient confidentiality is essential, necessitating stringent data protection measures. Additionally, the potential bias in AI algorithms, often stemming from insufficiently diverse training datasets, can lead to disparities in the quality of care delivered to different demographic groups. This risk underscores the importance of developing AI systems that are both fair and transparent.

Ethical considerations also play a critical role in the adoption of AI in healthcare. Decisions made by AI, such as treatment recommendations, must be transparent and explainable to ensure trust and accountability, particularly in life-or-death scenarios. While AI can reduce human error, the possibility of AI systems making errors introduces ethical dilemmas regarding accountability and the role of human oversight in automated healthcare processes.

As AI systems become more prevalent in healthcare, the role of healthcare professionals is evolving. While AI can augment clinical decision-making and improve efficiency, it is crucial to maintain the human element in patient care. Balancing technological advancement with compassionate care is essential to fully realize the benefits of AI without compromising the patient-provider relationship.

AI in healthcare is poised to continue its upward trajectory, with emerging technologies like AI-driven genomics, robot-assisted surgery, and AI-optimized clinical trials promising to modernize the field further. As AI technologies evolve, so too must the frameworks that govern their use, ensuring that AI-driven healthcare achieves its potential to improve patient outcomes and operational efficiencies while adhering to the highest ethical standards.

Assessing the Influence of Quantum Computing on Industries

In the financial sector, quantum computing is set to change how institutions manage risk, optimize portfolios, and detect fraud. Quantum algorithms, such as Shor's algorithm (Shor 1994), provide the theoretical basis for factorizing large integers efficiently, which is a critical aspect of cryptography. While this poses potential risks to current encryption methods, it also offers new pathways for developing quantum-resistant cryptographic systems. Moreover, quantum computing facilitates Monte Carlo simulations, a stochastic technique used to understand the impact of risk and uncertainty in prediction and forecasting models. By exponentially speeding up these simulations, financial analysts can achieve near-real-time risk assessment, enhancing decision-making processes.

The ability of quantum computers to simulate molecules and chemical reactions with high accuracy promises to accelerate the discovery of new materials and drugs. For instance, quantum simulations can model complex molecules at the atomic level, a task beyond the reach of classical computers due to the exponential scaling of required computational resources. This capability could lead to breakthroughs in developing high-performance batteries, more effective pharmaceuticals, and new materials with custom-made properties for specific applications.

In cybersecurity, quantum computers can break many cryptographic algorithms that secure our digital communications. However, this also drives the development of post-quantum cryptography, aiming to create security systems resistant to quantum attacks. Furthermore, quantum key distribution (QKD) presents a method for secure communication that uses the principles of quantum mechanics to ensure the security of encryption keys. This technology is already deployed in high-security applications, indicating the practical viability of quantum-enhanced security measures.

Beyond these areas, quantum computing is expected to influence numerous other sectors by enabling new types of computational problems to be tackled. In logistics, for example, quantum algorithms can optimize complex supply chains and distribution routes more efficiently than classical algorithms. The energy sector could benefit from improved models of molecular interactions, leading to better catalysts for chemical reactions that enhance energy efficiency.

Despite its potential, the widespread adoption of quantum computing faces significant hurdles. Quantum computers require extremely low-temperature environments, making them expensive and technically challenging to maintain. Additionally, the error rates in quantum calculations are currently high, necessitating further advancements in quantum error correction methods before these systems can be reliably used for practical applications.

Developing a skilled workforce to research, build, and maintain quantum computing systems is also essential. This requires educational institutions and industries to invest in quantum computing programs and partnerships to train the next generation of quantum scientists and engineers.

Recognizing the Challenges of Implementing AI Autonomous Systems

The implementation of AI agents within autonomous systems introduces a range of cybersecurity challenges that must be rigorously addressed, particularly as these systems are increasingly integrated into critical infrastructure sectors such as healthcare, transportation, and finance. The sophistication of modern cyber threats, combined with the complexity of AI technologies, creates a landscape where vulnerabilities can be exploited in novel and potentially devastating ways.

One of the most significant threats to AI systems is the risk of adversarial attacks where malicious actors manipulate input data to deceive AI models (Sun, Tan, and Zhou 2018; Qiu et al. 2019; Wallace et al. 2019; Ren et al. 2020; Liang et al. 2022). These attacks can be particularly insidious in high-stakes environments. For example, in autonomous vehicles, attackers can employ techniques such as pixel-level perturbation or physical alteration of road signs to cause the AI's vision systems to misinterpret objects, such as classifying a stop sign as a yield sign. This kind of attack, known as an *adversarial example*, leverages the AI model's sensitivity to small, carefully crafted perturbations, exploiting the nonlinear nature of deep neural networks. Defending against such attacks requires developing more robust AI models, incorporating adversarial training where models are exposed to manipulated inputs during training to increase their resilience.

Data poisoning represents another critical cybersecurity threat to AI agents. In data poisoning attacks, adversaries deliberately inject false or misleading data into the training dataset, corrupting the model's learning process. This can have dire consequences in sectors like healthcare, where AI systems are used to diagnose diseases or recommend treatments. For instance, an attacker could insert fraudulent medical records into a training dataset, causing the AI to misdiagnose conditions or suggest inappropriate treatments. A well-documented case of data poisoning involved manipulating an AI model used for spam detection by gradually feeding it poisoned data, which eventually caused the system to classify legitimate emails as spam. To mitigate such risks, it is essential to implement robust data validation protocols and employ techniques like differential privacy, which can help preserve the integrity of datasets even in the presence of malicious data.

Model inversion and data leakage attacks pose further challenges, particularly concerning privacy and the protection of sensitive information (Fredrikson, Jha, and Ristenpart 2015). In a model inversion attack, an adversary can infer private data by exploiting the outputs of an AI model. For example, by repeatedly querying a machine learning model trained on medical records, an attacker could reconstruct sensitive details about patients' health conditions. This threat is exacerbated by the deployment of AI models in cloud environments, where the attack surface is expanded. Techniques such as *homomorphic encryption* and *secure multi-party computation* are critical in mitigating these risks, as they allow for the computation of encrypted data without exposing the underlying sensitive information.

Cyber-physical systems (CPS) that incorporate AI agents, such as autonomous vehicles, smart grids, and medical devices, are particularly vulnerable to cyber attacks due to their real-time interaction with the physical world. For instance, in the case of autonomous vehicles, an attack on the vehicle's control systems through techniques like *CAN bus injection* could allow an adversary to take control of critical functions, such as braking or steering, leading to potentially catastrophic outcomes. Similarly, in smart grids, AI agents that manage energy distribution can be targeted through *denial-of-service (DoS) attacks*, disrupting the balance of supply and demand and causing widespread blackouts. To defend against such threats, a multi-layered security approach is necessary, combining real-time monitoring, redundancy in control systems, and robust fail-safe mechanisms.

The opacity of AI algorithms, particularly those based on deep learning, presents additional cyber-security challenges. The so-called black box nature of these models makes it difficult to predict how they will respond to certain inputs, which can be exploited by attackers. For example, by using *gradient-based attacks*, adversaries can iteratively probe the AI model to discover vulnerabilities, which can then be exploited to cause the system to behave erratically. Enhancing the transparency of AI models through *explainable AI (XAI)* techniques is crucial for identifying and mitigating these vulnerabilities. Moreover, adopting formal verification methods, which involve mathematically proving that a system adheres to specific security properties, can help ensure that AI models behave as intended under various conditions.

The security of the AI supply chain is another area of concern. The AI supply chain encompasses everything from data sources and model development to the software libraries and hardware used in deployment. Each component of this chain can be targeted by attackers to introduce vulnerabilities. For instance, compromised open-source libraries or software dependencies could be used to inject backdoors into AI models. A notable example is the *SolarWinds attack*, where a supply chain compromise allowed attackers to insert malicious code into widely used software, affecting numerous organizations worldwide. Ensuring the security of the AI supply chain requires rigorous vetting of all components, the adoption of secure development practices, and continuous monitoring for signs of tampering.

The advent of quantum computing introduces future challenges to the cybersecurity of AI systems. Quantum computers have the potential to break the cryptographic algorithms that currently protect AI models and data. For instance, *Shor's algorithm*, a quantum algorithm, could be used to factor large numbers efficiently, undermining the RSA encryption scheme that underpins much of today's digital security. Preparing for this eventuality involves developing and adopting quantum-resistant cryptographic algorithms, ensuring that AI systems remain secure as quantum computing technology advances.

AI agents that employ continuous learning mechanisms are vulnerable to dynamic threats that evolve over time. For example, an attacker could conduct a *concept drift attack* by subtly altering the input data over time, leading the AI agent to gradually adopt harmful or biased behaviors. Such attacks can be particularly challenging to detect because they exploit the ongoing learning process of the AI system. Defending against these threats requires the implementation of robust monitoring systems that can detect anomalous shifts in AI behavior, coupled with regular retraining of AI models on validated and secure datasets to ensure their integrity and reliability.

Analyzing the Economic and Social Implications of AI and Quantum Computing

Economically, AI and quantum computing drive innovation and create new markets while enhancing productivity across multiple sectors. They automate complex tasks, from data analysis to manufacturing processes, significantly reducing costs and improving efficiency. For example, AI-driven automation in manufacturing speeds up production, enhances precision, and reduces waste, resulting in a more sustainable manufacturing process. However, the rapid deployment of these technologies poses challenges to traditional employment structures. Many roles, particularly those involving routine or repetitive tasks, are at risk of displacement. This shift necessitates significant investments in workforce development and reskilling initiatives to ensure employees can transition to new roles requiring more complex and technology-oriented skills. Furthermore, the economic benefits of AI and quantum computing are distributed unevenly across all geographic regions or sectors, potentially widening the gap between high-tech and lower-tech areas or industries. This disparity can lead to economic imbalances, exacerbating regional inequalities and social tensions.

Socially, the deployment of advanced technologies like AI and quantum computing influences societal norms and interactions. For instance, AI technologies in social media algorithms can shape public opinions and cultural trends by controlling the flow of information and influencing user interactions. This power must be wielded responsibly, with an awareness of the potential for these technologies to propagate misinformation or biased content. Additionally, the increased use of AI in public surveillance and security raises significant privacy concerns. While enhanced surveillance can improve public safety, it also poses risks to individual privacy rights, requiring a careful balance between security and civil liberties.

Furthermore, the social integration of AI and quantum computing also impacts education and healthcare. These technologies have the potential to democratize access to high-quality resources. AI-driven educational tools can provide personalized learning experiences that adapt to students' individual needs, potentially overcoming traditional barriers to education. In healthcare, AI can facilitate the rapid analysis of patient data, helping to diagnose diseases more quickly and accurately, thereby improving patient outcomes.

To address the economic challenges posed by AI and quantum computing, governments and industries need to develop strategies focusing on economic diversification and innovation. Policies that encourage the development of new industries and support technological entrepreneurship can help mitigate the risks of job displacement while fostering economic growth. Socially, ensuring that the benefits of AI and quantum computing are accessible to all segments of society is crucial. This effort includes investing in educational programs that prepare future generations to thrive in a technologically advanced world and implementing policies that protect against the misuse of AI in areas like surveillance. Furthermore, public engagement and transparent governance are essential in shaping the development and implementation of these technologies. By involving diverse community stakeholders in decision-making processes, policymakers can better understand the societal impacts of technological advancements and create more inclusive and effective strategies.

Predicting Future Trends in Autonomous Technologies

Autonomous technologies are evolving rapidly, driven by advancements in AI and quantum computing. These technologies have the potential to transform many aspects of modern society. Industries and policymakers need to understand autonomous technologies' opportunities and challenges.

In the transportation sector, autonomous vehicles will significantly improve vehicular systems by enhancing vehicle-to-vehicle and vehicle-to-infrastructure communication, resulting in better traffic flow and fewer accidents. However, this requires the development of more advanced AI algorithms to navigate complex traffic environments.

The convergence of electric vehicle (EV) technology with autonomous systems will drive significant changes in automotive industry standards and consumer preferences, promoting sustainable urban mobility solutions and reducing carbon emissions.

Quantum computing will reform fields that rely heavily on solving complex computational problems. It will significantly impact drug discovery and materials science, enabling the simulation of molecular interactions at an unprecedented scale. Quantum-resistant encryption will also protect sensitive information against emerging quantum threats.

Integrating AI with the Internet of Things will transform connected devices' management and operational capabilities. AI's role in analyzing data generated by IoT devices will improve the functionality of smart homes, smart cities, and industrial IoT applications, yielding significant improvements in energy efficiency, public safety, and operational productivity.

However, the widespread use of autonomous technologies raises ethical and societal challenges. These challenges include governing AI decision-making, data privacy and security in interconnected environments, and the social implications of technological disruption.

Reflecting on the Need for Responsible Development

The advancement and integration of AI and quantum computing technologies require a thoughtful examination of their responsible development and deployment. As these technologies become increasingly ingrained in various societal and industrial frameworks, their potential to significantly impact both positively and negatively becomes apparent. This impact necessitates a robust approach to ensuring their development is guided by ethical principles and a deep consideration of long-term societal impacts.

Ethical frameworks and sustainability are crucial in developing AI and quantum computing technologies. They must adhere to established ethical frameworks that prioritize sustainability and the welfare of all society segments, guiding developers and policymakers in creating technologies that are innovative but also socially responsible. For instance, ethical AI frameworks in AI development focus on ensuring that AI systems are fair, transparent, and accountable. Developers must consider the implications of AI decisions and design systems that mitigate bias, ensuring that AI acts in the interests of all users.

Quantum computing introduces complexities, particularly in areas like cryptography, where the potential to disrupt security protocols exists. Therefore, the development of quantum technologies must be balanced with efforts to advance quantum-resistant cryptographic methods to protect data integrity and privacy. Additionally, the environmental impact of operating powerful quantum computers, which require significant energy resources, must be considered, pushing for innovations in energy-efficient quantum computing technologies.

The impact of AI and quantum computing on employment and social structures is profound, potentially leading to significant job displacement. Addressing this requires policies that support workforce transition through education and training programs, ensuring that individuals have the skills necessary to thrive in a new technological landscape.

Moreover, the benefits of AI and quantum computing should be accessible to all parts of society. This accessibility includes ensuring that underrepresented communities have equal opportunities to benefit from technological advancements, such as improved healthcare diagnostics, enhanced educational tools, and greater financial inclusion. Inclusivity in technology development also involves engaging diverse groups in the design and implementation phases, which helps create more comprehensive and universally beneficial technologies.

Responsible development also depends on effective regulatory oversight and international collaboration. Because AI and quantum computing do not adhere to traditional national boundaries, international guidelines and agreements are essential to manage their development and application globally. This collaboration can help standardize ethical norms and regulatory frameworks, ensuring a cohesive approach to addressing the challenges posed by these technologies.

For responsible development to be effective, long-term strategic planning is essential. This involves anticipating the technological capabilities of AI and quantum computing and understanding their potential societal impacts over decades. Strategic planning should include scenario planning exercises that explore various futures and the role of technology in shaping those futures. Such planning allows policymakers, businesses, and civic leaders to prepare for changes and design interventions that steer technology development in beneficial directions.

Responsible development ensures that AI and quantum computing technologies contribute positively to societal advancement while minimizing potential harms. Through ethical frameworks, inclusivity, regulatory oversight, and strategic planning, the promise of these technologies can be realized in a manner that respects and enhances human dignity and societal welfare. This approach ensures that as we advance technologically, we also progress in creating a fair and sustainable world for future generations.

Understanding the Evolution of Technologies

The evolutionary journey of AI, blockchain, and quantum computing showcases remarkable advancements in technology and innovation. Each field has developed independently, overcoming significant challenges and achieving remarkable milestones. As they continue to evolve, their convergence promises to unlock new possibilities and drive transformative change across various domains. This section consolidates the significant advancements discussed throughout the book, providing an integrated understanding of these fields.

The early days of AI were dominated by rule-based systems, where predefined rules and logic were used to perform specific tasks. The advent of machine learning marked a significant turning point, enabling computers to learn from data and make predictions without explicit programming. The rise of deep understanding, characterized by neural networks with multiple layers, modernized AI by significantly enhancing its ability to process and analyze large datasets.

Blockchain technology emerged with the introduction of Bitcoin in 2008, providing a decentralized and secure framework for digital transactions. The evolution of blockchain has been marked by the development of new platforms and frameworks, such as Ethereum and Hyperledger, which have expanded their capabilities beyond cryptocurrencies. Ethereum introduced smart contracts, enabling the automation of transactions and agreements, paving the way for decentralized applications that operate autonomously without intermediaries.

The theoretical foundations of quantum computing were laid in the early 20th century, but practical implementations began to emerge only in the late 20th and early 21st centuries. The development of qubits, quantum entanglement, and quantum algorithms has demonstrated the transformative potential of quantum computing, enabling parallel computations and vastly increasing computational efficiency.

Addressing Future Challenges in AI, Blockchain, and Quantum Computing

One of the primary challenges in AI is scalability. As AI systems become more complex and data-intensive, ensuring their scalability and efficiency becomes increasingly tricky. Developing algorithms that can handle large-scale data and perform real-time processing is crucial for the widespread adoption of AI technologies.

Another significant challenge is the interpretability and transparency of AI models. Many deep learning models, while highly effective, are often considered "black boxes" due to their lack of transparency. Ensuring that AI systems are interpretable and transparent is critical for building trust and ensuring accountability. This involves developing techniques for explaining AI decisions and making the underlying processes more understandable to users and stakeholders.

Blockchain technology faces several technical challenges that must be addressed to achieve broader adoption. One of the primary challenges is scalability. Many blockchain platforms, such as Bitcoin and Ethereum, need help with scalability due to the time and computational resources required for transaction processing and consensus mechanisms. It is essential to develop solutions that can enhance the scalability of blockchain networks for their widespread use in various applications.

Interoperability between different blockchain platforms is another significant challenge. The lack of standardized protocols and frameworks makes it difficult for different blockchain systems to communicate and operate seamlessly. Developing interoperable standards and frameworks is crucial for enabling cross-chain transactions and enhancing the overall functionality of blockchain technology.

Exploring Future Opportunities in AI, Blockchain, and Quantum Computing

One of the most significant opportunities is in healthcare. AI has the potential to transform healthcare by enabling personalized medicine, improving diagnostics, and optimizing treatment plans. AI algorithms can analyze large volumes of medical data to identify patterns and make predictions, providing valuable insights for clinicians and researchers.

Another significant opportunity for AI is in autonomous systems. AI-driven autonomous vehicles have the potential to transform transportation, reducing accidents, improving efficiency, and decreasing congestion. Autonomous drones and robots can enhance logistics and supply chain management, enabling more efficient and cost-effective operations.

Blockchain technology offers numerous opportunities for enhancing transparency, security, and efficiency across various sectors. One significant opportunity is in finance, where blockchain's decentralized and transparent framework can improve the security and efficiency of financial transactions, reducing fraud and increasing trust. Smart contracts can automate complex financial agreements, reducing the need for intermediaries and increasing efficiency. Another significant opportunity for blockchain is in supply chain management, where its transparent and immutable ledger can enhance the traceability and accountability of goods, reducing fraud and improving efficiency.

Quantum computing presents numerous opportunities for solving complex problems beyond the reach of classical computers. One significant opportunity is in the field of cryptography, where quantum computing's ability to factor large numbers and perform complex calculations at unprecedented speeds can modernize encryption methods, enhancing data security and privacy. Another significant opportunity for quantum computing is in material science. Quantum computers can simulate molecular interactions at a granular level, enabling the discovery of new materials and drugs, thereby revolutionizing industries such as pharmaceuticals, energy, and manufacturing, driving innovation and enhancing efficiency.

Examining Ethical, Legal, and Societal Implications of Emerging Technologies

One of the primary ethical concerns in AI is the potential for bias and discrimination in algorithms. AI systems are only as good as the data they are trained on, and if this data contains biases, the AI system may perpetuate and even exacerbate these biases. Ensuring fairness and reducing bias in AI algorithms is crucial to prevent discrimination and promote equity.

Another significant ethical concern in AI is transparency and accountability. Many AI systems, particularly those based on deep learning, operate as "black boxes" with little transparency into how decisions are made. Ensuring that AI systems are interpretable and transparent is critical for building trust and ensuring accountability. This effort involves developing techniques for explaining AI decisions and making the underlying processes more understandable to users and stakeholders.

With its transparent and immutable ledger, blockchain technology offers significant advantages in terms of security and trust. However, this transparency also raises privacy concerns. Ensuring that sensitive information is protected while maintaining transparency is a delicate balance that needs to be addressed. Developing privacy-preserving techniques and frameworks is crucial for safeguarding data privacy in blockchain applications.

The decentralized nature of blockchain technology means that there is often no single entity responsible for managing and regulating the network. Ensuring that blockchain networks are governed relatively and transparently is critical for building trust and ensuring the responsible use of the technology.

With its immense computational power, quantum computing has the potential to reform various fields; however, this power also raises significant societal implications that must be considered. One of the primary concerns is the potential impact on data security. Quantum computing's ability to break current encryption methods poses a significant threat to data privacy and security. Developing quantum-resistant cryptographic algorithms is essential for protecting sensitive information in a post-quantum world.

Another societal implication of quantum computing is the potential impact on employment and economic inequality. Deploying quantum computing technologies may lead to job displacement in specific sectors, exacerbating economic disparities. Ensuring that the benefits of quantum computing are distributed equitably and that workers are provided with the necessary skills and training to adapt to new technologies is crucial for promoting economic inclusion and equity.

The deployment of AI, blockchain, and quantum computing technologies raises several societal and ethical considerations that must be addressed to ensure their responsible and equitable use. To prevent perpetuating existing inequalities, it is crucial to ensure fairness and reduce bias in AI algorithms. Blockchain's transparency must be balanced with privacy concerns, particularly in sensitive areas such as healthcare and finance. Quantum computing's potential to break current encryption methods necessitates the development of quantum-resistant cryptographic algorithms to protect data privacy.

Addressing the potential societal impacts of these technologies, such as job displacement and economic inequality, is critical for ensuring their equitable and sustainable deployment.

Preparing for an AI-Integrated Future

Preparing for an AI-integrated future requires a commitment to continuous learning and adaptability. The fast pace of technological advancement means that individuals, organizations, and societies need to remain agile and open to new knowledge and skills. Through formal education, professional development, and self-directed study, lifelong learning will be essential to keep up with the evolving technological landscape. Developing technical proficiency in AI, blockchain, and quantum computing is crucial to thrive in an AI-integrated future. Understanding these technologies' foundational principles, algorithms, and applications will enable individuals to leverage their capabilities effectively. This includes proficiency in machine learning, deep learning, and natural language processing for AI. Blockchain involves understanding distributed ledger technologies, smart contracts, and decentralized applications. Quantum computing requires knowledge of quantum mechanics, qubits, and quantum algorithms. The convergence of AI, blockchain, and quantum computing emphasizes the importance of interdisciplinary collaboration. These technologies do not exist in isolation; they interact and complement each other, creating synergies that drive innovation. Fostering collaboration across different fields, such as computer science, engineering, mathematics, and ethics, will be essential in harnessing the full potential of these technologies. Experts from diverse disciplines can address complex challenges and develop integrated solutions by working together.

Enhancing digital literacy across all segments of society is another critical aspect of preparing for an AI-integrated future. As these advanced technologies become more pervasive, understanding their fundamental principles and implications will be essential for informed decision-making and participation in the digital economy. Educational institutions, governments, and private organizations must work together to promote digital literacy, ensuring individuals have the knowledge and skills to navigate an increasingly digital world.

To ensure their responsible integration, it is crucial to anticipate and address the broader societal impacts of AI, blockchain, and quantum computing. These technologies can reshape various aspects of society, including healthcare, education, finance, and governance. Understanding their potential positive and negative impacts will be critical in developing policies and strategies that promote societal well-being and prevent unintended consequences.

Innovation and entrepreneurship will play a key role in driving the integration of AI, blockchain, and quantum computing. Encouraging a culture of innovation involves creating an environment that supports creativity, experimentation, and risk-taking. This includes providing access to funding, resources, and mentorship for startups and entrepreneurs, as well as fostering collaboration between academia, industry, and government. By embracing innovation and entrepreneurship, we can accelerate the development and deployment of advanced technologies, driving economic growth and societal progress.

Harnessing the potential of AI, blockchain, and quantum computing for social good is a critical aspect of preparing for an AI-integrated future. These technologies can address the world's most pressing challenges, including climate change, poverty, healthcare, and education. Using their capabilities, we can develop solutions promoting sustainability, equity, and social justice. This involves supporting initiatives that use advanced technologies for humanitarian purposes, promoting corporate social responsibility, and encouraging public-private partnerships that address global challenges.

Engaging in policy and advocacy efforts is crucial for shaping the future trajectory of AI, blockchain, and quantum computing. This involves participating in discussions and debates on these technologies' ethical, legal, and societal implications; advocating for responsible and inclusive policies; and contributing to developing regulatory frameworks that promote innovation while protecting public interests. By actively engaging in policy and advocacy, individuals and organizations can help ensure that principles of fairness, transparency, and accountability guide the integration of advanced technologies.

Engaging with Emerging Technologies

Engaging with emerging technologies requires a commitment to continuous education and professional development. Staying informed about the latest advancements, trends, and best practices in AI, blockchain, and quantum computing is essential for remaining relevant and competitive in an increasingly digital world. Doing so involves participating in workshops, conferences, online courses, and professional certifications that provide up-to-date knowledge and skills. Educational institutions, industry associations, and technology companies are critical in providing these learning opportunities.

The convergence of AI, blockchain, and quantum computing emphasizes the significance of interdisciplinary collaboration. These technologies intersect and complement each other, leading to synergies that drive innovation. Collaborating across disciplines such as computer science, engineering, ethics, law, and business is essential for developing integrated solutions that harness the full potential of these technologies. Furthermore, collaboration across sectors, including academia, industry, government, and civil society, is crucial for addressing complex challenges and ensuring the responsible deployment of these technologies.

Proactive engagement with emerging technologies involves actively participating in research and development (R&D) efforts. This includes contributing to advancing knowledge and creating new technologies through academic research, industrial innovation, and public-private partnerships. By engaging in R&D, individuals and organizations can help drive technological progress, address critical challenges, and develop solutions that have a meaningful impact on society. Support for R&D initiatives in terms of funding and resources is essential for fostering innovation and technological advancement.

As we integrate AI, blockchain, and quantum computing into various aspects of society, advocating for ethical and responsible innovation becomes crucial. This involves promoting, developing, and deploying technologies that align with moral principles, such as fairness, transparency, accountability, and respect for privacy. Engaging in policy discussions, contributing to the development of ethical guidelines, and advocating for regulatory frameworks that ensure the responsible use of these technologies are essential actions for shaping a responsible technological future.

Engaging with emerging technologies proactively involves participating in public discourse and policy development. This effort includes engaging in discussions and debates on the ethical, legal, and societal implications of AI, blockchain, and quantum computing to raise awareness and inform public opinion. Contributing to policy development efforts ensures that the perspectives of informed individuals are considered in the decision-making process, shaping the future trajectory of these technologies in ways that promote public interest and societal well-being.

Another critical aspect of proactive engagement is supporting open innovation and open-source initiatives. This support involves collaborating with external partners, sharing knowledge, and leveraging collective expertise to drive technological progress. Open-source initiatives promote transparency, accessibility, and collaboration by making software, data, and research freely available to the public. Individuals and organizations can contribute to a collaborative and inclusive innovation ecosystem that accelerates AI, blockchain, and quantum computing development and application by supporting these initiatives.

Additionally, building and participating in communities of practice are essential for proactive engagement with emerging technologies. These communities provide opportunities for networking, knowledge sharing, and collaboration among individuals with shared interests and expertise. Community building involves participating in industry groups, professional associations, online forums, and local meetups focused on AI, blockchain, and quantum computing. By connecting with others in the field, individuals can stay informed about the latest developments, gain insights from diverse perspectives, and collaborate on projects that advance the state of the art.

Promoting diversity and inclusion in the development and application of AI, blockchain, and quantum computing is crucial to ensure that these technologies benefit all segments of society. Doing so involves creating opportunities for underrepresented groups to participate in and contribute to technological innovation. Efforts to promote diversity and inclusion include supporting educational initiatives, mentorship programs, and diversity hiring practices to ensure a wide range of perspectives and experiences are represented in the technology sector. By fostering a diverse and inclusive environment, we can drive innovation that is more equitable and reflective of society's needs.

Proactive engagement with emerging technologies is essential for shaping a responsible and inclusive technological future. By fostering a culture of curiosity and innovation, participating in education and professional development, collaborating across disciplines and sectors, engaging in research and development, advocating for ethical and responsible innovation, participating in public discourse and policy development, supporting open innovation and open-source initiatives, engaging in community building and networking, and promoting diversity and inclusion, individuals and organizations can actively contribute to the ongoing development and application of AI, blockchain, and quantum computing.

Providing a Forward-Looking Perspective

As AI systems become more sophisticated, they will increasingly enhance human capabilities and drive advancements in various fields. One significant development is the emergence of artificial general intelligence, where AI systems can understand, learn, and apply knowledge across a wide range of tasks, similar to human intelligence. Achieving AGI will require significant advancements in machine learning, neural networks, and cognitive architectures.

Another key trend is the integration of AI with the Internet of Things, leading to the proliferation of intelligent environments. AI-driven IoT systems will enable more efficient and adaptive resource management, from smart homes and cities to industrial automation and healthcare. These developments will enhance the quality of life, improve sustainability, and drive economic growth.

Blockchain technology will play an increasingly central role in the digital economy. As scalability and interoperability challenges are addressed, blockchain will become a foundational technology for secure and transparent digital transactions. One significant future development is the rise of decentralized finance (DeFi), where financial services are provided through decentralized platforms without intermediaries. DeFi has the potential to democratize access to financial services, reduce costs, and increase transparency.

Another key trend is the use of blockchain for digital identity management. Blockchain's immutable and transparent ledger can provide a secure and verifiable framework for managing digital identities, enhancing privacy and security. This development will significantly affect finance, healthcare, and government services.

Quantum computing has remarkable potential to transform the future. It can solve complex problems currently beyond the reach of classical computers' reach. As advancements in qubit technology, error correction, and quantum algorithms continue, quantum computers will become more practical and accessible. One significant future development is the application of quantum computing in drug discovery and material science. Quantum simulations can provide insights into molecular interactions at a granular level, accelerating the discovery of new materials and pharmaceuticals.

As we look ahead to future AI, blockchain, and quantum computing advancements, we must consider these technologies' broader ethical and societal impacts. It's essential to ensure that the development and implementation of these technologies are guided by principles of fairness, transparency, and accountability to build public trust and ensure their responsible use. Addressing issues such as bias in AI algorithms, privacy concerns in blockchain, and data security in quantum computing will be vital for promoting ethical and fair innovation. Preparing for an AI-driven future involves a multifaceted approach that includes continuous learning, interdisciplinary collaboration, moral frameworks, and proactive engagement. By staying informed about the latest advancements and trends, fostering collaboration across different disciplines and sectors, promoting ethical and responsible innovation, and actively participating in public discussions and policy development, we can effectively navigate the complexities of integrating AI, blockchain, and quantum computing into various aspects of society.

Looking ahead at the potential paths of AI, blockchain, and quantum computing underlines the transformative power of these technologies. Imagining and actively contributing to a future where technology enhances human capabilities and societal well-being can unlock new possibilities and bring about transformative change.

This book has offered insights into the evolution, applications, and implications of AI, blockchain, and quantum computing. By embracing adaptability, constant learning, and ethical responsibility, we can harness the full potential of these technologies to enhance human capabilities and societal well-being. The road ahead presents opportunities and challenges, but with the proper knowledge, skills, and commitment, we can navigate an AI-driven future and create a better, more inclusive world for all.

Moving forward, staying informed, fostering collaboration, and promoting diversity and inclusion are essential. Proactively engaging with emerging technologies allows us to contribute to their responsible and sustainable development, unlocking new possibilities and driving transformative change. The vision of an AI-driven world is within reach, and by working together, we can ensure that it enhances human capabilities, promotes societal well-being, and creates a brighter future for all.

Fictional Story (Part 2): The Story of Jovan

Jovan's Legacy:

Jovan passed away peacefully, leaving behind a legacy of innovation and a world transformed by his vision. The Quantum Consciousness AI he created became humanity's guide, drawing from Jovan's wisdom and the collective knowledge of centuries.

His story, taught in schools worldwide, inspired new generations to dream big and push the boundaries of technology. In memoriam, the first interstellar ship powered by Quantum Teleportation technology was named The Jovan Explorer, symbolizing the unending human quest for knowledge and exploration.

In the world that Jovan helped shape, technology was not just a part of life but a partner in creating a future where imagination knew no bounds. His story was a testament to the power of human curiosity, the transformative potential of technology, and the enduring spirit to explore the unknown.

References

Bartoletti, Ivana. "AI in healthcare: Ethical and privacy challenges." In *Artificial Intelligence in Medicine: 17th Conference on Artificial Intelligence in Medicine, AIME 2019, Poznan, Poland, June 26–29, 2019, Proceedings 17*, pp. 7–10. Springer International Publishing, 2019.

Fredrikson, M., S. Jha, and T. Ristenpart. 2015. "Model Inversion Attacks That Exploit Confidence Information and Basic Countermeasures." *Proceedings of the ACM Conference on Computer and Communications Security* (October): 1322–33. https://doi.org/10.1145/2810103.2813677.

Krizhevsky, A., I. Sutskever, and G. E. Hinton. 2012. "Imagenet Classification with Deep Convolutional Neural Networks." In *Advances in Neural Information Processing Systems 25*, Curran Associates, Incorporated. https://proceedings.neurips.cc/paper/2012/hash/c399862d3b9d6b76c8436e924a68c45b-Abstract.html

Krizhevsky, A., I. Sutskever, and G. E. Hinton. 2017. "ImageNet Classification with Deep Convolutional Neural Networks." *Communications of the ACM* 60 (6): 84–90. https://doi.org/10.1145/3065386.

Liang, H., E. He, Y. Zhao, Z. Jia, and H. Li. 2022. "Adversarial Attack and Defense: A Survey." *Electronics* 11 (8): 1283. https://doi.org/10.3390/ELECTRONICS11081283.

Panch, T., H. Mattie, and L. A. Celi. 2019. "The 'Inconvenient Truth' about AI in Healthcare." *NPJ Digital Medicine* 2 (1): 1–3. https://doi.org/10.1038/s41746-019-0155-4.

Qiu, S., Q. Liu, S. Zhou, and C. Wu. 2019. "Review of Artificial Intelligence Adversarial Attack and Defense Technologies." *Applied Sciences* 9 (5): 909. https://doi.org/10.3390/APP9050909.

Ren, K., T. Zheng, Z. Qin, and X. Liu. 2020. "Adversarial Attacks and Defenses in Deep Learning." *Engineering* 6 (3): 346–60. https://doi.org/10.1016/J.ENG.2019.12.012.

Shor, P. W. 1994. "Algorithms for Quantum Computation: Discrete Logarithms and Factoring." *Proceedings—Annual IEEE Symposium on Foundations of Computer Science, FOCS*, 124–34. https://doi.org/10.1109/SFCS.1994.365700.

Sun, Lu, Mingtian Tan, and Zhe Zhou. "A survey of practical adversarial example attacks." *Cybersecurity* 1, no. 1 (2018): 9. https://link.springer.com/article/10.1186/s42400-018-0012-9.

Wallace, E., S. Feng, N. Kandpal, M. Gardner, and S. Singh. 2019. "Universal Adversarial Triggers for Attacking and Analyzing NLP." *Proceedings of the 2019 Conference on Empirical Methods in Natural Language Processing and the 9th International Joint Conference on Natural Language Processing (EMNLP-IJCNLP)* (November): 2153–62. https://doi.org/10.18653/V1/D19-1221.

Test Your Skills

Multiple-Choice Questions

These questions are designed to test understanding of the key concepts, focusing on the societal impacts, challenges, and future implications of AI in autonomous systems.

1. What is the primary societal implication of integrating AI in autonomous systems?

    A. Increasing computational costs

    B. Enhancing security protocols

    C. Transforming transportation and healthcare

    D. Reducing the need for human intervention

2. Which technology is noted for its potential to reform diagnostics in healthcare by interpreting complex medical data?

    A. Blockchain

    B. Quantum computing

    C. Artificial intelligence

    D. Internet of Things

3. What is identified as a significant challenge in the implementation of autonomous vehicles?

    A. Cost of production

    B. Ethical decision-making

    C. Battery life of vehicles

    D. Wireless communication

4. What is a significant effect of quantum computing on global industries?

    A. Decreasing the relevance of traditional computing

    B. Facilitating faster Internet speeds

    C. Transforming sectors like finance and cybersecurity

    D. Simplifying data storage solutions

5. What challenge does quantum computing pose to current cybersecurity measures?

    A. It requires larger databases.

    B. It makes traditional encryption obsolete.

    C. It slows down computing processes.

    D. It increases the cost of security.

6. Which of the following best describes the economic impact of AI?

    A. Creates a monopoly in tech industries

    B. Drives innovation and reshapes labor markets

    C. Leads to a decrease in investments in technology

    D. Reduces the gross domestic product of tech-forward nations

7. What ethical consideration is emphasized when deploying AI in public surveillance systems?

    A. Cost-effectiveness

    B. Efficiency of data collection

    C. Privacy and individual rights

    D. Speed of data processing

8. How is AI expected to impact future transportation?

    A. By decreasing fuel efficiency

    B. By limiting route options

    C. By enhancing safety and reducing congestion

    D. By increasing travel time

9. What role does AI play in healthcare systems?

    A. Reducing the need for patient interaction

    B. Facilitating personalized treatment plans

    C. Decreasing the use of medical imaging

    D. Eliminating the role of healthcare professionals

10. What significant shift in AI development is marked by the transition from narrow AI to general AI?

    A. From rule-based systems to expert systems

    B. From machine learning to reinforcement learning

    C. From specific task performance to human cognitive ability mimicry

    D. From symbolic AI to machine learning

11. What is a primary ethical concern regarding the deployment of AI systems?

    A. The cost of implementing AI solutions

    B. The transparency and interpretability of AI models

C. The speed of AI data processing

D. The availability of AI programming languages

12. Which technology's foundational principle is the distributed ledger, ensuring transparency, security, and immutability?

   A. Artificial intelligence

   B. Quantum computing

   C. Blockchain

   D. Machine learning

13. What critical development in quantum computing allows it to perform complex calculations at unprecedented speeds?

   A. Neural networks

   B. Qubits and quantum entanglement

   C. Smart contracts

   D. Reinforcement learning

14. What significant opportunity does AI present in the healthcare sector?

   A. Enhancing entertainment and gaming experiences

   B. Enabling personalized medicine and improving diagnostics

   C. Improving social media algorithms

   D. Developing virtual reality applications

15. Which of the following is a technical challenge associated with blockchain technology?

   A. Quantum entanglement

   B. Scalability and interoperability

   C. Neural network training

   D. Data annotation

16. What does the term *quantum supremacy* refer to in quantum computing?

   A. The development of the first quantum algorithm

   B. The moment when quantum computers outperform classical computers in specific tasks

   C. The creation of the first quantum entanglement experiment

   D. The integration of AI with quantum computing

17. What is one of the primary ethical concerns about AI systems discussed in the chapter?

    A. The availability of AI software tools

    B. The potential for bias and discrimination in AI algorithms

    C. The speed of AI hardware development

    D. The cost of deploying AI systems

18. Which area is highlighted as a significant future opportunity for blockchain technology?

    A. Video game development

    B. Supply chain management

    C. Space exploration

    D. Food and beverage industry

19. What does integrating AI, blockchain, and quantum computing technologies create?

    A. A fragmented technological landscape

    B. A synergistic effect that amplifies their collective potential

    C. A decline in technological advancements

    D. An isolated application framework

20. What is a crucial aspect of preparing for an AI-integrated future mentioned in the chapter?

    A. Reducing the complexity of AI algorithms

    B. Continuous learning and adaptability

    C. Limiting the use of blockchain technology

    D. Avoiding interdisciplinary collaboration

21. How can quantum computing significantly impact AI and blockchain applications?

    A. By slowing down the data processing speed

    B. By providing advanced encryption methods and accelerating AI algorithms

    C. By increasing the need for manual data entry

    D. By reducing the overall computational power

22. What is the role of interdisciplinary collaboration in AI, blockchain, and quantum computing?

    A. To develop isolated technological solutions

    B. To harness the full potential of these technologies by addressing complex challenges collaboratively

C. To reduce the impact of technological advancements

D. To limit the integration of emerging technologies

23. What ethical principle is essential for gaining public trust in deploying AI, blockchain, and quantum computing?

    A. Speed of implementation

    B. Fairness, transparency, and accountability

    C. Cost reduction

    D. Limiting access to technology

24. What significant societal implication of quantum computing is highlighted in the chapter?

    A. Enhancing video game graphics

    B. Addressing the challenges to data security and privacy

    C. Reducing the need for renewable energy

    D. Improving social media engagement

Exercises

These exercises are designed to deepen your understanding of the specific societal impacts of AI agents, encouraging a critical assessment of these transformative technologies.

Exercise 10.1: Exploring AI and Quantum Computing's Societal Impacts

Read Chapter 10 and answer the following questions:

1. How has AI influenced the transportation sector, particularly in developing autonomous vehicles?

2. Describe how AI is utilized in healthcare systems for diagnostics and patient care.

3. Explain the role of quantum computing in revolutionizing industries such as finance and cybersecurity.

4. Identify and discuss the ethical challenges presented by deploying autonomous systems in society.

5. What are some economic implications of integrating AI and quantum computing into various sectors?

6. Predict the future developments in autonomous systems and their potential societal impacts.

7. Reflect on why responsible development and deployment of AI and quantum computing technologies are crucial.

Exercise 10.2: Detailed Analysis of AI in Specific Sectors

Read the designated sections in Chapter 10 and answer the following questions:

1. How do autonomous vehicles use AI to improve road safety and efficiency?

2. Discuss the impact of AI-driven systems like IBM Watson in healthcare.

3. What advancements in quantum computing could potentially disrupt current cybersecurity measures?

4. Examine the challenges of implementing AI in diverse and unpredictable environments, such as autonomous vehicles and healthcare systems.

5. How does integrating AI and quantum computing necessitate changes in policy and regulation at an international level?

Exercise 10.3: Reviewing Key Technological Advancements

Read Chapter 10 and answer the following questions:

1. What are the key advancements in AI discussed in the chapter?

2. How has blockchain technology enhanced digital trust?

3. Describe the significance of qubits and quantum entanglement in quantum computing.

4. How do AI and blockchain complement each other in a technological ecosystem?

5. What role does reinforcement learning play in the evolution of AI?

6. Explain the concept of smart contracts and their impact on digital transactions.

7. What advancements have been made in quantum computing algorithms?

8. How does integrating AI, blockchain, and quantum computing create a synergistic effect?

Exercise 10.4: Reflecting on the Evolution of Technologies

Read Chapter 10 and answer the following questions:

1. Summarize the evolutionary journey of AI from rule-based systems to deep learning.

2. How did the development of blockchain technology begin, and what were its initial applications?

3. What are the theoretical foundations of quantum computing, and how have they evolved into practical implementations?

4. Explain how the convergence of AI, blockchain, and quantum computing represents a powerful synergy.

5. What challenges did early blockchain platforms face, and how were they addressed?

6. How have quantum computing advancements demonstrated their transformative potential?

7. How does AI enhance blockchain's efficiency and security?

Exercise 10.5: Anticipating Future Challenges

Read Chapter 10 and answer the following questions:

1. What are the primary technical challenges associated with scaling AI systems?

2. Discuss the interpretability and transparency issues in AI models and their importance.

3. Identify the main scalability issues faced by blockchain platforms and potential solutions.

4. Explain the challenges of qubit stability and error correction in quantum computing.

5. What ethical concerns arise from the deployment of AI systems?

6. How do privacy concerns affect the implementation of blockchain technology?

7. What societal impacts might arise from the widespread use of quantum computing?

8. Describe the regulatory challenges in deploying AI, blockchain, and quantum computing technologies.

Exercise 10.6: Recognizing Future Opportunities

Read Chapter 10 and answer the following questions:

1. What opportunities does AI present in the healthcare sector?

2. How can blockchain technology transform supply chain management?

3. Discuss the potential impact of quantum computing on cryptography.

4. How can AI-driven autonomous systems update transportation?

5. Explain the role of blockchain in enhancing financial transaction security.

6. What are the applications of quantum computing in material science?

7. Describe how AI, blockchain, and quantum computing can be integrated into smart cities.

8. What opportunities do these technologies present for cybersecurity?

Exercise 10.7: Assessing Ethical, Legal, and Societal Implications

Read Chapter 10 and answer the following questions:

1. What are the potential biases in AI algorithms, and how can they be mitigated?

2. How does the transparency of blockchain technology raise privacy concerns?

3. Discuss the ethical implications of deploying quantum computing in various fields.

4. What legal challenges need to be addressed to ensure the responsible use of AI?

5. Explain the societal impact of job displacement due to quantum computing advancements.

6. How can regulatory frameworks promote the ethical use of blockchain technology?

7. Describe the importance of developing quantum-resistant cryptographic algorithms.

8. How can the benefits of AI, blockchain, and quantum computing be distributed equitably?

Exercise 10.8: Preparing for an AI-Integrated Future

Read Chapter 10 and answer the following questions:

1. Why is continuous learning and adaptability crucial in an AI-integrated future?

2. What technical proficiencies should individuals develop to thrive in a future with AI, blockchain, and quantum computing?

3. How can interdisciplinary collaboration enhance the integration of these technologies?

4. Discuss the importance of ethical and responsible frameworks in deploying advanced technologies.

5. What role does digital literacy play in preparing society for an AI-integrated future?

6. How can inclusive innovation be promoted to ensure equitable benefits from technological advancements?

7. Explain the impact of AI, blockchain, and quantum computing on workforce transformation.

8. Describe the potential of these technologies in addressing global challenges.

Exercise 10.9: Engaging with Emerging Technologies

Read Chapter 10 and answer the following questions:

1. How can fostering a culture of curiosity and innovation drive the development of AI, blockchain, and quantum computing?

2. What steps can individuals take to stay informed about the latest technological advancements?

3. Discuss the significance of interdisciplinary collaboration in addressing complex challenges.

4. How can participation in research and development efforts contribute to technological progress?

5. What actions can be taken to advocate for ethical and responsible innovation?

6. Describe the importance of public discourse and policy development in shaping the future of these technologies.

7. How can supporting open innovation and open-source initiatives accelerate technological advancements?

8. What role do diversity and inclusion play in developing AI, blockchain, and quantum computing?

Exercise 10.10: Concluding with a Forward-Looking Perspective

Read Chapter 10 and answer the following questions:

1. What are the future trajectories of AI, blockchain, and quantum computing?

2. How can artificial general intelligence impact various fields?

3. Discuss the integration of AI with the Internet of Things and its potential benefits.

4. What is decentralized finance, and how can blockchain facilitate its development?

5. Explain the role of quantum computing in drug discovery and material science.

6. How can the convergence of these technologies create powerful synergies?

7. What ethical considerations should guide the future development of AI, blockchain, and quantum computing?

8. How can continuous learning and proactive engagement shape an AI-driven world?

APPENDIX A

Test Your Skills Answers

Multiple-Choice Answers

Chapter 1

1. **Answer: C. Blockchain**. Blockchain technology plays a key role in ensuring the security and transparency of transactions within a decentralized system. By maintaining a distributed ledger that is cryptographically secure, blockchain allows for tamper-proof record-keeping, making it an essential technology for secure and transparent data management in various applications, including finance, the supply chain, and digital identity verification.

2. **Answer: C. Artificial intelligence (AI)**. Artificial intelligence is designed to mimic human intelligence, performing tasks such as learning, reasoning, problem-solving, and understanding language. This capability is what makes AI a cornerstone of modern technological innovation.

3. **Answer: C. Secure and transparent record-keeping**. Blockchain is known for its capability to maintain a secure and immutable ledger, where each block of data is cryptographically linked to the previous one. This capability ensures transparency and security in data transactions, making it ideal for applications where trust is essential.

4. **Answer: B. The employment of quantum bits (or qubits)**. Unlike classical computing, which uses binary bits (0s and 1s), quantum computing employs qubits that can exist in multiple states simultaneously due to quantum superposition. This allows quantum computers to perform complex calculations at speeds unattainable by classical computers.

5. **Answer: B. Facilitating machine learning from data**. Neural networks are a key component of AI, enabling systems to learn from vast datasets by identifying patterns and making decisions. This adaptive learning capability distinguishes modern AI from earlier rule-based systems.

6. **Answer: B. Finance and healthcare**. AI's predictive analytics have had a profound impact on both finance and healthcare, where they are used for risk assessment, fraud detection, and personalized medicine. These sectors rely heavily on AI's ability to analyze complex data and predict outcomes.

7. **Answer: C. Artificial intelligence**. AI has evolved from early rule-based systems, which were limited by predefined instructions, to modern adaptive learning models, like neural networks, which can learn and improve over time without being explicitly programmed for every scenario.

8. **Answer: C. Finance and healthcare**. The integration of AI and blockchain is transforming finance and healthcare by providing secure, efficient, and intelligent systems for managing sensitive data and complex transactions. This combination enhances transparency, security, and decision-making processes in these critical sectors.

9. **Answer: C. Job displacement risks**. As AI, blockchain, and quantum computing become more integrated into various industries, there is a significant risk of job displacement due to automation. This challenge underscores the need for upskilling the workforce and developing strategies to mitigate the social impact of these technologies.

10. **Answer: C. Provide secure, transparent record-keeping**. The defining feature of blockchain technology is its secure and transparent ledger system, which is resistant to tampering and ensures that records are immutable and traceable. This makes it particularly valuable in applications requiring high levels of trust and accountability.

11. **Answer: C. Facilitating machine learning from vast data**. Neural networks enable AI systems to learn from large datasets by identifying patterns and making predictions. This capability is essential for machine learning, allowing AI to improve its performance over time based on data inputs.

12. **Answer: B. Essential for guiding responsible development**. Governance and policy play a crucial role in ensuring that the development and deployment of technologies like AI, blockchain, and quantum computing are conducted responsibly. This involves setting standards, promoting ethical practices, and fostering international collaboration to mitigate risks and maximize benefits.

Chapter 2

1. **Answer: C. The introduction of Frank Rosenblatt's Perceptron**. The Perceptron, introduced by Frank Rosenblatt, marked the beginning of machine learning by laying the foundation for algorithms that could make predictions or decisions based on data input, moving away from the rule-based approach of symbolic AI.

2. **Answer: B. The development of the Perceptron in 1958**. The Perceptron was a pivotal development, demonstrating the potential of machines to learn from data and setting the stage for advancing neural networks in AI.

3. **Answer: A. It enabled AI to surpass the limitations of traditional machine learning algorithms**. Deep learning represents a leap in AI by using networks with many layers to learn from vast amounts of data, transcending traditional machine learning limitations.

4. **Answer: B. Focuses on learning through interaction and trial and error**. RL is unique because it involves an agent learning to make decisions within an environment to achieve a goal, guided by a system of rewards and penalties, akin to learning through trial and error.

5. **Answer: B. Difficulty in transfer learning and data efficiency**. RL models often require significant data to learn effectively, and transferring learned policies to new but related tasks remains a complex issue.

6. **Answer: C. Learning optimal policies through temporal difference learning**. Q-learning aims to learn a policy that maximizes cumulative rewards by iteratively updating its Q-values, focusing on temporal difference learning.

7. **Answer: B. Combine neural networks with the memory capabilities of traditional Turing machines**. NTMs are significant for their ability to process and store information, enabling them to handle complex tasks requiring memory.

8. **Answer: B. Drawing inspiration from human brain functionality, possibly through spiking neural networks**. The future of AI may include more complex neural network designs and learning methods, including those inspired by the human brain.

9. **Answer: B. The difficulty in interpreting the decision-making process**. The "black box" nature of deep learning models poses transparency and interpretability challenges, as it's often unclear how these models arrive at their decisions.

10. **Answer: D. It emphasizes temporal difference learning**. Q-learning is distinctive for using temporal difference learning to learn optimal policies, particularly in environments with uncertain outcomes.

11. **Answer: C. By improving diagnostic accuracy, such as in breast cancer detection**. Deep learning has notably impacted healthcare by enhancing the accuracy of diagnostics, as exemplified by Google Health's model for detecting breast cancer.

12. **Answer: C. Q-learning**. Q-learning faces challenges in high-dimensional state spaces, known as the "curse of dimensionality," which complicates the learning process in these environments.

13. **Answer: B. Combines external memory capabilities with neural networks**. NTMs represent a groundbreaking approach by merging the memory functionality of traditional Turing machines with the learning capabilities of neural networks.

14. **Answer: B. To develop artificial general intelligence (AGI) with capabilities similar to human thinking**. One of the significant goals of AI is to create systems that excel in various tasks, known as AGI, representing a substantial advancement in AI technology.

Chapter 3

1. **Answer: B. Immutable record-keeping**. Blockchain technology is renowned for its ability to create immutable records across a distributed network, ensuring data integrity and fostering trust.

2. **Answer: B. Turing-complete programming language**. Ethereum is distinguished by its Turing-complete programming language, Solidity, which enables the creation of complex smart contracts and decentralized applications.

3. **Answer: D. Hyperledger Fabric caters to enterprise solutions with permissioned networks**. Unlike Ethereum's public blockchain approach, Hyperledger Fabric is tailored for enterprise use with its permissioned network structure.

4. **Answer: B. To bridge external data with blockchain networks**. Smart oracles play a crucial role in integrating external data sources with blockchain networks, enhancing the functionality of smart contracts.

5. **Answer: C. By making data-driven decisions using machine learning algorithms**. Automated contracts use AI, particularly machine learning, to interpret data and automate decision-making processes.

6. **Answer: B. Data privacy and scalability concerns**. Integrating AI with blockchain technology presents challenges, including ensuring data privacy and addressing scalability issues.

7. **Answer: B. Transition from proof of work (PoW) to proof of stake (PoS)**. Ethereum 2.0 marks a significant transition to a PoS consensus mechanism, addressing energy consumption and scalability issues.

8. **Answer: C. Natural language processing (NLP)**. NLP enables automated contracts to understand and interact with legal documents written in natural language, enhancing the automation of complex legal processes.

9. **Answer: B. Predictive analysis using advanced machine learning models**. Future AI oracles are expected to demonstrate enhanced predictive capabilities, utilizing advanced machine learning models for more sophisticated data analysis and decision-making.

10. **Answer: C. A dynamic and innovative nature, constantly pushing technological boundaries**. The chapter highlights the blockchain ecosystem's evolving, dynamic, and creative nature, particularly its expansion and influence in various sectors.

Chapter 4

1. **Answer: C. Qubit**. A qubit, or quantum bit, is the basic unit of quantum information in quantum computing. It differs from classical binary bits' ability to embody quantum superposition and entanglement.

2. **Answer: C. Quantum entanglement**. Quantum entanglement is a phenomenon where qubits become interconnected in such a way that the state of one qubit is directly related to another, irrespective of the distance separating them.

3. **Answer: B. A quantum computer's ability to solve a problem that classical computers cannot solve in a feasible timeframe**. Quantum supremacy refers to the point where quantum computers can perform impractical tasks for classical computers.

4. **Answer: B. Breaking classical cryptographic codes**. Shor's algorithm is famous for efficiently solving the problem of integer factorization, which is the basis of many encryption systems, including RSA encryption.

5. **Answer: A. It provides a faster way to search unstructured databases**. Grover's algorithm significantly improves the efficiency of searching through unstructured databases by reducing the number of operations needed compared to classical algorithms.

6. **Answer: B. Quantum decoherence**. Maintaining qubit stability is challenged by quantum decoherence, where qubits lose their quantum properties due to environmental disturbances.

7. **Answer: C. Accelerating machine learning and solving complex problems efficiently**. The fusion of quantum computing and AI could dramatically accelerate machine learning processes, enabling AI to solve complex problems more efficiently.

8. **Answer: B. Detecting and correcting errors in quantum computations**. Quantum error correction is vital for addressing the intrinsic fragility of quantum states and ensuring accurate quantum computations.

9. **Answer: C. Various sectors, including healthcare, finance, and cryptography**. The advancements in quantum computing hold potential benefits for multiple sectors, including healthcare for drug discovery, finance for complex problem-solving, and enhancing cryptographic security.

Chapter 5

1. **Answer: B. To improve the efficiency and security of blockchain systems**. The integration focuses on leveraging AI for enhanced security, innovative contract automation, and optimization of blockchain functions.

2. **Answer: B. Quantum computing and AI on blockchain**. This combination is predicted to offer unprecedented data processing speeds and efficiency.

3. **Answer: C. Emergence of fully autonomous decentralized organizations**. AI is projected to manage entire organizations, with blockchain enabling decentralized governance.

4. **Answer: B. Allowing individuals to control their data**. AI-driven blockchain networks will empower individuals with greater control over their data.

5. **Answer: B. Legal and legislative systems**. AI will guide policy-making by analyzing vast amounts of data.

6. **Answer: B. Using personalized treatment plans based on AI analysis**. AI will enable tailored healthcare strategies.

7. **Answer: B. Decentralized network management across planets**. Blockchain will facilitate secure and efficient data transactions in space.

8. **Answer: B. Individuals being compensated for the data they generate**. This concept focuses on monetizing personal data.

9. **Answer: B. AI exhibiting consciousness-like attributes**. AI systems might show advanced decision-making and learning abilities.

10. **Answer: B. Ethical use of AI**. Ensuring AI aligns with human values is a significant concern in its integration with blockchain.

Chapter 6

1. **Answer: C. Utilization of quantum superposition and entanglement**. QNNs leverage core quantum concepts like superposition and entanglement, enabling them to handle and analyze data in ways classical computers can't.

2. **Answer: A. Faster and more accurate diagnosis**. Quantum-enhanced neural networks could analyze vast arrays of medical imaging data more rapidly and accurately than current systems.

3. **Answer: B. Quantum error correction and qubit stability**. These are significant challenges in the development of practical and sophisticated QML algorithms.

4. **Answer: B. They optimize the strengths of quantum and classical computing**, offering practical solutions by combining approaches.

5. **Answer: B. Protecting data against quantum-computing attacks**. PQC is crucial for maintaining data security and privacy in the quantum computing era.

6. **Answer: B. Quantum algorithms solve problems faster than classical algorithms** in specific applications, demonstrating superiority over classical counterparts.

7. **Answer: C. Healthcare, for drug discovery and personalized medicine**, where quantum computing could significantly accelerate molecular modeling and analysis.

8. **Answer: B. The creation of new learning theories and computational models** could reform the approach to AI and data processing.

9. **Answer: C. Difficulty in integrating quantum computing with renewable energy sources**. This challenge should have been mentioned explicitly in quantum AI development.

10. **Answer: B. Creating more stable and reliable quantum computers** is essential for running complex QML algorithms.

Chapter 7

1. **Answer: D. Designing cryptographic methods resistant to quantum computing attacks**. The goal of post-quantum cryptography is to develop encryption methods that remain secure even when faced with the advanced computational abilities of quantum computers. Quantum computers can solve certain mathematical problems much faster than classical computers, which could break traditional encryption methods. Therefore, new cryptographic methods must be designed to resist these quantum-specific threats, ensuring data remains secure in a future where quantum computing is prevalent.

2. **Answer: B. Lattice-based cryptography**. Lattice-based cryptography is considered promising for quantum resistance because it relies on mathematical problems that are currently unsolvable by both classical and quantum computers. The complexity of these lattice-based problems, such as the shortest vector problem, makes them a robust foundation for building secure cryptographic systems that can withstand the powerful capabilities of quantum computers.

3. **Answer: B. It utilizes the principles of quantum mechanics for secure communication**. Quantum key distribution (QKD) distinguishes itself from classical cryptographic methods by using the principles of quantum mechanics to secure communications. Specifically, QKD leverages the properties of quantum particles, such as superposition and entanglement, to detect any attempts at eavesdropping. This provides a level of security that is theoretically unbreakable, because any interception of the communication would disturb the quantum states and be immediately noticed.

4. **Answer: C. E91**. The E91 protocol is a type of quantum key distribution that employs quantum entanglement to secure communications. In this protocol, pairs of entangled particles are shared between two parties. The entangled state ensures that any attempt to intercept or measure the particles would alter their state, revealing the presence of an eavesdropper and maintaining the security of the communication.

5. **Answer: D. Utilization of one-way hash functions**. Hash-based cryptographic systems, such as the Merkle signature scheme (MSS), rely on one-way hash functions to secure data. One-way hash functions are easy to compute in one direction but extremely difficult to reverse, making them resistant to attacks, including those by quantum computers. This property ensures that even with advanced computational power, it remains infeasible to crack the cryptographic scheme by reversing the hash function.

6. **Answer: B. The threat posed by quantum computing to current cryptographic practices**. Quantum-resilient blockchain technology is developed to address the vulnerabilities that quantum computing introduces to current cryptographic practices. As quantum computers become capable of breaking traditional cryptographic methods, blockchain systems must incorporate quantum-resistant techniques to maintain security and integrity in the face of these new threats.

7. **Answer: B. Through cryptographic methods that involve complex lattice structures and problems**. Lattice-based cryptography secures data by using complex lattice structures and

problems that are computationally difficult to solve. These problems remain hard for both classical and quantum computers, making this type of cryptography a strong candidate for protecting data against quantum attacks. The intricate nature of lattice problems ensures that even powerful quantum computers cannot easily break the encryption.

8. **Answer: C. To detect and thwart eavesdropping attempts**. Decoy states in quantum key distribution are used as a security measure to detect eavesdropping. When random decoy signals are introduced into the communication, any attempt by an eavesdropper to intercept the communication will be noticed because the decoy states will reveal discrepancies in the received signals, indicating that the communication has been compromised.

9. **Answer: B. Enhanced security against quantum and traditional computational threats**. Integrating quantum mechanics principles into blockchain technology enhances its security by making it resistant to both traditional and quantum computational threats. Quantum-resistant algorithms ensure that blockchain remains secure even if quantum computers become capable of breaking conventional cryptographic methods, thereby safeguarding data and transactions on blockchain.

10. **Answer: A. It offers an efficient solution tailored for environments with limited resources**. The NTRU cryptosystem is a lattice-based encryption method that is both efficient and secure against quantum attacks. It is designed to work well in environments where computational resources are limited, making it a practical solution for applications that require strong security without demanding excessive processing power or memory. This efficiency, combined with quantum resistance, makes NTRU particularly valuable in resource-constrained settings.

Chapter 8

1. **Answer: B. Bias and fairness in AI algorithms**. AI algorithms can unintentionally perpetuate or even exacerbate societal biases, leading to unfair outcomes. This issue is particularly concerning in applications like facial recognition or loan approvals, where biased algorithms can lead to significant real-world consequences.

2. **Answer: C. Pre-processing techniques in data handling**. Pre-processing techniques aim to reduce bias before data is input into machine learning models by modifying the training data to ensure it is more representative of the population. This approach helps in mitigating biases from the outset, thereby promoting fairness throughout the AI system.

3. **Answer: B. Potential to break traditional cryptographic standards**. Quantum computing threatens current cryptographic methods like RSA and ECC, which are widely used to secure digital communications. The chapter discusses how quantum computing could render these methods obsolete, thus posing significant privacy challenges.

4. **Answer: B. Addressing privacy concerns and responsible use**. The ethical frameworks for quantum computing are primarily concerned with balancing the technology's powerful capabilities with the need to protect privacy and ensure responsible use. This includes developing quantum-resistant cryptography and establishing guidelines to prevent misuse.

5. **Answer: C. Impacts on surveillance and data security**. The advancements in AI and quantum technologies could enhance surveillance capabilities and affect data security. For example, quantum computing could potentially break current encryption methods, leading to significant data security concerns.

6. **Answer: B. Guiding ethical development and application**. Policy and regulation are crucial in ensuring that AI and quantum technologies are developed and applied ethically. The chapter emphasizes the need for regulations that promote transparency, accountability, and the protection of public interests while enabling innovation.

7. **Answer: B. A dual-use nature leading to both beneficial and harmful uses**. The dual-use nature of AI and quantum technologies, where they can be used for both beneficial and harmful purposes, will pose significant ethical challenges. This includes potential applications in surveillance and warfare, which require careful ethical consideration.

8. **Answer: C. Pre-processing modifications**. Pre-processing modifications involve adjusting the training data to reduce biases before it is used in machine learning models. This technique is crucial for ensuring that the model learns from a balanced dataset, thus promoting fairness from the start.

9. **Answer: B. It might lead to decreased accuracy in majority classes**. Integrating fairness into AI algorithms can sometimes result in decreased accuracy for majority classes. This trade-off occurs because efforts to ensure fairness for underrepresented groups may affect the model's performance on the data it is most accustomed to.

10. **Answer: C. They are in the early stages of development**. The chapter notes that ethical frameworks for quantum technologies are still being developed. Because quantum computing is an emerging field, the ethical guidelines are not yet fully established, and ongoing efforts are needed to address the unique challenges it presents.

Chapter 9

1. **Answer: B. To establish legal standards for AI systems based on risk levels**. The EU's Artificial Intelligence Act aims to regulate AI by categorizing systems into risk levels, ranging from minimal to high risk, and setting requirements accordingly. This framework ensures that higher-risk AI applications, which could impact fundamental rights or safety, are subject to stricter regulations, thereby protecting the public while promoting innovation.

2. **Answer: C. China**. China's AI policies are deeply intertwined with its broader national strategy, as outlined in the New Generation Artificial Intelligence Development Plan. This plan is part of China's ambition to become a global leader in AI by 2030, focusing on integrating AI into various sectors to strengthen technological dominance and national security.

3. **Answer: B. Developing AI standards and guidelines that influence industry practices**. NIST plays a crucial role in developing standards and guidelines for AI to ensure that industry practices align with national interests in innovation, security, and ethical considerations.

NIST's work helps establish a framework for responsible AI development that can be adopted across industries.

4. **Answer: B. Its potential to compromise data and national security frameworks.** Quantum computing poses a unique threat to current cryptographic systems, which could potentially compromise data security and national security infrastructures. This capability necessitates robust regulatory frameworks to prevent misuse and protect sensitive information.

5. **Answer: B. They enhance blockchain interoperability and security across different sectors.** ISO/TC 307 provides a set of international standards that promote interoperability and security, which are crucial for the widespread adoption and reliable integration of blockchain technology across various industries and geographical regions.

6. **Answer: B. Facilitating discussions on quantum computing's impact on global communications.** The ITU focuses on the implications of quantum computing for global communication networks, considering both the potential to disrupt existing systems and the opportunities for advancing secure communication technologies.

7. **Answer: A. Predictive regulatory frameworks.** Predictive regulatory frameworks are designed to be flexible and adaptable, enabling them to keep pace with the rapid evolution of technologies like AI and quantum computing. This approach allows regulators to anticipate and respond to new challenges proactively.

8. **Answer: A. Harmonizing international regulations with local demands.** Digital technologies often operate across borders, making it challenging for individual nations to align international standards with local regulations and priorities. Harmonization is necessary to ensure both global compliance and the protection of local interests.

9. **Answer: B. They provide a controlled environment for testing new technologies without full regulatory consequences.** Regulatory sandboxes allow innovators to experiment with new technologies like blockchain or AI in a controlled setting, fostering innovation while regulators observe and learn about potential risks before full-scale deployment.

10. **Answer: B. Technological neutrality.** The principle of technological neutrality ensures that regulations apply equally to all technologies performing similar functions, preventing biased regulatory frameworks that might otherwise favor one technology over another.

Chapter 10

1. **Answer: C. Transforming transportation and healthcare.** AI is driving significant changes in critical sectors like transportation and healthcare. In transportation, autonomous vehicles use AI to improve road safety and traffic efficiency. In healthcare, AI enhances diagnostics and treatment processes, fundamentally altering how these services are delivered and improving outcomes.

2. **Answer: C. Artificial intelligence**. Artificial intelligence has the capability to analyze large volumes of complex medical data, such as imaging and genetic information, with a precision that can surpass human ability. This makes AI a powerful tool for identifying patterns and making accurate diagnoses, thus revolutionizing healthcare diagnostics.

3. **Answer: B. Ethical decision-making**. Autonomous vehicles must make decisions in complex, real-world scenarios, which often involve ethical dilemmas. Programming these systems to handle situations where they must choose between different harms (such as during unavoidable accidents) is a major challenge that extends beyond technical concerns to deep ethical questions.

4. **Answer: C. Transforming sectors like finance and cybersecurity**. Quantum computing offers unprecedented processing power, which can modernize industries like finance by optimizing complex calculations and improving cybersecurity through advanced encryption-breaking capabilities. This transformation enables new possibilities but also presents significant challenges.

5. **Answer: B. It makes traditional encryption obsolete**. Quantum computers have the potential to break encryption algorithms that are currently considered secure. This ability threatens to render traditional encryption methods obsolete, prompting the need for the development of new, quantum-resistant cryptographic techniques.

6. **Answer: B. Drives innovation and reshapes labor markets**. AI stimulates innovation by automating tasks and enabling new technological advancements, which in turn reshapes labor markets. While AI creates new opportunities in tech-driven sectors, it also displaces some traditional jobs, requiring a shift in workforce skills and roles.

7. **Answer: C. Privacy and individual rights**. While AI-driven surveillance systems can enhance security, they also raise significant concerns about privacy and the potential infringement on individual rights. Balancing these concerns is crucial when deploying such systems to ensure that they do not undermine civil liberties.

8. **Answer: C. By enhancing safety and reducing congestion**. AI in transportation, especially through the use of autonomous vehicles, is expected to increase safety on the roads and reduce traffic congestion. This goal is achieved by improving decision-making and efficiency in traffic management, leading to smoother and safer transportation systems.

9. **Answer: B. Facilitating personalized treatment plans**. AI enables the creation of personalized treatment plans by analyzing a patient's unique medical data and predicting the most effective interventions. This capability leads to more personalized and effective healthcare, particularly in complex and chronic conditions.

10. **Answer: C. From specific task performance to human cognitive ability mimicry**. General AI aims to mimic human cognitive abilities across a broad spectrum, whereas narrow AI excels in particular tasks.

11. **Answer: B. The transparency and interpretability of AI models**. Ensuring that AI systems are interpretable and transparent is critical for building trust and accountability.

12. **Answer: C. Blockchain**. Blockchain technology is based on the distributed ledger principle, which ensures transparency, security, and immutability.

13. **Answer: B. Qubits and quantum entanglement**. Quantum computing leverages qubits and quantum entanglement to perform complex calculations much faster than classical computers.

14. **Answer: B. Enabling personalized medicine and improving diagnostics**. AI can modernize healthcare by analyzing large volumes of medical data to provide personalized treatment plans and improve diagnostics.

15. **Answer: B. Scalability and interoperability**. Blockchain faces technical challenges such as scalability and interoperability between different platforms.

16. **Answer: B. The moment when quantum computers outperform classical computers in specific tasks**. Quantum supremacy is achieved when quantum computers perform calculations faster than classical computers for particular tasks.

17. **Answer: B. The potential for bias and discrimination in AI algorithms**. Ensuring fairness and reducing bias in AI algorithms are crucial to prevent discrimination and promote equity.

18. **Answer: B. Supply chain management**. Blockchain's transparent and immutable ledger can enhance traceability and accountability in supply chain management.

19. **Answer: B. A synergistic effect that amplifies their collective potential**. Integrating these technologies enhances and complements each other, creating a synergistic effect.

20. **Answer: B. Continuous learning and adaptability**. Preparing for an AI-integrated future requires a commitment to constant learning and adaptability to keep up with technological advancements.

21. **Answer: B. By providing advanced encryption methods and accelerating AI algorithms**. Quantum computing's computational power can enhance AI and blockchain applications by offering advanced encryption methods and accelerating algorithms.

22. **Answer: B. To harness the full potential of these technologies by addressing complex challenges collaboratively**. Interdisciplinary collaboration is essential for developing integrated solutions that leverage the full potential of these technologies.

23. **Answer: B. Fairness, transparency, and accountability**. Ensuring these technologies are developed and deployed with fairness, transparency, and responsibility is crucial for gaining public trust.

24. **Answer: B. Addressing the challenges to data security and privacy**. Quantum computing's ability to break current encryption methods poses significant challenges to data security and privacy.

Exercise Answers

Chapter 1

There are no exercises in Chapter 1.

Chapter 2

There are no exercises in Chapter 2.

Chapter 3

EXERCISE 3.1: Exploring Blockchain Technologies and AI Integration

1. Vitalik Buterin developed Ethereum. It is distinguished from Bitcoin by its ability to support smart contracts and decentralized applications through its Turing-complete programming language, Solidity.

2. Hyperledger Fabric is renowned for creating permissioned networks for enterprise use, offering modularity and privacy, and being suitable for various industrial applications.

3. Smart oracles are intermediaries between blockchain networks and external data, enabling smart contracts to interact with and respond to real-world information.

4. Transitioning to proof of stake in Ethereum 2.0 is significant for addressing concerns over energy consumption and enhancing transaction scalability.

5. AI has the potential to revolutionize blockchain by enabling automated contracts to make sophisticated decisions, leveraging machine learning algorithms and natural language processing.

EXERCISE 3.2: Researching Deeper into Blockchain Technologies and AI Integration

1. The two principal blockchain platforms discussed are Ethereum and Hyperledger.

2. Smart oracles enhance intelligent contracts by providing access to external, real-world data, thus expanding their capabilities beyond blockchain.

3. Integrating AI with blockchain in supply chain management aims to address the challenge of dynamically adjusting to changing conditions, such as demand or supply disruptions.

4. A key challenge in integrating AI into blockchain technology is ensuring data privacy and managing scalability issues.

5. Future development could involve AI oracles with enhanced predictive capabilities and improved interoperability across blockchain platforms.

EXERCISE 3.3: Comparing Blockchain Technologies

1. PoET in Hyperledger Sawtooth is notable for its energy efficiency and suitability for permissioned and permissionless network configurations.

2. Layer 2 protocols like Arbitrum and zkSync improve Ethereum's transaction speed and reduce costs, addressing scalability issues.

3. A consequence of Ethereum's shift to PoS might include new considerations regarding validator incentives and network security.

4. AI-enhanced smart oracles could automate and optimize real-time trading decisions based on external financial market data.

5. An ethical consideration is the transparency and accountability of AI decisions, especially when integrated with immutable blockchain records.

EXERCISE 3.4: Assessing the Impact and Future of Blockchain and AI

1. Ethereum's support for dApps and smart contracts could lead to more decentralized, efficient, and transparent digital transactions across various industries.

2. AI-enhanced automated contracts could significantly transform healthcare, especially inpatient data management and personalized medicine.

3. Advancements in quantum computing could lead to faster and more accurate data processing in AI blockchain oracles, enhancing their predictive capabilities.

4. NLP integrated with blockchain in legal technology could automate complex legal processes, improving efficiency and reducing the need for manual intervention in contract analysis.

5. Maintaining data privacy is challenging when combining AI with blockchain due to the immutable nature of blockchain and AI's dynamic data needs.

Chapter 4

EXERCISE 4.1: Understanding the Fundamentals of Quantum Computing

1. Qubits can exist in multiple states simultaneously (superposition), unlike classical bits, which are either 0 or 1.

2. Quantum entanglement involves the interlinking of qubits such that the state of one qubit directly affects another, enabling simultaneous information processing.

3. Quantum supremacy is where a quantum computer can solve impractical problems for classical computers, marking a significant technological advancement.

4. Shor's algorithm can efficiently factor large integers, posing a threat to cryptographic systems like RSA that rely on the difficulty of factoring large numbers.

5. Grover's algorithm improves the efficiency of searching unstructured databases by reducing the number of operations needed compared to classical algorithms.

6. Maintaining qubit coherence and stability is a significant challenge, as environmental disturbances can easily disrupt qubits.

7. Quantum computing can process large datasets quickly, potentially enhancing AI and machine learning models' efficiency and accuracy.

8. Quantum computing could lead to more efficient drug discovery processes in healthcare and complex problem-solving in finance.

9. Error correction in quantum computing is crucial for correcting quantum errors and ensuring reliable outcomes from quantum computations.

10. Quantum coherence is essential for maintaining the quantum state of qubits long enough to perform calculations, a critical factor in the practical application of quantum computing.

EXERCISE 4.2: Probing Quantum Computing Concepts

1. Due to quantum superposition, qubits can exist in multiple states simultaneously, unlike classical binary bits, which are strictly 0 or 1.

2. Quantum superposition is a principle where a quantum system, like a qubit, can be in multiple states simultaneously.

3. Quantum entanglement is the phenomenon where the state of one qubit is directly related to the state of another, enabling simultaneous information processing.

4. Quantum supremacy is the point where a quantum computer can solve a problem that a classical computer cannot in a feasible amount of time, marking a significant advancement.

5. Maintaining the stability and coherence of qubits, which are highly susceptible to environmental disturbances, is a primary challenge.

6. Shor's algorithm can break current cryptographic codes, while Grover's algorithm significantly speeds up the search in unstructured databases.

7. Error correction in quantum computing is crucial for correcting quantum errors to ensure accurate computational outcomes.

8. Quantum computing challenges current encryption methods and could significantly accelerate AI processes.

9. Quantum computing has the potential to solve complex problems faster and more efficiently than classical computing.

10. Future directions include overcoming technical challenges like error rates and scalability and the impact of quantum computing on various sectors.

EXERCISE 4.3: Comparing Concepts in Quantum Computing

1. Quantum computing can process multiple states simultaneously due to quantum superposition and entanglement, unlike the sequential data processing of classical computing.

2. Due to quantum superposition, qubits can exist in multiple states simultaneously, unlike classical bits, which are either 0 or 1.

3. Quantum entanglement allows qubits to become interconnected, enabling simultaneous information processing.

4. Quantum superposition allows qubits to hold multiple states simultaneously, increasing the computational power of quantum computers.

5. Shor's algorithm demonstrates the potential to break current cryptographic codes, while Grover's algorithm significantly speeds up the search in unstructured databases.

6. Engineers should consider challenges like maintaining qubit coherence, quantum error correction, and the effects of environmental disturbances.

7. Quantum error correction involves complex algorithms and fault-tolerant architectures to rectify errors without collapsing the qubit's superposition.

8. Quantum computing can revolutionize cryptography by breaking existing encryption methods and enhancing AI with faster processing of complex datasets.

9. Coherence time is significant as it determines how long qubits can maintain their quantum state, which is crucial for completing quantum computations.

10. Future directions involve overcoming technical challenges like coherence, error rates, and scalability, with implications across various sectors.

EXERCISE 4.4: Assessing the Impact and Applications of Quantum Computing

1. Potential applications of quantum computing in drug discovery include (a) simulating molecular interactions, (b) designing new pharmaceuticals, (c) predicting drug efficacy, and (d) accelerating clinical trials.

2. Fields where quantum algorithms like Grover's and Shor's are expected to impact significantly include (a) cryptography, (b) database searching, and (c) complex problem-solving.

3. Quantum computing could enhance artificial intelligence by (a) processing massive datasets more efficiently and (b) improving the accuracy of machine learning models.

4. Challenges faced in developing quantum computing technology include (a) quantum error correction, (b) maintaining qubit coherence, (c) scaling quantum systems, and (d) developing quantum-resistant cryptographic methods.

5. Major technological hurdles in achieving practical quantum computing are (a) error rates in quantum computations and (b) quantum decoherence.

6. The implications of quantum computing for current cryptographic methods are (a) the potential to break encryption like RSA and (b) the need for quantum-resistant encryption.

Chapter 5

EXERCISE 5.1: Exploring AI-Blockchain Merging and Its Future Prospects

1. **b**. Enhanced security and transparency

2. **c**. Optimizing transaction throughput and security

3. **b**. Managing both individual contracts and entire organizations

4. **b**. Personalized treatment plans based on AI analysis

5. **c**. Individuals controlling their own data access through AI-driven blockchain networks

6. **c**. Enhancing the speed and efficiency of data processing

7. **b**. Ensuring AI systems are unbiased and aligned with human values

8. **b**. Conscious AI on blockchain networks.

EXERCISE 5.2: Assessing the Impact and Future of AI-Blockchain Integration

1. **a**. Automating and refining contract execution

2. **b**. Through real-time monitoring and response to network threats

3. **b**. Enabling trading of AI algorithms and datasets without central oversight

4. **c**. AI driving the overall management of DAOs

5. **b**. Giving individuals more control over their data through AI and blockchain

6. **b**. Shift in employment patterns due to new technological demands

7. **b**. By establishing decentralized networks for interplanetary communications

8. **b**. Ensuring ethical use and alignment with societal norms

EXERCISE 5.3: Exploring Innovations and Challenges in AI-Blockchain Synergy

1. b. To handle large-scale data analysis with unprecedented efficiency

2. c. Enhanced individual control over data access and usage

3. b. Using AI-driven, highly personalized treatment plans

4. b. Through complete and optimized resource management across cities or globally

5. c. Ensuring AI systems align with human values and are unbiased

6. b. Shifting the concept of work and compensation

7. b. AI provides data-driven insights, and blockchain ensures transparency

8. b. Addressing ethical considerations and equitable technology access

EXERCISE 5.4: Assessing the Potential and Risks of AI-Blockchain Evolution

1. c. Boosting blockchain scalability and efficiency

2. b. AI oversees intricate organizational structures on blockchain.

3. c. Enabling individual data management via AI-driven wallets

4. c. AI systems optimize global resources and are supported by blockchain.

5. c. Aligning AI systems with ethical and human values

6. b. Transforming concepts of work, remuneration, and data privacy

7. b. AI is analyzing data to guide policy-making, and blockchain ensures openness.

8. b. Addressing ethical use, equitable access, and sustainability in technology

Chapter 6

EXERCISE 6.1: Understanding Quantum Neural Networks and Their Applications

1. Quantum neural networks (QNNs) blend neural network theory and quantum computing. Unlike classical neural networks, which use binary data processing, QNNs use quantum superposition and entanglement, enabling them to process and analyze data in ways impossible with classical computers.

2. In the medical field, QNNs could reform how diseases are diagnosed and treatments are developed, mainly through enhanced medical imaging analysis, leading to faster and more accurate diagnoses.

3. Superposition allows QNNs to process multiple data states simultaneously, while entanglement enables instant correlations between qubits, irrespective of distance. These properties collectively allow QNNs to perform complex computations more efficiently than classical neural networks.

EXERCISE 6.2: The Impact of Quantum Computing on AI

1. Integrating quantum computing and AI can significantly enhance data analysis capabilities, enabling the processing and analysis of large-scale, high-dimensional datasets with unprecedented speed and accuracy.

2. Key challenges in developing QML algorithms include quantum error correction, maintaining qubit stability, and overcoming quantum computers' current hardware limitations.

3. Hybrid quantum-classical algorithms combine the strengths of quantum computing (such as handling complex calculations) and classical computing (like stability and efficiency in routine processing), making them a pragmatic solution in advancing quantum computing applications.

EXERCISE 6.3: Examining Quantum Advancements in Various Sectors

1. In healthcare, quantum computing could lead to significant advances in drug discovery and personalized medicine, such as modeling molecular interactions for drug development and tailoring treatments based on individual genetic profiles.

2. PQC is crucial for safeguarding data against quantum-computing attacks because current encryption methods are vulnerable to being broken by quantum algorithms. PQC aims to develop secure cryptographic systems that are resistant to quantum and classical computational attacks.

3. "Quantum advantage" refers to where quantum algorithms outperform their classical counterparts in solving practical problems. Achieving quantum advantage means quantum computing can offer solutions faster or more efficiently, impacting sectors like healthcare, finance, and cybersecurity.

Chapter 7

EXERCISE 7.1: Understanding Quantum-Resilient Cryptography

1. Post-quantum cryptography aims to develop cryptographic systems that are secure against an adversary with a quantum computer, using mathematical problems believed hard for quantum algorithms. Quantum cryptography, like quantum key distribution (QKD), uses principles of quantum mechanics to secure data transmission, ensuring any interception can be detected.

2. Lattice-based cryptography is significant because it is based on problems, such as the shortest vector problem (SVP) and learning with errors (LWE), that no efficient quantum or classical algorithms are known to solve, making it a robust choice for quantum-resistant cryptographic systems.

3. NTRU works by encrypting data using polynomials over a finite field, offering both speed and security against quantum attacks. Its operations include polynomial multiplication modulo, a fixed polynomial and an integer, capitalizing on the hardness of finding short vectors in a lattice, which remains secure against quantum attacks.

4. Hash functions in hash-based cryptography convert data into an almost unique fixed-size string. They are crucial for maintaining integrity and security in cryptographic systems, offering pre-image and collision resistance, which are properties not directly threatened by quantum algorithms.

5. The main challenges include the need for new algorithms to replace vulnerable ones like RSA and ECDSA, ensuring these new systems are both secure against quantum attacks and efficient enough for practical use. Also, integration into existing infrastructures without compromising operational efficiency poses a significant hurdle.

EXERCISE 7.2: Practical Application and Implications

1. BB84 uses properties of quantum mechanics, such as the no-cloning theorem and Heisenberg's uncertainty principle, to secure communications. It encodes information on quantum states or qubits sent over insecure channels, where any eavesdropping attempt would inevitably disturb the quantum states, thereby revealing the presence of an intruder.

2. The BB84 protocol is vulnerable to PNS attacks when weak coherent pulses emit multiple photons. Decoy-state protocols are used to insert random states with different photon intensities to detect and deter these types of eavesdropping attempts by causing noticeable discrepancies in photon statistics at the receiver's end.

3. Practical challenges include aligning and maintaining the polarization states over long distances, reducing photon loss in optical fibers, and integrating quantum systems with existing classical network infrastructures, which require new technological solutions and standards.

4. Integrating quantum cryptography with blockchain can enhance the security of blockchain against classical and quantum attacks. It can provide a robust method for achieving consensus and securing transactions, making blockchain more resilient to future technological advances.

5. The broader implications include ensuring long-term security for digital communications in various sectors, from financial services to governmental operations. It helps in safeguarding sensitive information against emerging quantum threats, thus maintaining confidentiality, integrity, and availability in a post-quantum world.

Chapter 8

EXERCISE 8.1: Understanding Ethical AI and Quantum Computing

1. Fairness and bias reduction are the two primary ethical considerations in developing AI algorithms. Fairness involves ensuring AI algorithms treat all individuals equally regardless of their inherent or acquired characteristics. At the same time, bias reduction focuses on identifying and mitigating biases that could be unintentionally embedded in AI systems through skewed datasets or flawed assumptions during the algorithm design phase.

2. Quantum computing poses privacy concerns primarily because it has the potential to break current cryptographic standards that secure digital communications. This could undermine encryption methods such as RSA and ECC, exposing sensitive data to potential security breaches.

3. Ethical frameworks govern the use of quantum computing by outlining principles and practices that ensure responsible development and deployment. These frameworks address privacy concerns, promote transparency in the development and deployment phases, and advocate for the early adoption of quantum-resistant cryptographic methods.

4. Two broader ethical implications of AI and quantum technologies on society include:

   Surveillance and Privacy: Enhanced AI capabilities, potentially augmented by quantum computing, could lead to more sophisticated surveillance systems capable of processing vast amounts of data at unprecedented speeds, raising significant privacy issues.

   Digital Divide: The advancements in AI and quantum technologies could exacerbate the digital divide by making cutting-edge technologies accessible only to well-funded, technologically advanced organizations and nations, thus widening global inequalities in technological capability and economic power.

5. Policy and regulation play a significant role in the ethical development and application of AI and quantum computing technologies by creating frameworks that balance innovation with moral considerations, public trust, and safety. These frameworks involve regulations around data usage, algorithmic transparency, and the protection of intellectual property while ensuring that the benefits of these technologies are accessible to all sections of society.

6. A potential future ethical challenge in AI and quantum computing is the dual-use nature of these technologies. For instance, while they can enhance security and efficiency in various sectors, they also raise concerns about privacy and civil liberties through enhanced surveillance capabilities that could be used to track individuals without their consent.

Chapter 9

EXERCISE 9.1: Regulatory Frameworks and Standards

1. c. Artificial Intelligence Act

2. ISO, through ISO/TC 307, develops international standards covering various aspects of blockchain technology, such as terminology, governance, security, and privacy, ensuring uniformity and interoperability across different sectors and regions.

3. c. Data security and national security

4. The United States follows a sector-specific approach without a single federal body overseeing AI, focusing on fostering innovation, while the European Union adopts a comprehensive and precautionary approach, emphasizing transparency, accountability, and users' rights under the proposed Artificial Intelligence Act.

5. The plan aims to position China as a global leader in AI by 2030, integrating AI policies with strategic goals for technological supremacy, focusing on enhancing state security and technological governance.

EXERCISE 9.2: Analyzing International and Regulatory Challenges

1. IEEE develops standards that guide the use of technologies like blockchain in IoT applications, ensuring that these devices interact securely and efficiently within blockchain networks, which is critical as quantum computing integrates with other digital technologies.

2. International bodies face challenges such as differing national interests, economic priorities, levels of technological advancement, and the rapid pace of technological change, which often outstrips the slower processes of international consensus-building.

3. Regulatory sandboxes provide a controlled environment for testing new technologies like blockchain without full regulatory consequences, which can foster innovation by allowing developers to experiment and adapt before these technologies are fully regulated.

4. Predictive regulatory frameworks anticipate future developments and challenges, allowing for more dynamic, adaptable regulations that can evolve with technological advancements, helping to ensure that regulations remain relevant and effective without stifling innovation.

5. Differing regulatory approaches can lead to fragmentation in global markets, create barriers to international cooperation, and result in competitive advantages or disadvantages depending on how restrictive or permissive those regulations are.

Chapter 10

EXERCISE 10.1: Exploring AI and Quantum Computing's Societal Impacts

1. AI has significantly impacted the transportation sector by enhancing the development of autonomous vehicles. These vehicles utilize AI technologies for navigation, safety, and traffic efficiency, improving road safety and reducing congestion.

2. In healthcare, AI is used for advanced diagnostics and patient care. It interprets medical data to diagnose diseases early and create personalized treatment plans. AI algorithms, particularly in radiology and pathology, enhance the accuracy and speed of medical diagnostics.

3. Quantum computing has the potential to transform industries by enabling the processing of information at unprecedented speeds. In finance, it enhances risk management and fraud detection, while in cybersecurity, it is pivotal in developing quantum-resistant cryptographic systems.

4. Deploying autonomous systems raises ethical challenges, including privacy, security, and decision-making autonomy concerns. Ethical dilemmas also arise from AI's role in critical decision-making processes, necessitating clear guidelines and regulations.

5. Economically, AI and quantum computing drive innovation, create new markets, and enhance productivity, but they also pose challenges like job displacement and the need to reskill the workforce. The economic benefits and challenges are not uniformly distributed, which can exacerbate social inequalities.

6. Future developments in autonomous systems, driven by AI and quantum computing, are expected to integrate these technologies further into daily life, enhancing efficiency and well-being while also requiring careful management of their societal impacts.

7. Responsible development is essential to ensure that AI and quantum computing technologies benefit society while minimizing potential harms. This effort involves adhering to ethical standards, promoting inclusivity, and engaging in long-term strategic planning.

EXERCISE 10.2: Detailed Analysis of AI in Specific Sectors

1. Autonomous vehicles use AI through computer vision, sensor fusion, and deep learning to navigate and react to the environment, enhancing road safety and traffic efficiency. AI algorithms process inputs from various sensors to make real-time decisions that prevent accidents and optimize traffic flow.

2. IBM Watson and similar AI-driven systems in healthcare analyze vast amounts of medical data to assist in diagnosis and treatment planning. These systems enable early diagnosis of diseases, such as cancer, through advanced pattern recognition techniques that surpass traditional diagnostic methods.

3. Advancements in quantum computing, such as the development of quantum algorithms, threaten current cryptographic methods by potentially breaking traditional encryption, necessitating the development of quantum-resistant cryptography to protect data security.

4. Implementing AI in diverse environments challenges AI systems to handle rare or unexpected events ("edge cases") that are not well represented in training datasets. This implementation requires robust AI models of high adaptability and reliability, especially in critical applications like autonomous vehicles and medical diagnostics.

5. The global nature of AI and quantum computing technologies requires international collaboration to develop standardized ethical guidelines and regulatory frameworks. This international approach helps manage the societal impacts of these technologies, ensuring they are developed and deployed responsibly.

EXERCISE 10.3: Reviewing Key Technological Advancements

1. The critical advancements in AI discussed in the chapter include deep learning, neural networks, and reinforcement learning. With its multilayered neural networks, deep learning has enhanced fields such as image and speech recognition, natural language processing, and autonomous systems. Reinforcement learning has enabled AI systems to learn and adapt through interactions with their environment, significantly advancing robotics and gaming.

2. Blockchain technology has enhanced digital trust by introducing a decentralized and immutable ledger system. This ensures digital transactions' transparency, security, and immutability, allowing for secure and transparent transactions without intermediaries. Smart contracts further automate and secure agreements, enhancing trust in digital interactions.

3. Qubits and quantum entanglement are fundamental to quantum computing. Qubits can exist in multiple states simultaneously due to superposition, allowing quantum computers to perform parallel computations. Quantum entanglement enables instantaneous information transfer between qubits, regardless of distance, significantly increasing computational power and efficiency in solving complex problems.

4. AI and blockchain complement each other by enhancing efficiency, security, and transparency. AI can optimize blockchain's efficiency by improving consensus algorithms and predictive analytics. Blockchain provides a secure and transparent framework for AI models, ensuring data integrity and provenance. The integration creates a robust system where AI enhances blockchain's functionality and vice versa.

5. Reinforcement learning plays a crucial role in the evolution of AI by enabling systems to learn and adapt through interactions with their environment. It allows AI agents to make decisions, perform tasks, and improve their performance over time based on feedback from their actions. This capability has been particularly impactful in robotics, gaming, and autonomous systems.

6. Smart contracts are self-executing contracts with the terms of the agreement directly written into code. They automatically execute transactions when predefined conditions are met,

eliminating the need for intermediaries. This automation increases efficiency, reduces the potential for errors or fraud, and enhances trust in digital transactions by ensuring transparency and security.

7. Advancements in quantum computing algorithms include Shor's algorithm and Grover's algorithm. Shor's algorithm can factor large numbers exponentially faster than classical algorithms, significantly impacting cryptography. Grover's algorithm provides a quadratic speedup for unstructured search problems. These algorithms demonstrate quantum computing's ability to solve complex problems more efficiently than classical computers.

8. Integrating AI, blockchain, and quantum computing creates a synergistic effect by leveraging the strengths of each technology to enhance overall capabilities. AI can optimize blockchain operations and improve data analysis, blockchain ensures secure and transparent data handling, and quantum computing provides immense computational power. Together, they create an interconnected ecosystem with amplified potential for innovation and problem-solving.

EXERCISE 10.4: Reflecting on the Evolution of Technologies

1. The evolutionary journey of AI began with rule-based systems, where predefined rules and logic performed specific tasks. The advent of machine learning marked a significant turning point, enabling computers to learn from data and make predictions without explicit programming. The rise of deep understanding, characterized by neural networks with multiple layers, improved AI by enhancing its ability to process and analyze large datasets, leading to significant advancements in various fields.

2. Blockchain technology started with the introduction of Bitcoin in 2008, providing a decentralized and secure framework for digital transactions. Its initial application was in cryptocurrencies, where it ensured secure and transparent transactions without intermediaries. The development of platforms like Ethereum expanded blockchain's capabilities, introducing intelligent contracts and enabling the creation of decentralized applications (dApps).

3. The theoretical foundations of quantum computing are based on the principles of quantum mechanics, such as superposition and entanglement. These principles allow quantum bits (qubits) to exist in multiple states simultaneously and enable instantaneous information transfer between entangled qubits. Practical implementations have evolved with the development of stable qubits, error correction techniques, and quantum algorithms, creating functional quantum computers capable of solving complex problems.

4. The convergence of AI, blockchain, and quantum computing represents a powerful synergy by combining their unique strengths to create a more robust and efficient technological ecosystem. AI enhances data processing and decision-making, blockchain provides secure and transparent data handling, and quantum computing offers unprecedented computational power. Together, they can address complex challenges and drive innovation in ways that are not possible with each technology individually.

5. Early blockchain platforms faced scalability, transaction speed, and energy consumption challenges. Scalability issues were addressed through sharding and Layer 2 protocols, improving transaction processing capabilities. Enhancements in consensus algorithms, such as proof of stake (PoS), reduced energy consumption. Developing interoperable standards and frameworks facilitated better communication and integration between blockchain platforms.

6. Quantum computing advancements have demonstrated their transformative potential through significant breakthroughs such as achieving quantum supremacy, where quantum computers outperform classical computers in specific tasks. Developments in quantum algorithms, like Shor's algorithm and Grover's algorithm, have shown the potential to improve cryptography and data analysis. These advancements highlight the immense computational power of quantum computing and its ability to solve problems previously deemed intractable.

7. AI enhances blockchain's efficiency by optimizing consensus algorithms, improving transaction validation processes, and providing predictive analytics for network performance. AI-driven intelligent contracts can be executed more efficiently and reliably. Additionally, AI enhances blockchain security by detecting anomalies and potential threats in real time, improving fraud detection, and ensuring data integrity within the blockchain network.

EXERCISE 10.5: Anticipating Future Challenges

1. The primary technical challenges related to scaling AI systems include handling large-scale data, ensuring real-time processing, and maintaining efficiency as the complexity of AI models increases. Developing algorithms that can scale effectively and manage vast amounts of data without compromising performance is crucial for widely adopting AI technologies.

2. Interpretability and transparency issues in AI models arise from the "black box" nature of many deep learning models, where the decision-making process is not easily understood. Ensuring that AI systems are interpretable and transparent is essential for building trust, ensuring accountability, and enabling users and stakeholders to understand and verify AI decisions. Techniques for explaining AI decisions and making underlying processes more understandable are critical for addressing these issues.

3. The main scalability issues faced by blockchain platforms include limited transaction throughput and high latency due to the time and computational resources required for transaction processing and consensus mechanisms. Potential solutions include sharding to divide blockchain into smaller, more manageable segments, using Layer 2 protocols to handle off-chain transactions, and adopting more efficient consensus algorithms such as proof of stake (PoS).

4. Qubit stability and error correction are significant challenges in quantum computing due to the sensitivity of qubits to environmental disturbances, which can lead to errors in computations. Developing robust error correction techniques, such as quantum error correction

codes, and improving qubit stability through advancements in materials and qubit design are critical for realizing the full potential of quantum computing.

5. Ethical concerns arising from deploying AI systems include potential biases and discrimination in AI algorithms, lack of transparency and accountability, and the impact on privacy and security. Ensuring fairness, reducing bias, making AI systems interpretable, and protecting data privacy are essential for addressing these ethical concerns and promoting the responsible use of AI.

6. Privacy concerns affect the implementation of blockchain technology due to the transparent and immutable nature of the blockchain ledger. Protecting sensitive information while maintaining transparency requires developing privacy-preserving techniques, such as zero-knowledge proofs and confidential transactions, to safeguard data privacy in blockchain applications.

7. Societal impacts from the widespread use of quantum computing include potential job displacement in specific sectors, increased economic inequality, and challenges to data security due to quantum computing's ability to break current encryption methods. Addressing these impacts requires ensuring equitable distribution of benefits, providing skills and training for workers, and developing quantum-resistant cryptographic algorithms to protect data privacy.

8. Regulatory challenges in deploying AI, blockchain, and quantum computing technologies include creating appropriate frameworks that address their unique characteristics, ensuring transparency, accountability, and fairness, and protecting privacy and data security. Developing standards and guidelines for these technologies' ethical and secure use is crucial for gaining public trust and ensuring responsible deployment.

EXERCISE 10.6: Recognizing Future Opportunities

1. AI presents numerous opportunities in the healthcare sector, including enabling personalized medicine, improving diagnostics, and optimizing treatment plans. AI algorithms can analyze large volumes of medical data to identify patterns, make predictions, and provide valuable insights for clinicians and researchers, enhancing patient care and outcomes.

2. Blockchain technology can transform supply chain management by providing a transparent and immutable ledger that enhances the traceability and accountability of goods. This effort reduces fraud, improves efficiency, and ensures the integrity of supply chain operations, allowing stakeholders to track products from origin to destination with greater confidence.

3. Quantum computing has the potential to improve cryptography by breaking current encryption methods through its ability to factor large numbers and perform complex calculations at unprecedented speeds. This necessitates the development of quantum-resistant cryptographic algorithms to protect sensitive information in a post-quantum world, ensuring data security and privacy.

4. AI-driven autonomous systems can improve transportation by enabling the development of autonomous vehicles that reduce accidents, improve efficiency, and decrease congestion. Autonomous drones and robots can enhance logistics and supply chain management, enabling more efficient and cost-effective operations and transforming the transportation industry.

5. Blockchain enhances financial transaction security by providing a decentralized and transparent framework that ensures the immutability and integrity of transactions. Smart contracts automate and secure financial agreements, reducing the need for intermediaries and increasing efficiency. Blockchain's secure ledger system helps prevent fraud and enhances trust in financial transactions.

6. Quantum computing applications in material science include simulating molecular interactions at a granular level, enabling the discovery of new materials and drugs. Quantum simulations can accelerate research and development in pharmaceuticals, energy, and manufacturing, driving innovation and enhancing efficiency in these industries.

7. In smart cities, AI-driven analytics can optimize urban planning and management, improving resource allocation and service delivery. Blockchain provides a secure and transparent framework for managing data and transactions, ensuring the integrity of innovative city operations. Quantum computing can enhance the efficiency and security of innovative city systems, enabling more sustainable and resilient urban environments.

8. AI, blockchain, and quantum computing present significant opportunities for cybersecurity. AI algorithms can enhance threat detection and response by identifying and mitigating real-time security risks. Blockchain provides a secure and transparent framework for managing digital identities and transactions. Quantum computing offers advanced encryption methods, ensuring the security of sensitive information in a post-quantum world.

EXERCISE 10.7: Assessing Ethical, Legal, and Societal Implications

1. Potential biases in AI algorithms arise from biased training data, leading to discriminatory outcomes. These biases can be mitigated using diverse and representative datasets, implementing fairness-aware algorithms, and regularly auditing AI systems for bias. Ensuring transparency and accountability in AI development processes also helps identify and correct biases.

2. Blockchain technology's transparency raises privacy concerns because all transactions are recorded on a public ledger, potentially exposing sensitive information. Balancing transparency with privacy requires developing privacy-preserving techniques such as zero-knowledge proofs, confidential transactions, and selective disclosure to protect sensitive data while maintaining the integrity of blockchain.

3. Deploying quantum computing in various fields raises ethical implications regarding data security, privacy, and economic inequality. Quantum computing's ability to break current encryption methods poses a significant threat to data privacy. Ensuring that the benefits of

quantum computing are distributed equitably and addressing potential job displacement and economic inequality are crucial ethical considerations.

4. Legal challenges in ensuring the responsible use of AI include developing regulations that address transparency, accountability, and fairness, protecting data privacy, and ensuring the ethical deployment of AI systems. Establishing standards and guidelines for AI development and use, as well as mechanisms for enforcement and compliance, is essential for addressing these challenges.

5. Quantum computing advancements may lead to job displacement in sectors where quantum solutions replace traditional computational methods. This effect could exacerbate existing economic inequalities. Ensuring that workers are provided with the necessary skills and training to adapt to new technologies and promoting financial inclusion are critical for mitigating the societal impact of job displacement.

6. Regulatory frameworks can encourage the ethical use of blockchain technology by establishing standards and guidelines for data privacy, security, and governance. Regulations should address issues such as transparency, accountability, and fairness in blockchain operations, ensuring that blockchain networks are managed to protect users' rights and promote trust.

7. Developing quantum-resistant cryptographic algorithms is essential for protecting sensitive information in a post-quantum world. Because quantum computing has the potential to break current encryption methods, quantum-resistant algorithms ensure that data remains secure and private, safeguarding information from potential quantum threats.

8. The benefits of AI, blockchain, and quantum computing can be distributed equitably by promoting inclusive innovation, providing access to education and resources, and addressing the digital divide. Ensuring diversity in technology development and deployment, creating opportunities for underrepresented groups, and implementing policies that promote economic inclusion are essential for equitable distribution of technological benefits.

EXERCISE 10.8: Preparing for an AI-Integrated Future

1. Continuous learning and adaptability are essential to an AI-integrated future due to the rapid pace of technological advancement. By staying informed and updating skills, individuals, organizations, and societies can effectively leverage new technologies, remain competitive, and address emerging challenges and opportunities.

2. Individuals should develop technical proficiencies in machine learning, deep learning, and natural language processing for AI. Understanding distributed ledger technologies, smart contracts, and decentralized applications is essential for blockchain. Knowledge of quantum mechanics, qubits, and quantum algorithms is crucial for quantum computing. These skills enable individuals to leverage the capabilities of these advanced technologies effectively.

3. Interdisciplinary collaboration enhances the integration of AI, blockchain, and quantum computing by bringing together expertise from different fields to address complex challenges and develop comprehensive solutions. Collaboration between computer science,

engineering, mathematics, and ethics ensures that the technologies are developed and deployed to maximize their potential and minimize risks.

4. Accountable and moral frameworks are essential in deploying advanced technologies to ensure fairness, transparency, accountability, and privacy. These frameworks build public trust, prevent misuse, and promote the sustainable and equitable use of AI, blockchain, and quantum computing. Developing guidelines, regulations, and best practices is essential for addressing ethical concerns and fostering responsible innovation.

5. Digital literacy is crucial for preparing society for an AI-integrated future as it equips individuals with the knowledge and skills to understand and navigate the complexities of advanced technologies. Enhancing digital literacy ensures informed decision-making, active participation in the digital economy, and the ability to leverage technology for personal and professional growth.

6. Inclusive innovation can be encouraged by creating opportunities for all individuals, regardless of background, to participate in and benefit from technological advancements. This effort includes addressing the digital divide, providing access to education and resources, promoting diversity in technology development, and implementing policies that ensure equitable distribution of technological benefits.

7. AI, blockchain, and quantum computing impact workforce transformation by creating new job opportunities, requiring new skill sets, and potentially displacing specific roles. Preparing for this transformation involves reskilling and upskilling workers, promoting job creation in emerging fields, and fostering an entrepreneurial ecosystem that supports innovation and adaptation.

8. AI, blockchain, and quantum computing have the potential to address global challenges such as climate change, poverty, healthcare, and education. AI can optimize resource use and improve diagnostics, blockchain can enhance transparency and accountability, and quantum computing can accelerate research and development. Leveraging these technologies for social good can promote sustainability, equity, and social justice.

EXERCISE 10.9: Engaging with Emerging Technologies

1. Fostering a culture of curiosity and innovation drives the development of AI, blockchain, and quantum computing by encouraging exploration, experimentation, and creative problem-solving. Valuing creativity and empowering individuals to take risks and challenge existing paradigms promote the development of novel solutions and technological advances.

2. Individuals can stay informed by participating in workshops, conferences, online courses, and professional certifications. Engaging with industry publications, research papers, and academic journals, as well as joining professional associations and online forums, also helps them stay up-to-date with new developments and trends.

3. Interdisciplinary partnership is significant in addressing complex challenges because it brings together diverse perspectives and expertise, enabling comprehensive solutions. Collaboration across fields such as computer science, engineering, ethics, law, and business ensures that technological developments are well-rounded, addressing technical, ethical, and societal considerations.

4. Participation in research and development (R&D) efforts contributes to technological progress by advancing knowledge, creating new technologies, and addressing critical challenges. Engaging in R&D through academic research, industrial innovation, and public-private partnerships drives innovation, fosters technological advancement, and develops impactful solutions for society.

5. Actions to advocate for ethical and accountable innovation include participating in policy discussions, developing ethical guidelines, and advocating for regulatory frameworks that promote fairness, transparency, accountability, and respect for privacy. Public awareness campaigns and collaboration with stakeholders can also promote responsible innovation practices.

6. Public discourse and policy development are essential for shaping the future of AI, blockchain, and quantum computing because they ensure that diverse perspectives are considered in decision-making processes. Engaging in discussions and debates on ethical, legal, and societal implications helps inform public opinion and develop policies that promote the responsible use of these technologies.

7. Supporting open innovation and open-source initiatives accelerates technological advancements by promoting collaboration, transparency, and accessibility. Sharing knowledge and resources through open platforms allows for collective problem-solving and accelerates the development and application of AI, blockchain, and quantum computing, fostering a more inclusive innovation ecosystem.

8. Diversity and inclusion play a crucial role in developing AI, blockchain, and quantum computing by ensuring that various perspectives and experiences are represented. Promoting diversity and inclusion in technology development leads to more innovative and equitable solutions, addressing the needs of a diverse society and reducing biases in technological applications.

EXERCISE 10.10: Concluding with a Forward-Looking Perspective

1. The future trajectories of AI, blockchain, and quantum computing involve continuous evolution and innovation. AI is expected to progress toward artificial general intelligence (AGI), enhancing human capabilities across various fields. Blockchain will play an increasingly central role in the digital economy, facilitating secure and transparent transactions. Quantum computing will become more practical and accessible, solving complex problems and improving subjects such as cryptography, material science, and optimization.

2. Artificial general intelligence (AGI) can impact multiple fields by providing systems that understand, learn, and apply knowledge across different tasks, similar to human intelligence. In healthcare, AGI can improve diagnostics and treatment planning. In education, it can personalize learning experiences. In finance, it can optimize investment strategies. AGI's ability to perform complex tasks and make informed decisions can drive significant advancements across multiple sectors.

3. AI-driven Internet of Things (IoT) systems can create intelligent environments that enhance efficiency and adapt to user needs. They can also optimize resource management in smart homes and cities, improve industrial automation, and strengthen healthcare services by monitoring patient health in real time. This integration enhances quality of life, sustainability, and economic growth.

4. Decentralized finance (DeFi) refers to financial services provided through decentralized platforms without intermediaries, using blockchain technology. Blockchain facilitates DeFi by providing a secure and transparent framework for financial transactions, automating agreements through smart contracts, and reducing costs. DeFi democratizes access to financial services, increases transparency, and enhances security.

5. Quantum computing plays a significant role in drug discovery and material science by enabling quantum simulations that provide insights into molecular interactions at a granular level. This accelerates the discovery of new materials and pharmaceuticals, driving innovation in healthcare, energy, and manufacturing industries and improving efficiency in research and development processes.

6. The convergence of AI, blockchain, and quantum computing creates powerful synergies by combining their strengths to enhance capabilities and drive innovation. AI optimizes data processing and decision-making, blockchain ensures secure and transparent data handling, and quantum computing provides immense computational power. Together, they can address complex challenges and create integrated solutions that amplify their collective potential.

7. Ethical considerations that should guide the future development of AI, blockchain, and quantum computing include fairness, transparency, accountability, and respect for privacy. Addressing biases in AI algorithms, ensuring data privacy in blockchain applications, and developing quantum-resistant cryptographic algorithms are essential for promoting ethical and responsible innovation. Establishing regulatory frameworks and ethical guidelines is crucial for gaining public trust and ensuring equitable and sustainable use of the technologies.

8. Continuous learning and proactive engagement shape an AI-driven world by ensuring individuals, organizations, and societies remain informed and adaptable to technological advancements. Lifelong learning, interdisciplinary collaboration, ethical frameworks, and active participation in public discourse and policy development enable effective integration and responsible use of AI, blockchain, and quantum computing. These efforts drive innovation, address emerging challenges, and promote societal well-being, creating a more inclusive and equitable technological future.

Index

R

Register Your Product at informit.com/register

Access additional benefits and save up to 65%* on your next purchase

- Automatically receive a coupon for 35% off books, eBooks, and web editions and 65% off video courses, valid for 30 days. Look for your code in your InformIT cart or the Manage Codes section of your account page.

- Download available product updates.

- Access bonus material if available.**

- Check the box to hear from us and receive exclusive offers on new editions and related products.

InformIT—The Trusted Technology Learning Source

InformIT is the online home of information technology brands at Pearson, the world's leading learning company. At informit.com, you can

- Shop our books, eBooks, and video training. Most eBooks are DRM-Free and include PDF and EPUB files.

- Take advantage of our special offers and promotions (informit.com/promotions).

- Sign up for special offers and content newsletter (informit.com/newsletters).

- Access thousands of free chapters and video lessons.

- Enjoy free ground shipping on U.S. orders.*

* Offers subject to change.

** Registration benefits vary by product. Benefits will be listed on your account page under Registered Products.

Connect with InformIT—Visit informit.com/community

 Pearson

informIT·

Addison-Wesley • Adobe Press • Cisco Press • Microsoft Press • Oracle Press • Peachpit Press • Pearson IT Certification • Que